MW00427537

Politics and the Urban Frontier

CRITICAL FRONTIERS OF THEORY, RESEARCH, AND POLICY IN INTERNATIONAL DEVELOPMENT STUDIES

Series Editors

Andrew Fischer, Naomi Hossain, Briony Jones, Alfredo Saad Filho, Benjamin Selwyn, and Fiona Tregenna

The contemporary world is characterized by massive wealth alongside widespread poverty, inequality, and environmental destruction - all bound up through class, race, and gender dynamics of inequality and oppression.
Critical Frontiers of Theory, Research, and Policy in International Development Studies, the official book series of the Development Studies Association of the UK, was established to contribute to critical thinking about local, national, and global processes of structural transformation. The series publishes cutting-edge monographs that promote critical development studies as an interdisciplinary and applied field, and shape the theory, practice, and teaching of international development for a new generation of scholars, students, and practitioners. As the series evolves, we wish to publish a diverse and inclusive range of authors whose work engages in critical, multidisciplinary, decolonial, and methodologically plural development studies.

Politics and the Urban Frontier

Transformation and Divergence in Late Urbanizing East Africa

TOM GOODFELLOW

OXFORD
UNIVERSITY PRESS

OXFORD
UNIVERSITY PRESS

Great Clarendon Street, Oxford, OX2 6DP,
United Kingdom

Oxford University Press is a department of the University of Oxford.
It furthers the University's objective of excellence in research, scholarship,
and education by publishing worldwide. Oxford is a registered trade mark of
Oxford University Press in the UK and in certain other countries

Published in the United States of America by Oxford University Press
198 Madison Avenue, New York, NY 10016, United States of America

British Library Cataloguing in Publication Data
Data available

Library of Congress Control Number: 2022935488

ISBN 978–0–19–885310–7

DOI: 10.1093/oso/9780198853107.001.0001

Printed and bound by
CPI Group (UK) Ltd, Croydon, CR0 4YY

Cover image: Tom Goodfellow

Acknowledgements

Writing acknowledgements for a book project like this, which has unfolded over fifteen years if I take the beginning of my PhD studies as the starting point, is easy to start but difficult to finish. The wealth of knowledge, support, companionship, and debate that fuelled this journey feels impossible to pin down. But here goes:

I want to begin by thanking my PhD supervisors, Jo Beall and James Putzel. Jo, without your encouragement and inspiration as I became drawn into your research world (while playing gigs by night!) I would never have even considered going into academia, or secured funding to return to study. James, without your steadfast support and the many opportunities you opened up through the Crisis States Research Centre, I would probably never have finished—or enjoyed it nearly as much. I also owe a great deal to Duncan Green for facilitating a collaborative scholarship with Oxfam GB, and all the opportunities that flowed from that.

I was lucky to have a fantastic cohort of fellow PhD students at LSE's Department of International Development with whom to share in the joys and agonies of the PhD experience, including Dominik Balthasar, Benjamin Chemouni, Lucy Earle, Chris Humphrey, Linnea Jonsson, Sheila Kamunyori, Stefan Lindemann, Megha Mukim, Praveen Priyadarshi, Charmaine Ramos, Prashant Sharma, and Alyson Smith. Special thanks to Sean Fox for his advice and friendship over the years, feedback on parts of the manuscript, and vigorous (if often drunken) debate back in our PhD days and since. As I juggled completing the thesis with my first experiences of teaching in the department, my research also benefited greatly from the broader academic environment and from discussions with LSE colleagues including Teddy Brett, Stuart Corbridge, Hazel Gray, Elliott Green, Kate Meagher, Dennis Rodgers, Ken Shadlen, and the late, great, Thandika Mkandawire. Surviving my time at LSE is also hard to imagine without the administrative support and good humour of Dru Daley, Steph Davies, and Sue Redgrave, and the moral support and friendship of Wendy Foulds and fellow researchers at the Crisis States Research Centre.

During my first experiences of field research in Kampala and Kigali, the following people were immensely welcoming and generous with their time, contextual knowledge (and sometimes accommodation!) as I found my feet and conducted research back in 2009–2011: Edgar Byamugisha, Camille Forite, Dennis Kabanda, Ayuub Kasaba Mago, Magloire Kindoki, Moses Mukundane, Vickie Nabwami, Andy Ratcliffe, Dalton Odomoch Oray, George Owor, and the late Matthew Wilson. My early research efforts were also aided at times by the assistance of Dennis

Bataringaya, Charles Rwabukumba, and Esther Kunda. In more recent visits to Kampala, Richard Kikonyogo has been a great source of historical knowledge and long conversations about the changing state of Kampala and its government. My research in Rwanda has also been enriched by various collaborative ventures (and the slow-burn plotting of papers and future projects) with Pritish Behuria. For my first foray into research in Addis Ababa, the advice and assistance of Marco Di Nunzio, Giulia Mascagni, Firew Woldeyes, and Wollela Yesegat was particularly valuable.

I would also like to thank all the academics and researchers in Ethiopia, Rwanda, and Uganda who have been so generous with their time and insights through conversations over the years. These include Berihu Assefa Gebrehiwot, Daniel Bwanika, Zegeye Cherenet, Fasil Ghiorgis, Frederick Golooba-Mutebi, Astrid Haas, Peter Kasaija, Meseret Kassahun, Shuaib Lwasa, Sabiti Makara, Andy Mold, Stephen Mukiibi, Antonia Mutoro, Amanda Ngabirano, Frederick Omolo-Okalebo, Frank Rusagara, and Elias Yitbarek. Special thanks to Paul Mukwaya, from whom I've learned so much about Kampala through research collaborations in recent years. In the United Kingdom, my knowledge of contemporary dynamics in Addis Ababa has also benefited hugely from engagements with Eyob Balcha Gebremariam, Alazar Ejigu, Ezana Haddis Weldeghebrael, Marjan Kloosterboer, Sabine Planel, Biruk Terrefe, and Sarah Vaughan, as well as my own PhD student Selamawit Robi, who has greatly enriched my understanding of the Ethiopian urban policy context.

Moving from the largely solo project that is a PhD into a range of collaborative projects has been a central part of my research trajectory, and one that has constantly required me to question my assumptions and understanding, to the inevitable benefit of the research. I offer profound thanks to my co-researchers and co-authors on various projects in Ethiopia, Uganda, and Rwanda who—in addition to various people already named above—include Sarah Charlton, Yohana Eyob Teffera, Zhengli Huang, Paula Meth, Susie Nansozi Muwanga, Metadel Sileshi Belihu, Kristof Titeca, and Alison Todes. Particular thanks to Zhengli for her remarkable quick learning, precision, and energy in relation to our ESRC project on Chinese influence in Addis Ababa and Kampala. Nolawit Teshome offered some very helpful research and logistical assistance on my first trip to Addis, as did Israel Tesfu on my last.

Since 2013 I have been fortunate to have as my workplace the supportive environment of the Department of Urban Studies and Planning at the University of Sheffield. In addition to many valued friendships, I have benefited from mentoring over the years from John Flint, Paula Meth, Glyn Williams, Rowland Atkinson, and Ryan Powell. The support I have received in terms of applying for grants and managing the complexities of research-funding bureaucracy is second to none, and I am very grateful in this regard to Simon Beecroft and Anisa Mustafa (as well as Mike Boultby and Gill Eyre for dealing with the horror that has been my post-research expense claims).

Parts of this book have appeared in journal articles in recent years, though there is little direct repetition of paragraphs or sections. Aspects of the argument in Chapter 1 on late urbanization feature in a co-authored article with Sean Fox in *Urban Studies*; parts of Chapter 5 made an appearance in an article in *Review of African Political Economy* and in a co-authored article with Zhengli Huang in *Environment and Planning C*; elements of Chapter 6 appeared in articles in *International Journal of Urban and Regional Research* and *Development and Change;* and parts of Chapter 8 draw on and update an article in *Oxford Development Studies.* The material in these chapters has, however, been substantially reframed, augmented, and drawn together in new ways through the book's overarching argument and analytical framework.

The research feeding into this book has been funded by a range of organizations, to which I am very grateful. These include the ESRC (through various channels), Crisis States Research Centre, International Centre for Tax and Development (with special thanks to Mick Moore), Effective States and Inclusive Development Research Centre (with special thanks to Sam Hickey), South African National Research Foundation, and more recently the Global Challenges Research Fund.

I want to emphasize the ways in which this book is indebted to other scholarship, and to be frank about the extent to which it would have been impossible without the academic labour of many, many others. Comparative work over any length of time can in no way substitute for the depth of ethnographic research; in my mind, comparative and ethnographic research perform distinct but complementary functions. Because my work has specialized in the former, I am immensely grateful for the scholarship of anthropologists and others who have conducted rich, in-depth qualitative research on the specific cities on which this thesis is focused. Of particular importance for this book has been the work of Marco di Nunzio and Ezana Haddis Weldeghebrael on Addis Ababa (as well as Daniel Mains' broader work on urban Ethiopia), of Anna Baral, Will Montieth, and Graeme Young on Kampala (as well as Andrew Byerley's remarkable historical study of Jinja), and of Samuel Shearer and Will Rollason on Kigali. Such work has been of great value when faced with the limitations and gaps in my own research. This, of course, only scratches the surface of the academic work to which this book is indebted, which is reflected in the bibliography and which includes a wealth of scholarship by Ethiopian, Ugandan, and Rwandan historians, political scientists, geographers, and planning scholars, several of whom are named above.

For comments on the book proposal and sections of the manuscript, I am deeply grateful to Claire Mercer, Matteo Rizzo, Tom Gillespie, and Sean Fox, as well as many anonymous peer reviewers of articles that fed into the book, and especially to Giles Mohan for his comments on the full manuscript when I finally delivered it. I am also grateful to Andrew Fischer and Uma Kothari, for their comments on the proposal as Series Editors and for giving the book the green light—and indeed to Andrew for inspiring me to submit it to this particular series. Adam Swallow at Oxford University Press has also been extremely helpful throughout, and I am also very grateful to Vicki Sunter who stepped in at the last minute to help me pull all the various aspects of the submission together (and for her help with my endless questions about maps) as well as the project management by Roopa Vineetha Nelson and copyediting by Susan Frampton. Special thanks also to journal editors who particularly went out of their way to feed into revisions and improvement of journal articles that, directly or indirectly, fed into aspects of this book—including Kenneth Shadlen, Jorg Wiegratz, and Lindsay Whitfield.

I cannot possibly end without thanking the hundreds of research participants who have given their time to talk to me about the past, present, and future of the cities with which this book is concerned, and their experiences of myriad aspects of living in these extraordinary, dynamic, and conflicted places. My memories of the intensity and excitement of conducting my earliest interviews (and many of them since), the confusion and ignorance I have so often had to work through, and the affective remnants of being 'in the room' with such an extraordinary range of people will always live with me, and certainly helped power me through the hardest bits of writing this book. I am so very indebted to you.

Finally, I must thank those closest to me. Embarking on a PhD in the first place would have been even more challenging if not for the support of my parents, Liz and Terry Goodfellow. Tess and Hal, you have brought me so much joy over the period of writing this, even if I had to set my alarm ever-earlier in an attempt to get just one more paragraph written before you appeared, demanding porridge, bleary-eyed, and wondering why I was already up. Sally, without your love, warmth, patience, and capacity to bring me happiness every day, I would have had no hope of completing a book. From the painstaking last-minute copyediting of my thesis to the travails of doing the heavy lifting of home schooling during the 2020 lockdown, during which much of this book was written, I am eternally grateful.

I dedicate this book to my father Terry, who died in 2015, ten days after my son Hal was born. You continue to inspire me every day. Doubtless you would have greeted the publication of this book with the usual hard-earned wry smile, and a casual question about why it took so bloody long.

Contents

PART III URBAN CURRENTS

PART IV CONCLUSIONS

List of Figures

Map of East Africa

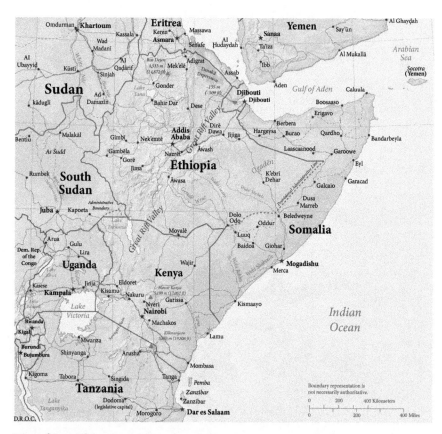

Map of East Africa

Source: adapted by the author from https://maps.lib.utexas.edu/maps/africa/txu-oclc-417699531-horn_of_africa_2009.jpg; courtesy of University of Texas Libraries, The University of Texas at Austin.

Impressions

It's February and I'm sitting in KFC just off Kampala Road, the main drag that separates Nakasero, the colonially planned government zone, from the throbbing commercial heart of Uganda's capital. Opposite me is the city's former acting chief town planner. By his account, he was forced out of office (an office in which he was already 'acting' after the previous incumbent was pushed out) for trying too hard to do his job. He looks exhausted. He's been out of work as a planner since 2006. No one is much interested in his expertise. With resignation he tells me about how his job was impossible: the more he tried to ensure land use regulations were implemented and planning taken seriously, the more resistance he faced. Inspecting new developments around the city was often rendered impossible by private security guards blocking construction sites, with guns. Attempts to pursue official processes invariably had the same outcome: 'Somewhere some politician will come and say, "you leave that to me, I'll handle it." And that's the end of it ... you'll never get to stop it now.'

Later that day, I find myself at the office of the city's former town clerk. He is more determined; he lays out to me his recipe for addressing the city's growing infrastructural decay, crippling congestion, and environmental degradation. Divorce management of the city from politics. Disband the council—bring in the technicians. No local democracy. 'Give me a year without politicians and I could turn this city around.'

In September, after weeks of haunting the shabby corridors of Kampala City Council, I'm talking to an officer responsible for markets and trade. The city's marketplaces have been in turmoil for several years, as politicians mobilize rival factions of vendors, riots flare up, and wealthy tycoons wield cash and influence to acquire title deeds to marketplace land in hope of lucrative redevelopment. I've been talking to the vendors in several markets about it, and about the lack of support and engagement the feel they get from the council. Today, as I discuss with the trade officer the challenges that she faces in trying to restore order in the markets, she repeatedly uses the same forlorn phrase: 'We are on the low bargaining side.'

Kigali, February 2010
I'm in a café in a large commercial block off the main roundabout in Nyarugenge, the commercial centre of Kigali. With me is a senior journalist at one of Rwanda's

opposition newspapers, which constantly fight harassment and threats of closure. He tells me about attempts on his life and shows me the scars. He points out the government agents sipping Coke and watching us, unsubtly, at a table nearby but out of earshot. Before we end our meeting, in which he recounts a host of grievances against the government, he tells me that there are many good things about what it is doing. There is development in some ways, he says. And security. When I ask him his thoughts about the Kigali Conceptual Master Plan, published with great fanfare a couple of years earlier, he says that it is a good thing, in itself. But the manner in which it is being implemented—rapidly and inflexibly, like some kind of development weapon—is a problem. 'The way the plan is moving, poor people are being eliminated from this city.' A few months later, he is forced into exile and moves to Kampala.

Kigali, December 2011

I heard that a delegation from Kampala—bureaucrats, planners, and engineers from the new Kampala Capital City Authority—are in town, and asked if I could join their tour of the city. Among them is Jennifer Musisi, the presidentially-appointed executive director of the new Authority, which earlier that year replaced Kampala City Council. She has her own vehicle and the rest of us follow along rather more raucously in a minibus, as the group from Kampala marvel at the Rwandan capital. One of the visitors from Kampala who works on drains is getting very excited about the design of Kigali's drainage channels. There is much discussion about the lack of encroachment by developers on road reserves and the removal of properties from the wetlands. The Ugandans can't understand how the government here can afford to relocate a bunch of industries from Kigali's existing industrial area to the new planned industrial zone in the peripheries. 'Where does your government get the money to move people like that?' Perhaps they haven't yet realized how small the industrial zone is, or how relatively little the government pays to compulsorily acquire land.

Ugandan delegates appear perplexed by the large expanses of green, unpeopled lawn scattered across the city: 'What *is* this—beautification?' 'They should have benches and let people sit—it's public money!' says someone else. We drive by some luxurious-looking real estate. Many of the owners of these don't live here, explains someone from the Kigali delegation. 'Holiday homes!'

When we reach 'CBD1'—the area adjacent to Nyarugenge where a large informal settlement has been razed to make way for the new central business district envisaged in the Master Plan—we disembark. Musisi steps out, resplendent in a sharp blue suit and sunglasses. As we gaze down the empty hillside, around us new roads are being carved across the huge expanse of cleared earth. We are told about fibreoptic cables being fitted. More questions about expropriation. When we get to Batsinda, an area of new low-cost housing designed to accommodate people relocated from CBD1, one of the Ugandans looks confused about whether this is a fair swap. 'But the value of land in the city centre is worth much more than the land here, and these houses are cheap—how does that work?' Later, when discussing the issue of compliance to urban rules and regulations, one of the delegates from Kigali just casually says, 'this is how we have to control our people.'

At the next stop, which is another vast expanse of land cleared for the free-trade zone and planned new industrial park, Musisi says, 'we would need a big space to do something like this. But they have sold it all off.'

The following week, I'm back in Kampala and so is Musisi. I manage to interview her. She tells me about the progress she has made so far since the new unelected Authority took control earlier in the year, and the obstacles. 'We need to establish the credibility of the institution,' she says. 'Without credibility we cannot have enforcement.' The politicians are a challenge, she says, but you can do many things without them. She is relaxed about the death threats she gets almost daily, particularly in relation to her efforts to wrest control of public transport away from the mafia-like association currently controlling it. 'It's part of the job.'

Addis Ababa, September 2014

It is my first visit to Ethiopia. The impression made by the city was deep and immediate, following the drive from the airport, where domineering over the road on both sides were a succession of vast half-finished tower blocks, grey hulking skeletons with scraps of tattered tarpaulin strewn across from top to bottom. Each day of walking its streets reveals new dystopic cityscapes. I'm attempting to head west on foot along Haile Gebre Selassie Avenue; down the middle runs the gargantuan concrete stripe of the near-completed Chinese-built light railway, while on either side are piles of macerated paving, in the shadow of further brooding cages of steel and cement. Although this is one of the main thoroughfares through the city, there is virtually no commercial activity and barely anyone on the road, either cars or pedestrians, as it has been rendered inaccessible to the former and non-functional for the latter. This whole part of the city centre feels not so much like an urban place as an abandoned speculative metropolis, looking neither actually futuristic due the variously cheap or half-finished structures, nor like a decaying city of the past.

As I make my way towards Meskel Square and traffic picks up, I get stuck under the light railway, wandering tentatively beside its colossal concrete legs with no sense of whether I am on legitimate pedestrian or vehicular territory. I chat with some street youths keen to practice their English. 'This city is like Baghdad after being bombed, right?' said one of them. 'But it means we're growing up,' said the other. His friend shakes his head vigorously in disagreement. Earlier in the year, the government had brutally suppressed student protests in Oromia, the region surrounding the city, over the proposed expansion of the city boundaries deep into Oromo farmland.

Kigali, January 2015
I'm catching up with a foreign investor who runs a small firm in Kigali. We're talking about his efforts to buy and develop a piece of land into apartments, which he's been trying to do since I first met him here in 2009. A short while back he managed finally to buy a plot, in one of Kigali's lush and elevated peripheries. In the Master Plan, the area was first zoned for hotels—specifically hotels with a 700-room capacity, to the amusement of many. The zoning was changed to allow residential development, and he purchased a plot, for which he paid a small fortune. But something has gone very wrong. Officers in Kigali's Singapore-inspired 'one stop shop' for investors, located high up in Kigali City Tower, are now telling him the area is zoned as forestry only. They told him it was too steep for building. 'Bullshit,' he says. 'It's a gold mine—there will be Rwandese houses up there in six months', belonging to someone 'high up'. After repeated complaints he has been given assurances that his plot will be re-zoned back to residential. But on his latest visit they tell him it is being held as forestry. 'It's had four zone changes in two years, and two in two days!' he laments. He tells me that he told them, 'I thought you guys wanted development and investment!' Later that year, in November, he's still waiting for the promised re-zoning, but says his trust has run dry. The moment it's re-zoned he'll sell it off immediately.

The following day I'm talking to a woman in the Ministry of Infrastructure, who is working on housing policy. She and her colleagues have been in Ethiopia, doing a detailed study of the condominium housing scheme there—one of the continent's leading examples of mass-scale state-provided urban housing. 'In Rwanda, we'll have to modify slightly,' she says. She explains that here they don't have all these government-owned small and medium enterprises. Local construction sector capacity is very weak. But also, while the programme is publicly financed in Ethiopia, partly through forced savings schemes, here the expectation is that it will be financed by private developers. I think about my investor from yesterday. The intention is that the housing will be affordable, says the housing specialist, but for this there will need to be good incentives in place. You can say that again.

The next day, I'm talking to an engineer about why almost nothing has been built on CBD1, despite infrastructure being in place for years now. The government has stepped in and bought a few plots. 'It was a bit ambitious,' he says. The plots were too big, and hugely expensive. He says he told them at the time. When asked about the rationale for the size, he defers to the Master Plan. 'But its OK, because tomorrow as the demand rises, the land will be there and it will get used.'

Kampala, May 2018
Someone who used to work for the Kampala Capital City Authority is reflecting on how things have changed since we first met in 2014. Back then, it really

seemed as though a major culture change was under way following the takeover by the new Authority in 2011. The marginalized planners, engineers, and environmentalists were suddenly in demand; waste collection had increased by 80 per cent in six months; revenue collection doubled in just a few years. 'I'm being consulted on everything, it feels good!' said another acquaintance in 2014, previously marginalized as an environmental specialist. 'Now, the law is the law!'

It doesn't feel so much like that in May 2018. Most of the people at KCCA are all 'in on the rot,' one contact tells me. KCCA has become part of the machine. It's just like the previous City Council if you scratch the surface. 'It's all about Jennifer, and she doesn't really have a grip on it.'

During a return visit in October, someone hands me a newspaper. Jennifer Musisi has resigned, in a twenty-one-page letter detailing her achievements and then explaining in detail the impossibility of reconciling 'competing interests between political decisions and the strategic plans of the KCCA technical team'. The plan to take politics out of the city, and to squash a political problem with a technocratic solution, has apparently failed. Even Musisi, who seemed so unassailable a few years back, found herself on the 'low bargaining side'.

Addis Ababa, June 2019
The atmosphere in Ethiopia is febrile, following a spate of political killings, alleged attempted coup, and total internet shutdown for over a week. Over the multiple visits I have made since 2014, the political situation had transformed, following years of protests in Oromia and a change of regime at the centre in 2018. A new law on expropriation and compensation, stimulated by the turmoil in Oromia and successive controversies over large-scale displacement for the government's housing programme, has been in the making for several years. It has still not materialized. Meanwhile, the government is set to stop rolling out its housing settlements in the contested urban peripheries.

We are visiting one of the condominium settlements on the very edge of the city for a focus group discussion, and to feed back findings from a research project. Many things about living in these far-flung settlements have improved, the residents tell us—even since our last visit there a year before. Once drab and brutal looking, social and commercial life is starting to thrive. Transport services are much improved. But electricity and water are still highly unreliable, the cost of living is increasing, and along with this so is crime and insecurity. Since the construction itself stopped, employment is a huge problem and it still takes hours to commute into the city proper. There are only three types of work available here, one man says: driving an auto-rickshaw, driving a mule cart, or being a broker for renters in the settlement's constantly churning rental market. This is certainly a city on the move, but perhaps not in the ways envisaged from above.

PART I
URBAN TECTONICS

1
East Africa and the politics
of late urbanization

Introduction

This book offers an explanation of differential trajectories of urban change within
one particular region of the world in the early twenty-first century. For those of
us who are fascinated by cities—seizing opportunities to walk their streets and
squares, cram into their public transport systems, hear their cacophony of sounds
and wonder at the power and capital behind their structures—comparison is often
a default mode of thinking, either explicitly or implicitly. Differences between
cities often strike us as mere curiosities handed down by history. Yet similarities
and differences in urban form and function, and the varying ways that control over
cities is organized and contested, offer powerful lenses onto socio-economic and
political change. Understanding drivers of urban similarity and difference matters intrinsically in terms of our understanding and theorization of such change,
but also instrumentally because there is a widespread desire by policymakers,
politicians, investors, and communities to *effect* change on cities.

Human attempts to change cities, and to control them politically, frequently
take as their reference point cities elsewhere; sometimes in far-flung regions of the
world, sometimes just across a border. The planners, investors, traders, engineers,
governors, and residents quoted in the 'impressions' preceding this chapter were
seeking to effect urban change, whether purely in their own interests or in pursuit of some larger stated goal. They often took comparisons to and connections
with other cities as reference points, but always found themselves constrained by
the realities of their own urban context. These cities could not be shaped in line
with some preconceived vision, let alone be intentionally moulded to more closely
resemble one another, beyond surface-level material forms. Efforts to effect change
were often as much about national power play as city-level priorities, and political agendas often existed in tension with the internationally sanctioned urban
imaginaries circulating in the world of policy and planning.

The idea that African cities have some intrinsic character is spurious, implying
a unified history when in fact they have been shaped by heterogeneous global and
regional influences (Fourchard 2011). This book unravels the forces that matter
when we want not just to interpret contemporary urban life but *explain* how the
conditions of urban life came to be as they are in specific places, and why these

Politics and the Urban Frontier. Tom Goodfellow, Oxford University Press. © Tom Goodfellow (2022).
DOI: 10.1093/oso/9780198853107.003.0001

conditions converge and diverge between cities, with important implications for economic development and social justice. It does so by examining the paths of urban development and change among a set of countries in East Africa: the least urbanized but most rapidly urbanizing region in the world. The book argues that this region is not only a geographical terrain of great urban dynamism and diversity, but because of its unique position within the broad arc of global urbanization is the place to which we should look if we want to understand the potentiality and peril of our urban future as a species.

Focusing on three of the region's countries—Ethiopia, Rwanda, and Uganda—the book is relentlessly comparative. These countries share many remarkable trajectories in terms of late urbanization, ancient histories of state-building and modern histories of conflict followed by significant economic growth. In the year 2000, the start of the period on which most of this book focuses, these three countries had virtually identical levels of urbanization: around 15 per cent of the total population lived in cities and towns. They were among the ten least urbanized countries in the world.[1] Yet, as the impressions shared at the start of this chapter have indicated and the book will explore in detail, the forms of urban development in each case and how these have evolved over the two decades since are starkly different in many important ways.

Comparative urban research has flourished in recent years, building particularly on the theoretical and methodological provocations of Robinson (2006; 2011; 2016). To compare is to enable ways of seeing that interrogate difference while also exploring resemblances, and experiencing uncanny concurrences of the two. Yet herein also lies the danger of comparison, which entails the risk of collapsing analysis into polarities and binaries. In order to unsettle the binarizing tendencies of comparing two things, this book opts for three. To compare three, rather than two, means keeping constant watch over easy polarities or received assumptions about what count as salient similarities and differences.

Close comparison also enables something else important that is of particular relevance to the fields of urban studies and development studies, between which this book finds its roots. Much recent research on urban development and change is 'split along lines of numerical or ethnographic reasoning' (Amin & Thrift 2017: 156). What is seen as important is either the identification of broad cross-country trends, or the description of embodied experiences of everyday urban life. Essential though these forms of understanding cities are, there is much that lies between. Neither numerical nor ethnographic reasoning can fully encompass the 'diversification of urban forms and outcomes' which demand that we take 'a differentiated view on the dynamics of urbanisation' (Schmid et al. 2018: 20). Offering an in-depth comparison of three cities, while embedding them in national, regional and global dynamics, this book advances approaches to urban research between the

---

[1] World Bank data available at: https://databank.worldbank.org/reports.aspx? source=2&series= SP.URB.TOTL.IN.ZS&country=#, accessed 3 December 2020.

poles of the numerical and ethnographic, in pursuit of better understanding these differentiated dynamics of urbanization.

This goal requires not only comparison but attention to analytical scale, and a commitment to interdisciplinary thinking. It requires pushing beyond generic approaches to global capitalist urban restructuring that dominate the meta-narratives of urban studies and development studies. This is sorely needed, because dominant paradigms even in the critical and heterodox traditions within these interdisciplinary fields are inadequate to explain different pathways of urban development. While comparative political economy is flourishing in both fields, extant analytical frameworks actually offer limited engagement with politics as a driver of change at the urban scale, and are beset with enduring problems relating to analytical scale itself—including both 'methodological nationalism' (Wimmer & Glick Schiller 2002) in development studies and 'methodological cityism' (Angleo & Wachsmuth 2015) in urban studies.

The book responds to two main concerns regarding our ability to analyse the drivers of urban change and, consequently, to better understand the prospects for urban economic development and social justice. The first and most obvious relates to the political naivety of prominent urban policy agendas, and the attendant assumption that any city can pursue a given package of strategies and achieve similar outcomes. The fact that urban development is back on the global development agenda, following significant activism over decades, is laudable (Parnell 2016). Both UN-HABITAT's 'New Urban Agenda' and Sustainable Development Goal No. 11 on making 'cities and human settlements inclusive, safe, resilient and sustainable' are packed with noble goals. Yet the circulating policy discourses of the entrepreneurial city, creative city, 'smart' city, and above all 'global' and 'world class' city remain among the strongest currencies used by national and city governments pursuing investment in a ruthlessly competitive global context (Acuto 2022). These ideas are questionable in themselves (Peck 2005; Robinson 2006; Pratt 2011; Marvin et al. 2015; Vanolo 2014). The main point here, however, is that they involve underlying assumptions that cities are economic and technological projects to be managed rather that terrains of political negotiation and contestation (Guma & Monstadt 2021). The quest for transferrable models of urban development will always fail without a deep and sustained engagement with urban politics.

The second concern this book addresses relates to academic trends in critical urban and development studies, and their limited utility for comparative analysis of urban change. This critique speaks to different threads of contemporary theorization in different ways. First, it addresses the general abdication of causality evident in dominant post-structuralist paradigms for interpreting the urban condition, notwithstanding the rich insights of this literature into the composition of urban life (Bennett 2010; Farías & Bender 2012; McFarlane 2011a). Such approaches can illuminate how particular urban policy agendas unravel through the socio-material conditions assembled 'at concrete sites of urban practice'

(Farías & Bender 2010: 2), but they rarely interrogate the wider causal dynamics that generate these concrete sites or drive the differential adoption of policy agendas. This aspect of the book's critique is developed in Chapter 2.

A further aspect of the academic critique speaks more directly to the tradition within which this book itself is associated: the political economy of urban development. This literature is still dominated by frameworks that place neoliberalism at their analytical core in ways that—even while highlighting the 'variegated' nature of neoliberal restructuring (Brenner et al. 2010; Peck 2015)—are limiting for the analysis of urban socio-economic and spatial evolution. The literature on neoliberal urbanism (He & Wu 2009; Peck et al. 2009a; Peck et al. 2013), municipal neoliberalism (Goldfrank & Schrank 2009; Karaman 2013), speculative urbanism (Goldman 2011; Goldman & Narayan 2021), urban entrepreneurialism (Harvey 1989; MacLeod 2002) and 'world city entrepreneurialism' (Golubchikov 2010) has surged, and for good reason. The adoption of market-driven approaches to economic restructuring has produced a 'cluster of recurring features, tendential characteristics, and family resemblances' in urban policies worldwide (Peck et al. 2010: 104). Recognizing the diversity of outcomes of these policies, the 'neoliberal urbanism' argument examines how this one-size-fits-all model of urban policy 'lands' in contextually specific regulatory and institutional landscapes, and suggests that the uneven development emerging from this is an integral facet of the neoliberalization process itself (Peck et al. 2009; Brenner et al. 2010; Sager 2011).

This acknowledgement of neoliberalism as necessarily variegated and 'always-incomplete' is important, yet still seeks to encompass political economy explanations within the neoliberal meta-narrative (Peck 2015). The way in which this prism has dominated analyses of diverse urban pathways obscures many of the political dynamics that shape urban agendas and their implementation. Differences in urban capitalist penetration and market processes are cast as *variegated impacts of neoliberalization*, rather than outcomes of politics in which neoliberalism plays only a partial role. By internalizing variation within its analytical ambit, the urban neoliberalism framing itself risks itself becoming a one-size-fits-all explanation for divergent trajectories among cities, to the exclusion of explanations beyond neoliberalism. Its underlying assumption is that all governments are essentially trying to do the same thing, with varying regulatory-institutional structures producing different outcomes (Peck et al. 2009; Brenner et al. 2010). However, as well as neoliberalism 'landing' in different regulatory landscapes we also need to take seriously the other urban political agendas and ideological projects which exist outside or in tension with neoliberalism, and which it is not helpful to subsume analytically within it. Not all governments and salient political actors *are* trying to produce the same kinds of city, even if their lip service to globalist neoliberal emblems suggests otherwise.

Emphasizing the need to look 'beyond neoliberalism' in theorizing cities—particularly in the global South—is not new (Ong 2006; Parnell & Robinson

2012; Baptista 2013). Yet the point emphasized in this book is not that theories of neoliberalization lack relevance to cities in the global South—clearly neoliberal policy approaches have swept across Africa in the decades since structural adjustment (Harrison 2010; Wiegratz 2016; Wiegratz et al. 2018)—or to suggest a 'post-neoliberal' perspective (Parnell & Robinson 2012). Nor is it to rehearse the critique levelled at Brenner and others that their approach to urbanization is too 'capital-centric' (see e.g. McCarthy 2005; Farías 2011; Gillespie 2016; Hartman 2020); indeed, capital is fundamental to the narrative of this book. The point is to emphasize that the focus on urban neoliberalism and its institutional-regulatory filters has thinned the attention given to the *politics of capital accumulation and distribution in specific urban places and times*.

In sum, if poststructuralist urban theory offers limited purchase on questions of what *causes* particular trajectories of urban development, dominant urban political economy approaches lack (ironically) sufficient attention to politics in their own analysis of causal drivers. This critique also chimes with some recent currents in development studies that highlight the deficit of political analysis in dominant approaches to political economy of development (Hickey 2013a; Hudson & Leftwich 2014). Even the 'political settlements approach' (Khan 2010; 2018; Kelsall et al. 2022), on which this book draws and which delves much deeper into arrangements of political power, remains partial in its engagement with politics—as well as struggling with how to engage at scales other than the national (Goodfellow 2018).

Positioning the book in this way is not intended to detract from the value of all the above literatures, which have advanced many aspects of our understanding of the contemporary urban condition. Yet they do not go far enough in facilitating an analysis of the politics that drives urban change, particularly in contexts such as East Africa where contemporary political settlements are layered onto precolonial and colonial institutions as well as globalized capital flows and longstanding regional dynamics. This book offers a new way of understanding the relationship between cities, global change, and the forces that we might locate somewhere in-between, not only at the national but also the regional scale. To understand why East Africa as a region is significant as a frame for urban analysis, we need to consider some fundamental aspects of this part of the world.

1.1 The peripheral frontier

East Africa—which in more expansive definitions includes Burundi, Djibouti, Eritrea, Ethiopia, Kenya, Rwanda, Somalia, Tanzania, and Uganda, as well as the eastern part of the Democratic Republic of Congo and South Sudan—might appear a strange place in which to ground a study of urban development and change. To many people elsewhere, this part of the world conjures up images of endless savannahs and rainforests, cattle herders and subsistence farmers, lowland tribes and parched highland communities, coffee and tea plantations, grinding rural poverty and famine. Its few large cities appear, in this image, as 'islands in a rural ocean', to use Lefebvre's (1970/2003) phrase about unurbanized societies. The image is not wholly inaccurate, and these rural connotations are unsurprising given that it remains, as a region, the world's least urbanized. It could be (and often is) therefore seen as peripheral in terms of urban development trends and patterns (Anderson & Rathbone 2000; Fourchard 2011); hardly a place through which to observe and theorize forces of urban change.

This sense of the region as being on the periphery of urbanization is also reflected in its status on the margins of academic debates and research on the urban. This point must be situated against the current sea change in how cities are being researched and theorized; a change that is, of course, part of a broader process of 'seeing from the South', sometimes conceptualized as the 'Southern turn' in the social sciences, embedded within a broader decolonization of scientific knowledge (Connell 2007 Mbembe 2016; Bhambra et al. 2018). The field of urban studies has helped to shape this turn,[2] with a number of scholars highlighting the need to theorize the urban from the South, building on longer traditions of postcolonial thought in critical urban geography, sociology, and planning (Roy 2005; 2009; 2016; Simone 2004b; 2010; 2018; Mbembe & Nuttall 2004; Rao 2006; Watson 2009b; 2013; Quayson 2014; Schindler 2017; Simone & Pieterse 2017; Lawhon & Truelove 2020). However, the journey to see cities differently based on the experience of the majority world has only just begun, and much of this work is rooted in a handful of countries such as South Africa, India, and other large, middle-income 'emerging economies' with comparatively industrialized cities and relatively balanced urban systems.

In contrast, East Africa's cities are located in countries that have high degrees of urban primacy,[3] minimal industrialization, and low *levels* of urbanization but high *rates* of urbanization and urban growth. In other words, they look very different in terms of their urban experience from places now at the forefront of 'Southern thinking' on urban development and change. There are cores and peripheries within 'the South', both economically and in terms of knowledge production.[4] Indeed, the economic surge in several large middle-income countries in recent decades, prompting renewed debates on the global geography

---

[2] It is perhaps because urban studies was so resolutely 'Northern' in its origins, and so fixated on the experiences of a handful of cities in industrialized or industrializing countries, that the pivot towards Southern perspectives was especially urgent.

[3] Urban primacy refers to the proportion of a country's urban population concentrated in its 'primate' (largest) city.

[4] This point was made incisively and to widespread agreement by a (non-South African) delegate to a major conference on African cities in Cape Town in 2018.

of development (Horner & Hulme 2019), arguably just recalibrated rather than erased core–periphery relations in the global economy (Fischer 2015; 2019).

East Africa has thus remained on the fringes of debate on urban development and the nature of the urban, despite urban studies' 'Southern turn'.[5] There is also no denying that demographically it *is* less urban than most other parts of the world. Eastern Africa is on average 28 per cent urbanized, placing it significantly below any other major world regions, including other relatively unurbanized regions like Southern Asia (36 per cent), Western Africa (46 per cent), Central Asia (48 per cent), and Central Africa (50 per cent) (UNDESA 2018).[6] Figure 1.1

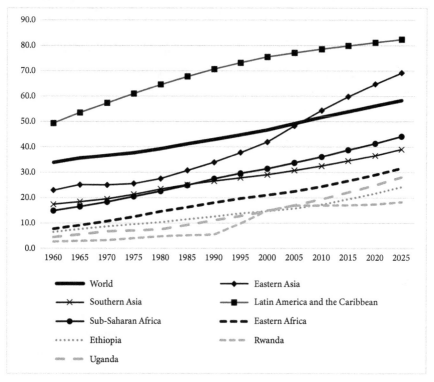

Figure 1.1 Percentage of population living in urban areas
Source: Based on data from UNDESA (2018).

[5] This does not mean it has been on the fringes of debates in development studies. On the contrary, here it has been disproportionately studied, partly reflecting the rural bias of the latter discipline until very recent years. It is also important to note that the scholarship on East African cities that speaks to the debates on decolonization and 'Southern urbanism' has started to grow in recent years, see, for example, McFarlane and Silver (2017a), Lawhon et al. (2018), Nagendra et al. (2018), Sseviiri et al. (2020), Guma (2021), Kimari (2021).
[6] These statistics are not without their problems, but they are the best available data we have for cross-country comparative studies of urbanization. See Brenner and Schmid (2014); Buettner (2015); Potts (2018), Fox and Goodfellow (2021).

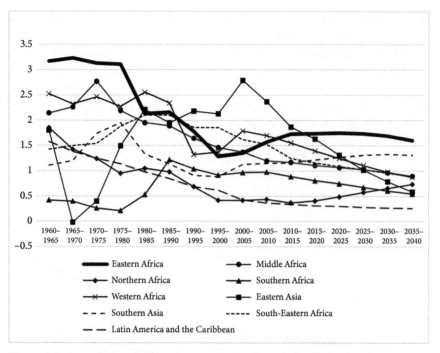

Figure 1.2 Annual rate of change in percentage of population living in urban areas, by region
Source: Based on data from UNDESA (2018).

illustrates the level of urbanization in East Africa (and the three focal countries of this book) relative to a range of other world regions.

It is also without doubt the world's fastest urbanizing region. Figure 1.2 illustrates regional averages of the annual rate of change in the percentage of national populations living in urban areas, comparing East Africa with other urbanizing regions. This demonstrates that—with the exception of a period around the turn of the twenty-first century—East Africa has been the world's fastest urbanizing region since the mid-twentieth century, and continues to be so.

East Africa's status in the least urbanized but fastest urbanizing region is precisely why it is such an illuminating place to study cities. Based on current population projections (which, though fallible, are important indicators of contemporary dynamics), no less than five of the top twenty largest cities *in the world* will be in East Africa in 2100: Dar es Salaam, Nairobi, Kampala, Mogadishu, and Addis Ababa (Hoornweg & Pope 2017). Currently none are in even in the top seventy. Meanwhile, significant changes are unfolding beyond the capital or 'core' cities: in places that until recently were just minor towns, which through border dynamics, new infrastructure connections, or nearby wars have mushroomed into major urban hubs.

The fact that this region is still predominantly rural today means that it holds the potential to avoid some of the worst pitfalls of urban sprawl, poor planning, and carbon-hungry development suffered elsewhere; in this regard, it presents opportunities to learn from past mistakes and innovate in ways that highly urbanized regions have constrained capacity to do (Nagendra et al. 2018). Yet it is also still among the poorest parts of the world, further underscoring the immensity of the challenge of charting a prosperous, sustainable, and inclusive urbanization path. East Africa has also been (and continues to be) the theatre of some of the most devastating conflicts of recent decades. Even its relatively stable states have been subject to the side-effects of conflict, including dramatic population displacement that has often catalysed urban growth. Despite all this, the region experienced remarkable levels of economic growth in the early twenty-first century, bolstered by new forms of aid and investment—most notably from China. These factors—rapid urbanization and urban growth from a low base, recent histories of violent conflict, and surging economic growth and infrastructure investment—render it a unique place for the study of how cities evolve in periods of wrenching change.

In this sense, peripheral though it may be in terms of its share of the global urban population or its place in debates on urbanism, it is a region that has much to offer the study of the contemporary urban condition and future urban development. This book flips the apparently peripheral nature of East African urbanism upside down: why would a region that is the world's least urbanized (but fastest urbanizing), with among the poorest (but fastest-growing) economies, yield anything but *vital* lessons for the understanding of how cities evolve under demographic, economic, and—increasingly—environmental pressures?

It is on this basis that we can conceive of East Africa as the world's urban frontier, not in the sense that it is the most advanced in this transition but rather the opposite. Frontiers involve the discursive construction of absences and spaces somehow 'waiting to happen'. Africa as a whole has sometimes been characterized as the 'last frontier' for capitalist development, being the continent in which the most significant number of people and communities remain outside capitalist relations of production (Moghalu 2013; Chitonge 2018). This book conceptualizes East Africa specifically not as the world's capitalist frontier but its urban frontier: a region where, from a low level of urbanization, the current pace with which new territory is being incorporated into urban processes is unparalleled globally. It is the ultimate region in which to contemplate what Simone (2004b) termed the 'city yet to come'.

The 'frontier' concept has long been associated with the North American colonial experience and with wild, rural, stateless spaces in which territory can be made and natural resources extracted (Tsing 2003; Rasmussen & Lund 2018). But if frontiers are 'novel configurations of the relationship between natural resources and institutional orders' (Rasumssen & Lund 2018: 388) they can just as well involve urbanization as mineral exploitation (Gillespie 2020). Geiger (2009) suggests that central to frontier zones is the destruction and recreation of property systems, political structures, and social relations to make way for new ones. Thus, as Rasmusssen and Lund (2018) argue, the dissolution of property regimes and social contracts in frontier spaces occurs only to facilitate their re-establishment and territorial re-ordering. Urbanization and urban growth are frontier processes in that they are *by definition* about the destruction and recreation of property systems; indeed, this is the very stuff of the impressions that started this book, and much of its content.

On the one hand, the idea of an urban frontier can be examined at the level of an individual city, with for example the urban periphery in Harare being conceptualized as a frontier zone for urban political control (McGregor & Chatiza 2019) and central areas of Accra as 'real estate frontiers' in which land is incrementally commodified to facilitate accumulation (Gillespie 2020). However, this book deploys the frontier concept differently, at the level of a global region in which the urbanization of property regimes and social contracts is happening at a pace faster than anywhere else at the present time. This renders the region not just a place abundant with urban frontiers but, in itself, *the global* urban frontier.[7] With mass urbanization taking place both relatively late and remarkably fast, it is the region on average most characterized by the conditions of 'late urbanization'.

1.2 Late urbanization

The idea of 'late urbanization' highlights the varied historical timing of the urban transition between countries and regions around the world, emphasizing that these differences in timing have far-reaching consequences (Fox & Goodfellow 2021). Recent debates over the nature of the urban have focused to a significant extent on geographical universality versus specificity, and on questions of urban epistemology, paying limited attention to the varied temporality of urban transitions around the world (Brenner & Schmid 2014; 2015; Scott & Storper 2015; Robinson & Roy 2016). Emphasizing the significance of 'late urbanization' involves foregrounding the fact that cities in different places have been made at different times, and the idea that *when* a society transitions towards more widespread urban living has a profound impact on *how* this transition unfolds.

Notwithstanding important difficulties in measuring urbanization across countries (Buettner 2015), there is now robust scientific evidence that the urban transition—defined as a secular, substantial overall increase in the proportion of people living in urban settlements—has happened significantly later in sub-Saharan African than many world regions (Dyson 2010; Fox 2012; 2017).[8]

---

[7] Bunnell et. al (2012) also discuss Asian cities with reference to the idea of 'global urban frontiers', though they are using this term to conceptualise Asian cities as frontiers of knowledge production, rather than framing a specific region as the current frontier of the global urban transition.

[8] Brenner and Schmid (2014; 2015) largely reject the idea of the 'urban age' on the basis that methodological approaches to measuring urbanization are flawed. We engage with these critiques in Fox and Goodfellow (2021).

Moreover, the nature of Africa's urban transition is distinct and unprecedented, both in terms of its pace and the fact that it has not primarily been driven by urban in-migration linked to industrialization, as was the case in many other regions of the world (Fox 2012; Gollin et al. 2016).

Urbanizing relatively late can have both negative and positive implications. On the one hand, some parts of the world reaped gains from early urbanization that cannot be replicated under current global economic and environmental conditions; but on the other, late urbanizers have a greater range of urban experiences and 'models' from elsewhere that are available for emulation, and in some ways have more scope to experiment and innovate (Nagendra et al. 2018; Marx et al. 2020). While the idea of 'late development' has pejorative connotations and is usually associated with stunted progress along a particular trajectory of modernization or structural economic transformation, the term 'late urbanization' does not imply anything teleological and has no normative emphasis. It simply serves to situate the experience of urbanization within geohistorical context: 'late' in this sense merely denotes taking place 'after' some other regions of the world urbanized, rather than implying that this process is somehow 'tardy'. Nor does urbanizing late imply the absence of deep urban history. Many parts of Africa, including some in East Africa, have urban histories dating back millennia, as will be discussed in Chapters 3 and 4. Nevertheless, the overall human population in the region remained predominantly rural.

While the intensity of demographic change is a key feature of late urbanizers, the condition of late urbanization is about much more than this. This demographic shift has coincided with unprecedented 'hyperglobalization', which has influenced how and where capital is accumulated, and the incentives of those who control it. Early postcolonial efforts to cultivate domestic industries through import substitution were cut off by the emergence of the 'Washington Consensus', imposition of Structural Adjustment Programmes and renewed focus on primary commodity exports (Arrighi 2002; Mkandawire, 2005; Chitonge 2015), even as urbanization rates soared. Meanwhile, urban labour markets became increasingly informalized and over time ideas of 'entrepreneurship' have become venerated in place of large-scale investments in urban productive capacity (Meagher 1995; Ochonu 2018).

Hyperglobalization has stimulated significant capital flight, but for holders of capital who cannot easily export it abroad, domestic high-end real estate markets are more appealing than investment in productive industries such as manufacturing (Goodfellow 2017a). One of the aspects that a focus on late urbanization highlights is the challenge of urbanizing at a time when opportunities for industrialization are 'running out' (Rodrik 2016: 1). This has affected late urbanizers in diverse ways, with a number of late urbanizing countries in Latin America and Asia (including China) managing to solidify their positions in global value chains early in the hyperglobalized period, partly due to the investment appeal offered by their large populations and relative political stability (Fox & Goodfellow 2021). Faced with such competition, many African late urbanizers have struggled to increase the share of manufacturing within their own economies (Gibbon & Ponte 2005). This difficulty has not held back urban growth, which requires us to radically decentre industrialization from our understanding about the functioning and significance of cities.

These dynamics have particular relevance in East Africa, where many countries have wholeheartedly embraced economic liberalization and accompanying deindustrialization in the context of soaring rates of urban growth. Indeed, the resurrection of the East African Community in 1999 (though corresponding only to part of East Africa as defined here) was rooted in principles of liberalization and market-led integration (O'Reilly 2019). While East Africa has seen substantial economic growth in the new millennium, much of it generated in and invested in cities, a high proportion of this has been chanelled into construction and real estate—the 'secondary circuit' of capital—rather than developing manufacturing or industrial capacity (Goodfellow 2017; Pitcher 2017; UN-HABITAT 2018; Gillespie 2020). These developments support Fischer's (2019) point that contemporary societies are often 'modernizing' and raising their technological consumption without really changing their position in the global economic hierarchy. Although the region attracts increasing amounts of foreign direct investment (FDI), it attracts a relatively small proportion of *manufacturing* FDI, which goes disproportionately to the southern, western, and northern regions of the continent (UN-HABITAT 2018).

Alongside this broad economic context for East African late urbanization, there is also a significant political dimension. The late twentieth-century Cold War context resulted in financial and political support being channelled to loyal regimes on both sides around the world, often accentuating the high levels of state centralization established through colonization (Mbembe 1992; Mamdani 1996). In this context, national governments in many postcolonial states claimed sweeping powers over land (see, for example, Larbi et al. 2004), while the militarized bureaucracies through which states sustained themselves sucked up the majority of resources available (Cheeseman 2015). The implications of this centralization for municipal government were profound. It stunted the development of strong municipalities at the very time when the demographic intensity noted above was gathering pace. This lack of municipal capacity combined with a small capitalist sector offered limited foundations for class-based political bargaining between state and society, fuelling the dominance of kinship and identity-based clientelist politics (Hydén 1983; Nelson 1979).

Since the 1990s, decentralization reforms and associated ideas of market-led urban governance have created new sites for clientelistic politics. Given the prior neglect of local state-building, decentralization has often occurred in the absence of the necessary political institutions to manage local competition, without sufficient resources at city level to enable urban authorities to act autonomously, and with significant political interference from the national state (Wunsch 2001).

Compounding this weakness of municipal government has been international donors' longstanding suspicion of planning, and receptiveness to ideas about 'urban bias' that fed disinvestment in cities (Rakodi 1997; Wekwete 1997; Mkandawire 2005; Potts 2007)—at least until early in the new millennium.

In addition to the economic and political conditions outlined above, late urbanizers face a global environmental regime that conditions urban possibilities in ways that were unheard of in previous times. These conditionalities, initiated in pursuit of a global shift away from carbon-based economies, derive in large part from the experience and priorities of early urbanizers. Late urbanizers thus face heightened intensity of environmental change alongside formidable challenges of building low-carbon economies—a process that city governments themselves are increasingly expected to lead (Lwasa 2010; Acuto 2013; Angelo & Wachsmuth 2020)—while also attempting to generate ongoing economic growth amid the relentless pressures of hyperglobalization.

East Africa is by no means the only region of the world that faces these conditions while undergoing intense urbanization and urban growth, but its frontier status and intensity of demographic change magnifies the challenges associated with both living in cities and governing them under these conditions. There is, however, significant diversity within the region in terms of both urbanization levels and many of the economic and political processes noted above, raising the question of why and how it constitutes a 'region', and what value there is thinking about urbanization in relation to the regional scale at all.

1.3 Cities in a world of regions

Cities exist, as Robinson (2011) has highlighted, in a world of cities; we gain something by looking at any city in relation to others, setting aside preconceptions about the directional flow of ideas or resources. But should cities themselves be the sole or even primary scale of analysis in our efforts to understand urban change? National policies and economies are integral to any city-level story (Sellers 2005), and many approaches frame cities in relation to global forces and flows (Sassen 1994; Brenner 2004; Roy & Ong 2011). Yet if we want to understand how cities develop and change, the three scalar units of the urban city, national, and global are insufficient. Particularly ignored in urban research is the space between the national and the global: in other words, the realm of supranational regions.

The word region requires some clarification. In the disciplines of geography and planning, 'regional' usually refers to subnational units, including city-regions, functional economic areas, or administratively created territorial units (see, for example, Scott & Storper 2003; Parr 2005; Hudson 2007; Pastor et al. 2009). In contrast, the idea of a region as a cluster of geographically adjacent countries has been associated with international relations (IR) and 'area studies', with geographers often denoting such areas as arbitrary and imperial in origin (Sharp 2019).

However, the demographic and economic changes affecting cities, and the processes through which these are governed, require us to take seriously certain
processes and institutions (colonial or otherwise) that transcend state borders but
are less than global.

The definition of 'region' is difficult to pin down even if we specify a focus
on the supranational rather than subnational. As Hettne (2005: 544) has noted,
'all regions are socially constructed and hence politically contested', and most
countries have plural 'regional logics' available to them (Agnew 2013). This book
adopts the perspective that regions matter for questions of urban development
and change, but not in the way that conventional approaches to international politics assumes that they matter—i.e. through concrete and intentional processes
of regional organization. As such, it draws on the emerging literature on 'global
international relations' that has evolved out of IR's own 'Southern turn':

> While the world is not fragmenting into regions, it is also not moving inexorably
> toward a seamless globality. Global IR calls for the acknowledgment of regional
> diversity and agency [and] views regions neither as wholly self-contained entities,
> nor as purely extensions of global dynamics.
>
> (Acharya 2014: 650)

There are good reasons to conceptualize East Africa as a region, beyond the
conscious project of 'regionalism' emerging through the East African Community (EAC). The regional logic underpinning this book relates to more expansive
and historically rooted regional dynamics, as well as contemporary processes of
de facto regionalization unfolding through infrastructure, trade, migration, conflict, and reconciliation well beyond the EAC. Indeed, 'Africa has always been
a deeply regionalized continent' in this sense (Clapham 1996: xiii). In Agnew's
(2013) terms, African regions mostly constitute 'macro regions' that developed
functional linkages and modes of production and exchange over time (including
through the slave trade and external orientations to the west, north, or east) rather
than necessarily being areas of similarity or shared political identity. There are also
reasons to believe that the global 'infrastructure scramble' now underway (Kanai
& Schindler 2019) is catalysing regionalism in Africa, with East Africa prominent
in this process (Otele 2020).

Despite this, delimiting East Africa is not unproblematic. The six countries of
the EAC[9] are now regionally grouped in a formal sense, but the Great Lakes Region
and Horn of Africa—both of which (by some definitions) contain states that overlap with the EAC—likewise have legitimate claims to coherence (Chrétien 2003;
Clapham 2017). The expansive definition of East Africa adopted in this book—
which effectively combines all three of these groupings—has a geographical rationale, being bound by the Sahara to the north, the Congo rainforests to the west,

---

[9] Burundi, Kenya, Rwanda, South Sudan, Tanzania, and Uganda.

the Indian Ocean to the east, and Red Sea to the north-east. The southern boundary has less geographical clarity, but there is a meaningful and accepted distinction between this cluster of states and their southern neighbours of Mozambique (with its distinct Lusophone heritage) and Zambia (with its distinct economic structure, rooted in mining, and a significantly higher degree of industrialization).

This version of East Africa, which corresponds quite closely to the grouping used by the African Development Bank,[10] is clearly a *loose* regional entity. But regions of any kind 'come with no automatic promise of territorial or systemic integrity, since they are made through the spatiality of flow, juxtaposition, porosity and relational connectivity' (Amin 2004: 34). The point is simply that historical and contemporary flows of people, resources, and ideas within this region are significant for understanding patterns of urbanization and trajectories of urban development in many of its individual states. In fact, this book posits that despite being porous and contestable, the scale of East Africa is more analytically salient here than that of 'Africa'.

Within East Africa we can identify three geographic nodes which, while all incredibly diverse, have a certain historical cohesion: the Horn of Africa, the Great Lakes Region, and the Swahili coast and its extensive hinterlands. The first two of these experienced many centuries of internal state- and empire-building, with their own distinct sub-regional dynamics prior to colonization (Mafeje 1998; Chrétien 2003; Reid 2011; Clapham 2017). The Swahili coast, meanwhile, gains cohesiveness through its long history of engagement across the Indian Ocean and internal struggles to control this, including through the formation of city-states (Horton & Middleton 2000). Although these three nodes remain distinct in important ways, the European 'scramble for Africa' and subsequent efforts towards regional economic organization, including through the EAC and Intergovernmental Authority on Development (IGAD), have in some respects brought them closer together. Moreover, the region's geographic alignments are being reshaped today as new railways snake from the Swahili coast to the heart of the Great Lakes, from Kenya to Ethiopia and South Sudan, and from Ethiopia to the Red Sea coast in Djibouti (Enns & Bersaglio 2020; Chome 2020; Aalders 2021). Much of the finance for these endeavours comes from China, underscoring how in addition to being one of the world's major ODA-receiving regions, East Africa plays a unique role in China's Belt-and-Road strategy (Johnston 2019; Otele 2020). None of this can be ignored when trying to understand the conditions emerging in any of the region's major cities.

The regional dimension of this book does not imply that any one country, or set of countries, speaks for East Africa as a whole. The aim is not to paint a picture of

---

[10] The AfDB definition also includes the island states of Comoros and Seychelles, which for obvious geographical reason it does not make sense to consider within my own analysis, as well as Sudan. I exclude Sudan for reasons relating to its predominantly desert geography and culture and strong links to North African Arab societies.

the region based on the experience of a handful of countries; it is rather to suggest that regional factors are central to the causal explanations of urban change in specific countries and cities. The countries the book focuses on—Ethiopia, Rwanda, and Uganda—are the primary focus within its broader concern with East African urbanization because of their distinct and extreme urbanization dynamics. With urbanization levels of 17.2 per cent, 20.8 per cent, and 23.8 per cent for Rwanda, Ethiopia, and Uganda respectively, all three countries are significantly below the East African average of 28 per cent, as illustrated in Figure 1.1 (UNDESA 2018). Yet over the past quarter century, they have been urbanizing even faster than the region as a whole. Uganda has for some time been the fastest urbanizing country in the world, bar none. Over the past twenty-five years its urban population growth rate has averaged at 5.98 per cent, with Rwanda close behind at 5.46 per cent (notwithstanding some significant fluctuation within this period, as indicated in Figure 1.3) and Ethiopia at 4.51 per cent—all above the regional average of 4.36 per cent and African average of 3.55 per cent (UNDESA 2018).

These countries are also of particular interest because of their very high population density, regardless of rural or urban classification. Their exceptional population clustering is clear if you look at any map of population density in sub-Saharan Africa; outside of Nigeria and some surrounding parts of West Africa, easily the most significant centres of population concentration and density are in inland East Africa—specifically, the Ethiopian highlands and the area around Lake Victoria (see Figure 1.4).

In sum, the regional dimension is an important part of the story of how cities in any of these individual countries are evolving. This emphasis helps to counter a tendency in urban theorization to sweep between the global, local, and

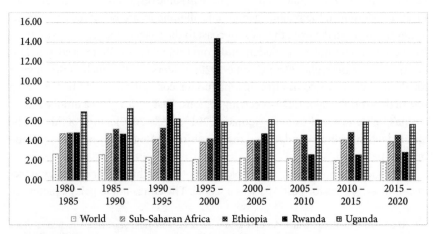

Figure 1.3 Annual rate of urban population growth 1980–2020
Source: Based on data from UNDESA (2018).

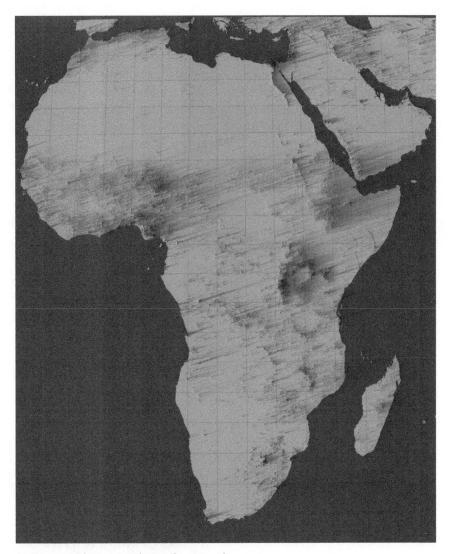

Figure 1.4 African population density spike map
© Alasdair Rae; reproduced with permission.

occasionally national levels without attention to differentiation between supranational regions (Taylor 1982; Brenner & Theodore 2002; Brenner & Schmid 2015). Attention to regional dynamics also challenges us to think carefully about how we understand the different scales at which politics shapes and responds to urban change.

1.4 Scaling the politics of urban development

This book is not a study of the fundamental drivers of urbanization. Often associated with structural economic change and industrialization, recent research has shown that urbanization is ultimately rooted in demographic change, with economic development playing only a supporting role that varies substantially by context (Dyson 2010 Fox 2012). The focus here is rather on how politics in its varying forms influences urban processes in urbanizing contexts, in ways that demand to be understood if attempts to generate more socially just and equitable urban futures are to succeed. Decades of ineffectual (or actively damaging) market-based and managerial urban reform programmes attest to ongoing failures to adequately engage with the politics of urban development. The kinds of politics *generated* by urban socio-economic and spatial development are discussed in Chapter 8. The majority of the book, however, is concerned with how political relations mould urban built environments and living conditions in different ways under conditions of late urbanization. To explore this requires reflecting on how we define politics, and how political relations at different scales impact on urban development and change.

One influential approach to politics in recent scholarship, which draws particularly on the work of Rancière (1995; 1998), draws a line between the instituted order of things and how this is governed ('the police' or 'police order') and the practices involved struggles for emancipation ('the political'). For Rancière, politics itself is where the 'police' and the 'political' meet, although the occlusion of the latter by the former through technocratic rule and the veneer of democratic consensus has created a contemporary 'post-political' condition. In this view, politics itself is effectively reduced to 'the police' through the tyranny of consensus (Rancière 2004; Mouffe 2005; Dikec 2005).

These conceptions of contemporary politics are rooted primarily in liberal democratic states in the global North and sit oddly with political conditions in East Africa. Despite donors' attempts to push de-politicized conceptions of 'good governance' onto governments of recipient countries (Doornbos 2001), the idea that East African societies are post-political and dominated by technocratic consensus does not withstand much reflection. Work by political scientists such as Resnick (2014a; 2014b; 2020) and Paller (2014; 2019) has explored how, with regard to Africa generally, political power recurrently subverts the formal instituted order of governance. In such contexts, the 'high' politics of political leaders and the coalitions they assemble in order to govern are frequently as informalized, and as transversal in their interface with formal governance structures, as the politics at street level (Helmke & Levitsky 2004; Bratton 2007; Mahoney & Thelen 2010; Radnitz 2011). Politics in such contexts is as much about *struggles among elites to settle the instituted order of things in their interests* as it is about struggles for emancipation and equality.

Even with respect to the global North, political scientists interested in urban contexts have long been concerned with the informal dimensions of elite politics, which are seen as central to how cities really work (Mills 1956; Stone 1989; 1993; Stoker and Mossberger 1994). Yet these approaches have tended to assume that city politics can be somehow 'sealed off' from broader national, regional, and global processes (Lauria 1997: 75; Sellers 2005). Meanwhile, the wealth of literature deploying Marxian political economy approaches to the city since the late twentieth century tends to privilege the global processes through which operations of capital hold sway over local politics and urban formations (Harvey 1978; 1985; Taylor 1982; Smith 2002). When trying to reconcile some of these diverse approaches to the politics of urban development, we cannot therefore ignore the question of scale.

Urban theory has long had a fixation with the problem of scale (Harding & Blokland 2014), particularly since Castells' (1977) pioneering work on the 'urban question'. One influential contribution was Taylor's (1982) tripartite approach to scale which frames the global as the scale of reality, the nation-state as the scale of ideology and the city the scale of experience. Written near the onset of late-twentieth-century economic globalization, this attached particular significance to the global scale in ways that have since attracted extensive criticism, leading to attempts to nuance Taylor's approach into less rigid conceptions of the vertical and horizonal 'scalar structuration' of social relations (Brenner 2000).

The question of scale became so fraught as to lead some geographers to suggest we now live in a world that 'post'-scale, due to the unsettling of territorial dynamics through globalization, the rise of networks, and the pace of flows (Amin 2004; Marston et al. 2005). The debate on scale is far from over however, as Brenner's recent work attests (Brenner 2019). I share Brenner's view that scale is analytically useful in understanding contemporary urbanization, and that the city is only one element within 'the multiscalar, polymorphic, and restlessly mutating geographies of capitalist urbanization' (Brenner 2019: 14). This is true for the politics of urban development as much as for other dimensions of urbanization. This politics is shaped by forces ranging from city-level planning frameworks to national political party competition, regional infrastructures and conflicts, and global architectures of capitalist investment and international development assistance. Rather than assign 'the juggernaut of globalization' a greater degree of significance than other scales, as Taylor arguably did (Marston et al. 2005: 427), we must take seriously a number of scales that can be justified as ontologically relevant when accounting for the tangled processes of causality in urban development.

This attention to scale also relates to the interdisciplinary endeavour at the heart of this book, because interdisciplinarity requires working across analytic frames in which scale is usually either implicit or explicit. To engage in analysis of the politics of urban development in East Africa is to draw from debates that span planning (which focuses primarily at the city scale), political economy (with its longstanding national framings), and the historical sociology of state-making through conflict and colonialism (which require thinking beyond nation-states), as well as the study of global capital flows. For the purposes of this book, attending to scale enables an analysis that accounts for some of the distinctive overall trends in the trajectory of urban East Africa as well as explaining divergent urban developments between its countries and cities. This is the central problematic to which we now turn.

1.5 Structure of the argument

This section first sets out the core empirical puzzle with which this book is concerned—how to explain significant emergent differences in urban development trajectories in East Africa—before turing to a summary of the analytical framing and argument.

The empirical puzzle

While global capitalism and regional conditions of late urbanization explain much about the general nature of urban development in East Africa, they cannot explain the different urban trajectories within it. It is these differences between urban contexts and outcomes that frustrated the planners, local officials, advisors, investors, and residents quoted at the start of this book. Such actors possessed varying capacities to implement rules and regulations, govern the urban economy, collect taxes, develop mass housing or large-scale infrastructure, acquire land, and mobilize collective urban dissent. These differences cannot be accounted for simply with reference to diverse regulatory-institutional structures through which neoliberalism is filtered (Peck et al. 2009; Brenner et al. 2010). Indeed, many such structures, having been shaped by European colonialism and subsequently Western development co-operation, are similar across the region. Understanding why shared global and regional dynamics can produce such varied urban outcomes is vital if we want to understand the prospects for shaping better urban futures.

Through a comparison of Kampala, Kigali and Addis Ababa, this book explores similarities and differences in four areas that are central to processes of urban change, and in which clear divergences are apparent. The first is the deployment of urban planning visions and major urban infrastructure projects. Here we see a stark contrast between a sustained commitment to high-level masterplanning processes in Kigali, with a service-sector-driven infrastructure push as the dominant urban economic paradigm, and a long-term 'anti-planning' political culture in Kampala in which major urban infrastructures are disembedded from the urban economy and targeted as sources of private gain. Meanwhile,

Addis Ababa has seen the most spectacular investments in large-scale mass-infrastructures, though these have taken on a life of their own due to widespread use by social groups for which they were not initially designed.

The second area relates to patterns of property development and housing provision, here conceptualized as *urban propertyscapes*. In the context of a remarkable construction boom across the region, the extent to which propertyscapes vary across urban and national contexts is often overlooked. Formal institutions for managing and regulating land and property have greater force in Kigali than either of the other cities, but it is also in the Rwandan capital that high-end residential property development has most dominated the transformation of the built environment, to the point of evident over-supply. In Addis Ababa, meanwhile, commercial property development is a relatively more salient feature of urban transformation, alongside a massive state-subsidized housing programme. Such a programme is virtually non-existent in the other two cities. In Kampala the state plays a far smaller role in any kind of property or housing development, which remains highly unregulated.

The third area of difference explored in the book relates to attempts to reshape urban marketplaces and regulate petty trade, with important impacts on urban life and livelihoods. Marketplaces and street trade are intensely political in all three cities, but in varying ways and with divergent outcomes. In Kampala, markets thrive all around the city despite factional disputes and a range of modalities of struggle in face of attempted privatization and redevelopment. Street vending has also been informally cultivated through clientelistic politics, despite periodic attempts to eradicate it from parts of the city. In Kigali, markets have been relocated and severely constrained in number and scale, with very limited scope for vendors to contest these changes, alongside a sustained repression of the street economy. Meanwhile, Addis Ababa's largest marketplace has become a site of significant collective power in the face of threatened redevelopment, and street trade has been incorporated into a state-driven entrepreneurship drive, rather than virtually 'invisibilized' as in Kigali or made a site of constant political bargaining as in Kampala.

The final area of difference to be explained relates to the ways that urban populations have responded to the changes discussed above through different registers of political mobilization. The difference in urban political registers is most immediately striking between Kampala and Kigali, but differs in significant ways between all three cities. In Kampala, the contestation of urban transformations has predominantly taken the form of protest, vocal collective negotiation, and at times periodic violent rioting—described here through the vernacular term 'noise'. In contrast, political dissent in Kigali has primarily taken the form of consciously 'silent' resistance and individualized acts of refusal in an environment of self-censorship and mutual policing. In Addis Ababa, political mobilization has oscillated between top-down incorporation of urban populations into an authoritarian political project, and the counter-mobilization of urban dissent with the potential to overthrow regimes in a way that seems unimaginable in the other two cities.

The explanation

This book argues that these different urban trajectories in each of the above areas can be explained through the intersection of four overarching causal factors, rooted in political economy and political sociology: i) the *distribution of associational power* within the wider nation-state; ii) the *pursuit of social legitimacy* by governing elites; iii) *modalities of political informality* at the city level and their relationship to formal governance structures; and iv) *legacies and practices of urban infrastructural reach*. These four factors—conceptualized in detail in Chapter 2—are situated against longer histories through which distinct forms of territory, property, and economy have been forged over centuries, often through processes of state-making and trade with a significant regional dimension (Chapters 3 and 4).

The first factor, the *distribution of associational power*, draws on the growing literature on the 'political settlements' approach within political economy analysis (Khan 2010; Gray 2013; 2018; Whitfield et al. 2015; Pritchett et al. 2017 Kelsall 2018), but with a focus on one central aspect: the structure of power relations between organizations and groups within a given national state. This distribution is shaped by historical dynamics of territorialization, property and economic structuring, as well as major conflicts and their outcomes. The resulting distribution of power, although never static, inevitably influences the distribution of resources and favours in a city, depending on which social and economic groups the city plays host to and how they are organized.

However, these political economy factors are not sufficient to explain why governing elites invest, regulate, control, and distribute resources in cities in the ways that they do—or why and how resistance emerges. This also requires attention to how coalitions of governing elites seek sufficient legitimacy to enable them to govern cities, and which sources of legitimation they appeal to in order generate enough support or acquiescence to govern effectively (Beetham 1991; Gerschewski 2013). The varying sources of legitimacy depend on historical paths to power and the constituencies they have gained and lost in the process, as well as their ideological orientations. The focus on distributions of associational power is therefore augmented with attention to the strategies elites deploy in *pursuit of social legitimacy* within cities, and how these respond to the legitimizing practices of opposition groups and movements.

Urban socio-economic and spatial outcomes are about much more than arrangements of power and the strategies of political leaders. They are also rooted in everyday processes, institutions and norms of state–society negotiation established over time, which condition the way urban transformations are bargained over and contested. The third factor, therefore, relates to *modalities of political informality*, calling attention to how informal institutions interact with formal frameworks for governance, planning, and regulation (Helmke & Levitsky 2004; Auerbach et al. 2018; Rubin 2018; Goodfellow 2020). Certain modalities of informal political negotiation may operate as a 'default' mode in a given context, building on particular histories of learning. Yet city-dwellers may also draw on diverse modes of political informality depending on what they are seeking to achieve, and how this is constrained or enabled by formal governance processes.

The fourth factor relates to both social and material infrastructures, and how these mediate the 'reach' of the state. On the one hand, ideas of 'infrastructural power' deriving from Mann (1984; 1986) facilitate analysis of the social relations that enable or constrain the implementation of governmental decisions across territories. These social networks of control and coercion are rooted in processes of territorialization and state-building, often evolving in parallel with control over land. Related to (but distinct from) these social relations is the deployment of *material* infrastructures by the state that generate lines of attempted and sometimes subverted control over both territories and populations. Such infrastructures continue to exert influence over development processes long after their inception (Winner 1980; Bennett 2010; Mains 2019; Aalders 2021). Infrastructural power and material infrastructures are interconnected: it is not mere coincidence, for example, that the Rwandan state has substantial implementation capacities and also one of the most developed road networks in Africa (Herbst 2000). Yet material infrastructures are not simply 'the long arm of the state' (Amin & Thrift 2017). They possess their own capacities to alter the course of urban change, as important but unpredictable mediators of the distribution of associational power and strategies of legitimation. This book approaches these complex infrastructural dynamics though the conception of *legacies and practices of infrastructural reach.*

Framing the drivers of differential urban development in relation to these four overarching factors does not preclude other things being significant. In particular, land tenure and economic history are central to any urban development story. These historical factors are accounted for in this book with reference to processes of territorialization, the evolution of property in land, and the operations of capital. These processes are examined in depth in the historical Chapters 3 and 4. However, the quadripartite framework outlined above provides a lens through which to understand how different *histories* in relation to land and capital filter into present day politics and translate into *active causal factors in a contemporary context.*

To conceptualize how these intersecting factors shape differential paths of urban transformation in the twenty-first century, this study combines attention to scale with understandings of causal force derived from critical realism. Critical realist approaches to causality, rooted in the foundational work of Bhaskar (1975) and Archer (1995), enable explanations that can assign meaningful causal force to social structures without seeing these as deterministic of human action. The framework adopted here, developed inductively over the course of long-term analysis of urban development in East Africa, embodies the perspective that causality is 'always the product of an unruly mess of interacting powers that happen to rub up against another at that particular moment and place' (Elder Vass 2010: 47). I argue that for heuristic purposes we can think of the factors that drive different forms of urbanization in the region as operating at different scales. While the dynamics of *global* capitalism and *regional* late urbanization account for many of the similarities between the cities studied here, their differences must be sought in the patterns of power, legitimacy, political informality, and infrastructure that are variously conceptualized at *national* and *urban* scales. How the causal factors are abstracted against scale is discussed at the end of Chapter 2.

As will be demonstrated throughout this book, the national-level distribution of associational power matters profoundly for urban development, particularly in terms of the relative ability of key social groups such as students or informal workers to make claims on the state that can divert attention and resources from other groups. We will see that the relative weakness of these groups in Rwanda (where the distribution of power is narrow) contrasts with a much broader distribution in both Ethiopia and Uganda, with important implications for urban propertyscapes and political mobilization. In all three cases, urban constituencies have grown in significance due to the pace of urbanization, and governing regimes increasingly seek legitimacy among urban groups. Yet the particular strategies for achieving and maintaining legitimacy they deploy are highly differentiated, depending on their pathways to power, ideological orientation, and the relative organizational capacities of different urban groups to mobilize opposition. This helps to explain the stark differences in infrastructural and livelihoods outcomes, including between Addis Ababa and Kampala, despite notable similarities in the breadth of power distribution.

However, the book also argues that dominant socio-political norms in a city, and how they intersect with the state's infrastructural 'reach', affect how these attempts to hold power and build legitimacy play out in urban space. In contexts such as Kigali, where state infrastructural power is relatively strong for historical reasons and collective political dissent is constrained, performances of compliance with state-sanctioned visions bolster regulatory enforcement and spatial control. Yet where levels of state infrastructural power are lower for historical reasons, as in Kampala, formal institutions and governance structures often act as a foil for informal political practices that gain their very legitimacy by discrediting state structures. Here the politics of building urban support and attempting to overcome opposition play out in ways that tend to further undermine already weak formal institutions for spatial regulation. Addis Ababa occupies an intermediary position in terms of infrastructural power and political informality. Here there is a remarkable capacity to roll out state-driven infrastructure projects and employment programmes, but limited capability for ruling authorities to control their use, and a wide range of social and political forces shaping the socio-economic trajectory in dynamic tension with the top-down visions implemented through this infrastructural reach.

In all cases, the presence of major material infrastructures generates opportunities and constraints for urban development, layering further unruliness onto the forces driving urban change. Unscripted practices associated with material infrastructure help to account for the perpetuation of spatial fragmentation in Kampala, the inhibition of foreign investment in Kigali, and the creation of new socio-spatial dynamics in the peripheries of Addis Ababa. This book argues that we need to take seriously the interaction of all of these forces to understand differential patterns of urban transformation. Only through this understanding can we hope to overcome past failures to support just and equitable outcomes on the world's urban frontier and beyond.

1.6 Organization of the book

This book is organized in three parts. Part I, 'Urban Tectonics', includes this opening chapter and Chapter 2, which sets out the book's analytical framework in detail. 'Tectonics' refers to the processes that control the structure of the earth's surface, and how these evolve through time through the rubbing together of tectonic plates. This book, and the discussion in its first two chapters, is likewise concerned analytically with the 'rubbing together' of things—of disciplines, causal factors, and scales of causal force—in pursuit of an explanation of contemporary urban form and function. I therefore use urban tectonics as a metaphor for the focus on structures and process that control and shape cities, as particular components of the earth's surface and as human, socio-technical, and political creations.

Chapter 2 begins with a discussion of some contemporary strands of urban theory, and how these engage with or deflect questions of causality. Drawing on critical realism, it explains this book's interdisciplinary approach to causal force, particularly in relation to questions of structure and infrastructure, and the human and non-human elements that shape urban transformations. It then sets out in detail each of the four casual factors used to explain divergent trajectories of urban development in this book: the distribution of associational power, the pursuit of social legitimacy, modalities of political informality, and legacies and practices of infrastructural reach. Finally, it discusses how these are conceptualized in relation to one another through a 'level-abstracted' analytical lens on the politics of urban transformation.

Part II of the book, 'Urban Foundations', draws primarily on secondary sources to develop historical narratives of urban development in the three countries under study here, in two distinct steps. Chapter 3 focuses on questions of urban territory and property. It begins by discussing the distinction between these two concepts, how they are interrelated and how each has played a different part in the evolution of East African states and cities. It then traces the making of urban territory from the emergence of the first kingdoms in the Great Lakes region, the internal imperial conquests of the Horn of Africa and the city-states of the Swahili coast. After this I consider the colonial encounter and its effects on land policy and on urban formations, examining varying forms of territorialization and property formation generated by colonial urbanism. Dynamics of urban land in the early postcolonial period are then examined, in the context of seismic changes and attempts to nationalize land and overcome colonial legacies in Rwanda and Uganda, as well as the radical transformations that shook Ethiopia after 1974. The chapter closes with a discussion of land policy and its urban ramifications under the victorious rebelled regimes that claimed power in Uganda, Ethiopia, and Rwanda in the closing decades of the twentieth century.

Chapter 4 turns to the making of urban economies, again taking in a broad sweep of history from the early modern period to the present. Framing the evolution of urban economies in relation to the idea of 'operations of capital', it traces the early evolution of a regional trading economy from the Indian Ocean to the interlacustrine zone, and the parallel economic integration within the Horn of Africa, before turning to the colonial period and the impact on cities of colonial railways and various forms of investment and disinvestment. It then examines the early postcolonial decades, tracing the journey from optimism and economic promise to revolutions, ruptures, and economic collapse. Finally, it examines the celebrated economic development achievements of the three case-study countries and their manifestations in the capital city, setting the scene for the divergent urban transformations to be discussed in the remainder of the book.

Part III, 'Urban Currents', turns to the core empirical material of this study, set out in four chapters that respectively explore the turn towards new urban visions and the urban infrastructure boom, the evolution of real estate and housing, the urban informal and street-level economy, and registers of political mobilization in the face of exclusion and marginality. Chapter 5 traces the path from urban neglect and, in some cases, clear rural bias towards a new enthusiasm for urban investment and engagement in the twenty-first century. It then sets out the context for international investment in African infrastructure, before discussing one major infrastructure 'mega-project' in each city. I argue that these projects typify the priorities and modes of infrastructure governance in each case, and explain their relationship to legacies of infrastructural reach and attempts to construct particular forms of legitimacy. However, the chapter also explores some of the more contingent and unanticipated outcomes of these infrastructures and their role in shaping urban change on the ground.

Chapter 6 turns to urban propertyscapes in the twenty-first century. After explaining how a real estate sector was developed in each case out of the ashes of conflict, it delineates the basic incentives and constraints in the sector and how these have served to channel ever more resources into the 'secondary circuit' of capital, further drawing capital away from more productive forms of investment.

I then consider questions of mass housing provision, particularly in Addis Ababa, which has been the site of one of Africa's most extraordinary state-driven housing experiments, and consider why so little urban housing has been built in the other cases. In a comparative discussion, I argue that different distributions of power and strategies of legitimation are central to accounting for the different emergent urban propertyscapes across the region.

Chapter 7 examines the economy of the marketplace and the street. In each of the three cities, major efforts to territorially restructure market trading have been undertaken in the early twenty-first century, but with divergent outcomes. I explore these before then considering the arena of street vending and hawking, and the different forms of marginalization, persecution, and negotiation that characterize street life in the three cities. The chapter argues that differences in both legitimation strategies and legacies of infrastructural power here combine with varying modalities of political informality to explain the variation in street economies, and consequently the experiences of vendors, hawkers, and hustlers. I argue that how these groups are connected to political regimes through negotiation, attempts at incorporation, or agendas of outright invizibilization provide a lens onto the broader politics of urbanization in each case.

Chapter 8 builds further on the analysis of modalities of political informality, interrogating the registers of political dissent and engagement among urban-dwellers at the receiving end of the urban projects explored in Chapters 5–7. After a discussion of questions of continuity and rupture in urban politics, it considers the historical evolution of political culture in each case. I then explore the dominant political registers that have surfaced and consolidated as ruling elites have pursued urban transformation alongside different forms of authoritarian control. Arguing against generic conceptions of 'resistance', I suggest that violent protest has become increasingly institutionalized as a political register in Kampala, in contrast to the relative silence of individualized refusal in Kigali and the more penetrative forms of mobilization and counter-mobilization in Addis Ababa.

Part IV consists of Chapter 9, the book's conclusion. Here I revisit the questions of capitalist globalization and late urbanization and the extent to which they can explain convergence and divergence in the region's urban trajectories, before reviewing the main findings of the book through the prism of its analytical framework. The chapter concludes by reflecting on the achievements, limitations and lessons of efforts to reshape territory, property, and social contracts at the global urban frontier.

2

Transformation and divergence

Explaining contemporary urban development trajectories

Introduction

This book is concerned with explanation. To some extent, it seeks to explain the historical trajectories of urbanization in East Africa and their distinctiveness globally; but for the most part it explains difference within this region at the level of states and cities. This chapter elaborates a framework for explaining urban divergence and differentiation in East Africa, setting out in detail four central explanatory factors, which represent a distillation of the various ways that politics—conceived as the organization and articulation of power and interests—drive urban change.

This attention to causality is at odds with much contemporary social analysis and urban theory, which through the influence of post-structuralist philosophy has become oriented towards questions of ontology and interpretation—a manifestation of a broader 'ontological turn' in the social sciences (Todd 2016). As an interdisciplinary field, urban studies has always been concerned with the fundamental nature of the urban, but today it is more preoccupied with this than ever. Questions of *what* are predominant: what is encoded in the very idea of the urban (or 'urbanism') today? What is actually going on in the places that we call urban that might previously have been overlooked, misconstrued, or simply absent?[1] Accompanying this has been a renewed focus on the epistemology of the urban, particularly in the context of the 'Southern turn', which justifiably demands that we question received wisdoms about how cities work and the basis on which this knowledge has been constructed (Roy 2005; Watson 2009b; Schindler 2017; Schmid et al. 2018; Lawhon & Truelove 2020). In this way, scholars are unpicking the long histories through which cities beyond the canonical 'blueprints' of the global North have been characterized as lacking, partial, incomplete, or simply failing.

This turn towards thick description, interpretation, and epistemology also reflects the exhaustion of totalizing structuralist accounts in which the explanatory

---

[1] See, for example, Amin and Thrift (2002), Roy (2011), Brenner and Schmid (2015); Scott and Storper (2015), Robinson and Roy (2016); Amin and Thrift (2017), Pieterse and Simone (2017), Schmid et al. (2018)

Politics and the Urban Frontier. Tom Goodfellow, Oxford University Press. © Tom Goodfellow (2022).
DOI: 10.1093/oso/9780198853107.003.0002

potential of 'neoliberalization' is yielding diminishing returns (Parnell & Robinson 2012; Venugopal 2015). There has been an understandable desire to further specify the urban experience through ethnographic detail, emphasizing what Simone and Pieterse (2017) term 'redescription'. A rich literature focused on new vernaculars for interpreting urban life is emerging, particularly with reference to the South (De Boeck 2015; Pieterse and Simone 2017; Bhan 2019). Partially overlapping with this is a concern with socio-material and socio-technical assemblages, which can be linked both to the diverse urban material conditions around the world and the rise of technologies that increasingly saturate urban life, generating widespread interest in 'more-than-human' forms of agency (Gandy 2005; McFarlane 2011a; Amin & Thrift 2002; Graham & McFarlane 2014; Amin & Thrift 2017).

This chapter begins by considering these recent currents in urban theory, and their limitations when it comes to questions of causality. Despite a deep concern with different forms of subjectivity, agency and relationality, the post-structuralist underpinning of many of these recent approaches to the city largely decentres a concern with *cause*. This consideration leads to a discussion of the approach to causal force adopted in this book. The chapter then turns to the four constituent elements of the book's analytical framework, exploring each of these in detail, before returning to the question of scale and reflecting on how these factors intersect to shape trajectories of urban development and change in East Africa.

2.1 Causal force and urban change

A significant fracture has opened within urban analysis between approaches that broadly sit within the field of political economy, and those rooted in theoretical and epistemological ideas that question the very foundations of this field. In particular, both Actor-Network Theory (ANT) (Law 1992; Latour 2005), and 'assemblage' theory (Deleuze & Guattari 1988) focus on processes of social composition and association (often conceived as being essentially 'flat', non-hierachical or 'rhizomatic') rather than on causal structures (Brenner et al. 2011; Rankin 2011). In contrast with political economy perspectives, these approaches generally treat the idea of 'interests' with suspicion (Michael 2016; 16), and ascribe significant agency to non-human entities or 'actants' including material objects (Bennett 2010; Farías & Bender 2012; McFarlane 2011a), reflecting a broader 'new materialism' in social thought (Coole & Frost 2010; Appadurai 2015). Notwithstanding the insightful conceptualizations of urban processes and urban life that have emerged through these lines of enquiry, this book is more concerned with explanation. While the book shares these authors' concern with processes, and the perspective that contemporary urban conditions are neither static nor fixed, it reaffirms the importance of understanding urban conditions as outcomes that can be subjected to causal analysis.

The problem for the analyst who is serious about causality is that theoretical approaches committed to exploring multiplicities of 'rhizomatic' and contingent connections leave one not knowing where to look for causal force. The risk when trying to think causally through these perspectives is that they present 'amalgams of "practices" which oscillate wildly between voluntarism and determinism' (Archer 2000: 6). We might therefore ask, as Appadurai (2015: 24) does, 'If the only sociology left is the sociology of association, then will the only guilt left be guilt by association?' A focus on causality necessarily amounts to a search for some higher-level 'guilt' (to use Appadurai's analogy), even if this is widely distributed and requires disentangling at different levels and scales.

While many post-structuralist approaches reject an explicit focus on scale, in practice their analytic lenses tend to be local or even microscopic: ANT is interested in 'discrete occasions of local interaction' (Michael 2016: 24), while to the extent that assemblage thinking engages with causality it does so 'not in wider or underlying contexts, but *within* particular contexts' (McFarlane 2011b: 383). Thus, even though assemblages may be 'translocal' (McFarlane 2009), the coming together of things *causally* to generate what Amin and Thrift term 'urban force' is a process situated at local scales within the city (Amin & Thrift 2017: 16). The idea that extra-urban causal forces can fundamentally shape the urban—without being constituted within it—has little place in these frameworks.

This study is concerned both with relations inside the city and with forces beyond that act upon it. A rejection of 'methodological cityism' (Angelo & Wachsmuth 2015) is especially important in contexts of late urbanization where economies (and cities) have been so vulnerable to vagaries of global capital flows and flight, and to seismic national revolutions, wars, and regional upheavals. This book centres both causality and scale because some of the most interesting differences between urban conditions emerging within East Africa can be explained through the interface of politics, social institutions, and infrastructures, and thinking about scale can enrich understandings of where similarity ends and difference begins.

The role of the causal analyst is to offer explanatory frameworks that can 'simplify and extract from the impossible complexity of actual causation' (Elder-Vass 2010: 53). In approaching this, I draw on the critical realist perspective that beneath 'actual' events and processes that we might empirically observe, there lie 'real' (if unobservable) causal structures and mechanisms (Bhaskar 2007/1975). Because of the disturbances that intervene between these causal mechanisms and the world of actual events, the former do not generate 'exceptionless regularities', instead merely operating as 'tendencies' (Fleetwood 2001). Furthermore, actual events are not produced by single causes, but by the complex interaction of multiple real causal forces (Elder-Vass 2010). These are often 'emergent', in the sense that social structures and groups can have causal force that is more than the sum of individual agency, though does not eradicate the latter (Archer 1995).

Since interdisciplinary analysis is fraught with misunderstanding around the use of key terminology, in this book I make a distinction between *causal force* and *power*. The former term is used to denote a whole range of causal influences combining to shape outcomes, while the latter is used here specifically in connection with human relations. This distinction is particularly important because of the ways that the concept of power (and relatedly, agency) will be deployed in this book, as discussed in the sections to follow. In many post-structuralist approaches, non-human force has been conceptualized in terms of the 'vitality' and 'liveliness' of matter, essentially attributing to it a form of agency (Bennett 2004; 2010). Thus, for Amin and Thrift, 'infrastructure is just as lively as the most enterprising city actors' (Amin & Thrift 2017: 115). While this book frames material infrastructures as being causally efficacious, it does not do so through attributing them agency; rather, it builds on Appadurai (2015) in conceptualizing infrastructures in terms of *mediation*. The material constitution and effects of infrastructure do not exist separately from infrastructure's role in mediation: mediation and matter are mutually interdependent (Appadurai 2015: 234). While infrastructure is a forceful mediant of human power, knowledge, and ideology, it is not a reliable mediant; it can strengthen or weaken those human flows and structures, and introduce new dynamics. In the framework of this book, infrastructure therefore can possess causal *force,* but does *exercise power* or agency in the same way that human individuals and groups do.

Part of the reason for delimiting the scope of non-human force here is that materialist and relational approaches to the city now sometimes argue for the capacity of material things not only to 'act' in causal processes, but to be sentient. The notion of infrastructures and machines being agents in 'subterranean plots' or 'machinic intrigues' (Bryant 2014: 81; Amin & Thrift 2017) is bolstered by forms of algorithmic intelligence that change how cities work. Yet many if not most cities are a long way from being governed by sentient computational infrastructures. Cities not (yet) engineered as 'smart' are no less complex, but their complexity and networked-ness is more about the roles and activities of *humans* than of algorithmic technologies, as Simone (2005; 2018) recognizes. It is the extent of human improvisation and creativity, which can be related in many respects to the lack of advanced infrastructural solutions, that characterizes much of the life in cities of the global South. In such cities, 'holding up the walls' is a metaphor for the jobs not of material infrastructures but of people, through lives of 'endless favours' (Simone 2018: 3). Rather than effectively assigning agency to material substrates, it resides largely within a 'substrate of residents', albeit one that exists within a complex ensemble of things (Simone 2018: 17; Lancione 2019).

None of this is to entirely reject insights from the new materialism, and this book builds on ideas about how socio-material forces can enrich political analysis (Bennett 2004; 2010; Coole 2005; McFarlane & Rutherford 2008; Mains 2019). Infrastructure is political in multiple ways; it can 'become the focus of political action' and it is able, as a mediating force, 'to convert often quite small interventions into very large gains' for certain groups (Amin & Thrift 2017: 6). How this feeds into the broader conceptual framing will be explored in the final section of this chapter. First, however, we turn to the element of the book's analytical framework that draws most clearly on political economy approaches, bringing these into conversation with critical realist ontologies of social structure.

2.2 The distribution of associational power

Debates on how the distribution of power among social groups and organizations affects development outcomes have been enlivened by the political settlements approach (PSA), particularly as developed by Mushtaq Khan (1995; 2010; 2018) and others including Di John & Putzel (2009), Whitfield et al. (2015), Gray (2013; 2018) and Kelsall et al. (2022). For the most part, the PSA has been used to explain differential economic growth and structural transformation outcomes (Hickey et al. 2015; Whitfield et al. 2015; Pritchett et al. 2017). This book focuses on a different set of outcomes, which are narrower in that they concern the city scale, but broader in going beyond economic indicators to encompass changes to physical form, the regulation of space and socio-political trajectories such as protest mobilization. The PSA is thus used here selectively, and in combination with other analytical approaches.

A political settlement is about much more than just the distribution of power; it also involves a particular institutional structure, highlighting the relationship between the former and latter.[2] Yet as Khan's more recent writings indicate, 'the distribution of organizational power' is the framework's central pillar (Khan 2018). This relates to the more general proposition in the PSA that how institutions function, particularly in terms of their capacity to generate economic growth, is a consequence of the relative 'holding power' of different groups and organizations who contest resources and shape formal and informal institutions in their interests (Khan 2010). This concept of 'holding power' requires greater critical attention than it has received in the PSA literature to date. Also, the idea that 'groups' possess power—reflected in regular references within the literature to 'powerful groups'—is assumed without much discussion. The terms 'group', 'organization', and sometimes 'class' or 'faction' are used by Khan and other PSA advocates with relative fluidity and interchangeability. This attention to the power of groups is not

---

[2] I consider institutional dynamics below, in the section on political informality. There are several other important aspects of the political settlement approach not considered in detail here—for example, the technological capabilities of different groups of capitalists and how these relate to rent distribution (see e.g. Khan 2010: 69–75 or Gray 2018: 64–66). I do not discuss these as they are not of central significance for the urban outcomes I seek to explain.

a weakness of the PSA; rather, it is one of its key strengths.[3] But the question of how the power of groups is constituted, and when power becomes 'holding power', are less well-developed dimensions of the framework. Here critical realism, rooted in sociology and concerned with the ontological basis for ascribing power to social structures generally as well as groups specifically, is of particular value.

Social groups and causal force

Some of the most significant fault-lines in the longstanding structure–agency debate relate to whether social structures are ontologically distinct external forms (as Durkheim believed) or exist only as embodied and internalized, as in the theories of Bourdieu (1977; 1990) and Giddens (1984). In contrast to post-structuralist perspectives that vest causal efficacy in agents (or actants) and their relations, or older structural approaches that subsume agency beneath structures almost entirely, critical realist approaches often see structure and agency as exerting their influence in different temporal moments (Archer 1995). There are 'external structural moments' in which structures themselves have causal force through their effect on agents' motivations and dispositions, though this does not mean that structures predetermine people's actions.

However, critical realism is also concerned with questions of *emergence:* how and when collective human agency becomes more than the sum of its parts to effect additional change in the world, through entities that we might consider as social structures. For Elder-Vass (2010), most of the structural powers that have usually been attributed to 'society' inhere in smaller and more clearly defined social groups, at the intermediate level between individual and society (Elder-Vass 2010: 82). This is predicated on the idea that groups, like any entity made up of different parts, are constituted in two ways: first by particular 'morphogenetic' causes that *generate* relationships between those parts to create the group, and second by 'morphostatic' causes that hold these parts together, thus accounting for the *maintenance* of this collective entity (Archer 1995). Relevant social groups for this book's purposes might include, for example, students, urban market vendors, petty bureaucrats, or landowners. A group such as market vendors is created 'morphogenically' by their coming together as actors pursuing similar livelihoods in a given spatial setting, but also maintained 'morphostatically' through everyday practices, relationships, and norms that bolster collective identity and interests. Such 'norm circles' are one of the ways that groups exert causal force (Elder-Vass 2010).

[3] Gray illustrates how the PSA is one of the few political economy frameworks that takes historically constituted social groups seriously, while other approaches—from traditional Marxist to neoclassical economics and New Institutional Economics—take as their core units of analysis either class, the state, individuals, or elites (Gray 2018).

While any group that generates a sense of continuing commitment and identity in this way can be thought of as an *association,* when such groups are structured through particular specialized roles involving relations of authority and hierarchy, they can be thought of as *organizations* (Elder-Vass 2010: 149–157). Some of the groups that exercise power within a given political settlement might be organizations, but others are merely associations—hence the framing of this dimension of the book's analytical framework as 'the distribution of associational power' (rather than Khan's 'organizational power'). To continue with the above example, whether or not market vendors are ordered into a structured hierarchical organization with clear specialized roles, they still have 'associational' qualities as a group (even if a politically or organizationally divided one) by virtue of a shared identity as vendors and a range of 'norm circles' and practices that have evolved over time.

Adopting a critical realist perspective that takes the causal force of social groups seriously helps us to move beyond a focus on 'elites' that dominates much contemporary political economy, enabling a recognition that what matters is the distribution of power between historically constituted groups (Behuria et al. 2017). Whether we think of groups as 'structure' or as forms of 'transpersonal agency' at one end of a 'spectrum of agentic capacities' (Coole 2005) is less important than recognizing that they have causal efficacy. Arendt goes so far as to argue that 'power is never the property of an individual; it belongs to a group and remains in existence only so long as the group keeps together' (Arendt 1970: 44). Yet once we accept that groups are ontologically relevant sources of causal force, we need to consider how this manifests, including in relation to Khan's idea of 'holding power'.

Political settlements and 'holding power'

'Holding power' is defined by Khan as the ability of a group to engage and 'hold out' in conflicts with other groups—particularly conflicts over institutional outcomes that affect the allocation of benefits (Khan 2010: 6; 2018: 640). Building on this, others have defined the term as the ability to assert or maintain claims to property and income flows (Gray & Whitfield, 2014: 11). 'Holding power' is therefore a specific conception of power linked to the capacity of groups to acquire and maintain material benefits relative to other groups whose interests may conflict. Alongside economic resources, factors affecting relative holding power include representation within institutional hierarchies, traditional sources of authority, the ability to mobilize ideologies, and histories of political mobilization and success in past conflicts (Gray & Whitfield 2014; Behuria et al. 2017; Khan 2018).

Previous political struggles leave groups with legacies and resources, both in terms of the normative institutions and practical capacities they generate but also their symbolic nature and capacity to inspire identity and commitment

(Gray 2018). But the relationship between resources and power itself is not always straightforward; unlike resources themselves, power cannot be 'stored up' or 'held in reserve' in particular places; nor does it simply 'flow' through networks. Rather, power is mobilized within and across space by actors and groups with particular associational capabilities (Allen 2003). For example, despite the disintegration of their formal organizational authority in the early 2010s, minibus-taxi owners in Kampala have retained a substantial capacity to mobilize urban associational power due to their ability to exert themselves collectively in the face of the city government's efforts to 'modernize' the transport sector (Goodfellow 2017c; Goodfellow & Mukwaya 2021a).

When thinking about the distribution of 'holding power' within a given setting, the PSA posits that in most developing countries pre-existing political and economic orders have been unsettled by the adoption of new—often capitalist—formal institutions, yet these do not align very well with the existing power distribution among groups (Khan 2010). There has long been a debate about the power and significance of domestic capitalists in Africa, and their role and relative strength varies substantially across the continent (Berman & Leys 1994; Whitfield 2018; Behuria 2019a). Yet it is widely accepted that the evolution of capitalists as a social *class* with distinct associational power has not been well-supported by the state, from their suppression under colonialism to various forms of marginalization under successive postcolonial approaches to development (Boone 1990; Mkandawire & Soludo 1999; Gray 2018; Behuria 2019a). In these circumstances, the power of many groups derives from sources outside capitalist (and democratic) institutions, not only through 'traditional' authority structures but other forms of informal institutions and patron–client relations through which land is allocated, economic opportunities generated, and services such as security and justice provided.

The power dynamics that matter depend on what it is that we seek to understand; 'we do not need a map of the relative power of *all* organizations to carry out a particular analysis' (Khan 2018: 643). The distribution of power relevant to the allocation of urban land rights may not involve the same groups as that which is relevant to security provision, for example. Depending on the specific setting and issue under consideration, groups relevant to the distribution of associational power in East Africa can include associations that consolidate the interests of people with ownership of key economic assets (e.g. major landowners); waged workers in specific sectors (including through unions); associations of self-employed/informal workers; students; religious groups; members of 'customary' or 'traditional' authorities; current and former members of the military; and organized diaspora exerting influence from overseas.

These groups often have porous boundaries, overlap and intersect, and may involve their own internal hierarchies. They are, however, nevertheless relevant in terms of both the 'norm circles' they generate and their systems of internal relationships, all of which give them the potential to mobilize associational power—or to *be* mobilized, for example by political parties. Parties themselves are of course a significant form of mobilizing collective, but much of East Africa is characterized by dominant party systems in which opposition parties are relatively weak (Randall & Svåsand 2002; Lebas 2011). Dominant parties establish such over-arching channels for the mobilization of power that within the PSA it is more meaningful to examine the coalitions of groups that they need to assemble in order to achieve this dominance, rather than putting parties themselves at the forefront of analysis (Khan 2018; Kelsall 2018; Goodfellow & Jackman 2020).

In this sense it is meaningless to just study 'ruling elites' without considering how they maintain their position by mobilizing and repressing groups that possess the potential power to destabilize it. The extent to which individuals and groups are linked into a ruling coalition differs in nature and degree. Some have 'thrown in their lot' with a political elite, pegging their political or economic fortunes to that elite's survival, while others more readily switch political allegiance (Goodfellow & Jackman 2020; Kelsall et al 2022). Excluded groups also vary in their potential to disrupt a ruling coalition's dominance; those with greater disruptive potential (i.e. strong enough holding power to threaten the ruling coalition in some way) may either be co-opted into the coalition, repressed, or potentially both at different times (Kelsall et al. 2022). In cases where they do manage to disrupt the ruling coalition's dominance—either through precipitating regime change or through a destabilizing event that demonstrates their potential to weaken that dominance—this can be viewed as a 'political rupture' that indicates a shift in the overall distribution of associational power (Behuria et al. 2017).

The extent to which the state itself possesses 'autonomous' power relative to social groups has been the subject of longstanding debate. Dating back to Marx and Weber, and associated particularly with Poulantzas (1980), the idea of the state's 'relative autonomy' in processes of economic transformation was revived from the 1980s (Evans et al. 1985; Evans 1995; Geddes 1994). In the framework of this book, the distribution of associational power that underpins the state, rather than state power itself, is central to explaining the kinds of urban investment and physical transformation that are promoted by governing elites, and how these are contested. Meanwhile the most significant question about the state's own power relates not to 'holding power' but to its 'infrastructural power'—in other words, the capacity for decisions by ruling elites to be *implemented* through populations and across territory. This is analytically distinct and considered separately below.

2.3 The pursuit of social legitimacy

The distribution of associational power alone cannot explain the specific decisions made by ruling elites about how to deploy resources, ideas and ideologies within urban areas. This also requires attention to what ruling elites in a given context perceive they need to do in order to secure sufficient popular legitimacy for cities to remain governable; a crucial issue given that cities—and especially capitals—are so often where regimes visibly rise and fall. The concept of legitimacy has been subject to continual debate in political science, political philosophy, law, and sociology. A common fault-line runs between normative conceptions (generally the preserve of political philosophers and legal scholars), and sociological ones focused on actual public consent and support rather than abstract principles (Barker 1990; Beetham 1991; Simmons 1999). Related distinctions are sometimes made between juridical and empirical legitimacy (Henderson 2015) or between legitimacy that is derived extrinsically and that which evolves intrinsically (Bereketeab 2020). While the normative/sociological binary is critiqued on the grounds that populations' beliefs about what is legitimate are themselves grounded in normative principles (Schmelzle 2016; Abulof 2016), there is value in highlighting the differences between abstract debates on legitimacy and more locally rooted understandings of it that play out on the ground.

The concern here is with the latter, drawing on a long tradition emphasizing the validity of subjective views in defining political legitimacy (Weber 1922/1968; Lipset 1959; Merelman 1966). I use the term 'social' rather than 'political' legitimacy because although political actors and organizations are the focus, the social foundations of their legitimacy and how they seek to bolster this are central factors in explaining urban development outcomes. The term political legitimacy holds associations with *state* legitimacy and with legitimation through particular kinds of institutions and political processes (Englebert 2002), but these constitute only of the means through which ruling coalitions achieve legitimacy. Importantly, the social foundations of legitimacy are often built outside formal political processes, and outside the state. Merelman emphasizes that 'the policy-making process in a society may be viewed as a gigantic process of communication and learning' through which legitimacy is constructed (Merelman 1966: 549). Social legitimacy is thus generated through positive and negative feedback in the processes of making, implementing (and strategically non-implementing) policies.

Within the PSA, legitimacy has sometimes been presented as part of an explanation for the holding power of a particular group (Khan 2010; Behuria et al. 2017). Yet legitimacy requires attention it its own right, because of the highly variable strategies and tactics that groups deploy in order to bolster their legitimacy, and the socio-economic effects of these. Legitimacy is a construct that requires active reproduction by governing coalitions (Beetham 1991). While the production and reproduction of legitimacy can make government more effective (Alagappa 1995; Schmelze 2012), it can also do the opposite because it does not necessarily involve working through and strengthening state institutions (Weyland 2001). On the contrary, a common mode of legitimation in certain urban contexts involves 'forbearance', defined as an 'intentional and revocable government leniency toward violations of the law' (Holland 2016: 233). For example, mayors in Chile often systematically prevent the police from using their legal powers and resources in relation to illegal street vending as a means of building political support (Holland 2016). This can erode the authority of state institutions while it builds the popular legitimacy of personalistic or populist leaders. Other mayors might vigorously support policing street vending to court urban middle-class groups and businesses who are opposed to it. A focus on the pursuit of social legitimacy therefore draws attention to the chosen *means* through which political elites attempt to bolster legitimacy, and how these impact on the built environment, state institutions, and the socio-economic fabric of cities.

Sources of legitimacy vary enormously, beyond the Weberian triad of traditional, charismatic, and legal-rational forms of authority to include specific sources from heredity and ethnic or socio-economic origin to democratic process, technical expertise, or the capacity to ensure security (Beetham 1991). Another approach classifies legitimacy in terms of input, output, or 'throughput' (Schmidt 2013; Chemouni 2016). The distinction between 'input' and 'output' legitimacy has become common in studies of governance (e.g. Scharpf 1999; Weiler 2012), with the former usually referring to democratic procedures and the latter to state performance. Although input legitimacy is generally associated with electoral processes, in authoritarian or semi-democratic settings it is often constructed in non-democratic ways, drawing instead on resources as varied as charisma, heredity, and rulers' roles in key historical struggles (Chemouni 2016: 207). A concern with 'throughput' legitimacy was added to the common input-output dyad to emphasize the way governance procedures themselves can become sources of legitimacy 'in terms of their efficacy, accountability, transparency, inclusiveness and openness to interest consultation' (Schmidt 2013: 2).

In seeking to grow or maintain their legitimacy, ruling coalitions and rival political groups may attempt to tap into these different forms, either singularly or in combination, depending on their predispositions, the constituencies they are courting, and the distribution of associational power. This generates specific kinds of actions, ranging from favours to particular socio-economic or religious groups to the pursuit of technical solutions or the ramping-up of the security apparatus. However, it is not only what actors and organizations do, or who they are, that gives them social legitimacy: it is also the how they mobilize ideologies and discourses to justify their actions (Gramsci 1971). In contexts of authoritarian rule specifically, where the legitimating meta-narrative of democracy is absent or patently hollow, the mobilization of other ideologies and legitimizing discourses is often necessary (Gerschewski 2013; Gebregziabher 2019a).

In the context of contemporary Eastern Africa, one such discourse is that of developmentalism, which can be conceptualized as a tenacious ideology of promoting state-led capitalist economic expansion against the odds (Harrison 2020). This can provide a powerful discourse of 'output legitimacy' (Schmidt 2013), which in authoritarian settings can distract from a lack of democratic 'input' into government. A second, contrasting legitimizing discourse is that of populism, defined as a political strategy based on anti-elite rhetoric, appealing to the masses, and the pursuit or exercise of power by a personalistic leader based on direct, unmediated support from mostly unorganized followers (Weyland 2001: 14). Here an emphasis on direct, personal connection with particular constituencies takes precedence over concrete developmental outcomes. Populist strategies can be effective in urban areas with highly informalized economies, where collective mobilization against wealthy elites gains a particular resonance, given the latter's proximity and visibility (Cheeseman & Larmer 2015; Resnick 2012; Resnick 2014a). A third legitimizing discourse of particular relevance is that of securitization, which can be particularly seductive in contexts afflicted by major civil conflict where 'conflict fatigue' has placed a large premium on territorial security. In cities more generally, securitization discourses are often used to crack down on aspects of everyday urban life such as informal street vending and squatting, when the overriding motive is often to disperse potential opposition as well as to build legitimacy with urban middle class groups (Potts 2006; Resnick 2019).

These discourses and associated practices of legitimation play central roles in urban politics, and their consequences for urban space are highly diverse, ranging from major housing programmes or targeted infrastructure investments to more subtle effects on urban form that unfold over time—including through 'forbearance' that weakens the regulatory strength of state institutions. However, strategies and tactics deployed in pursuit of social legitimacy do not exist outside of the urban institutions and norms that afford them value and efficacy in a given context; these too exert their own causal force.

2.4 Modalities of political informality

Shifts in the distribution of associational power, and the practices associated with constructing legitimacy, are filtered through place-specific normative environments through which urban social and political interaction have evolved over time. Informal institutions or norms are fundamental to political life. Within the PSA, the allocation of benefits informally is considered a defining feature of clientelist political settlements (Khan 2010), but there is little attention to the highly variable ways that informal political institutions operate and the extent to which they support or undermine formal governance processes. The idea of modalities of political informality captures salient variations in how informal political norms and practices relate to formal institutions. These can have a substantial impact on urban development outcomes and cannot be subsumed within either the distribution of power or pursuit of legitimacy.

Even where they are widely flouted, formal institutions matter in politics because official rules, regulations, and processes are part of the 'dynamic process of move, countermove, adjustment, and negotiation' that constitutes politics (Tarrow, 2012: 3). In much of Africa, the fact that legal and regulatory frameworks were often imported through colonialism (and subsequently, through donor support and intervention) creates particular challenges for postcolonial governance (Mabogunje 1990; Watson 2009a). Formal institutions therefore have often not evolved out of the kinds of historical struggles that bestow them with authority in developed capitalist economies (Gray 2018). In urban areas, constellations of institutions such as laws, ordinances, plans, and regulatory frameworks are particularly dense and complex, being the spaces in which colonization and formal authority generally establishes itself. Cities in the global South are thus thick with formal institutions, but are also places in which such institutions are widely undermined by informal institutions and practices. Yet the relationship between official procedures and the informal norms structuring urban life varies widely, both between and within urban contexts, with significance for urban spatial and economic outcomes. To unpack this variation, I here distinguish between four types of political informality: *pro-formal, anti-formal, para-formal,* and *a-formal.* Each of these is now considered in turn.[4]

Some political practices that occur outside official procedures are largely supportive of the formal political institutions in place. In their typology of informal institutions, Helmke & Levitsky (2004) include 'complementary' ones, which increase the likelihood that formal rules will be enforced. Building on this, Azari and Smith (2012) propose categories of 'completing' informal institutions (established norms that fill in gaps and ambiguities in existing formal political institutions) and 'coordinating' informal institutions (regularized practices that aim to resolve conflicts and overlaps among existing formal rules). Both of these can be considered as aspects of *pro-formal* politics, in the sense that they facilitate the better functioning of formal rules.

Analyses of the rise of Asian 'developmental states', for example, have highlighted how cronyism and informal bargaining between key firms and public authorities ensured the effective functioning of those states (Gerlach 1992; Evans, 1995). Tsai (2007), meanwhile, shows how local governance in China depends on collectively enforced informal norms of accountability to fill gaps in formal institutional capacity (Tsai 2007: 371). This focus on informal chains of accountability resonates with Tilly's (2005) work on the significance of informal 'trust networks' in public life, which through long historical processes often become partly integrated into the state.

However, given that many developing countries today have formal institutions generated extrinsically through colonialism and donor influence, there is often an extensive realm of informal practices that actively undermine or disrupt this formal framework. The second modality of political informality is therefore *anti-formal* politics. Political activities that deliberately challenge or weaken formal

---

[4] This section draws heavily on Goodfellow (2020a), though in abridged form.

institutions can be top-down in nature, involving elite practices to build political support through 'forbearance', or can involve popular mobilization against extant rules from below. Politicians managing their relationships with citizens under conditions of competitive clientelism often engage in highly anti-formal and anti-procedural behaviour. Indeed, populist legitimizing discourses often draw on and exacerbate anti-formal political cultures—particularly when they take the form of 'neo-populism', defined by Weyland (2001: 14) as involving a marked 'anti-organisational and anti-institutional orientation' that can involve consciously deprecating formal laws and systems to construct popular support (Weyland 2001: 14).

This vilification of the formal is particularly relevant to urban areas, where planning and regulation are convenient scapegoats for political figures positioning themselves as popular heroes pledging to 'protect' particular groups from rules and regulations through the generation of a 'state of exception' (Roy 2005). Through their power as voters, or mobilizers of popular discontent, urban groups can informally negotiate their political value in order to try and secure 'protection' from formal institutions, thereby playing their own part in the reproduction of anti-formal politics. Note, however, the contrast between these practices and those such as petitioning by a registered special-interest association for a change in the law, which is not anti-formal since it works *with* official process and seeks to formally change structures rather than subverting or seeking unofficial 'exemptions' to them.

Unlike the above two categories, some political practices co-exist with formal institutions without either actively supporting or undermining them. These often form distinct normative systems in their own right, here termed *para-formal*. Much clientelism and corruption fall within this category, including routinized forms of mutual exchange which operate alongside formal rules for political engagement, often contradicting but not seeking to challenge the latter. Corruption itself is regulated 'in accordance with complex rules, and tightly controlled by a series of tacit codes and practical norms' (Blundo et al. 2006: 5). This speaks to the extensive Africanist literature on varying conceptualizations of corruption, which has advanced concepts such as 'prebendalism'—the strategic allocation of public resource streams to supportive elites—in which rules governing the conduct of public officials remain in place but are of secondary concern (Joseph 1987: 8).

This echoes Ekeh's conception that postcolonial African societies are characterized by 'two publics' involving different moral foundations, but with the same political actors simultaneously operating in both (Ekeh 1975: 93). Similarly, but drawing explicitly on Weber, the literature on 'neopatrimonialism' in Africa proposes that politics is defined by two distinct but co-existing 'logics'—one patrimonial, and the other legal-rational (Erdman & Engel 2007: 105). These conceptualizations, however, frame all of politics through one essentializing binary. The approach taken here highlights a more nuanced range of logics through which informal politics operates, for example drawing attention to differences between informal political practices that actively subvert formal rules and those that merely co-exist and intersect with them.

The above three modalities describe systems of political interaction that have their own normative structure: in other words, though informal, they draw on and reconstitute social norms. In contrast, the fourth modality describes forms of political practice that exist largely outside of norms and shared expectations: a category of *a-formal*. The degree to which informal political bargaining and negotiation is bound by norms is often difficult to determine; there is no obvious moment when bargaining transitions from a space of unpredictability into one of order and stability, or vice versa. At one extreme, however, there exist informal political practices in which rules are unclear or non-existent, or where different norm systems clash to the point that no rules have effective force. The a-formal is a sphere of tactics, uncertainty, and unpredictability where institutions are withheld or break down, rather than a space of alternative institutions. In Tillyean terms, political negotiation and bargaining in such spaces occurs largely outside of 'trust networks'.

Human beings generally strive for certainty and stable expectations, so this mode of politics is rarely a 'natural' state of relations. Yet there are often active attempts to create a-formal political spaces by actors or organizers seeking to disable political opposition through the weakening of norms of trust and reciprocity. As Tapscott (2021) shows, in Uganda political leaders project their power in deliberately arbitrary ways to 'inject unpredictability' into the relationship between local authorities and citizens, in order to make it 'difficult to predict which rules will be applied in any given situation' (Tapscott 2021: 38, 199).

The complexity of urban contexts, in which mobility and transience can render human relations provisional and contingent (Simone 2004b; 2005), can also give rise to everyday micro-politics that are improvisational and 'rarely institutionalized into a fixed set of practices, locales or organizational forms' (Simone & Pieterse, 2017: xi). This is a state of flux, which in time would be expected to settle into new normative frameworks; yet in the cut and thrust of urban politics it can be reproduced, undermining trust and predictability, and exposing people to heightened risk and manipulation. The ways in which the previous three modalities of political informality emerge and consolidate relates to the earlier discussion of 'norm circles' (Elder-Vass 2010), and aspects of this are explored in Chapter 8. A-formality, however, alludes to situations in which norm circles have broken down, generating levels of socio-political precarity and uncertainty that can make surviving in the city especially hard.

The purpose of outlining these categories is not to suggest a rigid framework for putting particular practices in boxes. It is to offer a typological language for interrogating the forms of political negotiation prevalent to varying degrees in contemporary cities, training a lens on how informal negotiations and practices interact with formal governance. These varying modes of political informality often co-exist within cities, with some taking on particular salience in different places and times. An analysis of shifting political informality over time can illuminate features of what is sometimes just dismissed as the 'chaos' or fluidity of urban political life. But it can also help in explaining concrete urban outcomes, for example in situations where anti-formal politics is widely adopted as a populist tactic and undermines urban regulations, where ingrained para-formal norms render governance reforms ineffectual, or where collective action is hampered by a-formal contexts in which trust networks have been eroded.

2.5 Legacies and practices of infrastructural reach

As noted in the first section of this chapter, a growing literature argues that infrastructure is 'no longer an effect but a cause' (Amin & Thrift 2017: 34). Its role in causality is not straightforward, particularly if we think beyond its concrete impacts on urban space to consider its 'promises' and political symbolism (De Boeck 2011; Larkin 2013; Easterling 2014; Anand et al. 2018). Infrastructure carves deep legacies into territories and societies, intentionally or otherwise (Rodgers & O'Neill 2012; Appel et al. 2018). The experience of Apartheid renders South Africa a paradigmatic case for understanding the effect of infrastructural legacies on contemporary urban development, including in terms of infrastructure providing a site for the contestation of power and articulation of citizenship rights (von Schnitzler 2016; Lemanski 2019). The rejection of infrastructure's legacy can take the form of covertly mimicking the 'sly' forms of power embodied in its design, 'hacking into' its subversive potential (Easterling 2014).

To understand the causal force of infrastructure therefore involves attention to its past, present, and potential futures. Within political science and political sociology, infrastructural force has often been related to the transmission of political power. Rather than a focus in its own right, infrastructure is here relevant only as a means to mobilize power, or even as a metaphor for the dispersal of power. The latter is most obvious in Michael Mann's concept of 'infrastructural power'. The 'reach' of state power with which Mann is concerned cannot, however, be separated from the actual physical infrastructures and infrastructural legacies that enable it, and how these intertwine with the social networks and institutions that project such power. The remainder of this section discusses the idea of infrastructural power before considering some other ways that infrastructure is conceptualized as having causal efficacy, drawing these both into a broader articulation of infrastructural force.

Infrastructures of state reach

Mann's celebrated 1984 paper makes a distinction between 'despotic' and 'infrastructural' power. While his subsequent two-volume magnum opus explores four dimensions of social power—economic, military, ideological, and political (Mann 1986)—'despotic' and 'infrastructural' are framed as subcategories of the latter, and specifically of state power. Despotic power is about ruling coalition's freedom to make binding decisions; infrastructural power refers to the state's ability 'to penetrate civil society, and to implement logistically political decisions throughout the realm' (Mann 1984: 113). In his 'Alice in Wonderland' analogy, despotic power is the Red Queen's power to order Alice's head to be cut off, while infrastructural power is her logistical capability to hunt down Alice and execute her.

Infrastructural power is distinct from mere bureaucratic capacity or administrative efficacy, because the state's capacity to penetrate social life and implement decisions may have more to do with social control and societal communicative hierarchies than bureaucratic qualities (Soifer 2008; Soifer & vom Hau 2008; Goodfellow 2015). This echoes Foucauldian ideas about the 'capillary' nature of modern power, which instantiates self-disciplining subjects by circulating through everyday discourses and micro-practices (Fraser 1981). Yet the extent to which 'capillary' or infrastructural power has been achieved in different parts of the modern world is subject to debate. Mann sees states in the contemporary global North as characterized by high infrastructural power and low despotic power, because democratic politics has constrained executives while simultaneously institutionalizing structures that facilitate infrastructural reach. In the global South, degrees of both despotic and infrastructural power vary much more widely (Mann 2008). In many colonized African states, the intricate 'capillary' network on which effective infrastructural power depends was not achieved (or was actively undermined) by colonial rule, despite advancing despotic power (Comaroff 1998). It has thus been argued that power in colonial states was 'more arterial than capillary' (Cooper 1994: 1533).

In reality, the depth of infrastructural power in Africa varies widely. The historical origins of differential state 'reach' in Africa have been extensively explored by Herbst (2000) and Cooper (2002), with varying emphases on precolonial, colonial, and postcolonial heritage. Discussing Nigeria, Lucas (1998) notes that the impetus to build and maintain despotic power to dominate a fragmented postcolonial society actively impeded the development of infrastructural power, undermining the channels of social organization on which it depends. Yet in other African states such as Rwanda, the evolution of a territorially bound and densely populated precolonial kingdom (and subsequently colony and postcolonial republic) meant that structures of communication and organization were embedded in ways that make despotic and infrastructural power mutually reinforcing (Purdeková 2015). In Ethiopia, gradual and highly variable patterns of territorial augmentation over time mean that infrastructural power varies widely across the country (Lavers 2020).

Infrastructural power is then something that needs explaining in any given case, and is created and conditioned partly by other forms of social power, as well as by demographic and geographical factors. Mann's other sources of power—military, economic, and ideological—are all factors relevant to the earlier discussion of the distribution of associational power. The infrastructural power of the state itself is conditioned by this distribution of power, through a temporal relationship whereby past conflicts among groups and their outcomes have institutionalized a given degree of infrastructural state reach. Within East Africa specifically, the diversity of historical experience in terms of the distribution of power—examined in Chapters 3 and 4—has therefore contributed to producing differential infrastructural power.

Mann saw Africa as a continent in which variation in infrastructural power is especially pronounced within states as well as between them (Mann 2008: 363). Much attention to subnational variation has been directed towards rural areas in which state penetration is most self-evidently weak (Herbst 2000; Boone 2003; Jones 2008). However, there is also significant variation among and within urban areas (Davis 2009). The capacity to deliver services is confined to pockets of the urban space even in major cities like Lagos (Gandy 2006) and Durban (Schensul 2008), for reasons related to the reach of state infrastructural power in the face of organized interests, but also to legacies of partial, divisive, and ruptured forms of infrastructure provision.

Although Mann's distinction between two forms of power is a useful device, it thus raises the question of what the actual infrastructures are that transmit 'infrastructural' power, and how to analyse them in relation to historical legacies, present investments, and future aspirations. As well as enabling things such as bodies, materials, goods, energy, and communications to be transmitted, infrastructures enable the power of groups, organizations, and states to be conveyed. On the one hand, this involves 'soft' infrastructures like social networks for organization and communication; yet on the other, it enrols the 'hard' infrastructures on which such organization and communication depend. These infrastructures are not, however, always reliable transmitters of power. With implicit reference to Scott's (1998) idea of 'seeing like a state', which often involves 'high modernist' efforts to bludgeon cities into a new shape through top-down planning, Amin and Thrift counterpose the logic of 'seeing like a city' (2017: 29). This requires attention not only to the 'brute force' that states and other actors seek to exert over cities, but to the disruptions and feedback loops generated by urban infrastructures themselves.

Infrastructural 'vitality'

There no space here to do justice to the burgeoning critical literature on the 'infrastructure turn', itself part of a wider anti-anthropocentric turn in the human sciences (Boyer 2018). The discussion is therefore confined to a few threads of this literature that speak to questions of causality and politics. The idea that infrastructure itself exerts causal force has been extended into the study of politics through broader work on the political role of artefacts, including that of Bennett

(2010), whose aim was 'to see how analyses of political events might change if we gave the force of things more due' (Bennett 2010: viii). This builds on Winner's classic essay 'Do artifacts have politics?', which considered how machines and physical structures should be judged not only for their efficiency or productivity 'but also for the ways in which they can embody specific forms of power and authority' (Winner 1980: 121).

What does it mean, however, for artefacts such as infrastructures to 'embody' power? On the one hand, they *reveal* underlying forms of political rationality (Larkin 2013; Easterling 2014), being an 'embodiment of standards' that include some but exclude others (Star 1999: 381). In this sense, infrastructure is always socio-technical, incorporating some element of human design meaning that it can be read as a 'script' (Larkin 2013; Amin 2014). In Rodgers & O'Neill's (2012) terms, the exclusions of infrastructure can be through 'active' forms of 'infrastructural violence' on the part of infrastructure designers (from Hausmann's Paris to Robert Moses' New York), or through the more 'passive' ways in which infrastructure routes the power of, for example, capital. Urban political ecologists have thus explored how capitalist infrastructures redirect flows and circulations of things such as water, energy, food, and waste to make cities into socio-natural hybrids with inclusionary and exclusionary effects (Swyngedouw 2004; Heynen et al. 2006).

Yet the point being made by Bennett, among others concerned with infrastructure's capacities to engineer social change, is that infrastructure does not only channel and reveal power but can play its own autonomous role in shaping political outcomes. Hence infrastructural 'liveliness' (Amin 2014) or 'vitality' can be defined as the capacity of things to act as 'forces with trajectories, propensities, or tendencies of their own', and thus to 'make a difference, produce effects, alter the course of events' (Bennett 2010: viii). Among the things that infrastructure can be seen to 'do' is generate new patterns of behaviour when it provides a basis for use and alteration in ways far removed from (or actively contrary to) the goals of its designers (Mrázek 2002; Harvey & Knox 2012; Anand et al. 2018). As infrastructure unfolds over extended time periods, new interests, plans, and designs emerge. There is thus a 'subversive grain' within infrastructure (Amin & Thrift 2017: 123), linked to its often 'unruly and expansive promise' (Harvey 2018: 99) that generates a range of possibilities for repurposing and political action. However, as discussed previously, this need not lead to the attribution of *agency* to infrastructure, which instead can be conceptualized as a 'disturbance in a causal milieu, the material entity which motivates interferences, responses or interpretations' (Humphrey 2005: 43). This mediation by infrastructure can affect how political relations are enacted, offering 'a vital means of tracing the co-emergence of political and material histories' (Harvey & Knox 2012: 534).

Regarding cities specifically, Amin and Thrift place infrastructure at the centre of their critique of Scott and Storper's 'agglomerationalist' conceptualization of the urban (Scott & Storper 2015), arguing that it is not spatial propinquity but rather assemblages of intersecting infrastructures that 'define settlement as urban' (Amin and Thrift 2017: 102) and generate 'urban force'. This raises the question of whether cities with less infrastructure are somehow less urban. Yet it is the very absence of certain kinds of physical infrastructure that come to define urban life in parts of the South; as de Boeck notes in relation to Kinshasa, 'many activities become possible not because there is a well-developed infrastructure available to sustain them, but because that infrastructure is *not* there' (De Boeck 2013 mimeo, cited in Amin & Thrift 2017: 127). Infrastructural scarcity and absence provide new forms of struggle and politics, as Amin (2014) himself notes, with the consequent human 'conjunctions' rendering people themselves a more central part of the infrastructure (Simone 2004a).

Towards a holistic view of infrastructural force

In incorporating infrastructure within its explanatory framework, this book acknowledges that historical materialism and 'vital materialism' can and must be combined in order to fully understand urban outcomes (Mains 2019). Infrastructure is fundamental to the exercise of human political power, but is also more causally significant than that. It is not simply the state's 'long arm', working unambiguously for established power hierarchies (Chu 2014; Amin & Thrift 2017). Attentiveness to infrastructure's subversive potential and capacity to 'disturb' intentional projects is also helpful in the East African context in nuancing analyses that posit a return to 'high modernism', through which a range of socio-economic outcomes are attributed high modernist orientation of certain governing regimes (Bähre & Lecocq 2007; Newbury 2011). Such schemes certainly exist, but their intended infrastructures of delivery are not always compliant.

Because of the dual capacities of infrastructure both to embody power and disturb it, Mann's 'infrastructural power' and the force of physical infrastructure to shape practices and subvert intentionality often exist in tension with one another. Infrastructure can generate new coalitions, activities, and potentially poles of power that are at odds with the designs and plans through which it was conceived. This is one reason why infrastructural power is so difficult to build. Not all roads and pipelines become channels to effect state or elite power; infrastructure often finds alignment with the broader distribution of associational power, but also holds the potential to shift it by altering how groups can tap into flows and circulations.

Collier's (2011) book *Post-Soviet Social* provides an interesting example of how legacies of infrastructural power rub up against practices associated with contemporary infrastructural configurations to shape urban outcomes. The 'city-building' projects of Soviet planners from the 1920s were part of a broader project through which the Soviet regime sought to know, re-socialize, and ultimately control populations, with widespread infrastructure provision playing a key role. The state thus built its infrastructural power in part through the provision of material infrastructures. However, the material legacy of these infrastructures had important repercussions for later efforts to radically liberalize and privatize infrastructure provision. Neither the pipes and wires from the socialist planning period, nor the social networks and bureaucratic routines that cohered around them, were easily extinguished by neoliberal 'shock therapy' (Collier 2011). 'Handed down' infrastructures thus generated conditions and practices that frustrated the post-Soviet state's infrastructural power as it attempted to implement liberalization.

In this way, *legacies and practices of infrastructural reach* refers both to the building and enabling of infrastructural power in the past, and infrastructure's role in generating socio-material conditions that affect the possibilities of contemporary urban development. Infrastructural legacies have evident implications for the capacity of states to implement decisions on the ground: relative ease of access to pockets of territory, the ability to turn on or shut off supplies to certain areas, and the speed and effectiveness of communication are central to implementation capacity. These depend on hard and soft infrastructure. But in addition to channelling of state power, infrastructure exerts its own force on events—and on cities—by sparking new agendas and behaviours unforeseen by planners, and by constraining or enabling actors, sometimes in ways that interact with shifts in the distribution of associational power.

2.6 A level-abstracted view of the politics of urban transformation

The four elements of the framework presented here reflect processes of analysis, reflection, refinement, and distillation through the study of urban development and change in East Africa over a period of ten years. Explanatory frameworks are always abstractions in which the analyst makes decisions about what constitutes a causal factor, and at what level to aggregate such factors. Each of the four elements aggregates various economic, political, social, and socio-technical processes. This framework therefore represents a judgement about where such aggregation should end and the demarcation of distinct factors begin. It represents claims that, for example, legitimacy cannot be collapsed into power; political informality involves institutional processes that are analytically distinct from both power and legitimacy; and the effects of infrastructure cannot be reduced to power or institutions.

It also represents the claim that understanding the critical *interactions* between causal factors is more important than separating them in pursuit of 'ultimate primacy': the attempt to identify one all-powerful causal factor (Mann 1986: 3). This book builds on critical realist approaches that not only interrogate the interaction between causal factors but also consider how these factors are *laminated*, operating at different levels of social aggregation. Lamination in this context refers to how causal forces emerge and crystallize at the level of social structures, conditioning but not predetermining causal forces at 'lower' levels of human agency (Elder-Vass 2010: 49). The book argues that when interrogating divergent forms of urban transformation, this sociological approach to levels of 'emergent' causality can be put into conversation with geographical attention to scale. Lamination can thus help to avoid the problem of 'methodological cityism' (Angelo & Wachsmuth 2015), whereby explanations of outcomes in cities are overly focused on the city scale itself (see also Goodfellow 2018).

This book therefore takes a 'level abstracted' view of causality (Elder-Vass 2010) in which the drivers of similarity and difference among East African cities are framed heuristically in relation to scales of causal force. The framework set out in this chapter comprises one causal factor largely associated with the national scale (the distribution of associational power) alongside two that I argue are analytically significant at the urban scale (the pursuit of social legitimacy and character of political informality), and one that straddles these two scales (legacies and practices of infrastructural reach). This does not mean that each of these are *exclusively* relevant at these scales, but rather that they take on particular causal salience at these analytical scales when explaining urban outcomes.

For the most part, the political settlements approach has assigned significance to the distribution of associational power at the national level (Khan 2010; Whitfield et al. 2015). This is unsurprising, given that economies are primarily organized nationally, and the constitution of socio-economic groups such as social classes reflects this, making them difficult to isolate analytically within a subnational geographic space. In any case, understanding the politics of urban change *requires* attention to the national distribution of power in order to account for the political weight of urban classes relative to, for example, farmers or powerful elite groups with economic and land-based interests beyond the urban. Actors and groups based outside national boundaries—for example capitalist firms, international donors and financiers, or diaspora—also hold significant associational power to influence developments within a national territory (Hickey et al. 2015; Meehan & Goodhand 2018). However, it is at the national level that this associational power becomes politically significant when we wish to understand the relationship between these groups and government policy or political decision-making.

Despite the national framings of the distribution of associational power, strategies for gaining social legitimacy adopted by political actors are often differentiated by place. Urban 'political projects' are designed to speak to important constituencies in the cities in question. It is therefore useful to think of strategies for the pursuit of social legitimacy at the level of a city itself, even though we must keep the distribution of associational power nationally in view. Similarly, when considering modalities of political informality and how informal practices relate to formal institutions, the remit of many such institutions relevant to this study—such as regulations, planning frameworks, urban ordinances, or elections to a city council—sits at the level of the city. Analyses of political informality in urban analysis are therefore best considered at the city scale, where the interface between formal and informal institutions has concrete ramifications.

When it comes to legacies and practices of infrastructural reach, the scale for analysis is more complex. In some ways, the city is the natural scale at which to analyse the forces that existing material infrastructures exert on patterns of urban change, given that cities are themselves 'entanglements of infrastructures' (Amin & Thrift 2017). Infrastructures within cities play key roles in catalysing, obstructing, or refracting other drivers of urban change. Yet infrastructures beyond the city, such as major rail lines, also contribute to urban change. Moreover, understanding the evolution of infrastructural power requires attention to national histories of state-building the extent to which 'capillary' social networks have evolved within a political community, though these may differ substantially across territory. Attending to infrastructural legacies and practices therefore requires a dual focus on national and city scales, recognizing that hard and soft infrastructures are part of both state-building and the specific ways that it is pursued and resisted within urban space.

In addition to conceptualizing these causal forces at the level of city and nation-state, any explanation of similarity and difference in contemporary East African urban forms must attend to the role of global capital flows and how these relate to regional characteristics framed here through the lens of late urbanization. In this study, these factors constitute the 'context of context' (Brenner et al. 2010), accounting for much of the generic shape of East African urban development. These global and regional factors *cannot*, however, explain the often-striking divergences in urban form emerging within the region. This is where accounts of particular cities that emphasize the framings and homogenizing tendencies of 'world city-making' fall short.[5] While these processes are very real, they fail to account for why cities in countries subject to the very same global and regional forces and ideals evolve very differently.

Table 2.1 summarizes the 'level abstracted' view of the causal forces shaping urban transformation adopted in this study. The active abstraction involved in such a framework bears re-emphasis: as Elder-Vass notes, 'real powers can be described in a level abstracted form, while actual causation always occurs in the form of multi-levelled events' (Elder-Vass 2010: 53). Equally, the point is not that each element of the framework singularly explains one outcome of interest, but rather that they combine and intersect to explain differential outcomes in relation to the domains of urban change examined here.

---

[5] See for example Goldman (2011) and Shearer (2017)

Table 2.1 A level-abstracted analytical framework

Analytic scale	Explanatory emphasis
Global context	- Advanced capitalism
Regional context	- Late urbanization
National level	- Varying distributions of associational power
National/urban level	- Legacies and practices of infrastructural reach
Urban level	- Strategies in the pursuit of social legitimacy - Modalities of political informality

Before examining contemporary patterns of urban development and change with reference to this framework, we need to turn to the deeper historical processes that shaped the very emergence of cities in the countries under study. Central to these historical experiences, which are the focus of Part II of this book, are processes of territorialization, the evolution of property in land, and the operations of capital. Rather than explaining contemporary divergences in themselves—which is the role of the analytical framework just presented in this chapter—these processes are examined as part of the historical evolution of urban formations in each city. Historical narratives of territory, property, and operations of capital help to account for the divergent distributions of power, sources of legitimacy, patterns of political informality, and infrastructural legacies and practices that in turn can explain contemporary divergences in each case. The first two of these processes— the historical evolution of urban territory and its intersection with the evolution of property in land—are the focus of Chapter 3.

PART II
URBAN FOUNDATIONS

3

The making of urban territory

Introduction

> There seems to be a widespread assumption that the land question is
> mute in an urban context.
>
> (Chitonge & Mfune 2015: 210).

There is growing recognition that Africa's land institutions vary enormously across space and time, with significant implications for contemporary politics and development (Lund 2008; Onoma 2009; Boone 2014). However, much of this attention has been focused on the 'agrarian question' and how governments have extended their reach across expansive rural terrain (Mafeje 2003; Bernstein 2004; Lund & Boone 2013; Boone 2014). Understanding what land regimes and their evolution mean for urban Africa is an increasing priority. Notwithstanding the explosion of interest in urban Africa in recent years, much of the scholarship is focused on contemporary challenges, with little attention to how the historical evolution of land institutions conditions contemporary urban formations.

Research on urban Africa only gathered pace in the 1960s, and was initially characterized by modernization discourses depicting cities as the epitome of modernity alongside concerns that urban 'detribalization' was pulling apart traditional societies (Mayer 1962; Cohen 1969). Cities were thus seen as a break with the past and a breach of African tradition; in this view, 'History had little place in towns, because towns had little history' (Anderson & Rathbone 2000: 10). This belies the rich and fascinating history of urbanism across the continent. East Africa presents a particular paradox: while it had highly developed urban-based civilizations dating back to antiquity in places such as the Swahili coast and Ethiopian highlands, by the nineteenth century it remained significantly less urbanized than many other parts of Africa (Burton 2017). However, despite these low levels of urbanization, the evolution of social formations and institutions for land use and land ownership are crucial for understanding contemporary urban formations and the politics that shapes them.

This chapter is devoted primarily to providing a historical background focused on ideas of *territory* and *property in land*, and how this links to the differing manifestations of the urban question across the region. Notwithstanding ongoing debates about the definition of both these terms (Clare et al. 2018; Halvorsen 2019;

Politics and the Urban Frontier. Tom Goodfellow, Oxford University Press. © Tom Goodfellow (2022).
DOI: 10.1093/oso/9780198853107.003.0003

Obeng-Odoom 2020), territory and property are conceptually distinct, involving different institutions and ideologies, and implicating the state in different ways. How territorial authority has been constructed by public authorities, often over long periods of time, plays a central role in government legitimacy and infrastructural reach. It is thus part of the historical foundation for many of the political projects proposed by states within their cities, and their capacity to implement these. Relations of property, meanwhile, are fundamental to the distribution of associational power among different groups, and consequently to their relative ability to win in struggles over the transformation of the urban landscape.

In exploring these historical roots of contemporary East African cities, this chapter begins with a general discussion of the role of territory and property in the evolution of urban spaces. Following this, it dives deep into the precolonial histories of the region, with particular attention to the two sub-regions that gave rise to the cities that form the main focus of this book: the Great Lakes and the Horn of Africa. This is contextualized in relation to some of the broader trends in precolonial land regimes within the region. Next it turns to the colonial period, first exploring the general patterns of territorialization in the Great Lakes and Horn sub-regions, and then turning specifically to the urban dimensions of land policy and the foundations for urban property rights in colonial Uganda and Rwanda, as well as imperial Ethiopia. This is followed by an examination of the changes to land policy and urban land regimes after independence in the two colonized states (Uganda and Rwanda), and in the Ethiopian case during the communist period after the 1974 overthrow of the imperial regime. Finally, we turn to the period since the 1980s/1990s when in all three countries power was seized by a new rebel military organization after years of civil conflict, ushering in a period in which the relationship between property rights, urban territorialization, and state power was again transformed.

3.1 Land, territory, and property in the making of urban East Africa

History is shaped by misunderstandings about land, as well as active conflict over it. When different societies come into close proximity, either through imperial conquest or freer forms of interaction, the assumptions that they bring to their engagement with land can often clash. Struggles over land are as central to the 'urban question' as to the agrarian questions with which they are usually associated. The making of urban places requires that agricultural land produces a surplus to allow for urban populations to inhabit a non-agricultural existence (Childe 1950); but it also involves new ways of thinking about how land is governed, taxed, and regulated. The co-evolution of land institutions and cities thus has broader implications for the developments of states. Indeed, the words for 'state' and 'town' are difficult to disentangle in some African languages (Fourchard 2011: 242), suggesting that this link is particularly significant in Africa.

In the history of human societies generally—and urban areas specifically—we can broadly distinguish between how land becomes constituted as *territory*, which involves layering specific institutions, authority claims and hierarchies onto land's geographical characteristics, and as *property* through relations of ownership and tenure. Because property is generally the preserve of law and economics, and territory of geographers, the relationship between the two is rarely interrogated (Blomley 2016) despite vibrant debate on both these concepts and their meanings in postcolonial contexts. Yet considering the relationship between territory and property is important, especially given the highly territorialized nature of land across much of East Africa for centuries before land was widely conceptualized as property in the way it is understood today,[1] and the variation in territory–property relations across the region.

Territory is more than simply 'bounded space' (Elden 2010); it embodies social and political relations evolved through historical processes (Agnew 1995: 379). It can be seen as a 'triangular relationship' between i) a piece of land, ii) a group of people living on that land, and iii) the political institutions that govern those people in that place (Miller 2012: 1). Territory is not necessarily the property of those inhabiting or claiming political authority over the land—or indeed the property of anybody; it is possible for land to be territorialized without any clear ownership structure. Concomitantly, as property, land is owned but not necessarily governed or territorialized by its owners (Lund 2013: 14).

Territory is often associated with particular 'political technologies' deployed by states in relation to terrain, and therefore with ideas of sovereignty (Elden 2013), though this has recently been challenged by approaches seeking to decolonize the concept and emphasize counter-hegemonic territorial claims (Porto-Gonçalves 2012; Clare et al. 2018). Rather than necessarily being about establishing sovereign authority through legal and cartographic institutions, territory has thus been defined as 'the appropriation of space in pursuit of political projects', producing 'overlapping and entangled' territorial relations in which domination and resistance co-exist (Halvorsen 2019: 791). Yet even by this definition, territory is about political claim-making over space in which the state is usually a dominant player, and about efforts to *control* terrain. Property, on the other hand, is a social relationship between human beings constituted through social institutions of ownership and use (Obeng-Odoom 2020: 74–75). Though territory and property are distinct,

---

[1] Samuel (2021) argues that, contrary to mainstream literature on land in precolonial Africa, institutions of property were actually widespread. However, this varied significantly across the continent and scholars such as Mafeje have maintained more generally that 'the jural connotations of, and the incidence of personal power in, "property" are too specific and restrictive to describe accurately the inclusive and variegated rights in land as understood by Africans' (Mafeje 2003: 3). See also Moyo 2018).

the enhanced control of territory can be a stepping stone towards ownership as property, and vice versa (Lund 2013: 29). In this sense, building infrastructural power can proceed through a mutually supportive process of establishing territorial authority and intensifying control over property rights. The allocation of property rights can also play a significant role in constructing the legitimacy on which territorial authority depends, as well as in altering the distribution of power among social groups.

In many parts of Eastern Africa, territorial rights have historically been very strong even where property rights were weak. Questions of who has authority over land, who owns land, and how the two have intersected historically provide the foundations for urban development today. Through territory has often been thought about in terms of nations and states (Blomley 2016), other scales of space are also territorialized—including the urban. Urban areas, as institutionally complex bundles of land with distinctive characteristics, regulatory regimes, and uses, have been constituted as territory and property in different ways and at different times across East Africa. As this chapter will show, significant new forms of urban territorialization took shape through the colonial and imperial encounters. Before considering this, however, we turn to the much earlier period of history, and how land regimes facilitated political control alongside the evolution of urban life.

3.2 Precolonial dynamics and the emergence of land regimes

Along with parts of Southern and West Africa, the Ethiopian highlands, Great Lakes region, and East African coast are three of the zones within sub-Saharan Africa where urban settlements have existed for centuries or even millennia (Kusimba & 2006; Connah 2015). Early sub-Saharan urban settlements often differed from idealized West Asian, Mesoamerican, and ancient Egyptian forms (Mabogunje 1969; Anderson & Rathbone 2000; Connah 2015), but in terms of population size, archaeological studies have found precolonial African cities to be of similar size to those elsewhere in the world (Storey 2006). However, to understand the modern evolution of cities in East Africa requires going beyond a consideration of the region's early cities. As Fourchard (2011) notes, historical scholarship on *non-urban* dynamics may 'constitute a central, and sometimes more valuable, body of research on cities than urban history itself' (Fourchard 2011: 224). To understand contemporary cities we therefore need to examine the kinds of territorialization, land tenure and land-use relations that evolved over time across the region's primarily rural social formations. These are, after all, what many cities today have been layered onto.

As one of the first regions of Africa to develop forms of statehood, parts of East Africa were territorialized from a relatively early stage—in particular, the Great Lakes region with its clutch of historic kingdoms, and the Ethiopian plateau. In the context of such territorialization (and in the spaces beyond its reach) diverse forms of property relations emerged, particularly through varying relations between pastoralists and agriculturalists. In this context, warfare between kingdoms and empires played a key part in the evolution of early urban centres (Reid 2001). The following sub-sections explore these dynamics in the Great Lakes and Horn sub-regions in turn, before briefly considering the Swahili coast and broader East African region.

The Great Lakes

The kingdoms that emerged in the early modern period between the Lakes now known as Victoria, Albert, Edward, Kivu, and Tanganyika were preceded by the empire of Kitara—an enormous entity stretching from present-day Northern Tanzania to South Sudan, and Eastern Congo to Western Kenya. Kitara was believed to have a series of impressive capitals; archaeological work has revealed sites with 'an extensive urban layout', probably dating back to the early centuries of the second millennium (Reid 2017: 107). Relatively undocumented, Kitara is shrouded in mystery; but the subsequent rise of a cluster of kingdoms from the 1400s is attributed to the existence of settled agriculturalists in the abundant fertile land around Lake Victoria, providing the basis for the exchange of goods and services (Mafeje 1998). The fact that land was abundant but cattle scarce rendered the latter prestige goods, elevating the status of cattle-herders over cultivators in ways that shaped structures of bureaucratic organization and political control (Chrétien 2003). This was a particular feature of the evolution of social formations in Bunyoro and Nkore (now in Western Uganda), Burundi and Rwanda, and Buhaya and Buzinza (now in North-Western Tanzania).

Meanwhile, Nilotic pastoralists migrated southwards from present-day South Sudan, bringing clan structures and evolving into the societies such as the Alur, Acholi, and Langi of Northern Uganda. Bunyoro was the first kingdom to consolidate into state-like form, with increasingly centralized and bureaucratic political organization from the fifteenth century, and territorial chiefs rather than kinship as the main mode of political organization (Mafeje 1998: 39; Maxon 1994). Ideas about the centralization of power filtered from Bunyoro to many of the other kingdoms to its south, including Rwanda (Chrétien 2003).

Buganda in central Uganda flourished from about 1650 through its banana and fishing-based economy and links to the Indian Ocean coast, becoming Bunyoro's greatest regional rival and outnumbering the latter's population tenfold by the nineteenth century (Kiwanuka 1972; Maxon 1994; Reid 2017). Mono-ethnic and entirely agriculture-based, it had no division between pastoralists and agriculturalists but nevertheless developed comparable centralized structures, partly through conflict with and emulation of Bunyoro. State formation in the region thus resonates with Tilly's (1992) argument about how tightly organized violence, and the need to finance it, can produce rapid sate formation (Reid 2017: 117). Warfare became professionalized among the kingdoms in the eighteenth and nineteenth centuries, funded in part by trade in slaves and ivory (Médard & Doyle 2007; Reid 2017).

In Rwanda, hierarchical structures of social control developed around the time of the Nyiginya dynasty in the seventeenth century (Vansina 2004). The following century, population densification and the shrinkage of available land across the sub-region necessitated what Vidal terms 'sedenterization', precipitating new strategies of territorial control (Vidal 1984). Scaled forms of administration proliferated, in Rwanda comprising a system of local 'hill chiefs' who tightly controlled the population and reported upwards to land, cow, and army chiefs (Chrétien 2003: 175). In this way, territorialization and building infrastructural power proceeded in tandem, as the central state gradually eroded the autonomy of local chiefs, whose main responsibilities were to collect in-kind taxes in the form of agricultural, pastoral, or artisanal products (Newbury 1988). This facilitated some accumulation and significant filtering back of resources to the centre. The reach of such taxation was, however, significantly lower than in feudal Europe (Mworoha 1981; Vidal 1974).

Across the interlacustrine zone, land rights were generally use rights, founded either on claims of being the first land clearers or the granting of familial rights to 'vacant' land by a chief. However, the power of royally appointed chiefs was limited in practice, and—despite perceptions of feudalism popularized by European anthropologists—in none of the kingdoms did chiefs equate to feudal lords of medieval European type (Goody 1971; Amin 1980; Coquery-Vidrovitch 1975; Mafeje 1998; Chrétien 2003). Although the precolonial Great Lakes institutions were 'tributary' (Amin 1980), many specific institutions associated with feudalism were largely absent, including heritability of landed estates and serfdom—though in an exceptional case, forms of bonded agricultural labour were introduced in late nineteenth-century Rwanda (Chrétien 2003: 180).

Mafeje (1998) even argues that the interlacustrine zone was largely devoid of relations of property; economic value extraction was shaped by political domination of territory rather than property relations. Moreover, with limited possibilities for inheritance, and tribute largely comprising perishable goods, little accumulation took place. The organization of production was based on use value rather than exchange value, and peasants were mobilized for political and military purposes rather than production (Mafeje 1998: 79–86). At the eve of colonialism therefore, the kingdoms were characterized by a widespread absence of property in land, and despite remarkable strides in terms of territorial domination had weak foundations for accumulation.

These generalities aside, important differences existed between the kingdoms. In the western kingdoms with their distinctive pastoralist/agriculturalist divide, institutions that explicitly privileged cattle-keepers emerged as land pressure grew, with farmers often paying fees for the use of land granted in fief to pastoralists.

In Rwanda, this led to the elevation of Tutsi over Hutu in status, with a similar dynamic between Hima and Iru in the kingdom of Nkore to its north (New-bury 1978; Maxon 1994; Chrétien 2003). The elevation of pastoralism limited the significance of land as either property or capital, while cattle constituted a form of inheritable wealth, leading to increased inequalities (Mafeje 1998: 60–61). Everywhere in Rwanda apart from the north-west, the *mwami* (king) was the holder of all land rights and granted usufruct rights through local representatives in exchange for fees and labour, and could withdraw these rights at his pleasure (Musahara & Huggins 2005: 293).

Meanwhile in Buganda, in the nineteenth century the *kabaka* (king) usurped the role of clan heads to make himself custodian of all land, monopolizing the right to distribute it (Mafeje 1998: 51). Chiefs' estates were not heritable and reverted to the Kabaka on death or dismissal. As such, there was much greater royal control over land than in the western kingdoms (Maxon 1994: 87). However, this was the territorial control of sovereign over subject rather than landowner over labour-ing tenant, creating an economy of predation by an elite interested in the utility value of land rather than exploiting it to generate a surplus for potential capitalist investment (Wrigley 1957; Coquery-Vidrovitch 1975).

The consolidation of kingdom bureaucracies necessitated substantial non-agricultural settlements, and growing regional trade also began to generate multi-functional urban spaces. Sedenterization meant that by the mid/late-nineteenth century the royal capitals were no longer itinerant but settled in sites such as Nyanza in Rwanda, Bukeye in Burundi, and above all at the Kabaka's capi-tal (*Kibuga*) in Buganda (Chrétien 2003; Reid & Medard 2000). By the mid-nineteenth century, the *Kibuga* housed over ten thousand people. It was highly spatially stratified, with distinct zones for traders, junior chiefs, and the *Kabaka's* wives before entering the royal core (Reid and Medard 2000: 102). European mis-sionaries arriving in the city also brought new ideologies of spatial organization. Historians have debated whether these capitals were really urban: some argue they held 'no special economic milieu distinct from the surrounding agro-pastoral countryside' (Chrétien 2003: 166), while others depict them as crucibles of socio-economic and political change (Coquery-Vidrovitch 1993). Whatever their level of specialization, administration and service functions were substantial in these places (Mukwaya et al. 2010: 272) and they also became increasingly central to region-wide trade networks (see Chapter 4).

The Horn

The Horn of Africa is no less remarkable in its history of state formation. The sub-region's political history is often seen as rooted in its dramatic topography and varied landscapes, with Markakis (2011) distinguishing between three zones of

Ethiopia: the 'highland core' in the northern and central highlands (historically termed Abyssinia), the 'highland periphery' to the south, and 'lowland periphery' stretching out to the north-east and east—a categorization of the landscape that Clapham (2017) extends to the sub-region as a whole, including Somalia and present-day Eritrea and Djibouti. The highland core was the site of a powerful classical empire based in the ancient city of Aksum, which became one of the world's earliest Christian civilizations from the fourth century AD. Following Aksum's gradual decline from the seventh century, the Zagwe dynasty took control of part of the highlands, making its capital at Lalibela in the eleventh century. This was followed by a dynasty of kings that traced their lineage back to Aksum and, beyond that, to Solomon himself, thus beginning a new 'Solomonic line' of kings and emperors that effectively continued right through to Haile Selassie in the twentieth century.

Topographically, the highland core broadly corresponds with the contemporary Ethiopian regions of Tigray and Amhara—a zone which has, unusually within sub-Saharan Africa, long been characterized by ox-plough agriculture (McCann 1995). This facilitated levels of arable farming comparable with Europe in the medieval period, generating a surplus and rendering land central to political organization and identity (Markakis 2011; Clapham 2017). It also fostered high levels of territorialization from an early stage; something that has shaped the region's turbulent history ever since (Markakis 2011). Again, the system has often been described as 'feudal'—and despite the Eurocentric nature of this term, with respect to Abyssinia there is wider agreement that patterns of surplus extraction and hierarchy were comparable to those termed 'feudal' elsewhere (Zewde 1984; Clapham 2017).

This surplus-producing agricultural economy was rooted in the relative land scarcity and labour abundance in the highland core, which was also a driver of early urbanization (Connah 2015) and generated particular forms of land tenure. Abyssinian land tenure involved linking usufruct rights to kinship group, vested in family heads, through a form of communal tenure known as *rist*. These rights were very strong (though could be revoked on failure to pay tax to the crown) and could not be alienated outside the kinship group; land was therefore not commoditized. This gave peasants significant tenure security, and their rights were heritable (Zewde 1991; McCann 1995). The state claimed tribute administered through bureaucratic hierarchies, the burden of which fell entirely on the peasantry, A system of surplus appropriation known as *gult* enabled officials to collect tribute from *rist*-holding peasants and pass it upwards, retaining part of it in lieu of a salary. *Gult* was a major instrument of state patronage, granted sometimes in exchange for military service and sometimes heritable (Pausewang 1983; Zewde 1991; Jembere 2000). Peasants were also subject to corvee labour and a burdensome range of taxes (Markakis 2011: 34).

This evolution of hierarchical social structures rooted in agriculture starkly contrasts with the lowlands, which were inhabited by a diverse array of ethnic groups. Most of these lowland areas are poorly suited to agriculture and primarily characterized by animal husbandry; hence even today the Horn is home to the largest concentration of mobile livestock producers in the world (Markakis 2011: 15). This livelihood necessitates low population densities, which in turn gives rise to very different social structures. The lack of territorial fixity limited processes of territorialization and consequently the development of internally driven states (Clapham 2017:15). The imperial regimes in the highland core made little effort to fully integrate the lowlands due to their limited potential to produce a surplus, compounded by Abyssinian conceptions of the landless pastoralist way of life as somehow sub-human (Markakis 2011: 39). The most significant social formation in lowland societies was and remains the clan, with lineage structures stretching over long distances and remaining largely non-hierarchical, though with elaborate relations of age and gender-based authority (Clapham 2017).

The third zone, the highland periphery, permits settled agriculture and more structured forms of political organization but has been largely excluded from, or dominated by, the state structures emanating from the core. The largest group here is the Oromo, based in central and southern Ethiopia and constituting the Horn's largest ethnic group. Oromo political culture has long involved distinct governance systems, and at particular points in history they have formed small kingdoms (Zewde 1991: 18–19). However, their role in Ethiopia's broader political story was thwarted by the strength of the Christian empire to the north, which progressively attempted to conquer and integrate the highland periphery in pursuit of new arable land due to over-farming in the core (Markakis 2011: 26–27). Meanwhile, other parts of the highland periphery in south-western Ethiopia were suitable for settled agriculture but contained such high levels of ethnic diversity that there was little shared identity through which to organize, facilitating relatively easy incorporation into the Abyssinian state.

It is notable that in contrast to the interlacustrine sub-region, settled agriculture and pastoralism largely remained in separate geographic zones, with the former seeking to impose dominance over the latter. Meanwhile, arable land scarcity became much more of an issue in the Horn, driving constant expansion, whereas the Great Lakes developed a violent and fluctuating balance of power between kingdoms, alongside varying internal relations between settled and nomadic populations. These differences have impacted the roles that land plays in the politics of various parts of East Africa, as well as emergent forms of tenure and the degree of centralization in land distribution.

When it comes to urbanization itself, Ethiopia was the site of some of the most significant ancient, medieval, and early modern cities in Africa, from Aksum to Harar, Lalibela and Gondar. The Zagwe dynasty had a flourishing urban culture (Negash 2003), but after Lalibela's decline the Ethiopian empire lacked a fixed capital for centuries, as the emperors moved around their territory to maintain internal control through a succession of 'wandering capitals' (Horvarth 1969). Eventually Gondar was established as the fixed capital in the seventeenth century, followed by a period of division with a major regional capital at Ankober, until the founding of Addis Ababa by Emperor Menelik in the late nineteenth century (Burton 2001: 7). Yet Ethiopia under the emperors was far from an urban society, with cities and towns remaining small and relatively insignificant until the twentieth century. In the lowlands, the nomadic pastoralist lifestyle was antithetical to settling in towns—though since classical times a number of small maritime city-states had flourished on the Somali coast (see Chapter 4). Layered onto this history, a number of significant ports such as Baraawe and Mogadishu emerged in the medieval period (Ahmed 1996; Maxon 1994: 41), while Massawa in Eritrea had flourished as a port since Aksumite times. However, the most significant coastal urban culture was predominantly south of the Horn, along the Swahili coast.

The Swahili coast and wider region

There is a rich an extensive literature on the Swahili societies and urban settlements of the Indian Ocean coast.[2] Although this book does not focus on the coastal zone or the modern states of Kenya and Tanzania, the precolonial evolution of the Swahili coast set the foundation for region-wide trade and transport links, as well as exhibiting distinct forms of territorialization in which cities played a significant role. The East African coastal zone did not have the same fertile soils as the Great Lakes zone or Ethiopian plateau, though was rich in ocean resources. The most valuable land was confined to a narrow coastal strip, resulting in significant competition for land, as evidenced by early forms of territorial demarcation and the presence of double-storied houses (Kusimba et al. 2006: 149; Connah 1987: 176–177). Urbanism itself a key component of cultural identity along the coast, as the towns competed with one another for trade and land, and came to perceive their urban-based, Swahili civilization as superior to the rural communities of the African interior (Horton & Middleton 2000; Burton 2017). The role of Swahili city-states in shaping the regional economy, and concomitantly the nascent urban economies of the Great Lakes region, is considered in Chapter 4.

Meanwhile, in inland Kenya there was a constant movement of people, with Nilotic pastoralists coming to dominate much of the north and west of the country, and Bantu-speakers settling on the eastern side of Lake Victoria. Ancestors of the Oromo (Galla) also inhabited parts of central Kenya. Unlike in the interlacustrine region, no centralized kingdoms developed within this territory,

---

[2] e.g. Chami (1994; 1998); Horton & Middleton (2000); Kusimba (1999); Ochieng & Maxon (1992); Maxon (1994); Middleton (1992; 2004); Spear (2000a); Chittick (1965; 1974); see also Spear (2000b) for a full bibliography.

perhaps partly because the Bantu agriculturalists were progressively pushed away from the lakeshore by the Luo (Maxon 1994: 64–70). These developments were significant in terms of limiting the scope for urban development across parts of the Kenyan interior. There were, however, a range of tenure systems emerging across the country, with Kikuyu tenure relations forming a particularly unusual example because 'every inch' of Kikuyu territory 'had its owner, with the boundary properly fixed and everyone respecting his neighbour's' (Kenyatta 1938/2015: 18). Land was often communally *used,* with eight carefully specified and named forms of tenure, but unlike many other parts of East Africa was not communally held (Kenyatta 1938/2015: 15–21). It bears repeating however this conception of land as individual property was very rare within precolonial East Africa (Colson 1971: 198).

In Tanzania, meanwhile, Bantu-speaking agriculturalists dominated the inland areas by 1650, with particular concentrations around Kilimanjaro and south of Lake Victoria, where a number of kingdoms evolved. Much of the rest of the terrain was organized into small, relatively unstable chieftaincies (Maxon 1994: 77). It was however subject to wrenching change in the nineteenth century as international trade intensified, strengthening a tendency towards the creation of larger, more centralized forms of authority, and more militarized forms of power (Maxon 1994: 77). Firearms spread throughout the region, the Indian Ocean slave trade took hold and the industrial revolution provided new stimuli to the regional trade economy (see Chapter 4). These transformations consolidated the development of territorialized states and their royal capitals across the Great Lakes region (Burton 2017), bolstering the infrastructural power of ruling elites. However, the increasing penetration of European colonists would soon fundamentally reshape territory–property relations, and with them the distribution of associational power within and among kingdoms, with long-term urban implications.

3.3 The colonial encounter and urban territorialization

Despite rich urban histories and accelerating urbanization by the mid-nineteenth century, on the eve of European colonialism there were no urban-based civilizations on the scale of those in North or West Africa, and East Africa remained overwhelmingly rural (Anderson & Rathbone 2000: 5). Colonialism indisputably shaped land rights and institutions across the region, making new demands on land, introducing new forms of mobility and immobility and creating centres of population clustering. Colonial legal architectures generated particular forms of territorialization, while also introducing land tenure principles that often conflicted with extant norms.

Colonialists generally assumed that ownership rights must exist in Africa, and the official search for the 'owners' of all land encouraged the 'confusion of sovereignty with proprietary ownership' (Colson 1971: 197). This in turn intro-duced a false rigidity between communal land rights in 'customary' (rural) areas, which applied to the vast majority of the population and were administered by tribal authorities, and individual private property rights administered by the state, primarily in urban areas. In reality, communal and individual rights in pre-colonial Africa 'were not mutually exclusive' (Joireman 2008: 1242). The colonial bifurcation between the collective/customary realm on the one hand, and the indi-vidual/private on the other (Mamdani (1996), was never complete and obscured more nuanced understandings of property. It did, however, imprint a rural/urban citizenship divide, whereby urban direct rule served to exclude the native majority from rights and freedoms enjoyed by the (largely foreign) citizens of colonial cities, while rural indirect rule incorporated that majority into a colonially enforced 'customary' order (Mamdani 1996).

The general thrust of colonial policy involved an elevation of economic relative to social relationships in the formal governance of land, as property relations were layered onto territorial ones. As well as being privileged sites for individualized property and citizenship, urban areas were subject to new forms of territorial con-trol in the form of zoning and residential segregation (King 1976; Home 1997). Many precolonial urban forms in East Africa gradually faded away or were subor-dinated under colonial urban systems, in contrast to West Africa where the 'old' city often remained a substantial part of the new (Southall 1971: 236). Kampala-Mengo forms a significant exception, being in many ways the prototype of the colonial 'dual city' in which indigenous settlement and colonial city co-evolved together, as discussed further later in this section.

The colonial nature of most East African cities meant that they emerged 'after legal claims to territoriality had been established' rather than 'as part and parcel of state and nation building', as had been the case in Europe (Schatz 2004: 114). Consequently, Africans were treated as though they did not belong in urban areas (Southall 1971). The idea that urban life would result in the 'detribalization' of African populations, precipitating social dislocation and crime, generated signif-icant moral panic (Mayer 1962; Gluckman 1960; Cohen 1969). The sense that Africans in the city were displaced and temporary meant that colonial land gover-nance paid little attention to the prospect of substantial urban expansion (Home 1997; Fox 2014). Since colonial planning was only ever confined to a core intended for a small population, this proved hopelessly inadequate as cities came to expand rapidly into their peripheries.

The great exception to these colonial developments was, of course, Ethiopia. However, the aspirations of the emperors, along with transformations initiated during the brief Italian occupation, mirrored some of the dynamics unfold-ing in colonized East Africa. As Therborn (2017) notes, countries that escaped colonialism often did so through forms of 'reactive modernization' from above, replicating some of the urban effects of colonial domination (Therborn 2017: 147).

While there were important differences, the evolution of land policy under the Ethiopian emperors from the late nineteenth century also involved forms of territorial colonization and attempted imposition of private property rights. The following sub-section thus examines the evolution of land policy from the late nineteenth to mid-twentieth century in the Great Lakes and Horn sub-regions, with particular attention paid to the three countries that form the focus of this book. This is followed by a discussion of the specifically urban dimensions of colonial and imperial territorialization.

Imperial land policy

The Great Lakes

Buganda was central to colonial fantasies about East Africa from an early stage: a reputed land of milk and honey characterized by abundant fertile land, stable bureaucratic political organization, and increasing interest in Christianity. In 1890, amid conflict between Muslim, Catholic and Protestant missionaries (Chrétien 2003: 207–211), the Imperial British East Africa Company entered into a military alliance with the kingdom (despite earlier hostility on the part of Kabaka Mwanga), and used this to subjugate and incorporate surrounding territories (Jørgensen 1981; Doyle 2006), leading to the establishment of the Uganda Protectorate in 1894. Buganda's key role in allying with the British in its assault on Bunyoro and other surrounding areas meant that the kingdom was privileged in various aspects of colonial governance, including land policy (Apter 1967; Kasfir 1976; Twaddle 1993).

In 1900 the colonial government passed the 'Buganda Agreement', which provided the kingdom elite with large amounts of private land (Nkurunziza 2006; Mutibwa 2008). Of Buganda's estimated 19,600 square miles, the Agreement gave the British control of 9,000, designated 'Crown Land', alongside 1,500 of forest. The remainder was granted as freehold to the Kabaka and around 3,700 chiefs and royals (Englebert 2002: 352). The British assumed they were formalizing individual property rights that already existed, but in fact they were instituting a fundamental shift (West 1972; Okuku 2006: 7). The new form of private land tenure—which came to be known as *mailo*, due to the measurement of land allocations in square miles—had profound implications for Uganda's future. It institutionalized legal inheritance and created a new hereditary ruling class (Richards 1963), which rapidly grew as plots were subdivided (Troutt 1994: 20). Other kingdoms within Uganda demanded similar agreements, but although estates were granted to ruling families, there was no wider distribution of freehold land.[3]

---

[3] In this respect, the majority of land in Uganda (75 per cent)—both within and outside its kingdoms—is actually customary land (Batungi 2008; Obeng-Odoom 2020). The issues discussed in this book relate specifically to Buganda, in which Kampala is based.

In some ways, the Buganda Agreement weakened the link between the Kabaka and ordinary people, since most land was no longer his to control. Simultaneously instituting private property and territorializing colonial control through crown land thus doubly disembedded the Kabaka from the territorial domination that had been a source of both infrastructural power and legitimacy, and shifted the distribution of power in favour of Baganda landowners. Settlement by European farmers was difficult, given the widespread distribution of land to nobles alongside restrictions on Baganda selling their *mailo* to non-Baganda, and difficulties in identifying available crown land (Zwanenberg & King 1975: 62). Distance from the coast also posed challenges. The colonial administration thus eventually gave up on developing significant European enterprise and large-scale plantation agriculture in Uganda (Brett 1973). The institution of *mailo* meant that in theory Baganda landowners were able to develop their plots along capitalist farming lines, assured of permanent ownership (Zwanenburg & King 1975). Yet there were limits to what they could do on the land, particularly after a law passed in 1927 imposed certain restrictions on the eviction of peasant tenants (Bazaara 1997; Okuku 2006). These restrictions, alongside an absence of credit and incentives to invest in large-scale farming, were partly rooted in colonial fears of the political instability that African capitalist farming might stimulate (Zwanenburg & King 1975).

Relatively abundant high-quality land meant that there was little incentive to increase productivity, but also that land did not dominate Uganda's internal politics during the colonial period (Brett 1973; Zwanenburg & King 1975). This contrasted with the situation in Kenya, where a struggle to dominate the peasantry by establishing large-scale farming estates brought prosperity to European-settled areas but severely held back other areas, in the process fomenting major political unrest (Zwanenburg & King 1975: 33). However, the landlord–tenant relations codified in colonial Buganda sowed the seeds for a dramatic intensification of land politics in the late twentieth and early twenty-first centuries, when the effort to limit Buganda's power by maintaining a stalemate between landlords and tenants became politically explosive in Kampala (see Chapter 6).[4]

Other kingdoms within the protectorate, such as Nkore (subsequently renamed Ankole), were increasingly reordered along 'Bugandan' lines and supervised by administrators from Buganda, in a typical mode of indirect rule (Chrétien 2003). Buganda was controversially awarded territory from neighbouring Bunyoro (Doyle 2006), while Luganda became a quasi-official language across the protectorate—all of which nurtured growing anti-Buganda sentiment. Meanwhile, colonial development policy rested on a division between productive regions in southern Uganda and labour-sending areas of the North. By the 1950s, income per capita in Buganda was twice as much as any other region of the country, and these disparities were increasing over time (Zwanenburg & King 1975: 71).

---

[4] For a fuller discussion, see Goodfellow and Lindemann (2013).

As Britain established its authority in Uganda, Germany conquered several small kingdoms in north-west Tanzania before incorporating Rwanda and Burundi into German East Africa in the 1890s. Amid intensifying European interest, Rwanda's royal court carefully played one camp off against another before accepting the German flag (Chrétien 2003: 218). Nothing like the 'Buganda Agreement' was instituted here, reflecting the insignificance of land relative to cattle, but also the fact that Germany was relatively uninterested in Rwanda and Burundi and viewed them primarily as depositories of ivory and bastions against Belgian expansion (Chrétien 2003: 247). The only land in Rwanda not governed by customary law consisted in urban areas and church plots, which were held in freehold (Pottier 2002: 181). Influenced by the British in Buganda, the German colonial administration moved towards indirect rule in 1907 but assumed the kingdoms were more centralized and feudal than they actually were, and through indirect rule instituted increased centralization in the hands of the Tutsi monarchy (Chrétien 2003: 256). Land policy thus became increasingly 'statist' in the colonial period, with lineage-based controls undercut by central authority (Boone 2014: 234).

After Germany's defeat in World War I, Belgium was granted a 'trusteeship' over Rwanda and Burundi and governed them jointly as Ruanda-Urundi from the colonial capital Usumbura (now Bujumbura). The centralization and 'pyramidal feudalization' initiated under the Germans and backed by the Christian Church was deepened, with royal landed estates parcelled into chiefdoms and conferred on princes (Chrétien 2003: 256, 268). This served to 'intensify a system of political oppression' (Newbury 1988: 207) with the Tutsi aristocracy acting as key intermediaries, implementing various forms of forced labour and territorially based taxation (Newbury & Newbury 2000; Pottier 2002; Vansina 2004; Erlebach 2006). In Rwanda the very idea of Tutsi came to be equated with power and chiefship (Chrétien 2003; Mamdani 2001), while the majority Hutu were mostly landless and resentful (Lemarchand 1982; Newbury 1988; Pottier 2002). The central state was the locus of power to a degree that is unusual in Africa, relatively undiluted by more local social institutions (Van Hoyweghen 1999; Boone 2014). In this respect, unlike in Buganda where the colonial institution of new property relations partly undercut the Kabaka's territorial authority, in Rwanda social relations of property proceeded hand in hand with deepened territorial control. Infrastructural power and dominance in the distribution of associational power were fused in the structures of the Tutsi monarchy.

From 1926 to 1936 the colonial state was reorganized and racialized, making chiefship explicitly a Tutsi privilege and framing Tutsis as a superior race from the Horn of Africa (Mamdani 2001: 105). By 1959, every chief in Rwanda was Tutsi, as were all but ten of the 559 sub-chiefs (Straus 2006: 181). Meanwhile, land escalated in importance as the population grew and densified. Plots were subdivided through father-to-son inheritance of use rights, resulting in increasing numbers of tiny parcels (RoR 2004); an institution called *umunani* facilitated flexible use of plots and allowed for subdivision during the owner's lifetime to ensure farmland for every male heir (Shearer 2017: 47). Meanwhile, the principalities of the Kivu zone to Rwanda's West densified as Rwandans fled *corvee* labour to areas largely beyond the reach of Belgian rule in the neighbouring Congo (Chrétien 2003). The perceived need to police flows in and out of the Congo influenced evolving patterns of policing and territorial control within Rwanda as a whole (Lamarque 2017), further building institutions of infrastructural power.

The Horn

The Ethiopian imperial state's success in fending off colonizers built on concerted efforts towards Ethiopian unification by successive emperors in the nineteenth century. After important but limited gains under Emperors Tewedros II and Yohannes IV, Emperor Menelik II executed ruthlessly effective campaigns of military expansion during the 1880s and 1890s (Zewde 1991; Markakis 2011). Menelik played colonial powers off against one another, mobilizing a formidable force of over 100,000 men to defeat the Italians at Adwa in 1896, and emulating aspects of the design of European states to entrench Ethiopia's dominance of the Horn, harden its national boundaries and modernize its bureaucracy (Zewde 1991; 2002; Clapham 2006).

Often described as a form of 'internal' colonialism (Donham & James 1986; Clapham 2017: 33), Menelik's imperial rule privileged certain indigenous groups and languages over others, and ensured that the surrounding European colonies of Eritrea, Somalia, and Somaliland remained fragmentary (Clapham 2017). While the Italians colonized Eritrea from 1889, the French claimed a small port territory around Djibouti, and Somali territory was divided between four distinct zones: British Somaliland to the north, Italian Somalia facing the Indian Ocean, part of British Kenya, and a large zone within eastern Ethiopia. Colonizers considered the Somali zones relatively unimportant in comparison with their other African territories, and most borders were never formally demarcated (Clapham 2017: 37).

Ethiopia's expansion into its diverse peripheries produced one of the most complex constellations of land-use systems in Africa (Donham & James 1986; Joireman 2000). Under Menelik, the system through which both tribute and labour were extracted from peasants (*gabbar*) was expanded, as many farmers in both the highland and lowland peripheries were obliged to offer a third of their labour time in *corvee* and a tenth of their harvest in tribute (Zewde 1991: 87–88; Jembere 2000). The state also increased its appropriation of land to distribute it as property to royals and nobles. Land measurement and registration increased for the purposes of both taxation and sale; hence in the twentieth century land privatization began to emerge (Crewett et al. 2008; Zewde 1991: 90). Private property rights were very limited however, and both European would-be investors and Ethiopian intellectuals campaigned for the reform of the dominant quasi-feudal land system in favour of national capitalist development emulating Japan's experience (Zewde 1991: 92).

On becoming emperor, Haile Selassie took heed of these concerns and buttressed private property rights, as well as eventually abolishing the *gabbar* system in 1941 (Pausewang 1983; Zewde 1991). The period after the 1936–1941 Italian occupation saw increased penetration by foreign capital as the United kingdom and United States increased their influence, alongside the consolidation of absolutist rule.

Private land tenure increasingly became the norm, particularly in southern Ethiopia, as settlers from the 'highland core' claimed ownership (by purchase or seizure) of land that they previously had tributary rights over (Pausewang 1983) and the government doled out land grants convertible to freehold. This was a strategy of political patronage that ramped up as opposition to Haile Selassie intensified: most land grants were targeted towards exiles, soldiers, and civil servants on whose support the regime's survival depended (Zewde 1991: 191). Meanwhile tenants on the new privately owned land commonly had to bear the triple burden of pre-existing tithes *(asrat)* and land taxes as well as rent to their landlords. The increasing pressures on the peasantry, combined with famines, were crucial to the regime's eventual demise. From 1965 onwards the urban-based student movement gathered pace, with the slogan of 'Land to the Tiller' at the heart of annual demonstrations amid broader ongoing activism (Markakis & Ayele 1986; Zewde 1991). The late imperial period in Ethiopia thus sought to use institutions of private property to consolidate territorial domination in ways that would ultimately generate a radical rupture in the distribution of power through socialist revolution.

Colonial urbanism

Towns in East Africa were seen by colonists as places where traditional authority and customs risked breaking down, which promoted a general colonial hostility towards African urbanization (Burton 2005; 2017). As their presence in the city was seen as temporary, if not aberrant, most urban Africans were subjected to 'shameful' housing conditions (Southall 1971: 245). There was no sense that urban tenure relations required dedicated attention from colonial authorities, outside the European areas in which churches and other institutions were granted freehold tenure and non-Africans could lease plots from the crown. Governance structures for cities were generally ad hoc, and urban land legislation remained vague (Home, 1990, 1997).

Nevertheless, the territorialization of colonial cities proceeded through a range of approaches including racist spatial segregation (Mamdani 1996; Myers 2003; Freund 2007; Njoh 2008), surveillance and social control (Njoh 2009), and the separation of Europeans from Africans by green belts ('cordon sanitaires') and other perceived barriers to disease (Home 1997; Fourchard 2011). Urban Africans were subject to much more direct colonial supervision than in the countryside (Burton 2017; Southall & Gutkind 1957). Yet the colonial ordering of urban space was always incomplete (Fourchard 2011), with African urban populations finding ways to at least partially resist colonial 'enframing' strategies (Myers 2003). Meanwhile, in many East African cities, the Indian population that came to dominate urban commerce (see Chapter 4) found themselves in liminal urban areas aligned with their socio-economic position in colonial society: sandwiched between rulers and ruled (Burton 2005; 2017). Viewing colonial cities as 'dual' cities is misleading in that a 'European versus indigenous' dichotomy oversimplifies colonial society (Fourchard 2011), though some colonial cities were much more spatially 'dualized' than others, with Kampala being a prominent example. The following sections explore dynamics of colonial-era urban territorialization and property within the countries and cities that are the focus of this book.

Uganda

Colonial Kampala originated in 1890 when Captain Lugard built a fort on a hill close to Mengo, the Buganda kingdom capital thought to have been the most populous urban agglomeration in the East African interior in the nineteenth century. Although the colonial authorities based their administrative capital at Entebbe, trade flourished around Lugard's camp and the two urban settlements—colonial Kampala and indigenous Mengo—evolved side by side (Southall & Gutkind 1957; Nuwagaba 2006; Omolo-Okalebo 2011). The spatial arrangement of the emerging dual city became increasingly influenced by religious missionary rivalries, through 'battle for urban symbols' in which cathedrals were built on hilltops formerly territorialized by the *kabakas* (Reid & Medard 2000). Rubaga hill was the site of the Catholic mission and cathedral, with Namirembe hill fulfilling the same function for the Protestant missionaries (see Figure 3.1). Religion was increasingly placed above the *kabaka*, both symbolically and physically, as the protectorate took shape. The intensity of religious and political conflicts that shaped Kampala-Mengo in the late nineteenth century were unparalleled in the interlacustrine region, and 'The new political balance of Buganda could be seen by all' in the layout of the city (Reid & Medard 2000: 105). On slopes of hills surrounding the *kibuga* were estates belonging to the chiefs of each province of Buganda, further divided into plots for sub-chiefs held through *bibanja* occupancy rights.

The growth of Kampala-Mengo along with other towns around Uganda normalized processes of buying and selling land, as the expansion of urban areas increased land values and led to nascent urban land markets (Gutkind 1963). Planning regulations were instituted by the colonial regime, including Township Ordinances in 1903 and 1914 regulating plot size and coverage (Mukwaya et al. 2010: 273), though these were generally only applied in colonial towns and not their indigenous counterparts. Most significant was the Town and Country Planning Act of 1948 (modified in 1951), which was based on typical principles of British colonial governance and was especially concerned with maintaining

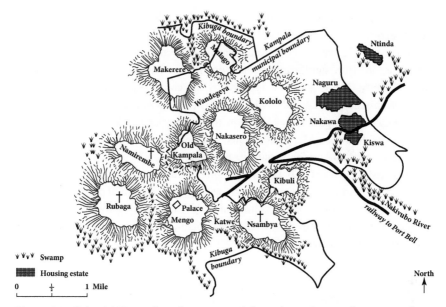

Figure 3.1 Colonial Kampala and Mengo, with boundary of Kampala municipality indicated

Source: Adapted from Southall (1967: 298).

standards of urban health and sanitation through formally established Sanitation Boards in urban areas (Mukwaya et al. 2010).[5]

Kampala was the Protectorate's core city by the 1940s (Munger 1951: 76). The ideas that filtered through colonial planning policy had concrete spatial impacts on Kampala and solidified the distinction between municipal Kampala, which included the European/Asian residential areas and commercial centre, and the *kibuga* and its surrounding African residential areas in Mengo (O'Connor 1983; Omolo-Okalebo 2011). Property rates, infrastructure, the Sanitation Boards, and elaborate rules and regulations were introduced in the colonial areas only (Elkan & van Zwanenburg 1975). Shanty towns soon developed around Mengo as the colonial authorities largely ignored established systems of land governance within these areas (Mukwaya et al. 2010),[6] while placing them under unprecedented strain due to the labour demands emanating from Kampala. Meanwhile, the perceived dangers of young men living in slums on the urban periphery were explicitly highlighted in colonial reports from the 1940s, driving a concern to 'stabilize'

[5] For a particularly thorough discussion of planning in Kampala and the ideas that guided it from the early colonial period until the early 2000s, see Omolo-Okalebo (2011).

[6] Nkurunziza (2006: 165) argues that in fact the native government consistently protested against colonial interference in Mengo itself.

urban populations (Byerley 2005: 237) and giving impetus to a new focus on industrial development (see Chapter 4).

The duality of governance in Kampala-Mengo produced distinct forms of territorialization, with significant implications for the state's infrastructural power across the city. The disparity is typified by the colonial government's expenditure on Kampala in 1954–1955, which was *two hundred times* the amount spent by the Buganda kingdom on Mengo in the same year (Makara 2009: 103). By mid-century, Kampala-Mengo combined had 36,000 residents, including around 1,500 Europeans and 15,000 Asians in Kampala alongside some 20,000 Africans in Mengo (Munger 1951: 17–19).[7] Provision of housing for Africans within Kampala itself was minimal even by the 1950s, as the 1951 residential plan in Figure 3.2 shows, though of course tens of thousands of Africans were living in the areas outside the Kampala boundary that appear blank here because 'huts of African squatters are not indicated'.

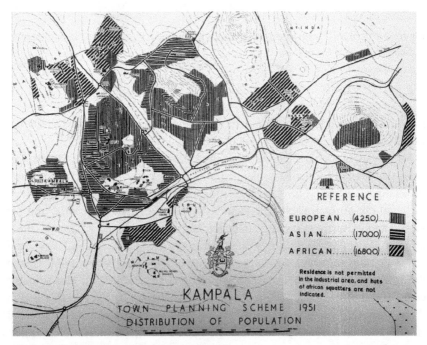

Figure 3.2 1951 Kampala residential plan
Source: Kendall (1955).

[7] There is significant inconsistency in the statistics available; other sources suggest that the population of the *kibuga* had already reached 32,441 by the 1911 census (Gutkind 1963: 14–15). Temple (1968) documents 4,250 Europeans, 17,000 Asians and 38,250 Africans in Kampala township alone by 1951.

The 1959 census indicates that a couple of years before independence, there were 47,000 people living in Kampala alone. The fact that only 10 per cent of these were Baganda illustrates that while some Africans were allowed to settle in the colonial city, the vast majority were still outside its municipal boundary (O'Connor 1983). Here Mengo formed its own capital, centred on the Kabaka's palace (visible in the bottom left-hand corner of both Figures 3.1 and 3.2) and complete with its own modern parliament (*Lukiiko*), housed in the modern *Bulange* building from 1958 onwards (see Figure 3.3).

Figure 3.3 Buganda's *Bulange*, with statue of Kabaka Mutebi II in the foreground
Photograph © Tom Goodfellow.

Rwanda

While a settlement located at present-day Kigali may have existed some five hundred years ago (Vansina 2004), the city is generally considered a colonial creation. Its official foundation dates to 1907, when Richard Kandt was appointed Resident of Rwanda. The site was chosen because, at the centre of the country, it maximized potential both for broadcasting power and acting as a crossroads for national and regional trade. Under the Germans and during early Belgian rule, Kigali remained a small colonial outpost, with the capital for Ruanda-Urundi being at Usumbura. It therefore grew slowly, even as the Belgians embarked on a road-building programme linking Kigali to other towns and the neighbouring colonies through hundreds of kilometres of roads by the mid 1920s. Settlement remained confined largely to the top of Nyarugenge hill, which remains the commercial centre today (see Figure 3.4). More generally, urbanization in Rwanda only really began at all

Figure 3.4 Kigali city centre and surrounding hilly terrain
Photograph © Tom Goodfellow.

in the colonial period (Sirven 1984), prior to which settlements were scattered in a context of general population density throughout the kingdom, and commercial trade involved barter without the need for trading centres (Jaganyi et al. 2018).

The colonial government was little interested in fostering urban development, and the Catholic Church actively hostile to it due to its perceived detrimental effects on Christian behaviour. Migration into urban areas required the authorization of local leaders and payment for an urban living permit, which was only open to formal workers (Sirven 1984; Jaganyi et al. 2018). Unlike in Buganda, the seat of the kingdom was some distance away in Nyanza, and from the 1920s much colonial interest within Rwanda centred on the new colonial town and prominent religious centre of Astrida (subsequently called Butare, and now Huye) in the South of the country, so there was little interest in Kigali.

Kigali's growth was given some impetus by the expansion of the cassiterite trade in the wider area from the 1930s (Dorsey 1994), but nevertheless by mid-century its population was a mere six thousand (Manirakiza 2014)—much smaller than Kampala around the same time. Yet the settlement continued to grow slowly due its value as a transport hub for commercial activities between Usumbura, Kisangani in the Belgian Congo, Kampala and the lakeside towns of Kigoma and Bukoba in Tanzania (Jaganyi et al. 2018). Colonial vagrancy and pass laws kept most Rwandans out of the town, with the Church also keen to limit contact between the general population and the mostly Muslim Tanzanian and Omani traders who dominated urban trade (Shearer 2017: 44). At the time of independence in

1962, Kigali was still 'just a small village with primarily administrative functions' (Jagyani et al. 2018: 25). Neither the complex territorial dualism nor widespread indigenous freehold land ownership that characterized Kampala were features of the city.

Ethiopia

The evolution of cities and towns in Ethiopia under the unifying emperors of the nineteenth and twentieth centuries diverges from the colonial experiences in Uganda and Rwanda because of Ethiopia's multi-national configuration and the process of internal colonization. Large numbers of Abyssinian highlanders migrated south, particularly from the early twentieth century, and came to form a landholding ruling class and significant presence in towns across the country. Meanwhile, in a very different kind of population movement, masses of people migrated from the peripheries to the geographic centre of the new state in and around Addis Ababa in search of economic opportunity (Markakis 2011: 8). This produced high levels of diversity in the urban areas, underlain with steep hierarchies and legacies of domination and resistance (Pankhurst 1961; Levine 1965a; Markakis 1974).

Although—as in the rest of East Africa—the population remained overwhelmingly rural, there was a proliferation of urban centres and by the mid-1960s Ethiopia had around two hundred towns of various sizes, which concentrated state power and housed 10 per cent of the population (McCann 1995: 240). Land rights played a central role in urban growth patterns, and the post-war period increasingly revealed the incompatibility between traditional forms of rural landholding and new notions of private urban property emerging from the highland core (Seyoum 2000: 235). Taking the town of Bahir Dar as an example, Seyoum (2000) argues that prior to the Italian occupation there was no distinction between rural and urban lands in and around the town, with heritable communal land rights also allowing for rental to commercial actors. However, the Italian occupiers sought to strengthen their control by seizing land in the urbanized area and redistributing it to commercial and residential owners, as well as subjecting it to new forms of taxation, undermining a wide range of traditional use rights and payments. The creation of a class of private landholders imposed acute divisions between the urban and rural, processes that were consolidated when Haile Selassie returned to power. These developments, echoed in many cities and towns, meant by the 1960s a new spatial order had emerged in which urban and rural land were sharply distinguished and the majority of people were shut out of the opportunities associated with the former. The territorialization of urban areas as spaces for state allocation and control, and the proliferation of private property, were thus introduced simultaneously.

Following its founding in 1886 and adoption by Menelik as his permanent capital, Ethiopian nobility rapidly settled in Addis Ababa along with foreign diplomats sent to establish contact with Menelik's court (Zewde 1991; Burton 2001). The city grew extremely fast, with a population of around fifty thousand by 1903 (Burton 2001: 16), though it was almost abandoned due to a lack of timber until the mass planting of eucalyptus trees in the first decade of the twentieth century. Despite its growth, around this time it was still something of a 'rural city' in nature, composed of 'houses scattered amid eucalyptus groves, often clustered into villages, themselves separated from one another by belts of trees' (Pankhurst 1961: 116). It has been termed the 'least colonial metropolis' in sub-Saharan Africa, with a highly dispersed layout and its central nodes such as the palace and market located far apart (Southall 1971: 240).

The growth of Addis Ababa and increasing sense of its permanence as capital— unusual in much of Ethiopia's history—transformed patterns of land ownership and use. Starting with the more traditional Ethiopian pattern in which land was made temporarily available to nobles and royal servants at the sovereign's pleasure, land grants soon became permanent and land values rapidly escalated (Pankhurst 1961: 115–116). A real-estate market of sorts operated under the emperors, whereby dignitaries possessing large land concessions gradually sold parts of these off to the growing administrative and commercial classes, who in turn constructed at the rear of their lots to offer buildings for rent to new urban-dwellers (Duroyaume 2015: 398). Hence the city became characterized by an unusual pattern of 'sumptuous dwellings alongside hovels of wattle and daub' (Duroyaume 2015: 398). While some elites gravitated towards suburban living by the 1960s in the last years of the imperial regime (Zewde 2005), the intense spatial mix in central Addis Ababa persisted, despite continuously increasing social inequality[8]—a phenomenon characterized by Di Nunzio (2019: 36) as 'segmented conviviality'. The city's population continued to soar in the last years of the imperial regime, reaching around 800,000 by 1970 (Burton 2001: 21). Although the overall level of urbanization in Ethiopia remained low, the size of Addis Ababa's population helped to grow the associational power of the urban and educated classes, despite their widespread exclusion from the benefits of property ownership.

3.4 Independence and revolution

The widespread achievement of independence across Africa from the 1960s ushered in a period of sweeping changes to land laws and policies, and a continent-wide acceleration of urbanization. Yet there were vast differences in the ideological orientation of post-independence regimes (including with regard to land and property), the role of violence in postcolonial regime transitions, and how changes

---

[8] In 1962, 58 per cent of land in the city was owned by just 1,768 individuals (UN-HABITAT 2011: 2).

to the territorial order affected both the state's infrastructural reach and the distribution of associational power. Postcolonial Rwanda was born in a violent overturning of the colonial power structure, while Uganda's postcolonial settlement initially reflected an attempt to assemble a fragile balance of powers, necessitated by its complex ethnic and regional structure, before this too was violently disrupted. Meanwhile in Ethiopia, the imperial regime's foundations were also shaken from 1960 onwards, before being destroyed by the 1974 revolution. All of these changes were accompanied by radical land reforms with highly variable degrees of implementation, and varying political economic consequences for the capital city.

Uganda

As independence loomed, *Kabaka Yekka*—the party of the Protestant Mengo-based Baganda elite—entered an improbable alliance with the Uganda People's Congress, the nationalist (and also Protestant) party that had largely formed to *oppose* Mengo's demands for Buganda to retain privileged status in the post-independence order (Mutibwa 2008). This 'marriage of convenience' (primarily based on shared hostility towards the Democratic Party, a Catholic organization) won the elections at independence in 1962. Consequently Uganda entered independence on the back of a very fragile coalition, with Milton Obote from northern Uganda as its first prime minister and Kabaka Mutesa II as president. The monarchy secured federal status for Buganda under the independence constitution (Mukholi 1995), which papered over acute differences between the parties (Karugire 1980).

Before long, the alliance unravelled: in 1966 Obote unilaterally abrogated the independence constitution and assumed the role of president. When the Kabaka appealed to the UN for help, Obote sent troops to occupy his palace, killing hundreds or possibly thousands in the 'Battle of Mengo' and sending the Kabaka into exile (Kasfir 1976; Kasozi 1994; Rubongoya 2007). In 1967 Obote introduced a new republican constitution, abolishing kingdoms and vesting vast powers in the presidency, before banning opposition parties two years later (Mukholi 1995). These events precipitated two decades of dictatorship, instability, and violence under Obote (1967–1971 and 1980–1985) and Idi Amin (1971–1979), for which Uganda became infamous across the globe.

The 1966 crisis and subsequent Public Lands Act (1969) stripped the Buganda Land Board of the control over former crown land it had won at independence. *Mailo* was then formally abolished in 1975 by Amin's Land Reform Decree, which nationalized all land in Uganda and converted *mailo* titles into ninety-nine-year leases (Okuku 2006; Batungi 2008). However, the decree was barely implemented, and when Obote returned to power in 1980 land policy was in considerable disarray (Okuku 2006: 11). Baganda landlords' attachment to *mailo* was as strong as ever in the 1980s, with peasants occupying *mailo* land being heavily exploited, though it was still difficult for landlords to legally remove them.

As the capital of the newly independent nation, the municipal boundaries of Kampala were finally expanded to include Mengo in 1968. From this point Kampala City Council (KCC) attempted to establish territorial authority over the half of the city that had developed outside of colonial planning, having been governed through the kingdom's institutions and consisting mainly of *mailo* land owned by chiefs (Nkurunziza 2006; Nuwagaba 2006). This was no mean feat, and important elements of dualism remained with respect to land tenure as city growth spiralled after independence. Most slums proliferated in the *mailo*-dominated areas and land that had been held by the kingdom itself, where the state's infrastructural power—as well as infrastructure provision itself—was particularly weak (Nuwagaba 2006). Importantly for the future relationship between KCC and the city population, the municipal state lacked historical legitimacy in these areas.

These challenges were exacerbated by subsequent neglect and civil war: a potent indication of the decimation of state infrastructural reach is the fact that having possessed 227 items of engineering equipment in 1970, KCC had only forty-four left by 1988 (KCC 1997). Meanwhile, the city's growth and development was thwarted under Amin and during the war years of the early 1980s, when many people retreated into subsistence in the hinterlands (Bryceson & Potts 2006). Even within the city, urban farming became a primary source of food and income (Amis 2006; Nuwagaba 2006). Overall, the Amin and 'Obote II' period saw the state's infrastructural power within the city weaken despite extreme despotism, both of which undermined the legitimacy of the state and its institutions.

Rwanda

Rwanda's tragic postcolonial history, from the violent events of 1959–1964 that caused several hundred thousand Tutsis to flee into exile to the slaughter of over half a million (mostly Tutsi) Rwandans in the 1994 genocide, has been extensively documented (Prunier 1997; Uvin 1998; Des Forges 1999; Mamdani 2001; Straus 2006). The implications of these upheavals for politics in Rwanda, and political mobilization and subjectivities in Kigali specifically, are discussed in Chapter 8; here the discussion is confined to major postcolonial developments concerning land policy, particularly as these affected Kigali. Conflicts over land were central to Rwanda's postcolonial story, though the role of land in the 1994 genocide itself is contested (André & Platteau 1998; Musahara & Huggins 2005; Verpoorten 2012; Boone 2014).

In the context of land scarcity, population pressure, and heightened ethnic tension after independence and the 1959–1961 'Social Revolution' that saw

Hutu–Tutsi power relations effectively reversed,[9] many Rwandans were subject to repeated forced relocations as large parts of the population were resettled by the state. Juvenal Habyarimana—Rwanda's second post-independence President from 1973, following Grégoire Kayibanda—was particularly concerned with the impacts of farmland fragmentation on agricultural development (Nezehose 1990), prompting an escalation of resettlement programmes. Boone (2014) thus argues that the 'statist' nature of Rwanda's land regime provides the key link between land scarcity and the all-encompassing national scale of Rwanda's violent conflicts. The postcolonial state saw itself as a pioneer of new land relations, flexing the muscles of its infrastructural power through resettlement programmes that made many Rwandans dependent on the state, rather than social or 'neo-customary' institutions, for their land rights. Moreover, uprooting populations and moving them to new territory actively undermined historically rooted forms of associational life, making people particularly 'exposed to social pressures exerted by the local-level agents of the state' (Boone 2014: 249). These processes of territorialization further enhanced infrastructural power through the weakening of social networks outside the state, and bolstered the state's capacity to exert pro-formal political control through 'microlevel levers of influence' (Boone 2014: 240). Interestingly, the area around Kigali was especially affected by government-sponsored land reallocation from the 1960s to the 1980s (Boone 2014: 241).

In terms of property relations, legislation passed after independence attempted to formalize the land market, but to little effect. A 1976 law shifted ownership of land from 'the community' to the state, though this made little difference to the informal nature of local land transactions, which remained primarily unregistered and unregulated (Pottier 2002: 181; Sagashya & English 2009: 3). Meanwhile, local officials and, increasingly, urban elites bought up agricultural land, further diminishing the amount available to ordinary farmers. By 1984, 15 per cent of landowners owned half of Rwanda's land (Uvin 1998; Musahara & Huggins 2005). When economic crisis hit in the late 1980s, panic sales of plots through the informal land market precipitated an escalation of land conflicts in the run-up to the genocide (André & Platteau 1998).

It was also only in the post-independence period that the first substantial growth of Kigali's population occurred. Between 1962 and 1984, the population grew from around 6,000 people to nearly 160,000 (Oz Architecture 2007: 17), with other sources suggesting the city's population even reached 250,000 by 1988 (Bizmana 1989). In the mid-1980s, the population density in Kigali was higher than at any other point in its history, including today. This was facilitated in part by the bringing of the institution of *umunani* into the urban context, where its function involved mitigating the economic precarity of town life, and through which periodic phases of urban expansion were then followed by densification (Shearer

[9] For more detail on the 'Social Revolution' and politics of the postcolonial transition, see Chapter 8.

2017: 47–48). In this context there was a growing tension between *akajagari*—a term that refers to disorder and messiness in dense proximity—and the drive to make the city a space of 'modern' development.

More generally, there was an increasing fissure between the rural majority and urban-based elite (Jefremovas 2002). Bizmana notes that Kigali in particular was 'the town which rural Rwandans call AMAHANGA (abroad): not only because it looks foreign but also because of the widespread European mentality of its inhabitants' (Bizimana 1989: 160). Kigali was already the hub of Rwanda's international donor community, which had a generally cosy relationship with Habyarimana's regime (Uvin 1998). Yet at the same time, Kigali prior to 1994 was described by the city's first post-genocide mayor as 'really like a big village'.[10] Although increasingly territorialized as a space of state-led modernization projects and outward-facing elite projects, there was little by way of a distinct urban property regime and the city was growing primarily through the adaptation of existing informal and rural institutions.

Ethiopia

Ethiopia's land tenure regime transformed fundamentally after the 1974 revolution, one of the most radical revolutionary upheavals ever to take place in Africa (Zewde 1991; Markakis 2011). Despite a decade of radical activism, it surprised almost everyone when a mutinous group within the armed forces, popularly known as the Derg (committee), capitalized on growing urban unrest (discussed further in Chapter 8) to seize power and depose Haile Selassie (Zewde 1991; Markakis 2011). Rising public anger was compounded by outrage at the emperor after the devastating famine in Wollo in 1973, exposed internationally in a famous report by Jonathan Dimbleby, subsequently intercut with scenes of Haile Selassie at a royal feast and disseminated on national television. The incoming military junta, while not initially ideological aligned with the student activists, turned to radical leftists for ideas to substantiate its rule. This resulted in an agenda that aimed to do no less than put the entire economy 'in the hands of the state' (Markakis 2011: 169).

A central pillar of this was the 1975 land reform, which was by far the most lasting of the Derg's legacies. These proclaimed all rural land to be the property of the state, without any compensation for previous rights holders, and prohibited all tenancy relations (Crewett et al. 2008; McCann 1995), following the 'Land to the Tiller' demands that had been growing in volume since the 1960s (Pausewang 1983; Markakis 2011). Unlike the laws nationalizing land in Uganda and Rwanda around the same time, this one was ruthlessly implemented. The reforms largely crowded out both imperial and customary land institutions in the highlands,

---

[10] Interview with Rose Kabuye, 12 February 2010.

though this was less the case in lowland areas, and the bundles of rights held by tillers in different parts of the country remained diverse (Crewett et al. 2008: 6). However, throughout the country farmers were legally prohibited from transferring their usufruct rights by sale, mortgage, or lease, plot sizes per family were limited to ten hectares, and the use of hired labour was prohibited (Crewett et al. 2008: 12).

Meanwhile, principles of agrarian socialism were implemented including the collectivization of small-scale farms and establishment of state farming (Joireman 2000), as well as the state control of land redistribution through Peasant Associations *(gabbar kebele)*. Possibilities for migration were limited, because usufruct rights were tied to the membership of Peasant Associations in a particular place of origin (Clapham 1988). These associations effectively became instruments of the Derg regime to control the countryside. Despite the rural imagery of 'Land to the Tiller', the revolution was a very urban-based phenomenon (Tiruneh 1993; McCann 1995), and almost sixty thousand students and teachers from cities and towns were sent to the countryside to design and implement rural reforms, including villagization programmes (Tiruneh 1993). The redistribution was very real, but land tenure insecurity increased for many people due to ongoing redistribution and compulsory resettlement programmes (Rahmato 1984). The *kebele*, which initially had an unclear status within government structure, was rapidly turned into the official unit of local government with tax-collecting powers, armed defence and policing functions.

Urban areas were also revolutionized in distinct ways, with major long-lasting consequences. Following the rural land reform of March 1975, in July both urban land and all 'extra houses' were nationalized (Tiruneh 1993). Since Ethiopian towns were constituted primarily of nobles' grand houses surrounded by many smaller ones they had built to rent out (and less privileged city-dwellers also supplemented their income by building shacks of wattle and daub), the nationalization of extra houses was an extremely radical step, abolishing landlordism overnight. New housing construction also virtually ground to a halt, and the imperial urban structure was effectively 'frozen' (Duroyaume 2015: 400). The rents that city-dwellers had paid to landlords were now paid directly to the state, at rates fixed by the Ministry of Urban Development and Housing, through a two-tier system: rents over 100 Birr were paid to the National Housing Authority, while those under 100 Birr were paid to the *kebele*. Because rent levels were frozen, and the development of properties without special permission was prohibited, most city-dwellers paid small and in real terms diminishing amounts of rent to their local *kebele* to live in extremely substandard housing. Meanwhile urban *kebele* became instruments of mass control and surveillance (Tiruneh 1993; Markakis 2011: 172), facilitating a state presence of 'leviathan proportions' (Zewde 1991: 424).

Through the Derg's reforms, the property regime of Addis Ababa was completely overturned, and the city was re-territorialized as a space of surveillance and control, executed to a significant degree through the state's new local organs, the *kebele*. The significance of this political juncture can therefore hardly be overstated. As well as expanding the state's infrastructural reach through close regulation of land and housing markets and intensified policing, bolstered through the trauma of the 1976–1978 'Red Terror' (see Chapter 8), there was a fundamental rupture in the balance of power, with major landowners stripped of assets and heightened sense of the collective power of the urban masses.

3.5 Land and urban territory under the new rebel statesmen

Between 1986 and 1994, the governing regimes in Uganda, Rwanda, and Ethiopia were overthrown following years of civil war, which in the Rwandan case culminated in one of the world's most devastating and rapid genocides. There are important similarities and differences between the nature and motivation of the rebel groups which, in each case, fought sustained armed struggles against the central government and eventually won, subsequently metamorphosizing into new ruling parties. In Uganda, rebel forces led by Yoweri Museveni's National Resistance Army (NRA) built on a long history of struggle against both the Amin and Obote regimes by numerous rebel groups. While Museveni and many of his key allies hailed from south-western Uganda, his strategy for overthrowing Obote's second regime involved a protracted 'people's struggle', which meant building an alliance with the Buganda kingdom's leadership and progressively incorporating Baganda into the NRA (Museveni 1997; Amaza 1998: 28–35). Much of the 'Bush War' was fought from 1981 to 1986 in an area known as the Luweero triangle in central Uganda, just north of Kampala.

The even longer struggle against the Derg in Ethiopia was primarily based on an alliance between two liberation movements from northern regions of Ethiopia (which at the time included Eritrea): the Tigray People's Liberation Front (TPLF) and Eritrean People's Liberation Front (EPLF). Although the TPLF went on to form the umbrella Ethiopian Peoples' Revolutionary Democratic Front (EPRDF) in a bid for national legitimacy, the civil war that swept it to power was very much a revolt of the excluded northern peripheries against the Amhara core that had dominated (and internally colonized) Ethiopia since the time of Menelik (Tareke 2009; Berhe 2020). In Rwanda, meanwhile, the guerrilla war waged by the Rwandan Patriotic Front (RPF) was not rooted in a peripheral region but among excluded Tutsi factions who had been living in exile, mostly in Uganda (Waugh 2004; Straus 2006). The RPF enacted much of its struggle from across Rwanda's northern border, before marching through the country to take control of Kigali in the midst of the genocide.

Thus, while all three civil wars involved rural-based guerrilla warfare waged by rebels fighting on behalf of excluded or marginalized groups, their relationship to core–periphery dynamics within the country—and by extension to the capital city on arrival in power—differed in significant ways. The NRA largely fought its war from the heart of Uganda, and in so doing needed to gain favour and support from the local population in Buganda, the core of the Ugandan state surrounding Kampala. The RPF, by contrast, fought their war mainly from the outside, with Kigali as the goal. Given the historical dominance of the Tutsi monarchy prior to independence, the sense of 'returning' to Kigali after decades of exile—in some cases, a whole lifetime of exile—was significant in terms of the territorialization of RPF rule. In Ethiopia, the people of Tigray and Eritrea who overthrew the Derg had never been at the heart of power in the modern state of Ethiopia. The much longer history of rule emanating from the mountains in Tigray—dating back to Aksum—gave them a sense of restoring the historical power of the northern high-lands; yet they were somewhat unfamiliar with Addis Ababa and to urban life as it had evolved under the emperors. The remainder of this section teases out the differences between the cases through some salient aspects of land reform under the rebels-turned-statesmen in these three countries, particularly with respect to the urban land question.

Uganda

The fact that both Amin and Obote had failed to resolve the landlord/tenant impasse in Buganda—and that during the 'Bush War' the NRA had allied them-selves with *both* Baganda landed elites and the peasants occupying their land—made the land question one of the thorniest issues facing Museveni's government once it achieved power (Oloka-Onyango 1997; McAuslan 2003; Kasfir 2005). The National Resistance Movement (NRM - peacetime successor to the NRA) needed to maintain its alliance with the kingdom by officially reinstating *mailo* and pro-tecting the interests of powerful landlords, yet also had to be careful not to alienate Baganda peasants by entrenching their position of virtual serfdom (Green 2006). In attempting to balance these conflicting goals, once in power the relationship between the NRM government and the Buganda kingdom became increasingly strained. This was exacerbated by the 1998 Land Act, which legally protected occupants and holders of *kibanja* (a form of usufruct right on *mailo* land) from eviction on the simple condition that they paid an annual 'peppercorn' rent of 1,000 Shillings. Resistance from Baganda landlords was fierce, heightened by the fact that increasing numbers of occupants on *mailo* land were believed to be non-Baganda from Museveni's region in south-west Uganda (Green 2006). The dispute over land in Buganda worsened with the tabling of the Land (Amendment) Bill in 2007, passed into law amid acrimony at the end of 2009, which further strengthened the rights of 'bona fide' occupants against eviction (Goodfellow & Lindemann 2013).

While the debate on Buganda's land question was raging, Kampala's population was booming following its wartime contraction, with the population reaching a million by the mid-1990s, around two million by 2010 and an estimated 3.3 million by 2020 (UNDESA 2018). Planning of any kind held little sway; a preparatory study for the 1994 plan stated that 'since 1971 ... virtually all growth in Kampala has been unplanned' (Kampala Urban Study 1994), and the 1994 plan itself fared little better (Omolo-Okalebo 2011). Kampala's primacy within the national urban system continued to grow, as discussed further in Chapter 4. The economic boom in Museveni's Uganda—celebrated internationally and supported by enthusiastic donors (Kuteesa et al. 2010; Tripp 2010; Wiegratz et al. 2018)—was thus centred on Kampala and sent its land values soaring, which raised the stakes in the battles over land policy noted earlier. While the associational power of landowners remained substantial, it was also circumscribed by the NRM's political hedging on land reforms, all of which served to fuel informal land markets operating through para- and anti-formal processes that further undercut state infrastructural power. The implications of this are explored in Chapters 5 and 6.

Rwanda

Rwanda's post-1994 framework for urban land and planning evolved in a very concentrated period, necessitated by the new land crisis following the return of successive waves of refugees and the fact that the RPF inherited very little by way of a legal and regulatory framework for urban development. In rural areas, the new land crisis prompted the government to launch its controversial *imidugudu* villagization campaign in December 1996, in a further attempt to address low agricultural productivity and dispersed settlement (Van Leeuwen 2001; Ansoms 2008). At the level of national land policy, the need for reform was considered extremely urgent given high population densities, growing landlessness, and continued conflict in much of the country (Van Hoyweghen 1999). In 2001, more than 80 per cent of court cases involved land disputes (Ngoga 2019). The 2004 National Land Policy (amended in 2012) set out to consolidate plots, ensuring equal access to land regardless of gender or 'origin', and establishing mechanisms for land registration and tenure regularization. The extreme nature of land fragmentation bears repeating: by 2008 the average parcel size was just 0.35 hectares (Sagashya & English 2009: 1), and by 2011 there were around ten million registered land parcels in Rwanda—almost equivalent to one per member of the population.[11]

The 2005 Organic Land Law (OLL) set the new policy in stone, introducing a system whereby investors in urban land meeting certain specifications are entitled to freehold titles, while all other landholders can acquire an 'emphyteutic

---

[11] Interview with land official, Kigali, 9 December 2011.

lease' of variable length (three–nintety-nine years). This granted them leasehold rights in exchange for paying a lease contract fee and developing the land in accordance with lease conditions, which relate to its classification (as commercial, residential, etc.) and zoning rules. In order to implement the new legal framework, from 2009 the government rolled out a major Land Tenure Regularization Programme supported by the UK Department for International Development. Through this process, most urban residential and commercial plots were granted leases of twenty to thirty years depending on location, with those in the city centre mostly just twenty years.[12] While the LTRP has generally been considered a success (particularly in stimulating the urban land market), the parcelling up of land has not eradicated the informal *umunani* system and informal land transactions in practice (Ngoga 2019).

Kigali itself had an extraordinary range of challenges to deal with after the genocide: as survivors emerged and 'old caseload' (primarily Tutsi) returnees flooded into the city, they often occupied houses in a pattern described by the first post-genocide mayor as 'random settlement. People would just open a house and go in, and stay in. Because there was nowhere else you could put them.'[13] Two years later, with the return of the 'new caseload' refugees from DRC, the city felt the strain of post-conflict urbanization under the most extreme circumstances imaginable. While the RPF attempted to discourage 'new caseload' refugees from overwhelming Kigali given its acute housing shortage,[14] many headed there due to the relative anonymity of the large city context.[15]

The growth of the city in this period spiralled, surpassing even its soaring growth in the 1980s, with an average urban population growth rate of 18 per cent from 1995 to 2000, something virtually unprecedented anywhere in the world in the last sixty years.[16] The population exploded from around fifty thousand immediately after the genocide to six-hundred thousand by 2000 (KIST 2001). The government did not prevent people from returning to properties they rightfully owned, even though these were now being inhabited by other people. In some cases, genocide perpetrators and survivors even had to share the same property.[17] Unsurprisingly, crimes relating to ongoing property disputes were bitter and plentiful in the late 1990s. The prevalence of violent disputes gradually dissipated as the RPF turned its military intelligence levers towards enhancing urban security as a central part of its legitimation drive, further deepening the state's existing infrastructural power through an intensification of community-based policing (Lamarque 2017). The RPF was therefore able to build on the long history of infrastructural power to gradually re-territorialize Kigali in its own image, and in

---

[12] Interviews with various city officials, June 2014.
[13] Interview with Rose Kabuye.
[14] Interview with Rose Kabuye; see also Prunier (2008).
[15] Interviews with local officials, 17–18 February 2009.
[16] According to UN statistics, the only time a (marginally) higher growth rate has been seen anywhere since 1950 was in Western Sahara in the late 1970s (UNDESA 2009).
[17] Interview with Rose Kabuye.

response to the demands of powerful groups on whom its power and legitimacy depended, as explored further in Chapters 5 and 6.

Ethiopia

Contrary to much international expectation, the EPRDF did not seek to privatize land ownership after taking the reins of power in 1991. Instead, Meles Zenawi's government announced the continuation of the Derg's land policy, and state ownership of land was cemented in Article 40 of the 1995 Constitution (Crewett et al. 2008; Markakis 2011). The fundamentals of collective ownership, passed down through *rist* to the post-revolutionary system of state-controlled Peasant Associations which largely continued into the EPRDF period, remained in place. As well as preventing the emergence of a landholding class, part of the reason for maintaining state control of land was to limit rural–urban migration that might cause political instability (Rahmato 2009; Lavers 2018). However, unlike the 1975 land reforms, the 1995 Constitution did not prohibit the leasing of land or specify minimum plot sizes. The new Constitution also provided for individual rights to the immovable property on land (Article 40).

The EPRDF adopted a historically unprecedented approach to dealing with Ethiopia's 'ethnic question' by instituting a new federal system, through which the country was divided into seven federal regions and two federal cities, Addis Ababa and Dire Dawa. This gave Federal states significant autonomy over land policy (within the limits set by the Constitution), for example over issues such as inheritance rights and the link between land use rights and *kebele* residence (Crewett et al. 2008: 16–17). This generated contradictions with principles embedded in the countrywide policy of universal access to state-owned land (Lavers 2018). The regional government of Oromia granted higher levels of tenure security than other regional governments, granting lifelong usufruct rights to agricultural land, free of all payment (Crewett et al. 2008: 17). But significantly, given the location of Addis Ababa as a federal city surrounded by Oromia, the Oromia government's proclamation also allows for state expropriation of farmland for 'more important public uses', subject to compensation (Article 6.4). While in theory land rights improved relative to the situation under the Derg, in reality the land situation in Oromia under the EPRDF was riddled with festering tensions that would come to a head with the plans to extend the Addis Ababa city boundary in 2014 (see Chapter 8).

In urban areas, the EPRDF was faced with a land-use system that neither yielded much revenue nor provided the foundations for the rapid development it sought to promote. Existing land use was governed by a permit system, in which the government would issue permits to use particular plots of land for indefinite periods in exchange for rent, which (as noted previously) bore no relation to market value. The EPRDF wanted to combine continued state land ownership with market-driven development, and in pursuit of this objective soon began investigating the possibilities for a system of land leasing along the lines of other countries transitioning from socialism.[18] Based on a series of study visits including several to China, the Addis Ababa City Authority led the way in developing a leasing system designed to unlock the market value of land. Proclamation No. 80/1993 provided for government to transfer rights over land for specified periods of time while retaining the ultimate title. A revision of the law in 2002 made it feasible to acquire land with much lower upfront payments, or even for free if the purpose of acquisition was to develop large numbers of housing units, unleashing a wave of land purchases and transfers and feeding rampant speculation.[19]

In 2011, a further revision (Proclamation No. 721/2011) attempted to address this by subjecting all new land leases to auction, which sent land prices shooting upwards. This revision also took the leasing system a step further through a controversial measure to try and incorporate *all* urban land gradually into the leasing system. This meant that whenever a plot held under the old permit system was sold, instead of the permit transferring as part of the sale the new landholder was required to take out a lease at the benchmark price (updated every two years) which dramatically increased the cost of formal land transactions.[20] This, along with the 2005 proclamation on expropriation, unsettled the pre-existing system in which land-use rights were cheap and easily transferrable, and created an unstable and asymmetric system with potential to generate great inequality (Frew Mengistu 2013). It resulted in substantial increases in government revenue through the land-lease system,[21] but also allowed for government to expropriate land for leasing with minimal compensation (Kloosterboer 2019; Weldeghebrael 2020). The institution of leasehold ownership provided a new tool for distributing resources to powerful groups that might seek to destablize EPRDF rule, while retaining strong powers of expropriation facilitated the rapid rollout of new forms of infrastructure. The ways in which these policy levers were deployed in the context of the growing power of a range of urban interests, and the EPRDF's heightened pursuit of urban legitimacy, will unfold in Part III of this book.

3.6 Conclusions: Land regimes, urban territory, and violent transitions

The land regimes in Uganda, Rwanda, and Ethiopia all involved centuries of territorialization and the evolution of complex systems of land-use rights that

---

[18] Interview with land expert, 4 October 2014.

[19] Interview with land specialist, 1 July 2019.

[20] Leases in Addis Ababa are ninety-nine years for residential housing, science and technology, research and study, government offices, charities, etc; seventy years for industry; sixty years for commerce; and fifteen years for urban agriculture (Article 18).

[21] For a discussion of the effects of the land-lease system on peri-urban areas in different parts of Ethiopia, see Adam (2014; 2020). For an discussion of the land-lease system and its relationship to land value capture in Addis Ababa, see Goodfellow (2015).

were subsequently overlain with capitalist notions of property. The extent of this territorialization, whereby land-use rights were linked to territory and enforced through rigid hierarchies and tributary systems linked to a spatial order, was relatively unusual in Africa. This reflects extensive bureaucratic development and relatively strong infrastructural power across the Great Lakes kingdoms and Ethiopia constructed over hundreds of years, linked to the abundance of fertile land and unusual levels of population density. In all three countries, colonialism or imperial rule saw increasing moves towards private land ownership, though the extent and depth of this differed substantially, with freehold land coming into play most significantly and earliest in Uganda.

Despite these similarities, the divergences between Uganda, Rwanda, and Ethiopia in relation to policies affecting urban land became increasingly stark over time, notwithstanding parallel attempts to nationalize land in the mid-1970s. In Uganda the chaos of the Amin and Obote years meant that the contradictions of Uganda's colonial land regime—rooted in a partial transition to private owner-ship and incomplete settling of landlord–tenant relations—intensified, while in Rwanda there was an increasing use of state control to shift populations across territory and centralize the allocation of land rights. These different trajectories drew the relationship between land and infrastructural power in opposite direc-tions in the two countries, while also further cementing the associational power of private landlords in Uganda. Meanwhile in Ethiopia, the rapid proliferation of private property in the later decades of Haile Selassie's rule was radically over-turned by the 1974 revolution, providing the state with unparalleled formal levers over land but doing little to address the fundamental inequalities that had already surged in both urban and rural Ethiopia.

The socio-spatial legacies of these histories were profound for the evolution of their capital cities. Kampala was the archetypal colonial 'dual city' in terms of its spatial divide between colonial and indigenous capitals, while Kigali and Addis were 'dualized' in very different ways: in Kigali, the postcolonial city's role as an aid hub and space of privilege jarred against the gaping absence of a broader economic foundation through which urbanization could benefit ordinary people (explored further in Chapter 4), while in Addis the growing inequality between landown-ers and tenants produced a more spatially mingled form of inequality. While the territorialization of Kampala was contested between the national government, for which it was the capital, and the Buganda kingdom for which it was a central power base and economic hub, Kigali was territorialized as a space for the state bureau-cratic elite. Addis Ababa, meanwhile, formed a multi-ethnic bundle of political and economic interests that would come to pose substantial challenges for the legitimacy of both the emperor and successive post-imperial regimes, as well as fomenting an explosive situation regarding its territorial boundaries with Oromia.

In addition to these long-term trends of property rights and territorialization, Kampala, Kigali, and Addis Ababa were shaped by the extraordinary levels of violence and bloodshed affecting the three countries in the late twentieth century.

As well as direct effects on urban stagnation and growth, civil wars reconfigured the national balance of associational power fundamentally—albeit with important continuities—with long-term implications for urban development. In Kampala, the associational power of Baganda landlords persisted, though a new elite from south-western Uganda gravitated to the capital and Museveni's land reforms bolstered the counter-power of occupants on *mailo* land, who were legally empowered to resist eviction. Meanwhile, despite being formally restituted in 1993, the power of the Buganda kingdom authorities themselves were progressively eroded. In Kigali, the shoots of an urban capitalist class that emerged under Habyarimana was largely destroyed or expelled through the civil war and aftermath of genocide, while a class of returnees from the mostly Tutsi diaspora was catapaulted into Kigali after 1994 with an international outlook and determination to transform Rwandan territory and society. Many ordinary urbanites, including genocide survivors, were marginal to this vision, as subsequent chapters will show. In Ethiopia, the coming to power of a new, rural 'outsider' elite from the mountains of rural Tigray—alongside growing angst of a substantial Ethiopian diaspora around the world—produced new arrangements of power, including through the institution of ethnic federalism, which would struggle to contain the aspirations of the capital city's population.

Given their distinct, often uncomfortable relationships with urban populations, the victorious rebel forces that took the helm of government in each case needed to seek legitimacy in the capital city with a range of important and potentially destabilizing groups. In so doing, the use and distribution of land were always close to the surface; but the infrastructural reach of the state, and political modalities through which land benefits and rents could be best be distributed, differed substantially. Before exploring how this played out with respect to investment and lived realities of infrastructure, real estate, and housing, we need to examine the parallel story of the making of urban economies, which intersects with questions of territory and property but requires its own historical analysis.

4

The making of urban economies

Introduction

> Capitalism does not spring from the womb of pre-capitalist society
> like the Greek Goddess Athena from the head of Zeus, its features fully
> formed and looks easily identifiable to one and all. Neither is it like a
> flag planted from outside in a single clean swoop. Capitalist relations
> assume a variety of historical forms, depending on both the concrete
> character of the pre-capitalist soil in which it grows or on which it is
> foisted, and the overall international context.
>
> (Mamdani 1985: 185).

The preceding chapter focused on land to explain how, over time, East African
cities came to exhibit different property regimes and dynamics of territorialization.
However, despite the integral role of land as a factor of production and central element in group-based identification and political mobilization, East African cities
were not only made by the politics of land but the politics of capital and labour.
They were shaped by decisions about urban investment, but also by patterns of
commerce, employment, and entrepreneurialism. This chapter therefore turns to
the flows of capital, the constitution of urban labour, and related shifts in dominant
ideas about urban economic development. The colonial period was particularly
important—even in the case of the very brief Italian occupation of Ethiopia—in
laying the foundations for capitalist urban development, albeit in highly exclusionary and racist ways. But in order to understand the deeper foundations of urban
economies and how these were networked into regional relationships, we need
again to look deeper into history and consider precolonial commercial dynamics
and the gradual ploughing of trade routes from coastal regions to the centre of
Africa. Through these networks and practices, the colonial investments and regulations that followed them, and the subsequent (often path-dependent) patterns
of urban economic development, particular 'operations of capital' (Mezzadra &
Nielsen 2015) came to shape the urban landscape.

The idea of 'operations of capital', although developed in relation to contemporary processes of financialization and their relationship with extraction and

Politics and the Urban Frontier. Tom Goodfellow, Oxford University Press. © Tom Goodfellow (2022).
DOI: 10.1093/oso/9780198853107.003.0004

logistics, enables a focus on how capital has historically shaped East Africa without getting into debates on whether or not these societies were (or are) truly 'capitalist' in themselves (see e.g. Saul & Leys 1999; Chitonge 2018). For Mezzadra and Nielsen, 'An operation always refers to specific capitalist actors while also being embedded in a wider network of operations and relations that involve other actors, processes, and structures' (Mezzadra & Neilson, 2015: 6–7). This is helpful in characterizing the relationship between global capitalist processes—which were central to the very foundations of colonialism—and the local territories and materialities through which they unfolded in contexts such as East Africa.

As East African territories became enrolled into patterns of regional commerce and then global trade relations, followed by full-fledged colonialism itself, the operations of capital reshaped territories in distinct ways. As Ouma notes, 'the coming into being of capital hinges upon establishing often far-flung connections that enroll and reformat organizations, economic relations, labor and nature itself at different sites in often surprising configurations' (Ouma 2016: 89). When it comes to urban areas, factors such as the land regime, different population densities across territory, and the insertion of major infrastructure projects conditioned how capital has reworked organizational and economic relations. The 'reformatting' wrought by operations of capital in East Africa's nascent urban centres has helped to produce new modalities of politics as well as reshaping distributions of power.

This chapter begins with a discussion of the precolonial trade links that formed region-wide networks across East Africa, linking inland kingdoms to the coast and providing the basis for early urban settlement. I then turn to the colonial encounter, paying particular attention to how major regional railways galvanized economies as well as the patterns of colonial investment in manufacturing. Important differences emerged within the region not only regarding the extent of manufacturing but in terms of how industrial development related to issues of race and ethnicity. Following this, I consider a period that has sometimes been termed a 'golden age' of urban society in parts of East Africa—the 1950s and 1960s—when the urban educated classes were growing and exerting their cultural and political presence around the time of independence or, in the Ethiopian case, in the run-up to revolution. Beneath this, however, was an increasingly pressing question of urban labour and how it might be absorbed in rapidly urbanizing postcolonial economies. After considering this I turn to the violent ruptures and economic shocks of the 1970s and 1980s, and how these reshaped urban economic development trajectories in different ways in all cases. Finally, the chapter returns to the period since a triad of new regimes emerged victorious from civil wars in Uganda, Ethiopia, and Rwanda, embraced by the donor community and pursuing varying forms of economic transformation with important implications for the urban present.

4.1 The early foundations of a regional trading economy

The making of an economic region from the coast to the lakes

Despite being some five hundred miles inland, we cannot comprehend the economic foundations of the Great Lakes region without attending to the role of the Indian Ocean and the vast stretch of coastline that for millennia formed the main point of contact between Africa and Asia. It was along this coast that some of the earliest urban centres emerged in places now encompassed within the modern nation-states of Kenya and Tanzania, as well as southern Somalia and northern Mozambique: a thousand-mile stretch of coastline and archipelago that came to be known as the Swahili coast. These city-states constituted centres of elite merchant activity, trading locally and regionally as well as across the Indian Ocean (Middleton 1992; Kusimba et al. 2013). Swahili coastal city states flourished from around the second century AD, gathering pace around the ninth century as urban settlements were increasingly rebuilt in coral stone (Chami 1998; Kusimba et al. 2013). Much attention has been devoted to the precise nature and timing of Persian and Arab engagement with the coast, and the degree to which Swahili urban culture was Shirazi (Arabic/Persian) relative to Bantu in nature (Chittick 1965; Chittick & Rotberg 1975; Chami 1994; 1998). Yet the key point about these early Swahili towns is that they represented dynamic *interaction* between local, regional, and international forces (Spear 2000a; Pouwels 2002): something that would continue to shape East Africa through its evolution and often abrupt transformations up to the present day.

Islam was a distinguishing feature of the Swahili towns from the eleventh century onwards, and was central to how they constructed their identity relative to inland communities as the city-states became cultural arbiters between Africa and the Islamic world (Fourchard 2011; Pouwels 2002; Burton 2017). Trading centres along the coast were linked together in urban clusters which each had a specialization in production and trade, and the region's trade links reached as far as China and South East Asia (Sinclair 1995). The Swahili coast has thus been seen as a dynamic 'middleman society', with cities and towns acting as brokers between the commercial world of the sea and the productive world of the hinterland (Spear 2000a; Middleton 1992). Especially important in early Swahili coastal urbanism were towns such Mogadishu in the north and Kilwa in the south, which by the fourteenth century surpassed Mogadishu as the coast's major trading town (Chittick 1974). These however later paled in comparison to great centres of Swahili Indian Ocean commerce at Lamu, Mombasa, Malindi, Bagamoyo, and the island town of Zanzibar.

With the arrival of the Portuguese in the sixteenth century, rivalries between coastal towns undermined any co-ordinated response to Portuguese expansionism, which sent some of the most prominent towns (including Kilwa) into swift decline (Burton 2017). By contrast, Portuguese and later Omani Arab penetration bolstered the relative rise of Mombasa, which in the seventeenth and eighteenth centuries was unrivalled as the pre-eminent power base on the coast. This was partly due to its success in building commercial links with the inland communities and kingdoms (Maxon 1994; Burton 2017). A new era of coastal prosperity from the late eighteenth century was to have significant implications not only for the coast but for the whole of East Africa and its emerging urban centres. This prosperity was linked both to the rise of the Busaidi dynasty in Oman from the mid-eighteenth century, and the global effects of the industrial revolution in Europe and North America, which drove unprecedented levels of demand for East African commodities (Burton 2017).

Britain emerged after the Napoleonic wars as the dominant power in the Indian Ocean, and allied itself with the Omani rulers, supporting their claims to the coast while also attempting to enlist them in limiting the Indian Ocean slave trade (Nwulia 1975). Cities such as Kilwa, Lamu, Mafia, and Zanzibar submitted to Omani sovereignty to shield themselves from Mombasa's dominance. By 1837, Oman's ruler, Seyyid Said, had secured dominance of Mombasa too and united the whole stretch of coast into a single customs unit (Maxon 1994: 113–114). After shifting his permanent residence to Zanzibar, the island superseded even Mombasa in importance in the nineteenth century. Elites from the coastal city-states 'managed and financed a complex and extensive interregional trade network' including 'long-distance trading expeditions to the African interior to procure ivory, leather, rock crystal, beeswax, rhinoceros horn, and other products for export' (Kusimba et al. 2013: 400–401).

Through the expansion of trade between the coast and mainland, the Zanzibari commercial empire spurred unprecedented urban growth as new trading centres emerged on caravan routes inland, often financed by Indian bankers that Said invited to East Africa (Maxon 1994). These towns included several on Lake Victoria and Lake Tanganyika. While the dramatic increase in trade with the coast inevitably changed mainland Tanzania and Kenya, heightened demand for products such as iron implements and food also galvanized production deeper into East Africa. The royal capitals emerging in the interlacustrine region increasingly developed into sites of economic specialization in the face of these sweeping economic transformations (Burton 2017). In this sense, coastal developments reverberated wide across the region and its emerging urban formations. Meanwhile, Buganda itself was effectively operating as a maritime society, benefiting from mobile ideas as well as people and goods across the extensive networks criss-crossing Lake Victoria (Kiwanuka 1972). Swahili and Arab merchants from Zanzibar and beyond established themselves within the interlacustrine region in the 1830s and 1840s, often trading in firearms in exchange for slaves and ivory (Chrétien 2003; Mworoha

& Mukuri 2004; Reid 2017). From the 1840s, the region began to be transformed by integration into trade and production at the global scale.

Britain played an increasingly significant role after the opening of a British consulate in Zanzibar in 1840, and from the 1870s onwards took increasing interest in penetrating beyond the coastal region itself. European commercial interests layered onto existing networks of missionary and anti-slavery activity (Nwulia 1975; Maxon 1994). Christian missionaries of varying stripes had been actively invited in by Kabaka Mutesa of Buganda, who sought to bolster his kingdom against the threat of Egyptian expansion into the interlacustrine region. This was to have far-reaching consequences, both in terms of entrenching Christianity within the kingdom for generations to come, and because of the conflicts between Christians, Muslims, and Mutesa's hostile son Mwanga that generated turmoil within the kingdom on the eve of British colonialism (Maxon 1994: 123). Shortly after missionary penetration of Buganda, the Roman Catholic 'White Fathers' entered Burundi and Rwanda from the east, as competitive regional religious missions intensified (Chrétien 2003: 212–213).

Growing trade relations between Europe and East Africa meant the latter being drawn into a highly asymmetric role within the unfolding global economic transformation, positioned as a supplier of raw materials while being introduced to cheap manufactured goods that undermined local artisanal production (Maxon 1994: 119). However, while trade is often considered to undermine the foundations of pre-capitalist economies and pave the way for capitalist accumulation, Mafeje argues that in the Great Lakes region trade did little to undermine the tributary/non-capitalist foundations of economy. Both short- and long-distance trade 'led neither to capital accumulation nor to technological investment or increased production relying on existing technologies' (Mafeje 1998: 86), partly due to dynamics of land and property discussed in Chapter 3. Even those Kingdoms that were more intensively involved in trade (like Buganda, Bunyoro, and Buzinza) did not see any appreciable difference in the level of development of their material capacities (Mafeje 1998). The incorporation of the region into global operations of capital in the nineteenth century did not therefore foster capitalist transformation internally.

Nevertheless, market towns flourished across the kingdoms, trading in goods such as ivory, livestock, bark cloth, salt, iron, and jewellery across regional borders (Chrétien 2003: 191; Reid 2017: 201). Hawkers transported these products to rulers' courts, and the royal capitals grew into impressive and highly organized cities—particularly the Kabaka's enclosure at Mengo. Nineteenth-century European visitors to Mutesa's court describe the royal enclosure alone as being mile long, surrounded by neatly arranged huts in lines covering an area of up to twenty square miles (Gutkind 1963; Reid & Medard 2000). The expansion of the *kibuga* at this time was partly due to the regular influx of foreign visitors, missionaries, and traders as the economy became increasingly monetized. An Arab quarter was present in the capital by the 1850s, and markets sprung up across the city as the century wore on (Reid & Medard 2000: 102). The *kibuga* became a 'supranational' centre and important destination both for Zanzibari traders and European missionaries decades before colonialism, and the kingdom's rulers actively encouraged both in an attempt to strengthen themselves (Reid & Medard 2000: 106).

The Horn and its regional economic relations

In parallel to the above developments, trade routes emerged between the coastal territories, the Great Lakes region and the Horn. Although the Abyssinian high-lands were less directly integrated into the caravan routes snaking inland from the Swahili coast than many other parts of Eastern Africa, Somali traders coming inland from the northern coastline passed goods along east–west chains of traders until they reached the Ethiopian interior. Similarly, north–south routes emerged, whereby ivory from Equatoria (contemporary Northern Uganda and South Sudan) was exchanged for metal goods and beads from the Abyssinian high-lands. In this way, groups such as the Acholi of Uganda and Oromo of Ethiopia were linked into patterns of regional exchange, mediated by other groups (Kurimoto 1995). Ethiopia was also deeply integrated into the East African slave trade, both through export of slaves across the Red Sea and through flourishing internal trade within the region.

Like other East African trade routes, those linking Ethiopia to the wider region intensified in the nineteenth century. The emergence of a 'common market of microbes' became particularly significant in the 1890s with a spate of severe epidemics including an epizootic originating in the Horn that devastated cattle herds in Rwanda and Burundi, with the effect of further concentrating livestock within aristocratic circles and thus consolidating their power (Mworoha & Mukuri 2004). A further way in which Ethiopia and the Great Lakes became region-ally interlaced was at the level of discourse, particularly with missionary clerics and subsequently colonial authorities themselves developing and perpetuating the 'Hamitic hypothesis'—the idea that interlacustrine cattle-herding groups such as the Tutsi had originated in the Christian kingdom of Ethiopia to the north, and were therefore superior (Mamdani 2001; Mworoha & Mukuri 2004). This discursive construction of regional movements, based on highly contested histor-ical evidence, was later to feed into the rhetoric of ethnic hatred and genocide in Rwanda and Burundi.

Within the Horn itself, two major nineteenth-century trade routes developed the link between the northern and southern areas of Ethiopia. One passed from south-western Ethiopia up through the highlands to the port of Massawa (now in Eritrea) on the Red Sea, while the other traced a line west to east, through a series of commercial centres including Harar, the Muslim political and commercial centre of eastern Ethiopia with its origins in the seventh century, and on to the Somali coast (Zewde 1991: 21–22). This became an extremely important artery of commerce in the nineteenth century, leading to the increased significance of the port city of Berbera (Geshekter 1993; Stepputat & Hagmann 2019).

Within inland Ethiopia, however, urbanization was minimal, despite the long and distinguished urban history of places such as Axum, Harar, and Gondar. The division and conflict that characterized the period known as *Zemene Mesafint* (the 'Era of the Princes') from the mid-eighteenth to mid-nineteenth century reduced many cities to being defensive hubs, as the emperors struggled to exert authority beyond the capital at Gondar and little was possible by way of capital accumulation and urban economic development. Abandoned by Emperor Tewodros II in the mid-nineteenth century, Gondar itself was then repeatedly ravaged by his soldiers and went into steep decline (Pankhurst 1969; Crummey 1971). Ankober, capital of the Shewa region from which Menelik rose to prominence, never grew very large, and declined in significance when Menelik moved south to Entoto and subsequently founded Addis Ababa.

4.2 Limits to economic transformation in the imperial period

Across Africa, as in much of the world, urbanization was one of the most important and lasting impacts of colonialism (Southall 1971; Mabogunje 1990; Home 1997; Fox 2014). It was in the early twentieth century particularly that a geographically extensive network of interconnected urban centres first emerged in the East Africa region (Burton 2017). Despite this, the initial growth of towns in colonial Africa was relatively slow, both due to limited manufacturing activity and colonial mobility restrictions (Elkan & van Zwanenberg 1975; Fox 2012). While colonial territories such as Northern Rhodesia (Zambia) and the Belgian Congo developed extensive mining towns, in much of East Africa, which held fewer mineral resources, the slower urban growth of inland colonial towns rested on the gradual expansion of administration, transport linkages, and trade (Elkan & van Zwanenburg 1975).

These processes were exemplified by Nairobi and Kampala, though the latter city's dual nature and the extensive pre-existing settlement at Mengo complicated the situation. In the Horn of Africa, meanwhile, a major reorientation of trade routes took place as Menelik shifted his attention southwards and established the capital at Addis Ababa, and the north–south route to Djibouti took precedence over the east–west route through Harar to the Somali coast (Zewde 1991: 94). In the remainder of this section, we first explore the urban impact of a crucial colonial infrastructure intervention—the railways—before looking at the operations of capital in relation to industrial development, and then consider some of the specificities of Imperial Ethiopia.

The coming of the railways

The colonial railway system introduced to East Africa initiated a major transformation in economic geography, radically reducing the significance of caravan trade and ushering new cities onto the map (Mworoha & Mukuri 2004). The first colonial railway in the region was initiated by the Germans in 1891 from the port of Tanga in German East Africa (now Tanzania), with the aim of ultimately connecting it to Lake Victoria. Progress was slow, though the initiation of a second railway (the Central Railway) in the early 1900s proved to be the making of the city of Dar es Salaam (Gann 1975). Meanwhile, the British were working on their own competing line through Kenya: the 'iron snake' (Kenyatta 1938/2015: 32) that was to prove central to the evolution of cities in both Uganda and Kenya, in both direct and indirect ways.

The 'opening up' of Africa through railways was at the heart of the British colonial vision. More specifically, building a track from Mombasa to Lake Victoria was central to the rationale for the Uganda Protectorate even before it was created in 1894 (Byerley 2005: 124). The British railway was initiated in Mombasa in 1896, reached lake Victoria at Kisumu (in Kenya) in 1902, and only reached Kampala in 1931; yet it was always called the 'Uganda Railway', with Kenyan terrain seen as less valuable and 'merely transit territory', and the route was chosen on the basis of the lowest construction costs (Jedwab et al. 2017: 89). The economic effects of the railway are difficult overstate when writ large: it cut travel time from Mombasa to Lake Victoria from over two months to around two days, reducing freight costs by 90 per cent, boosting the insertion of cheap imported goods into local markets, and generating Indian merchant dynasties as well as driving monetization of the economy (Chrétien 2003: 237). However, beyond its galvanizing impacts on the lacustrine commercial economy, the spatial effects of the railway as it extended into Uganda protectorate itself were more mixed.

Towns along the line inevitably grew, and the colonial government encouraged settlement stabilization to bolster centres for the collection of rural commodities, administrative activities, and trade (Mukwaya et al. 2010). However, unlike in Kenya where the railway *preceded* the development of a commercial economy, and a number of new urban centres (including Nairobi) emerged as a consequence of it, within Uganda commercial patterns were already well established and the railway's route did not generate many new economic hubs (O'Connor 1965: 26). Figure 4.1 shows the extent of the traffic on different parts of the railways in British colonial East Africa. The Uganda Railway's subsequent western extension to the Kilembe mines in 1956 largely failed to live up to its promise, and did little to

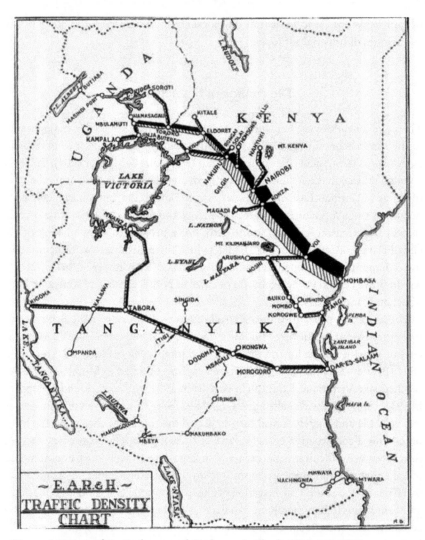

Figure 4.1 East Africa Railways and Harbours traffic density map, 1953
Source: EAR&H Magazine 1(6), September 1953.

stimulate the town of Kasese (O'Connor 1965: 26–27). Indeed, from the 1920s onwards the augmentation of the railway network in British-controlled East Africa was rooted more in British job creation and steel production interests than transport needs (Brett 1973: 296). Moreover, the railways were so capital-intensive that although some development was fostered along the line, anywhere more than a few miles away was starved of resources (Brett 1973: 297).

The long-term consequences of building the Uganda railway extend well beyond its effect on the country's economic geography, however—particularly in terms of the extent of South Asian settlement it generated as large numbers of Indians (mainly from Gujarat) were brought in to construct the track, and the privileged role that South Asians subsequently acquired in the economy (Reid 2017). As Byerley (2005: 125) notes, the railway introduced the 'Asian' as an 'agent of striation in the production, regulation and reproduction of colonial space.' The trading centres along the line also attracted Asian traders in significant numbers, though these were not the only foreigners who arrived in significant numbers to engage in trade; Swahilis, Arabs, and Greeks also arrived and opened shops (Mukwaya et al. 2010).

Under German and Belgian rule, there were no such efforts to develop railways in Rwanda and Burundi. Germany was much more focused on their Tanzanian line, and Belgian extractivism focused primarily on mineral extraction from Katanga in the Congo southwards to Northern Rhodesia, where it could connect with other British railways. Meanwhile in Ethiopia, Menelik rapidly seized the opportunity to engage with processes of colonial railway construction. A commission was granted for the Addis Ababa-Djibouti railway in 1894 (see Figure 4.2), to be constructed by the French from their small territory at Djibouti, which reached the new Ethiopian city of Dire Dawa in 1902 and eventually Addis Ababa in 1917. Significantly for integration of regional trade, plans to extend it to the

Figure 4.2 The original railway from Addis Ababa to Djibouti
Source: Addis Ababa Museum.

Nile were abandoned in the face of British opposition (Zewde 1991: 101). The extent to which Djibouti came to dominate Ethiopia's trade—amounting to some 75 per cent after the railway was constructed, despite major existing routes through Eritrea, Somalia, and Sudan—is testament to the force the Addis-Djibouti railway, as it became 'the chief means through which Ethiopia was drawn into the world economy' (Zewde 1991: 96–101). It also gave rise to the new towns of Nazareth and Mojo as well as Dire Dawa.

Emerging patterns of production and urban industry in Uganda and Rwanda

As soon as the railway from Mombasa reached Lake Victoria's shore in 1902, Uganda was opened up for cash-crop production—something also facilitated by Buganda's relatively good pre-existing road system (Brett 1973: 219). The first ginnery was opened in 1904 (Kilby 1975: 476) and cotton output, primarily produced by Ugandan peasants rather than European planters, rose from 1,000 bushels in 1906 to 180,000 in 1926 and almost 380,000 on the eve of independence (Chrétien 2003: 238). Alongside crop production, facilities for secondary activities such as processing and marketing grew in importance, and could in theory enable Ugandans to move out of purely agricultural activities into trade, processing, and even basic manufacturing (Brett 1973: 238).

However, in reality this was limited by the privileged role of European and, increasingly, Asian capitalists. The Indians rapidly superseded the British in terms of ownership of ginneries, such that by the 1920s two-thirds of cotton ginneries were Indian-owned and the vast majority of cotton exports went to India (Kilby 1975: 476). Colonial limitations on African participation in processing and manufacturing was quite deliberate; if sufficient numbers of Africans moved into these roles, the very foundation of the colonial enterprise would have been challenged (Brett 1973: 261; Rodney 1972). This in turn limited the ways that Africans could participate in the country's emerging urban economies, cementing the key role of the Asian trading class in the urban centres, particularly in the south and east of the country (Reid 2017).

The desire to build colonial economies that 'complemented' rather than competing with British manufactures meant that investment in manufacturing was virtually ignored up until World War II. The population of many East African cities declined during the Great Depression, often by as much as 30–40 per cent (Burton 2001: 19). In all of British-controlled East Africa, out of almost £8m allocated by the Colonial Development Advisory Committee by March 1939, only £151,000 was for industrial projects and only £23,000 of this had actually been spent, almost all in Kenya and Tanganyika (Brett 1973: 268). Colonial records document concerted efforts to limit the extent of manufacturing industry in Uganda (Brett 1973:

270–274; Jorgensen 1981), contrasting with the situation in Kenya, where the settler community pushed a higher level of industrialization in part to secure markets for their cash crops. This played a decisive role in cementing Kenya's position as the leading manufacturing centre in the region.

Nevertheless, some agri-processing industries were established in Uganda, particularly in Jinja, the famed source of the Nile that by 1908 had been identified by Winston Churchill as a future industrial centre (Byerley 2005: 10). Here a British American Tobacco cigarette factory was established, alongside the Mehta and Madhvani families' sugar refineries, by the late 1930s (Kilby 1975; Chrétien 2003). Nascent industrialization by Asian capitalists was partly driven by colonial restrictions preventing Asians from buying land outside of towns, only allowing them to trade in gazetted trading centres (Byerley 2005: 242). Over time, Jinja became the obvious location for industrial development due to its strategic location on the railway and, from 1954 onwards, the opening of the Owen Falls hydroelectric dam (Byerley 2011).

A much more positive attitude to industrialization emerged after the war, influenced in part by the Colonial Office's growing concern with labour stabilization (Cooper 1996) and creating urban job opportunities to 'avoid the creation of slums in the townships' (quoted in Brett 1973: 280). Anticipating future industrial growth, a 1946 colonial plan for Uganda allocated an unprecedented amount of funding for urban development—more than any other single sector—in addition to funding a major housing estate in Jinja (Byerley 2005: 234). The Uganda Development Corporation was established in 1952, and from the 1950s onwards Jinja became Uganda's leading industrial centre, with facilities such as the Nyanza Textiles factory, Sikh Sawmills Ltd., Nile Breweries, and the two sugar factories, as well as a copper smelter. Other cities were also targeted for industrial growth, notably Tororo (further east along the rail line towards Kenya) for the Ugandan cement industry, and Kasese near the Kilembe copper mines. Labour migration from northern parts of the country to centres such as Jinja was also substantial (Byerley 2005).

Despite this, in the two most significant cities—Jinja and Kampala—capitalist enterprise remained overwhelmingly in European and Asian hands. In Jinja, of fifty-two major employers listed in 1951, twenty-two were European and twenty-eight Asian (Byerley 2005: 260). Similarly, an enumeration of Jinja-based traders in March 1953 found that 351 out of 404 were Asian while only twenty-two were 'African' (Byerley 2005: 259). The dominance of Asians in the productive and commercial economy fomented anti-Asian sentiment as early as the 1930s, ultimately sowing the seeds for Idi Amin's 'economic war' and consequent economic turmoil (Reid 2017: 232). In all, the operations of capital in colonial Uganda created an urban system in which land ownership was divorced from the ownership of productive assets through a strongly racialized split. The associational power of Baganda landlords was limited by their inability to effectively become capitalists, while the Asian capitalist sector grew in power but in ways that were largely de-linked from territory and land politics due to their inability to purchase most forms of land. Meanwhile, the colonial government sought more 'penetrative' forms of governmentality, attempting to inculcate ideas and practices associated with 'modern colonial subjects' in order to stabilize labour (Byerley 2005: 244). Yet the colonial state's infrastructural power in Buganda was limited by widespread private *mailo* ownership and strong powers retained by kingdoms, complicating governance in the institutionally dense 'dual' city of Kampala-Mengo.

In Ruanda-Urundi, the Belgians persevered with building the coffee-based economy initiated by the Germans. However, unlike in Buganda or other colonial cash-crop economies such as the Gold Coast, the coffee boom was driven less by reinvesting capitalist profits and more by a 'combination of coercion, tax, intimidation, and corporal punishment' (Chrétien 2003: 278). Indeed, now that pre-existing power structures were underpinned and augmented by the colonial state, chiefs were able to water down the reciprocal character of their authority, resulting in greater exploitation of the (predominantly Hutu) peasantry (Erlebach 2006: 53–54). The consolidation of cash-based taxation enhanced the need for people to engage in wage labour, which played a significant role in helping European-owned plantation enterprises source cheap workers (Newbury 1988). The sense of the kingdom colony being a 'vast camp of forced work', to quote the Rwandan historian Alexis Kagame,[1] was augmented by the fact that people were still expected to maintain their obligatory cultivation and tribute (at least until 1933), as well as engage in colonially driven reforestation and road-building projects (Newbury 1988).

The Germans had done very little to stimulate manufacturing in its interlacustrine colonies; Rwanda barely gets a mention in one overview of economic transformation in German East Africa (Gann 1975). The Belgians also oversaw minimal investment and growth manufacturing in Ruanda-Urundi, in contrast to the Congo which by the time of independence had the second largest manufacturing output in sub-Saharan Africa, outside of South Africa (Kilby 1975: 472). Small-scale manufacturing did, however, start to emerge in Rwanda through minor enterprises such as brick factories by the 1940s (Erlebach 2006: 55). The dominance of foreign capital severely limited the evolution of an indigenous capitalist class, though to some extent a state bourgeoisie emerged. Indeed across East Africa generally, administration itself became central to class formation, being imbued with significant social status as well as providing a high percentage of non-agricultural employment. While central control and decision-making was monopolized by Europeans, over time Africans were able to take up lower-level

---

[1] Cited in Mamdani (2001: 9).

positions in increasing numbers, rendering administrators a significant class in the late colonial structure (Brett 1973: 301–303).

The need for cash incomes drove many Rwandans to seek work in neighbouring countries, including in the mines of eastern Congo and the emerging industries of Uganda where wages were higher (Byerley 2005: 229). Tens of thousands of people migrated out of Rwanda either temporarily or permanently each year (Gouvernement Belge 1960: 194; see also Mworoha & Mukuri 2004). British territory and Buganda in particular were seen by many peasants in Ruanda-Urundi as a 'brighter' world, as Figure 4.3 indicates, more modern and free than their own; many travelled there and returned with crates of clothes and even manufactured

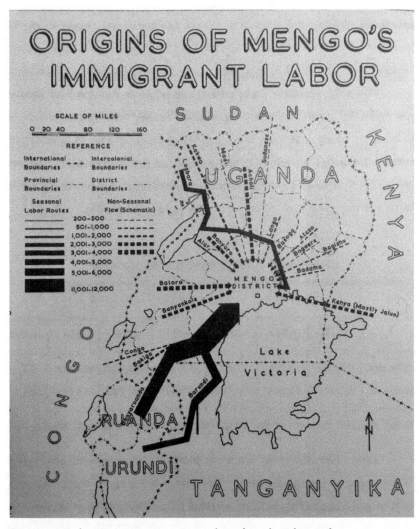

Figure 4.3 Labour migration into Buganda in the colonial period
Source: Munger (1951: x).

goods (Chrétien 2003: 280). This reflects both the greater investment and nascent capitalist development in Buganda and the extent to which the infrastructural power of the Rwandan kingdom, harnessed by the colonial state, was primarily channelled towards population control and the extraction of labour and tribute. Meanwhile, the increased land scarcity noted in Chapter 3 generated a class of landless, semi-proletarianized peasants (Lemarchand 1982; Erlebach 2006).

Whatever the moves towards capitalist production within colonial East Africa, which as noted above were limited and racially stratified, there was a conscious effort by colonial authorities to resist social (and hence political) structures changing too much in line with economic ones. Paralleling the concern with 'detribalization' in the cities, both civilian and religious colonial authorities believed that native populations should be 'introduced to economic development alone'—with change to their political institutions to be avoided as far as possible (Linden 1977: 136). Jorgensen (1981: 109) notes that 'A European-style proletariat seemed morally repugnant to colonial administrators, who naively sought to preserve an idealised rural "tribal order" from the horrors and vice of slums.' Yet the colonizers' approach to urban populations was also riddled with contradictions; while worrying about urban 'detribalization', they commonly also attempted to treat urban areas as 'laboratories of modernity' and to transform African urban labour forces into disciplined, time-keeping workers (Byerley 2011; Fourchard 2011; Burton 2017). This fomented resistance to colonial rule, as the evasion and negotiation of the colonial regulating impulse became a feature of urban life for colonized Africans. By the 1950s, neat and manageable colonial towns were no longer achievable as unemployment and informal economies burgeoned, alongside growing anti-colonial ferment (Burton 2017).

Urbanization and industry in Imperial Ethiopia

Under Menelik's regime, Ethiopian towns became economic hubs for traders and craftspeople as well as sites of administration and education. Urban areas were increasingly inter-ethnic melting pots, albeit accompanied by 'Amharaization' as Amharigna was imposed as the language of instruction, administration, and commerce (Markakis 2011: 13). Meanwhile, coffee became the principal export crop, but there was little investment in agricultural processing or manufacturing. Despite substantial efforts to modernize the Ethiopian state, the 'full scale assault' of capital from colonial metropoles that was unfolding in many European colonies was absent in Ethiopia under Menelik, as was direct access to the sea, leading many Ethiopian commentators in the early twentieth century to bemoan independent Ethiopia's relative economic backwardness (Zewde 1991: 84). Little changed in this regard in the early years of Haile Selassie's rule. Domestic life was also still characterized by slavery well into the twentieth century (Zewde 1991: 92).

During their brief occupation, the Italians attempted to intensify wheat production for urban consumption (McCann 1995) as well as investing substantially in manufacturing in Addis Ababa and some other urban areas, stimulating the production of manufactures including tyres, hessian and rope, oxygen, shoes and boots, flour and biscuits. A major textile mill and cement factory were also developed in Dire Dawa (Zewde 1991: 198). The extent of Italian investment in Ethiopia in just five years, along with Mussolini's grandiose fascist visions for the colony, came as a great surprise to the British; they had not adopted anything like this approach in their East African colonies (Pankhurst 1996). However, it counted for little in the long run, because when the British assisted in liberating Ethiopia from the Italians they pursued an active and very rapid policy of 'dismantling' the most substantial Italian industrial investments. This meant literally removing equipment and Italian-built factories, on the grounds that Ethiopian industrialization was 'artificial' and the equipment would be wasted once the Italians left, as well as the racist colonial attitude that Ethiopia's industrial potential was 'far in excess of what befitted a "native" state' (Pankhurst 1996: 41).

In the postwar period of heavy American influence, Haile Selassie's Ethiopia remained primarily rural, with 80 per cent of the population still working in agriculture and 90 per cent of export value deriving from agricultural commodities (Zewde 1991: 191). Small renewed efforts towards industrialization were realized, dependent on foreign capital and concentrated in the three major imperial cities: Addis Ababa, Dire Dawa, and Asmara in Eritrea. Import substitution in textiles was introduced, with the Dire Dawa textile mill being among the few spared by the British, and new mills opening in Addis Ababa and Bahir Dar (Zewde 1991: 198). Post-war industrialization was, however, still entirely dependent on foreign capital—in 1951 all sixty-three manufacturing enterprises in Ethiopia were foreign-owned—and comprised a mere 1 per cent of GDP (Oqubay 2019: 608).

Meanwhile, increased penetration of the rural economy by the state and by urban interests changed the nature of urban economies, as urban centres became places where one could buy and sell food—a dimension of urban trade that had barely existed in the nineteenth century (McCann 1995: 240). This further expanded the cash economy and investment in urban development, with an intensification of the built environment. Haile Selassie's drive to expand the education system as a centrepiece of modernization led to the growth of an urban technocratic class, all of which contributed to Addis Ababa's growing identity from the mid-twentieth century as the 'diplomatic capital of Africa' (Clapham 2017: 39–40; Zewde 1991). The emperor's aim was for the new urban bureaucratic elite to be liberated from earlier forms of patron–client relations and steward Ethiopia's transition into a modern economy (Markakis 1974).

The commercial centrality of Addis Ababa was also consolidated in the post-occupation period. Italian interventions left a lasting stamp on the city, particularly in terms of the dominance of the *Merkato* area for commerce, which was

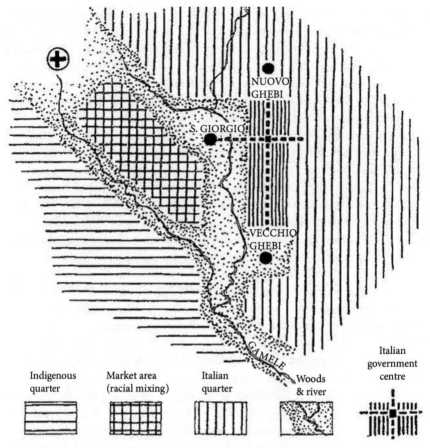

Figure 4.4 1936 Guidi and Valle plan for Addis Ababa
Source: Adapted from Guidi and Valle (1937).

established as the new 'indigenous market' and where Muslim traders had been encouraged to operate under the Italian approach to 'divide and rule'. As the schematic plan proposed by Guide and Valle (Figure 4.4) demonstrates, the market itself was inevitably a place of racial mixing but would be located next to the 'indigenous town', segregated from the government area and Italian quarter in the east of the city centre. The Grand Mosque was built near *Merkato* to attract Muslim traders to the area (Vrscaj & Lewis 2016: 122). A tight grid-iron street layout was built west of the market, as part of the *Addis Ketema* (new township) into which most of the city's indigenous population was forcibly relocated under the 1937 Italian segregationist resettlement programme (Truneh 2013: 304; Garvin 2020). The legacy of this is clearly evident in the street layout of Addis Ketema to this day (See Figure 4.5).

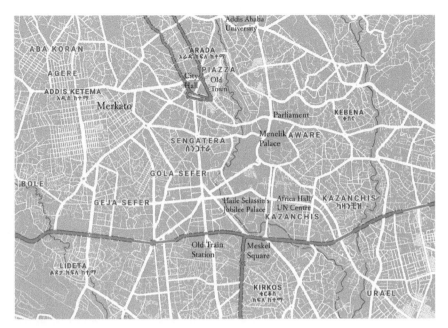

Figure 4.5 Contemporary Addis Ababa street plan
Map data © 2020, Google.

4.3 From high hopes to crisis

The 'halcyon days of city life' and the developmentalist impulse

As the period in which most African states achieved independence, the 1950s and 1960s were a time of heightened optimism. In the run-up to independence, elections in many countries and the emergence of nationalist elites set to take the reins of power fostered a sense of inevitable progress and democratization, although the extent to which the decolonization process was planned is still highly contested (Cooper 1996; Nugent 2012; Cheeseman 2015; Gopal 2019). Meanwhile, shifts towards a more 'developmentalist' approach within many colonies after World War II had ushered in heightened efforts towards industrialization as well as greater attention to the bargaining structures and working conditions of the growing urban workforce (Cooper 1996; Austin et al. 2016). Notwithstanding significant differences across the continent, in many countries the period from the mid-1950s to the mid-1960s was therefore one of apparently great promise, not only politically but in terms of industrialization and urban development prospects. In non-colonized Ethiopia too, this period saw an increased vibrancy in urban society and sense of potential that ultimately contributed to the dissolution of

Haile's Selassie's regime. The 1960s have thus been characterized as the halcyon days of city life in East Africa (Bryceson 2006).

In Uganda, the Uganda Development Corporation (UDC) continued to play an important role after independence. A World Bank report at the time praised the UDC as 'the most important entrepreneur in Uganda' (Davis 1962: 105), and its developmental role was indeed remarkable: by 1966, it had investments ten times the size of its equivalent in Kenya (Zwanenberg & King 1975: 13). This reflects the extent to which capital was already accruing to Kenya without the need for such state entrepreneurialism, but also indicates how central the state was in Uganda's overall system of production. The UDC was considered 'probably Africa's most successful development corporation' (Kilby 1975: 477), playing a leading role in import substitution. Manufacturing as a share of GDP at the time of independence was higher in Uganda than countries such as Ghana, Nigeria, Zambia, and Côte d'Ivoire, as well as Ethiopia (Kilby 1975).

At independence there were around six hundred light industrial enterprises registered in Kampala, producing goods such as soap, furniture, retreaded tires, window frames, doors, pre-cast concrete blocks, and soft drinks, and again mostly run by Asians with little machinery and few employees (Davis 1962: 105). Over two-thirds of the companies in Uganda by the early 1960s with a capital invest-ment of over £50,000 were Asian owned (Byerley 2005: 257). The development promoted by the UDC was also highly geographically uneven, with almost all fac-tories being located in Kampala and Jinja. Yet industrial growth was substantial, reaching 14 per cent of GDP by 1971 (Kitabire 1994). Urban populations boomed, not only due to industry but because of substantial populations moving into ser-vice sector work (such as vehicle repair) in what would soon come to be known as the urban informal sector (Davis 1962: 272).

In Rwanda, meanwhile, efforts towards industrialization continued to be extremely minimal in the decade after the 'Social Revolution' of 1959. Under the first president, Kayibanda, the economy remained heavily focused on coffee, along with minerals, tea, and some investment in other crops such as the pesticide pyrethrum (Behuria 2015a). Even by the standards of African countries at the time, Rwanda was highly dependent on primary commodity exports. Kayibanda was too preoccupied with the dual threats he perceived to be facing him from the rem-nants of the Tutsi monarchy overseas and rival Hutu elites in northern Rwanda to develop any concerted focus on industry; instead his efforts were geared towards supporting patronage in his home region of south/central Rwanda through cof-fee marketing boards and other state and parastatal institutions (Behuria 2015b: 202–203).

Rwanda had to wait until the 1970s for anything approximating developmen-tal promise. After Juvenal Habyarimana staged a successful coup in 1973 in response to the marginalization of elites from northern Rwanda, a period of devel-opmentalist discourse and international donor enthusiasm ensued (Uvin 1998;

Verwimp 2000). This lay behind a façade of national unity, as Habyarimana reframed Hutu–Tutsi relations as an intra-national ethnic issue, rather than a racial one in which Tutsis were foreigners (Mamdani 2001). Meanwhile, the developmentalist approach itself remained focused on agriculture; although a small industrial area was developed in Kigali from the 1970s, industrialization remained nascent. This was partly due to the expense of importing materials to a landlocked, resource-poor country (Verwimp 2000; Behuria 2015b), but there was also active resistance: urban capital was associated with the feudal power of the Tutsi monarchy (Verwimp 2000). Consequently, 'The very modest Rwandan efforts towards industrialization were undertaken only after intense outside pressure' (Verwimp 2000: 337).

In Ethiopia, by contrast, Haile Selassie's modernizing efforts and concern with generating an educated middle class had produced a flourishing of urban culture by the 1950s and 1960s, leading to a 'golden age of Ethiopian urban society' (Di Nunzio 2019: 35). Although industrialization remained a small component of the economy, this was changing quite rapidly. Manufacturing grew from 1.5 per cent pf GDP in the 1950s to 5 per cent by the 1970s, by which time around three hundred foreign firms accounted for over 75 per cent of the industrial sector (Oqubay 2015: 62). The proliferation of students was also a major feature of mid-century urban society: numbering around seven-hundred thousand by the 1960s (Zewde 1991: 221), they were a distinctly urban group with weak links to the countryside. Ultimately, the generation of this new educated urban class, with its urban sensibilities, political awareness, and heightened associational power, was to prove the emperor's undoing.

The urban labour question

Despite this atmosphere of developmental potential, large-scale unemployment was a pervasive feature of the region's growing cities in the postcolonial period due to the late and limited nature of the industrialization push, and the fact that colonial governments only took African presence in cities seriously from the 1950s (Southall 1971; Burton 2017). Rates of natural population increase gradually rose through the 1960s and 1970s, coming to outstrip migration as the main cause of urban growth in Africa (O'Connor 1983). From constituting a fifth of the total population in the early 1960s, the urban population of Africa overall rose to a quarter by 1975 and a third by 1990 (Gilbert & Gugler 1992). Some of these urbanites found waged work, and in the 1960s urban wage labourers increasingly identified themselves in relation to their roles as workers, including through increased trade-union membership (Sandbrook & Cohen 1975). Yet simultaneously, practices of 'gatekeeping' by postcolonial regimes, which sought to maintain tight control over the economy and allocate economic opportunity to key allies, constrained economic expansion and foreclosed substantial 'proletarianization' (Cooper 1996; 2017).

Women began to find niches in urban petty production and services, taking on important roles in supporting male 'breadwinners' (Cooper 2017). Although there were still significantly more men than women in most cities (though less so in Ethiopia), gender ratios had significantly declined since the early/mid colonial period (Burton 2001). The change in gender ratios fed substantial gender-based tensions, as women were able to benefit from an opening up of opportunities for 'modern' urban lives in jobs in services sectors and trade, while male youth struggled in contexts of growing unemployment. Despite this opening up, women's jobs were overwhelmingly informal in cases where they could work, and often they were confined to the home (Little 1973).

More generally, there was a growth of small-scale, unregistered economic activities which, after Keith Hart's (1973) and the ILO's (1972) celebrated interventions became known as the 'informal sector'. This reflected the limited reach of large-scale capitalist production, despite the late-colonial investment push and efforts to build an industrial workforce. Indeed, as Mabogunje notes, postcolonial states inherited many of the social and political relations of the colonial economy, which were beset with tensions that 'undermined the further penetration and rationalization of capitalist relations, while the mass of poor rural migrants seeking wage labor in the cities had to create other sorts of productive relations in order to survive' (Mabogunje 1990: 123).

In Uganda, part of the reason that operations of capital did not generate widespread capitalist social relations (and consequently an urban proletariat with strong class consciousness and associational power) relate to the land tenure regime and racial bifurcation of land and capital in Buganda, discussed previously. In the view of a 1962 World Bank report, Ugandan rural land tenure incentivized being physically present on one's land in order to maintain claims to it, which led to livelihoods that straddled rural and urban areas and generated high levels of worker turnover, in primarily Asian-owned firms (Davis 1962: 271). Capitalist wage labour thus co-existed with a range of other networks and economic relations. In any case, any growth and consolidation of an industrial working class that did unfold in the first decade of independence, as the UDC flexed its muscles, was cut brutally short by Amin's coup in 1971.

In Rwanda meanwhile, capitalist relations barely entered the city at all, despite the shoots of industry in Kigali from the 1970s. In the first decades after independence almost everyone was working in agriculture, the degree of urbanization was the lowest in the world, and youth unemployment was rife as Habyarimana romanticized the peasantry (Verwimp 2000: 348). The small proportion of people working in cities and towns mostly engaged in informal artisanal and service activities, along with agriculture (Munyaneza 1994). Things were quite different in Ethiopia, where as noted above the urban economy was relatively vibrant despite very low levels of urbanization. With the concentration of industry in a handful of cities and half of it in Addis Ababa, labour concentration also followed, leading to increased organization of the urban labour force and fully fledged unions emerging in the 1960s (Zewde 1991).

The situation in terms of urban labour therefore varied quite substantially in the three countries and their capitals at the time the crises of the 1970s hit. While there was a proliferation of informal, piecemeal work in all cases, in Ethiopia this was combined with the gradual growth of industrial labour and the expansion of a bureaucratic urban class, patterns to some degree echoed in Uganda but over a shorter, intensive time-period of state developmentalism. While the growing urban sector was to be radically distorted in Uganda under Idi Amin, the nascent power of Addis Ababa's urban classes was itself a driver of the revolution that shook Ethiopia several years later. In Rwanda meanwhile, there was little by way of either substantial capital or wage labour in the Kigali, which would later help to ease the near-total reinvention of the city following cataclysmic violence at the century's end.

Revolutions and ruptures in economic structure

The widespread optimism among many African post-independence elites and in the broader international community in the 1950s and 1960s had 'mostly evaporated by the 1970s' (Nugent 2012: 8). While the downturn in the global economy and successive waves of capitalist crisis that unfolded during that decade clearly came to play a role, in much of Africa the effects of these were primarily felt in the second half of the decade (Arrighi 2002) by which time Uganda, Rwanda, and Ethiopia had already been shaken by military coups, ethnic pogroms, and, in the latter case, a genuine revolution. These national political crises were paralleled by an unravelling of the urban economic promise, though in different ways and over different time-periods in each case.

In Uganda, the process of urban informalization, particularly among the non-Asian urban population, were fuelled and refuelled over fifteen years of conflict and turmoil following Idi Amin's 1971 coup, which resulted in the explosion of Uganda's notorious *magendo* (black market) economy (Kasfir 1983; Prunier 1983). In the context of Amin's 'economic war' and the expulsion of Asians in 1972, the formal sector contracted, government authorities were starved of revenues and the state was debilitated while informal networks and cronyism flourished (Kasfir 1983: 86). In this period wage-earners 'lost their viability as a group' (Hansen & Twaddle 1991: 11) and new forms of 'occupational pluralism' emerged as urban-dwellers increasingly found themselves seeking livelihoods in 'interstitial jobs' (Obbo 1991; Wallman 1996).

By 1980, two-thirds of Uganda's GDP consisted of *magendo*, a remarkable increase from the 3 per cent estimated a decade earlier (Green 1981). In one study, Green argued that *magendo* created its own class structure, with up to 500 very wealthy *mafutamingi* ('dripping with gold') at the top, some 2,500 *magendoists* in the middle and vast numbers of *bayaye* ('thugs') who comprised the labourers, drivers, street vendors, hustlers, and thieves at the bottom (Green 1981). Top-level *magendo* often involved informal production and smuggling, while for *bayaye*, livelihoods centred on petty trade. The typical *magendoist* 'distributed his stock to "his" *bayaye* to retail at every nook and corner of the town at *magendo* prices' (Mamdani 1983: 53–54). While these conceptualizations of the *magendo* economy were highly gendered and focused on men, petty trade was especially critical for urban women, for many of whom the Amin period was not one of economic crisis but a time when they first came to have a major role in the urban cash economy (Ahikire and Ampaire 2003).

Significantly, economic informalization did not end with the ousting of Amin; the *magendo* system grew even larger when Obote returned to power in 1980 (Kasfir 1983: 92). Uganda's first Structural Adjustment Programme (SAP), introduced in 1981, did little to slow this growth, even though it was barely implemented in the context of ongoing civil conflict. While the 'Obote II' regime expanded public-sector employment, *magendo* reinvented itself in the context of salaries so low that even formal workers sought other ways to earn money in order to survive; indeed incomes were falling fast in this period (Jamal 1991; Gombay 1994). Under Obote II the state grew 'more porous', enabling new linkages between informal activities and state actors who either partook in them directly or took bribes to facilitate them (Kasfir 1983: 101). The implications of this shift for the evolution of para-formal systems of bargaining over access to resources and opportunities in Kampala were substantial, as explored in Part III of this book. The hub of urban activity became ever more focused on Kampala, as Jinja fell into sharp decline with the Expulsion of Asian capitalists (Byerley 2011). However, Kampala barely grew in size during the Amin years and subsequent civil war as people retreated into subsistence agriculture to survive (Bryceson 2006).

In Rwanda, despite Habyarimana's lack of interest in urban industry there was evidence of a growing rural–urban divide in the 1970s and 1980s (Jefremovas 2002: 125); urban primacy was extreme, with 57 per cent of Rwanda's urban population living in Kigali by 1990 (UNDESA 2018). This was a tiny proportion (3 per cent) of the overall population, exacerbating perceptions of a disjuncture between the capital and the masses. Beneath a layer of urban elites fed on state salaries, there was barely any formal urban economy and Kigali was the site of extensive informalization from the 1970s onwards, even without anything as ruptural as Amin's 'Economic War'. From 1970 to 1990, amid growing land scarcity Rwanda's urban growth rates consistently outstripped the African average (UNPD 2009), despite very little by way of formal employment to absorb this population. A 1990 report confirmed that most inhabitants of Kigali worked in the fields or in other 'unregistered' activities, also highlighting how urban unemployment was leading to 'deliquency of all kinds' (RoR 1990: 40). The city authorities did 'everything in their power' to organize petty traders and limit the presence of informal activity on the streets, however (RoR 1990: 28). The control exerted over urban space was perhaps best exemplified by the institution of a weekly 'poor people's day', whereby poor people were allowed to come into the city on Fridays only and beg for money.[2]

The attempt to control the informal economy became increasingly difficult as Rwanda was hit by a wave of economic crises in the late 1980s. Between 1985 and 1992, the prices of virtually all Rwanda's exports fell catastrophically—coffee by 72 per cent, tea by 66 per cent, and tin by 32 per cent—leading to a 59 per cent drop in export earnings and calamitous effects on public finances (Woodward 1996: 19–21). By 1989, around a sixth of Rwandans were suffering from famine (Pottier 1993: 5). As the crisis escalated, a Structural Adjustment Programme was adopted in 1990, precipitating a devaluation of the Rwandan Franc and inflation that led to 50 per cent increase in prices for basic goods in Kigali (Waller 1993: 33). Moreover, from 1990 as the Rwandan Patriotic Army launched its assault from across the Ugandan border, the country was also plunged into civil war, generating both massive population displacement and the diversion of public funds to the military (Storey 1999: 50). Throughout all this devastation and impoverishment, the sense of Kigali as a privileged elite hub, insulated from Rwanda's wider problems and sucking up foreign aid through salaries and infrastructure spending, persisted right up until the eve of the genocide (Waller 1993).

Ethiopia's historical trajectory was fundamentally realigned by the 1974 revolution, which in contrast with Uganda and Rwanda's upheavals was rooted in growing urban malaise and activism. The Derg quickly realized the importance of keeping urban-dwellers onside with both cheap food and cheap rent, through agricultural price controls and centrally determined rents (Tiruneh 1993; McCann 1995); the sweeping post-revolutionary agricultural reforms of 1975 were to a significant extent about feeding the cities (McCann 1995: 250–252). These developments made the urban population increasingly dependent on systems of state support and distribution (Clapham 1988). In this respect, Addis Ababa and other Ethiopian cities became (and have in many ways remained) cities in which it is relatively feasible to engage in urban life even when very poor. The Derg's policies, including the control over rents that enabled the city's distinctive socio-economic mix to persist throughout the urban landscape, enabled large numbers of people to live in situations of 'secure poverty' (Di Nunzio 2019: 40). This, as we will see in Chapters 7 and 8, fed into a situation where the urban masses were at times able to mobilize substantial associational power even while continuing to be subjugated on a day-to-day basis.

---

[2] Interview with a local land broker, 11 December 2009.

The Derg began with the aim of emulating Eastern European-style communism, but this evolved into a unique approach to agricultural reform centred on large-scale and ultimately disastrous population transfers and villagization (Prunier 2015). Their 'cocktail of misguided economic politics', which combined the nationalization of firms in key sectors with the allocation of huge amounts of resources to the military and 'virtually no investment in physical infrastructure', led to urban economic stagnation and very little technological innovation (Oqubay 2019: 609). There was an exodus of foreign capitalists and banks (Vaughan & Gebremichael 2011: 18). Unlike in Uganda, where a new economic structure emerged in the form of the *magendo* economy with significant implications for political informality and the distribution of power (see Chapter 7)—the upheavals in 1970s Ethiopia effectively froze the existing economic structure. This economic stagnation was accompanied by increasing state penetration of all dimensions of city life, as infrastructural power was extended through the *kebele* system.

4.4   East Africa's development labs

When the NRM, EPRDF, and RPF took control of Uganda, Ethiopia, and Rwanda respectively, a new chapter in the urban economic life of these countries was opened. This was connected to, but also distinct from, the new economic chapter in Africa as a whole from the 1980s onwards, whereby a series of new agendas on the part of international donors and financial institutions came to strongly influence patterns of economic development. On the one hand, the three countries of focus here were the quintessential 'donor darlings' of the 1990s, enthusiastically adopting (albeit in different degrees) liberalization, privatization, decentralization, export agriculture-led development and donor-sponsored poverty reduction strategies. But they also diverged from the Washington agenda in distinct ways, particularly over time as their economic confidence increased and new development partners such as China grew in significance. As such, Uganda, Rwanda, and Ethiopia have been the sites of some of the most intensive efforts towards developmental reform and experimentation, constituting celebrated laboratories for Western donor policies as well as efforts to emulate successful late industrializers in Asia.

Ethiopia and Rwanda in particular were by the late 2000s increasingly associated with efforts to generate state-driven development in the mould of the East Asian 'developmental states', despite significant differences in both context and political-institutional structures (Goodfellow 2017b; Behuria 2018; Gebresenbet & Kamski 2019; Goodfellow & Behuria 2019b). Uganda also became associated with substantial levels of economic growth and poverty reduction, but its fidelity to donors' twin focus on liberalization and poverty alleviation, and lack of a concerted focus on structural economic transformation, mark some clear differences in approach (Hickey 2013b; Wiegratz et al. 2018). There is no space here to do justice to the economic strategies and transformations that emerged in these countries after the violent regime changes of the 1980s and 1990s, but this section briefly overviews some of the ways that each of them pursued a new developmental path, with significant consequences for urban areas.

Uganda

The NRM arrived in power with high levels of international and internal goodwill after two decades of civil conflict. Though Marxist in origin and a sharp critic of international financial institutions before taking power, Museveni's regime became increasingly reliant on Western donor support and advice in the face of a dire economic situation (Hansen & Twaddle 1998: Wiegratz 2010). The tenor of reform was initially focused on macroeconomic stabilization, with a new round of structural adjustment introduced in 1987. Because of the economic growth that followed, with rates of around 6 per cent per annum on average over an extended period, Uganda was considered one of the most successful 'adjusters' of the 1990s (Makokha 2001). Its economic progress has continued to be celebrated by international financial institutions in the decades since (Wiegratz et al. 2018). Yet from early stage, there were widespread concerns about the exclusionary consequences of SAPs and their lack of capacity to promote economic and societal transformation (Mamdani 1990; Makokha 2001).

In relation to questions of industry and urban labour, structural adjustment 'undermined the very sectors of the economy where labour had become the most stabilized' (Cooper 2017: 138): in other words, it had a very negative effect on urban industry and urban employment, further reversing the gains made by the UDC. Industry had already been decimated under Amin; of 930 manufacturing enterprises registered in 1971, only 300 remained operational by the early 1980s (Livingstone 1998). While some manufacturing sectors recovered significantly under the NRM, such as food processing, drinks, and construction materials, there was a notable failure of any 'bounce back' in labour-intensive industries such as textiles, leather, and footwear (Livingstone 1998: 40). Textiles continued to decline quite steeply after 1987, and virtually none of the proceeds of privatization were earmarked for industrial investment (Tukahebwa 1998: 71). Over the longer term, 'industry' as a share of GDP did increase, rising from around 10 per cent when Museveni took power to around 27 per cent in 2019—but much of this was in construction rather than manufacturing, which comprised only 15 per cent in 2019.[3] Most manufacturing involves small enterprises with fewer than five employees, and productivity levels remained low by regional standards (Tukahebwa 1998: 80).

[3] World Bank data, available at https://data.worldbank.org, accessed 11 November 2020.

Uganda came to thus exemplify a neoliberal model of development that amounts to 'growth without meaningful transformation' (Asiimwe 2018: 146). The small-scale nature of enterprise is reflected in the fact that it is in the top three countries in Africa in terms of the number of small and medium enterprises per capita.[4]

Meanwhile, the share of services in GDP continued to grow, rising from 34 per cent in 1986 to 52 per cent in 2004, though dropping down again and stabilizing around 43 per cent in the period 2013–2019.[5] This was driven partly by government services such as health and education, financed primarily by aid through forms of conditionality that simultaneously limited the scope to invest in industry and infrastructure (Hansen & Twaddle 1998: 9). There was also growth in service sectors such as telecommunications and tourism, and a further explosion of service activity in the informal service economy (Whitfield et al. 2015) through enterprises of the kind depicted in Figure 4.6. The continued mushrooming of the informal economy is one of the most significant urban legacies of the economic reforms of the NRM period; amid celebrated poverty-reduction strategies in rural areas, inequality and precarity increased in the urban sphere (Wiegratz et al. 2018: 16). The new urban roles that women had already started to carve out for themselves in services, trade, and petty commodity production became even more important in the context of structural adjustment and its consequences for household incomes (Tripp 1997; Meagher 2016; Cooper 2017). Urban economic informalization was further bolstered by the active slashing of formal employment opportunities, not only in industry but in the state bureaucracy and public-service provision. As part of the SAP there was massive public-sector retrenchment from 1992, with numbers of public-service employees more than halved from 320,000 in 1992 to under 125,000 in 1997 (Ssonko 2008: 160).

State capacity more broadly had been decimated by the decay of the Amin and Obote years, and as the NRM pursued its agenda of state withdrawal and privatization there was an increased reliance on NGOs and community-based organizations (Lateef 1991; Hansen & Twaddle 1998). This attempt to limit the power of the central state was both donor-sanctioned and a response to the brutal uses to which state power had been put under Obote and Amin. The state under the NRM was thus itself 'informalized' through the evolution of parallel structures of authority and power (Khisa 2013). In this respect the NRM's approach involved the active weakening of infrastructural power, as state structures were hollowed out and a range of social and economic forces bolstered. Regan (1998) argues that the NRM sought to encourage the emergence of a wide range of economic forces that could help to constrain future state action; the welcoming back of Asian capitalists and restitution of their properties was symbolic in this regard. While Museveni has himself deployed state coercion with great force and brutality,

---

[4] Interview with World Bank representative, 17 November 2020.
[5] World Bank data, available at https://data.worldbank.org, accessed 11 November 2020.

Figure 4.6 Local enterprise in Kampala
Photograph © Tom Goodfellow.

time and time again, the active limiting of state capabilities in the economic sphere
has had a substantial legacy in terms of both infrastructural power and the nature
of political informality. Thus, even when an agenda for more concerted state-led
structural economic transformation was adopted in the 2010s, there was very little
capacity to implement this as well as generally weak political commitment (Hickey
2013b; Kjaer 2015).

Layered onto the informalization and civil conflict since the 1970s, the opera-
tions of capital in Uganda therefore transformed substantially in the NRM period.
From a situation in which the state was among the most economically activist in
Africa, and where private-sector investment and profit were actively constrained,
Uganda was by the turn of the twenty-first century an arena in which the state

had been slashed back and private capital roamed freely across the terrain. More-over, a marked shift away from industrial capital occurred as private capital was intensively invested in service sectors but also in land and urban real estate, as the pressure on urban land and concentration of economic activity in urban hubs intensified. This also had significant implications for the distribution of power. In effect, Museveni's early liberalizing reforms allowed the *magendoists* to consoli-date their position (Mamdani 1990), while also empowering a new generation of 'tycoons' with political connections to the NRM (Wiegratz 2016). While the eco-nomic trends embodied in NRM reforms were to some degree regional in scope, with similar reforms playing out in Tanzania and Kenya for example (Wiegratz et al. 2018), the unqiue legacy on which NRM reforms built—both in terms of Amin's shadow economy and state decay, and in terms of the distinctive charac-teristics of land tenure in Buganda—produced a form of neoliberal development that burned with particular ferocity.

Kampala occupies a curious position in the post-1986 development narrative. Despite being a hub of great wealth, a Participatory Poverty Assessment in 2000 indicated insidious poverty in Kampala that Uganda's celebrated macro-level indi-cators had not captured (Amis 2006). Moreover, the urban farming mainstay of the 1970s to early 1990s was largely unavailable by the mid-2000s due to overcrowding and increasing land prices (Amis 2006: 178–80). Nevertheless, Kampala contin-ues to dominate the economy as well as hosting just over a third of the total urban population (Mukwaya et al. 2012: 6), with the Greater Kampala Metropolitan Area comprising almost a third of national GDP and 65 per cent of non-agricultural GDP (COWI 2020). No other city therefore comes even close to its economic importance.

There are, however, other cities that have grown in significance in the NRM period for specific reasons. Gulu in the north rapidly expanded in size in the context of civil war, become a significant humanitarian hub; Mbarara in the south-west grew to become a significant site of investment, which is often associated with its location in Museveni's home region; Hoima in the west became a resource boomtown in the late 2010s following the discovery of substantial amounts of oil near Lake Albert; and Jinja has continued to grow despite relative industrial stagnation, including through some recent attempts to revive manufacturing in the area. Meanwhile, the towns and cities within Kampala's orbit have experi-enced intensive growth as the built-up area around the capital and its economic magnetism continue to grow.

Rwanda

Since 1994, Rwanda's economic narrative has echoed Uganda's in several key respects. The RPF itself was virtually a Siamese twin of the NRM, having emerged when Rwandan exiles based in Uganda joined Museveni's National Resistance

Army and subsequently formed their own Rwandan force within it, before launching a war on Habyarimana's regime (Mushemeza 2007). Like Museveni's movement, they were schooled in scepticism of Western donors but on achieving power had little choice but to embrace donor support, and as in Uganda the incoming regime rapidly stabilized the economy and achieved economic growth averaging around 6 per cent per year. This generated substantial amounts of praise from certain quarters of the international community (Tumwebaze 2014; Collier 2015; Lagarde 2015). However, behind these similarities in terms of growth trajectories and donor-supported macroeconomic policy measures, there are important differences in terms of national economic strategies and how these have played out in urban areas given a very different distribution of power, longer history of infrastructural reach, and differing priorities for building social legitimacy.

If Uganda for a few short years in early independence looked like a sort of proto-'developmental state', it is Rwanda—along with Ethiopia—that has in the twenty-first century drawn comparisons with the East Asian developmental experience. The RPF on coming to power was heavily dependent on Western donor support, but its approach to the economy has been distinctive in combining substantial privatization and liberalization with features that do, to some extent, echo state-driven approaches to economic transformation in East Asia, as famously analysed by authors such as Johnson (1982), Amsden (1989), and Wade (1990). The unusual levels of developmental drive among the RPF's leaders are rooted in part in contextual factors that resemble those of pre-transformation North-East Asia, including a lack of major natural resources for easy export revenues, and a persistent sense of regime insecurity engendered both by limited internal legitimacy and the presence of hostile armed forces in the wider region. In this respect, Rwanda under the RPF has been characterized by conditions of 'systemic vulnerability' (Doner et al. 2005), which have functioned as a major driving factor in spurring particularly approaches to state intervention in the economy (Chemouni 2016).

Despite these similarities, there are many important structural and contextual differences with the East Asian 'developmental states'. These include Rwanda's landlocked geography, its small pool of bureaucratic expertise and associated problems of governmental coordination, and its heavy dependence on OECD donors at a time when the latter were opposed to heavy state intervention in the economy, including with respect to promoting manufacturing (Goodfellow 2017a; Behuria 2018). With agriculture-led development already hitting hard constraints in terms of land scarcity, the RPF was driven to spur radical economic transformation in ways that often sat uncomfortably with the influence of international donors, who for much of the post-1994 period have provided 30–40 per cent of Rwanda's GDP and 70 per cent of government expenditure (Ezemenari et al. 2008; World Bank indicators). The diverse range of influences and agendas feeding into economic strategy produced an approach that Behuria (2018) characterizes as 'incoherent emulation', as the RPF aimed to emulate Singapore's economic model and promote extensive investment by party and military-owned firms, at the same time as adopting wholesale liberalization in some sectors (Booth & Golooba-Mutebi 2012; Behuria 2015a).

For most of the period since 2000, central to this ambitious vision of economic transformation and to state-led operations of capital has been the service sector. In 2000 the government published Rwanda's 'Vision 2020', which centred services and a 'knowledge-based' society, with particular reference to financial services, ICTs, and tourism (RoR 2000). Although the government has pivoted towards a focus on manufacturing in very recent years in recognition of the difficulties of achieving broad-based development based on services alone, very little action has been taken on manufacturing in much of the period since 1994 (Behuria 2019b). Even in its revised economic development strategy of 2013, 'manufacturing' was mentioned just eight times compared to sixty-six mentions for tourism and financial sectors combined (Government of Rwanda 2013).

The neglect of industry is clearly reflected in economic statistics; between 1994 and 2019, industry (including construction) declined as a share of GDP from 21 per cent to 18 per cent, and manufacturing specifically reduced from 17 per cent to 8 per cent over the same period.[6] The disparity between these two sets of figures also clearly indicates the substantial proportion of 'industry' embodied in the construction sector, as explored further in Chapters 5 and 6. Meanwhile, the trajectory of the service sector—Rwanda's great development showpiece—is somewhat deceptive. While services made a rapid recovery after 1994, reaching 50 per cent of GDP by 1999 and remaining around that level ever since, service sectors had been on an upward trajectory prior to the genocide and had already reached 48 per cent of the economy by 1992,[7] so the RPF period has not actually witnessed much continued relative growth of services. In real terms, of course, the service sector has boomed along with the economy as a whole. However, a closer look at the nature of this growth indicates that it is driven by revenues from high-end services such as tourism and real estate, as well as (mostly aid-funded) expenditure on government services such as health and education, with relatively little linkage between the two and an enduring problem of labour absorption (Behuria & Goodfellow 2019).

Though Rwanda remains a largely rural society—with 70–80 per cent of its population working in the agriculture sector and a heavy dependence on coffee, tea, and minerals (as well as tourism) for export earnings—urbanization rates have soared, as noted in Chapter 1. The urban Rwanda presented to the world is of growth in sectors such as international conference tourism and luxury real estate, yet the vast majority of the urban population—82 per cent of women and 78 per

---

[6] World Bank data, available at https://data.worldbank.org, accessed 11 November 2020.
[7] World Bank data, available at https://data.worldbank.org, accessed 11 November 2020.

cent of men—eke out a living in the informal economy (Adams et al. 2013: 211). One report even claims that 98 per cent of the poor in Rwanda work in the informal economy (Bonnet et al. 2019: 17).

In Kigali itself, while the economy was already highly informalized, the most intense period of informalization was probably in the years immediately after 1994. A 2001 study found that in areas outside the CBD up to 94 per cent of businesses were unregistered (KIST 2001a: 28). In the early RPF period but before the renewed efforts to cleanse and transform the city in the 2000s (see Chapters 5 and 7), the streets in central Kigali were lined with informal kiosks, vendors, and orphans; indeed, there was a 'rapid increase' of street children after 1994 (KIST 2001: 34–35). Older youths would engage in informal service activities such as sitting on the street with typewriters to type up documents for people and providing telephones for use for a small fee.[8] By the late 1990s, street traders operated more or less as they pleased, flooding the city centre (Shearer 2020).

As in Uganda then, the capital city holds a dual role as showpiece and engine of the country's new, increasingly urbanized economy while also being a place in which the majority of people exist in a state of intense precarity in the informal economy, explored further in Chapter 7. Yet the operations of capital and how these have reflected the distribution of power and pursuit of legitimacy differ substantially. While manufacturing investment and urban mass employment have lagged behind in both cases, in Rwanda there has been a much more sustained effort to promote a particular kind of urban economy, overwhelmingly aimed at international investment in service sectors in the absence of a substantial pool of domestic capital (or indeed a relatively significant capitalist class to bring back in, such as the Ugandan Asians). In this context the government also sought to stimulate investment and build capitalist capacities through a more closely governed economy, strategically targeted towards certain sectors and led by party and military-owned firms whose support is crucial for the government's survival (Behuria 2016a) . The need to ensure a flow of benefits to a powerful, albeit small group of domestic capitalists exists in tension with the pursuit of an outward image of being liberalized and 'open for businesses' (Behuria and Goodfellow 2017; Behuria 2018).

Overall, the urban economic context in Rwanda by the 2000s was one in which informal, small-scale and self-employed activity was dominant, but largely excluded from the urban vision and associated government support. Kigali remained the overwhelmingly primate city, hosting 49 per cent of the urban population and accounting for 40 per cent of GDP (World Bank 2017: 17, 19), while a number of secondary cities in Rwanda increased in significance, but with little by way of solid industrial foundations. These include the border towns of Rubavu (formerly Gisenyi) and Rusizi (Cyangugu), which rub up against the conflict and

---

[8] Various interviews, Kigali 2009–2010.

humanitarian hubs of Goma and Bukavu in the eastern DRC, and the northern town of Muzanze (Ruhengeri), close to the tourism draw of mountain gorillas. Other major towns that were already significant prior to the genocide, such as the university town of Huye (Butare) and Muhanga (Gitarama), have seen relatively little growth and investment.

Ethiopia

Comparisons with East Asian 'developmental states' were made with even greater confidence for Ethiopia from the mid-2000s to 2018 under the EPRDF (Gagliardone 2014; Di Nunzio 2014; Lefort 2015; Clapham 2018). While the EPRDF regime's 'developmental orientation' and commitment to structural transformation echoed that of Rwanda, its efforts to discipline capital, control finance, and guide foreign investment were more marked and more consistent (Vaughan & Gebremichael 2011; Weis 2014). Meanwhile, Meles Zenawi himself explicitly invoked the aspiration to follow the developmental state model, both in speeches and academic writings (Zenawi 2012; De Waal 2013). Gebregziabher (2019a) has recently argued that the adoption of this rhetoric was actually a pragmatic move to legitimize what was essentially an ethnic vanguard party-state. In reality there have been many tensions within the EPRDF's declared 'developmental state' approach, including regarding its relationship to ethnic federalism and excessive political control at the expense of bureaucratic expertise (Abebe 2018; Gebresenbet & Kamski 2019). Nevertheless, the parallels and aspirations are clear (Hauge & Chang 2019).

Ethiopia, of course, also began its post-1991 journey towards developmental transformation from a very different place in terms of the ownership (and potential operations) of capital, given the widespread nationalizations instituted under the Derg—including of land and housing but also of vast swathes of the economy. When the EPRDF took power in 1991, the majority of the economy including 48 per cent of construction, 72 per cent of transport and communications, 89 per cent of mining, and 100 per cent of electricity, banking, and insurance were in the hands of the state (Lefort 2015: 359). Clinging to its Marxist-Leninist origins, the TPLF-led EPRDF government initially maintained that shifting to a market economy would constitute a 'dead end'. In fact, it did accept some of the conditions of the World Bank and IMF and reluctantly adopt a Structural Adjustment Programme, and some economic sectors were gradually opened up (Demissie 2008). However, land, banking, insurance, communications, and electricity remained in state hands (Vaughan & Gebremichael 2011; Clapham 2018; Oqubay 2019).

The political shocks of the early 2000s, following a regime crisis in 2001 that saw left-wing elements of the TPLF expelled, led to a shift in emphasis that was further reinforced by the election crisis of 2005 (Lefort 2015). From this point onwards, a policy of economic 'renewal' was initiated, involving a marked turn towards a growth agenda and aspiration to build a society of entrepreneurs (Vaughan & Tronvoll 2003; Di Nunzio 2015; Lefort 2015). Despite this shift, unlike in Rwanda or Uganda, the state retained its tight grip on key economic sectors and on land. Moreover, while there was a new enthusiasm for market logics, it was the party-state that was to remain the key player in constructing a market economy (Lefort 2015; Weis 2014). In this sense, centralized rent management played a key role (Kelsall 2013), including through party-owned firms with links to specific regions under the system of ethic federalism. As for the private sector, there is a sense that despite holding greater potential than in Rwanda due to greater population size, market size and educational legacies of previous regimes, it has been actively stifled by the extent of government control over finance and the limitations imposed on private investment (Vaughan & Gebremichael 2011; Weis 2015). Indeed, Meles was notoriously suspicious of private actors in specific sectors, making a distinction between productive and parasitic, rent-seeking forms of capitalists (Vaughan & Gebremichael 2011; De Waal 2013; Kelsall 2013).

The change of tack from the early 2000s achieved results at the level of growth; between 2004 and 2011 average rates of 10.6 per cent annually were achieved, making it one of the fastest-growing economies in the world (Lefort 2015: 368). Meanwhile, Ethiopia has made sustained progress in manufacturing, especially since the shift from a relatively unsuccessful 'Agricultural Development-Led Industrialization' (ADLI) strategy initiated in 1994 towards a more concerted focus on industrialization from 2003, culminating in the Growth and Transformation Plan of 2011 (Oqubay 2019). Exports of manufactured goods grew twenty-one-fold from 2004 to 2015 (Hauge & Chang 2019: 837). Industrial strategy was further ramped up with the establishment of the Industrial Parks Development Corporation (IPDC) in 2014 to drive forward a programme of national industrial park (IP) development (Oqubay 2015; Oya 2019). This has also been followed by a wave of private industrial parks, many of them Chinese-owned (Goodfellow & Huang 2021).

Of the three countries, the rise in share of industry within GDP is the most striking in Ethiopia, where it increased from 6 per cent in 1992 to 27 per cent by 2018. However, once again the lion's share of this category of 'industry' involves construction; indeed infrastructure consumes an incredible 40 per cent of all government spending (Hauge & Chang 2019: 837). Manufacturing alone merely rose from 3 per cent to 6 per cent over the same period. While this constitutes a doubling form a very low base, and in absolute terms Ethiopia demonstrates the steepest and most consistent rise in manufacturing output (especially in the 2010–2019 period), this low percentage also highlights the feeble manufacturing effort under previous regimes and the mountain that remains in terms of transformation to a manufacturing-based economy. As in Uganda and Rwanda, it is services that dominate GDP, averaging around 40 per cent since the early

2000s—but with a notable tip to around 36 per cent since 2016, reflecting relative increases in industry.

Cities occupied a curious position in the EPRDFs Ethiopia; on overthrowing the Derg in 1991, the incoming government was initially uninterested in cities and actively suspicious of urban capitalist interests. As McCann (1995: 255) notes, if the 1974 revolution was 'an expression of urban power against an archaic landed elite', the 1991 regime overthrow was 'a resounding rejection by farmers of the domination of their lives by urban imperatives'. Housing continued to be neglected and, as the state retained land ownership, there was no formal property market to speak of. All of this was to change in the early 2000s and especially after 2005, as documented in the chapters that follow. In Addis Ababa as well as many other cities, there has been a persistent attempt to generate self-employment and small firm development through a range of entrepreneurship schemes, though these have been extensively criticized (Di Nunzio 2015; Getahun Fenta Kebede 2015: Gebremariam 2017). Rather than promoting economic transformation, these schemes primarily served to bolster the EPRDF party-state's infrastructural power, as well its pursuit of urban legitimacy once it became clear that this was an urgent priority (discussed in Chapters 7 and 8).

Given the growing urban population in need of employment, operations of capital in urban Ethiopia under the EPRDF were guided to a significant degree by the imperative of labour-intensivity, both in terms of generating waged employment through manufacturing and also through labour-intensive infrastructure such as a major cobblestone road-building programme (Mains 2019). However, as in much of its history, moves towards capitalist development have remained highly dependent on foreign capital with limited linkages to local economies and domestic firms (Whitfield & Staritz 2021). Meanwhile, much as the government attempted to guide domestic and diasporic investment towards what it considered to be 'productive' sectors, in reality real estate has sucked up substantial amounts of resources (see Chapter 6), with limited capacity to absorb urban labour.

In addition, where major urban industrial projects have been initiated, the relationship between industrial zones, existing cities, and urban planning has been a weak link in government policy. Concerns about the creation of 'enclave economies' have been expressed by a number of observers (Giannecchini & Taylor 2018; Fei & Liao, 2020), but as well as a lack of economic linkages there are enduring problems of spatial and infrastructural connectivity between industrial zones and urban areas, in both the nationally owned industrial parks and private ones.[9] Poor transport and housing continue to provide challenges to worker retention, and building an industrial workforce remains one of the overriding challenges for urban Ethiopia (Oya 2019). Despite these challenges, the IPs have

---

[9] Various interviews with industrial park representatives and government officials in Addis Ababa and Hawassa, 2017–2019. See Robi (forthcoming) for a detailed discussion.

generated substantial employment. The Eastern Industrial zone to the east of Addis Ababa houses over ninety factories and employed 14,700 people in 2017 (mostly living in the nearby towns of Dukem and Bishoftu), with a further 3,600 employed in a related Chinese industrial park within Addis Ababa—the Huajian Light Manufacturing Zone—mostly in a single factory.[10] While these figures are small by the standards of the city's population, they far exceed anything achieved in Uganda or Rwanda.

In addition to these developments in the capital, it is in secondary cities that the real employment boom from IPs was set to play out, though the collapse of the EPRDF in 2018 and descent into civil war two years later has called this into question. A number of major industrial parks were at varying levels of development around the country, in line with the ethnic federal system. The first such IP to open (following the first national industrial park at Bole Lemi, also within Addis) was the Hawassa Industrial Park in the south of the country, which in 2019 was employing over 20,000 workers, with a projected capacity of 90,000—which could ultimately mean employing 270,000 people over three 8-hour shifts. This has the potential to increase the city population by over 50 per cent, from an estimated half a million today to a projected 750,000 by 2035, posing an enormous challenge to the city's capacity in terms of resources and planning.[11] In addition, a series of other national IPs were operational by 2019, though at varying levels of completion and population, including in Dire Dawa, with links to the new Chinese-financed railway (following the route of the old colonial one), Mekelle in Tigray, Kombolcha and Bahir Dar in Amhara region, and Adama and Jimma in Oromia. Partly as a consequence of manufacturing investments, but also due to growth and clustering of medium-sized firms, many secondary cities are now actually growing faster than Addis Ababa, the primacy of which—while still very substantial—is declining in terms of both size and proportion of urban employment (World Bank 2015; Gebre-Egziahber & Yemeru 2019).

4.5 Conclusions: Towards a contemporary urban political economy

The past two chapters have set out the historical foundations of urban territory, property regimes, and economic structure in Uganda, Ethiopia, and Rwanda. There is a significant regional dimension to these narratives, but they also involve national-level junctures spurred by new trading relations, state formations, imperial domination, independence, and revolution. These histories underpin twenty-first-century urbanism in each case and contextualize the contemporary circumstances to be analysed in Part III of this book. As well as partly accounting

---

[10] Interviews with senior industrial park management staff, 2017–2018.
[11] Presentations and discussions at stakeholder workshop, Hawassa, 26 June 2019.

for the lateness of urbanization itself in these societies—which all inherited high levels of urban primacy through colonial rule and imperial domination, and were held back from industrializing through imperial policy and conflict—these histories generated particular distributions of power among social groups in each case.

The relevance of the shared regional conditions of late urbanization characterizing these historical narratives is evident. The difficulty in competing in manufacturing sectors in a globalized world, high level of dependence on foreign capital, and the inheritance of highly centralized power structures alongside a major demographic boom are common features in late urbanizing societies (Fox & Goodfellow 2021). Relatedly, the rapid growth and economic expansion that has been evident in all three capital cities has been backed and shaped by foreign aid, particularly from the Anglophone global North but also more recently from China, which has fuelled growth in construction and infrastructure development, as well as basic services. Yet if the overall shape of these economies indicates a shared regional trajectory, many significant differences lie beneath. These include differential foundations for capitalist production—which, while relatively weak in all three cases, have been historically the least developed in Rwanda and the most in Uganda—but also the varying extent to which the state has been at the forefront of capital investment, employment generation and efforts to structurally transform economies.

In Uganda, a colonial legacy of industrialization and urban investment in a specific period, led by Asian capitalists and the state, gave way through processes of state collapse, structural adjustment, and post-conflict liberalization to a heavily deregulated and informalized economy that has fostered substantial growth but posed major limits to structural transformation. The distribution of associational power is relatively diffuse in a context where pre-colonial and colonial land relations, early Asian and UDC investments, *magendo*, aid-funded growth, and the return of Asian capital have dispersed economic opportunity beyond any one particular elite group. Meanwhile, processes of state decay followed by active decisions to liberalize the economy and downsize the state have constrained infrastructural power—including within the capital city, where infrastructure itself was allowed to fall into serious disrepair, as discussed in Chapter 5.

In Rwanda, a much starker distribution of power characterized the precolonial and colonial settlements in the context of a single kingdom with two major ethnic groups and unusual levels of hierarchy that persisted under successive postcolonial regimes. Always governed colonially as part of a broader set of (German or Belgian) territories, major urban investment was never a priority in Rwanda and path-dependent processes of agricultural investment were set in train. While the power relations between Tutsis and Hutus flipped in the early postcolonial period, the urban remained a space primarily for the state bureaucracy and trickling in of foreign capital. Since the genocide and RPF takeover—and consequent further 'resetting' of ethnic relations—there has been substantial continuity in these dynamics alongside heightened interest in transformation towards urban service sectors and infrastructure, and an enhanced need to secure regime legitimacy through palpable state-driven development achievements.

Ethiopia has a particularly unusual historical narrative, reflected in its urban evolution. A quasi-feudal system developed through centuries of conquest and coercive national integration attempted to incorporate elements of capitalism, industrialization, and state modernization after the Italian occupation, but this was radically interrupted by the 1974 revolution. One legacy of Haile Selassie's long reign was the relatively substantial holding power of the urban classes, which despite the Derg's ruthless repression and catastrophic economic policies remained substantial under the communist regime, and resurfaced after 2005. Meanwhile, the Derg's sweeping nationalizations and increased state penetration of society facilitated a particularly pronounced form of state-driven economic development under the EPRDF, which depended to a significant extent on foreign and diasporic capital but also subjected private investment to substantial constraints.

These different economic legacies in Uganda, Rwanda, and Ethiopia created divergent conditions under which contemporary political regimes have found themselves managing the challenges—and reaping the benefits—of urbanization. As the forces unleashed by decolonization and globalization swept across the world, late but rapid and insistent urbanization in East Africa has been fashioned into a varying urban formations as ruling elites, wielders of capital, and urban populations striving for better lives have tried to make cities in their image and interests. It is to these twenty-first-century urban realities and the associated urban fortunes that we now turn in the third part of the book.

PART III
URBAN CURRENTS

5

New urban visions and the
infrastructure boom

Introduction

This chapter examines changing urban visions and infrastructural priorities in East Africa, through the lenses of Addis Ababa, Kampala, and Kigali: cities that have transformed virtually beyond recognition in recent decades. While urban growth has been a feature across the continent, in East Africa specifically this has mushroomed from a background of particularly low levels of urbanization (see Chapter 3), combined with high levels of economic growth and donor engagement—particularly since the conflicts that ravaged the region in the late twentieth century. Kenya and Tanzania, while spared the worst of this conflict, have experienced their own economic struggles and transitions (Branch 2011; Gray 2018), which have also fed into patterns of explosive and highly inequitable urban growth (Bryceson et al. Potts 2005; Kombe 2005; Mercer 2017; Kimari 2021). Meanwhile Uganda, Ethiopia, and Rwanda have been sites of celebrated but often controversial economic and urban change as the NRM, EPRDF, and RPF each courted and channelled post-conflict investment in distinctive ways.

At the dawn of the twenty-first century, the capital cities of all three countries were in a state of growing crisis. The economic and political ruptures, civil wars, and regime transitions of the 1970s to the 1990s had been immediately followed by continued urban neglect due to the focus on securing rural territory and quelling pockets of ongoing insurgency, alongside the imperatives of structural adjustment and the generally rural priorities of incoming regimes. But this was to change, albeit more radically in some cases than others, as the extent of urban growth and the proliferation of urban interests became ever more apparent to governing regimes. Attention to reworking urban territory through projects seen as pivotal to bolstering urban legitimacy and control ramped up in the first decade of the new century, and even more in the second. Meanwhile, as cities both expanded and densified, urban land soared in value. This created new opportunities and challenges for both city-dwellers and governments, with popular economies around trade, transport, and the appropriation of public space often in conflict with state-sanctioned urban visions.

The preceding chapter showed how economic growth has been a major feature of all three countries in the early twenty-first century, but it has been growth

Politics and the Urban Frontier. Tom Goodfellow, Oxford University Press. © Tom Goodfellow (2022).
DOI: 10.1093/oso/9780198853107.003.0005

of a particular type. While footloose capital should theoretically flow to places of capital scarcity, in late twentieth-century East Africa it initially fled from cities, particularly in the crisis-ridden Horn and Great Lakes sub-regions, before returning to manifest increasingly in infrastructure and high-end real-estate developments. Aside from a few scattered efforts to seriously stimulate manufacturing industry across the subcontinent—most notably in Ethiopia—much of the capital in African cities today is therefore invested in construction and real estate (UN-HABITAT 2018: 61).

The concentration of growth and investment in these sectors is perhaps unsurprising in late urbanizing countries where manufacturing cannot easily compete, stock markets are non-existent or small, and other service sectors are nascent and under-developed. Yet it also presents a paradox in relation to major currents of twentieth-century urban theory, which posited that countries with *advanced* levels of urbanization are the places where we would expect to see this kind of intensification of investment in the built environment. For Lefebvre, the flow of capital into urban land, infrastructure, and real estate—conceptualized as the 'secondary circuit' of capital—was a symptom of societies that had already been through the 'urban revolution', in which urbanization pervades society and cities no longer appear as islands 'in a rural ocean' (Lefebvre 1970: 11). In such societies, he argued, 'Real estate functions as a second sector, a circuit that runs parallel to that of industrial production [...] where capital flows in the event of a depression' (Lefebvre 1970: 159). Harvey further developed these ideas, arguing that overaccumulation in the primary (industrial) sector leads to the 'switching' of capital to the secondary sector (Harvey 1978: 107). The paradox we face when contemplating East Africa is that even though advanced industrial urbanization has not occurred in societies such as Uganda, Ethiopia, and Rwanda—in fact they are among the *least* advanced globally in these economic sectors, and most people are still rural farmers—capital is rapidly coalescing around urban land and real estate as if they were highly urbanized societies.

Against these general conditions of late urbanization and the apparent draw of the 'secondary circuit', all three cities have experienced remarkable construction booms in recent decades, with structures at varying degrees of completion and usage typifying the urban landscape. Despite some surface similarities however, the distribution and function of the construction boom is quite different in the three cities. We can broadly distinguish between the boom in urban infrastructure—which has been notable in all cases, but in very different ways—and the boom in real estate. This chapter focuses on the former, with particular attention to large-scale 'flagship' infrastructure projects promoted by the state in each city and how these relate to the broader processes of urban planning and 'visioning' in each case, while Chapter 6 focuses on emerging urban 'propertyscapes'.

The extent and nature of large-scale 'mega'-investments in infrastructure differs substantially between the three cities. Varying ambitions with respect to physically transforming cities, and divergent capacities to implement these visions, are rooted both in legacies of infrastructural power and different priorities in the pursuit of social legitimacy. By examining how urban visions and large infrastructure investments play out in the three cities, we can further unravel how 'operations of capital' typical of late urbanization interact with place-specific legitimation strategies and structures of power. The chapter begins by examining the transition from a politics of urban neglect to a hunger for urban transformation. Following this, it discusses the growing interest in financing large-scale infrastructure, particularly in the context of the dominant twenty-first trope of the African 'infrastructure gap'. This is followed by a dedicated discussion of a specific mega-infrastructure project in each city, and the dynamics of investment and use in each case. The infrastructure megaprojects chosen for discussion in Addis Ababa, Kampala, and Kigali are purposively selected on the basis that they reveal distinctive dynamics at play in terms of the nature of legitimation strategies, the capacity to implement large-scale urban projects, and the consequences of infrastructure for the urban fabric.

5.1 The politics of urban neglect

In countries and regions where the urban transition has been relatively late in global terms, the adoption of positive attitudes towards urbanization has also tended to come late. The countries considered here are no exception. The neglect of cities in terms of policy and planning in the early years of EPRDF, NRM, and RPF rule provides a clear counterpoint to the idea, popularized in the 1980s, that late twentieth-century developing countries exhibited patterns of 'urban bias' through which city-dwellers were systematically privileged (Lipton 1977; Bates 2014). In fact, across postcolonial Africa a rural bias has often been prevalent in terms of heightened attention to political patronage in the countryside (Green 2010; Boone & Wahman 2015), which often bred a wider disinterest in cities. The story of a senior urban advisor to one African government who was given ten minutes to convince an uninterested cabinet of the merits of urban policy is emblematic of this (Jones & Corbridge 2010: 10).

How things change. By 2020, it was typical for an East African country not only to have a national urbanization policy but for central government be taking a much more direct role in managing the capital city, channelling substantial amounts of its own funds to urban infrastructure as well as playing host to major World Bank programmes on urban institutional reform, EU and African Development Bank loans for urban Bus Rapid Transit, Chinese infrastructure loans worth billions of dollars, and further urban infrastructure and governance programmes supported by British, German, Japanese, and French donors. Since the mid-2000s, through a combination of environmental concerns, changing donor agendas and inspiration from emerging economies in Asia, planning and urban infrastructure finance have thus seen a resurgence across the continent (Fox & Goodfellow 2016; Parnell 2016). In the East African cases examined here, the indifference towards urban interests that was evident in the early years of NRM, EPRDF, and RPF rule gave way in the 2000s to a concerted focus on dominating and transforming urban space. To understand the significance of the shift requires a closer look at the state of these capital cities by the turn of the millennium, and the factors that prompted each regime to sharpen their urban focus.

Kampala provides the starkest example of urban degradation in the early twenty-first century. Although some infrastructure was built in the early NRM period after its decimation during the civil war, there was little sustained attention to this and by the turn of the twenty-first century the extent of neglect was becoming clear. Sanitation and waste management were extremely limited; in the year 2000 just 9 per cent of Kampala's population were served by a central sewer system (Makara 2009: 15). Tens of thousands of people each year suffered from intestinal infections and acute diahorrea, and cholera was on the rise.[1] Infrastructure was in constant need of repair and flooding regular and widespread (see Figures 5.1 and 5.2). Kampala's innumerable potholes were notorious across the region, coming to symbolize government corruption and neglect. One of many articles on this subject that littered the newspapers by the late 2000s reported how trade nose-dived for several businesses due to a single pothole within the city that evolved into a 'lake' of twenty-five metres in length, deep enough to bring vehicles to a total standstill in the rainy season.[2] Infrastructural decay combined with a traffic problem of similarly legendary proportions, reckless driving and the prevalence of *boda-boda* motorcyclists combined to contribute to soaring traffic fatality rates (Goodfellow 2015b). All these issues were central to public discourse and city politics, providing endless fuel for the passing of blame between the NRM and the opposition—particularly the Democratic Party, which had a majority of councillors within Kampala City Council and provided a string of city mayors.[3]

Income levels certainly increased under the NRM, but factors such as disease burdens, environmental degradation, inadequate infrastructure, and the need to constantly bribe authorities were perceived by many to have worsened their overall condition (Amis 2006). Moreover, unlike in cities such as Nairobi where Kibera and other major 'slums'[4] are concentrated in particular areas, almost forming cities-within-cities, Kampala's slums are dispersed around the whole capital. Residents would commonly refer to the city as one huge slum, with one journalist

---

[1] 'Without planning, urban areas wallow in filth and disease' *Daily Monitor*, 6 April 2010.

[2] *The Monitor*, 27 August 2010.

[3] For a more detailed account of the sense of crisis in service delivery and infrastructure in the city at this time, see Goodfellow (2010; 2013a).

[4] Although there is an ongoing debate about the use of the term 'slum' (Gilbert 2007), I use the term here in recognition of the importance of highlighting living conditions in these areas rather than just their mode of production (as is implied by 'informal settlement') and the extent to which 'informal settlement' actually extends beyond the geographic areas usually associated with the term. See Dovey et. al (2021) for a discussion.

Figure 5.1 Infrastructural repair in Kampala
Photograph © Tom Goodfellow.

memorably dubbing Kampala the 'executive slum'.[5] Despite being the seat of power and the main engine of the economy, investing in Kampala's infrastructure had clearly been a low priority; instead, it was effectively a site of lootable resources. Rural areas took precedence as the sites of visible 'development' initiatives, while in Kampala, the large amounts of former 'crown land' in the city, now held by a range of government institutions, provided ample opportunities for rent-seeking and competitive clientelism. In the context of the political struggles between the NRM and the Democratic Party, land was illicitly distributed and sold off with

[5] *The Monitor*, 10 May 10 2009.

significant disregard for planning and regulation.[6] The sense that planning was beyond the control of any one institution was exacerbated by the continued significance the old dualism between Mengo and the colonial government, with the restored Buganda kingdom strongly influencing cultural norms around the use and transfer of *mailo* land. Kampala was, in the words of one political figure, 'to put it crudely, the bastard child of nobody ... an orphan that no-one quite wants to deal with properly'.[7]

In Ethiopia, despite a very different urban history, the TPLF's origins as a rebel force rooted in the rural peripheries was similarly reflected in an initial lack of attention to urban problems in Addis Ababa. Prior to the 2000s, the prioritization of rural support and rural development was very explicit and the incoming regime knew very little about the city and its institutions (LeFort 2007, Di Nunzio 2014; 2019). Some observers even suggest that neglect of the capital involved deliberate political disengagement whereby Addis Ababa was allowed to develop into a site of political opposition, thus showcasing the EPRDF regime's democratic credentials (Pausewang et al. 2002; Di Nunzio 2014).

Figure 5.2 Flooding in Kampala
Photograph © Tom Goodfellow.

---

[6] This is particularly starkly illustrated by a 2006 report into land leasing and sales in Kampala (RoU 2006)—though the politicized nature of this report in the context of the tussle between central government and the then-opposition-run Kampala City Council is important to bear in mind.

[7] Interview with Ugandan lawyer, Kampala, 13 February 2009.

In this context, severe urban problems inherited from the Derg regime, including poor-quality housing stock and high proportions of people living in slum conditions, continued to worsen as the government focused its energies elsewhere and partially adopted punitive structural adjustment reforms (Demissie 2008). In 1994, total unemployment had soared to an alarming 34.7 per cent, up from 10.5 per cent in 1984 (Demissie 2008: 530). The built environment also suffered distinct problems related to the virtual freeze on investment in the 'secondary circuit' of capital under the Derg. The extent of dilapidation of *kebele* housing meant that much of it was beyond repair; basic infrastructures such as water pipes were characterized by constant leakage and interruptions in supply; and only 16 per cent of the population had private toilets, with 30 per cent forced to practice open defecation (Ayenew 1999).

Meanwhile in Rwanda, the RPF-led government took the 'urban question' more seriously early in its rule than did either the NRM or EPRDF—or indeed most African governments (DFID 2007). This is unsurprising both in view of the origins of the regime and the situation it faced on arrival in government. Though the RPF achieved power through rural guerrilla struggle like its Ugandan and Ethiopian counterparts, the core of the organization comprised Tutsi exiles who had grown up outside the country, and the fight to oust the Habyarimana regime was largely fought from across the border in Uganda and from the hostile and relatively isolated Virunga volcanoes (Waugh 2004; Straus 2006). This meant that their connections with rural constituencies were weak, and on arrival in power Kigali was intrinsic to the government's political and economic vision (Goodfellow & Smith 2013). Far from being their core constituents, the rural population was viewed with some suspicion, being predominantly Hutu (Prunier 1998; Mamdani 2001; Mkandawire 2002). The government therefore took a more positive view of urbanization, incorporating this into its overall framework for land reform (ICAS 2010). The RPF's development plans envisaged the country's level of urbanization increasing from 17 per cent to 30 per cent by 2020 (RoR 2009): an active encouragement of urbanization that was atypical of African governments at the time. One minister even commented in 2009 that 'in the long term, Rwanda will probably be 100 per cent urban' given its population density and land scarcity.[8]

Nevertheless, urban conditions in Kigali by the turn of the century were highly challenging. The existing limitations of the city's infrastructure had been compounded by the city's decimation during the 1990–1994 civil war and genocide, and subsequently the influx of (mainly Tutsi) returnees in 1994, followed two years later by the 'new caseload' (primarily Hutu) refugees from the DRC. In this context, *akajagari* took over the city: most people lived in densely packed informal housing, and one local official described Kigali at the turn of the twenty-first century as being 'like Kampala' in terms of its absence of planning and unenforced

---

[8] Interview with former minister of infrastructure, 9 September 2009.

development regulation.[9] Moreover, the RPF-led government inherited a virtual vacuum of legislation pertaining to urban development (MININFRA 2008: 19). Due to overwhelming security concerns, questions of how to manage and plan cities were barely addressed until around 2000, when a raft of policy documents and new legislation appeared in rapid succession.

Before examining how the new zeal for investment in urban infrastructure has subsequently unfolded in these three cities, it is important to highlight the politicized discourses underlying the dynamics discussed in this section: narratives of cities run into the ground, now rising from the ashes into a shiny, modern twenty-first-century future. In all of these cities, the symbolism of urban investment and renewal, rhetorically contrasted with what came before, has played a role in legitimizing discourses for governing elites as specific times. As explored in this chapter and Chapter 6, many of the problems noted above, including poor housing and service delivery, lack of effective planning, and severe congestion persist into the present, and the fact that there has been a greater prioritization of these issues should not obscure this reality. Nevertheless, the shifting of both rhetoric and investment towards cities has been remarkable, proceeding in distinctive and revealing ways in each case.

5.2 Growing urban appetites

The shift towards a pro-urban stance in Uganda, both discursively and in terms of investment, was a long time in the making. It fermented through the ramping-up of media narratives in the late 2000s that framed the city in a state of crisis (see Figure 5.3), with the finger usually pointing to opposition-controlled Kampala City Council (Goodfellow 2010). In the context of ongoing contestation over the city's status, relating in particular to its location within Buganda and debates over federalism and land, the government pushed through a 2005 constitutional amendment that provided for the possibility of the central government taking control of the administration of Kampala. This was initially put on hold, but as the 2000s wore on and the sense of crisis in the city deepened, plans to realize it were developed, despite evidence of widespread opposition.[10] The effort to take control of Kampala was carefully calculated (Gore & Muwanga 2014). In mid-2009, the government tabled the 'Kampala Capital City Bill', which proposed an entirely new structure of governance for the city, alongside proposals that Kampala's boundaries be radically expanded. This fuelled the flames of existing anger among Baganda elites, which was rapidly growing due to a range of other rifts between the Buganda kingdom and the government.[11]

[9] Interview with local official, Kigali, 26 November 2009.
[10] 'Ugandans Don't Want Govt to Run City.' *Daily Monitor*, 15 November 2008.
[11] See Goodfellow and Lindemann (2013); Goodfellow (2014a).

Figure 5.3 Typical newspaper headlines about the state of Kampala, 2009–2010
Newspaper cuttings assembled by author; photograph © Tom Goodfellow.

In order to allow the bill to pass, the provision about expanding the boundaries to create a new metropolitan area was removed. However, the passage of the Bill in 2010 still generated huge controversy and marked a watershed moment for Kampala, stripping the democratically elected City Council of most of its powers and ushering in the new technocratic Kampala Capital City Authority (KCCA), accountable to central government, in 2011. This was headed by an executive director, Jennifer Musisi (see the 'impressions' at the start of this book), who was directly appointed by Museveni to lead the city's transformation. Commended for toughness and effectiveness during her tenure as the commissioner for legal service and board affairs at the Uganda Revenue Authority, she was seen as having the capacity to steward the transformation in governance that the city required (Gore & Muwanga 2014). The creation of a Ministry of Kampala and Metropolitan Affairs from 2015 was further testimony of the shift in power away from the city to the central government.[12] Meanwhile, the popularly elected mayor of Kampala, opposition Democratic Party stalwart Erias Lukwago, was downgraded to a lord mayor with largely ceremonial functions.

After decades of neglect, exploitation of urban resources and a lack of serious policy engagement with urbanization, the foregrounding of urban policy by the central government was epitomized by Uganda sending a very substantial delegation of government representatives at the UN-HABITAT World Urban Forum

---

[12] This ministry served an important political function in further undermining the power of the opposition mayor and providing a platform for further prominent NRM-aligned figures to loom over urban governance. However, in reality the ministry was a shell with virtually no staff, though as of 2020 it was beginning to develop a more substantial office (interviews with international donor and government adviser, November 2020).

in Brazil in 2010—including the president himself. The decision to ramp up the rhetoric and branding of an urban renewal agenda was visible in other ways, too. While in 2009 the Kampala City Council premises were severely run down, with ancient equipment and a general spirit of low morale, by 2014 the corridors were filled with slickly branded posters detailing Musisi's achievements. In an attempt to build urban civic morale, KCCA instituted an annual Kampala City Festival, with themes such as 'Regenerative Urban Development' (2014), 'Colour and Climate Change' (2015), and the particularly self-referential 'Celebrating 7 Years of Rebuilding Kampala City' (2018). Meanwhile, urban planners and environmental specialists who had been sidelined and even intimidated by politicians in previous years were now finding their expertise in high demand.[13]

This major governance overhaul represented a new commitment to, and opportunity for, much more concerted and streamlined urban policy supported by a substantial increase in resources. With the opposition's role in the city's governance enfeebled, central government stepped up direct transfers of resources to the city, particularly for infrastructure. In addition to the transfers received, internally generated revenue within the city received a major boost, more than doubling from 30bn to 68bn Ugandan Shillings between 2010 and 2014.[14] In the first five years of her rule, Musisi racked up a number of substantial accomplishments in the city, including the redesign of a number of particularly problematic traffic intersections, advances in sanitation and water supply, and a large-scale road improvement programme: 145km of roads in the city were paved in the first three years under KCCA, as compared with just 15m in the previous decade.[15] More controversially, Musisi pursued the removal of street vendors from various parts of the city through ongoing 'clean-up' operations (see Chapter 7). These activities continued to be vigorously contested by Lord Mayor Lukwago.[16] The new agenda under KCCA was, in many respects, a reflection of the growth in associational power of the urban middle classes after over two decades of economic expansion under the NRM—a group that was often particularly angry about the poor quality of urban infrastructure. In order to legitimize the central government takeover of the city, Musisi thus had to strike a balance between appealing to the growing middle classes and not alienating NRM elites who were profiting very well from the city as it was. In the words of an official working for her at the time, 'Jennifer is trying to get people to understand that even as a corrupt person you could make more money if you organize efficiently.'[17]

[13] Various interviews, 2014.
[14] Interview with revenue official, KCCA, 10 June 2014.
[15] Interview with transport official, KCCA, 11 June 2014.
[16] For an extended discussion of the governance dynamics in Kampala from 2010–2020, see Muwanga et al. (2020).
[17] Interview with KCCA official, 10 June 2014.

The new urban agenda in Kampala paled into significance, however, with the scale of ambition and urban visions in both Addis Ababa and Kigali, where in very different ways and for different reasons, cities shot up the domestic policy agenda. The turnaround towards a more concerted urban policy focus also came notably earlier in Ethiopia than in Uganda. EPRDF interest in Addis Ababa grew from the early 2000s in the context of an internal political crisis within the ruling coalition in 2001 and loss of parliamentary seats in the capital. Despite the sense that urban areas were turning more concertedly against the EPRDF, the party decided to allow a significant opening of political space in advance of the 2005 election, leading to the loss of virtually all their seats in Addis Ababa. The events surrounding this election and the subsequent violence are discussed in Chapter 8, but the key point here is that this electoral shock prompted an acute awareness of the power of the city's population to mobilize and inflict serious political damage, and consequently a new appreciation of the potential for urban investment to limit opposition and bolster the regime's social legitimacy (Lefort 2007; Di Nunzio 2014; Planel & Bridonneau 2017; Gebremariam 2020).

The new governmental attention to Addis Ababa manifested in range of policy initiatives that unfolded on a grand scale over the subsequent decade, alongside a dramatic closure of democratic space (Aalen & Tronvoll 2009). Even EPRDF regime insiders acknowledge that the 2005 election was a central motivation for the government to pivot decisively towards urban areas across a range of policy domains (Oqubay 2015: 74, 128). From this point onwards urban areas became a priority in the national development plan, the Plan for Accelerated and Sustainable Development to End Poverty (PASDEP) (MOFED 2006; Asnake 2011). The government established the Ministry of Urban Works and Development in October 2005, and the seeds were sown for large-scale urban transformation.

The EPRDF's emerging vision for Addis Ababa was sophisticated and multi-faceted, encompassing not only the continent's most striking housing programme (UN-HABITAT 2011; 2017; Planel & Bridonneau 2017), examined in Chapter 6, but also investment in health and education facilities (Duroyaume 2015), new microfinance and entrepreneurship schemes for small-scale businesses and urban youth (Di Nunzio 2015), and subsidized urban food distribution (Gebremariam 2020). Most striking of all was the wholesale renewal as parts of the city, which effectively combined a global vision of Addis as the 'diplomatic capital of Africa' with the dispersal of the urban poor (Kloosterboer 2019; Weldeghebrael 2019; 2020), as well as major new investments in urban roads and rail, examined later. Fuelled by the land-lease system discussed in Chapter 3, in the early 2010s the city was in a process of constant transformation as vast construction projects overturned the city's history of largely incremental and low-rise development—even though more traditional means of transporting construction materials were still sometimes required (see Figure 5.4). Meanwhile, the process of producing a new integrated plan for the city and surrounding urban areas was rather slow, and in

Figure 5.4 Four-legged construction workers in Addis Ababa
Photograph © Tom Goodfellow.

2014 stalled amid huge controversy and rising protest over the implications of this
for the extension of central authority into Oromia region.[18]

In Rwanda, meanwhile, the RPF was pursuing its own vision of an urban future
guided by principles of cleanliness, order, spatial regulation, and zero tolerance
for crime and corruption. Foregrounding these principles was central to efforts to
legitimize its rule in a country where it had a very limited social base. The production of a new masterplan for Kigali was accorded the utmost priority; after
commissioning the plan in 2005, in 2007 the government published the Kigali
Conceptual Master Plan, designed by the American firm Oz Architects at a cost
of US$1.7m (Oz Architecture 2007). The Conceptual Master Plan, which bears
the clear influence of 'new urbanist' ideas about accessible, multifunctional public spaces, embodied the growing emphasis on creating a city that is a paragon of
environmental conservation, public order, and social harmony, as well as being an
ideal site for investment.

---

[18] Despite the controversy, the planners involved maintain that this was rooted in a fundamental
misunderstanding, since the plan was never to actually annex surrounding land or extend the boundaries of the city but rather to integrate the master plans for each surrounding area with that of Addis
Ababa (interview with planner in the Addis Ababa Integrated Development Plan Office, 30 September
2014).

From the moment of its publication, the plan and the very idea of transforming Kigali through planning wielded enormous influence. With the Conceptual Master Plan in place, the government brought in a Singaporean firm, Surbana, to develop detailed area plans (see Figure 5.5). The choice of Singapore was not accidental; the island state holds a particular significance in the RPF developmental vision, and its founding father Lee Kuan Yew acted as an adviser to president Kagame.[19] Foreign consultants who have worked in both countries were emphatic about the similarities between Rwanda's predicament and the one that had faced Singapore some half a century earlier,[20] while a presidential advisor spoke of Kagame's personal notes scribbled in the margins of Lee's autobiography, *From Third World to First*.[21] Oz had also used Singapore as an indicative case study when designing the Conceptual Master Plan.[22] The plans developed by Surbana were explicitly geared towards transforming Kigali into a sort of 'model' city and secure site of investment, free of the volatility, conflict, and corruption affecting many surrounding parts of East and Central Africa. This dovetailed with the broader aim of making Rwanda a high-end services hub for the region (Goodfellow & Smith 2013; Behuria & Goodfellow 2019). As well as being more detailed for specific parts of the city—including the proposed new Central Business District (CBD)—Surbana's plans were based on more of a 'tabula rasa' approach (Shearer 2017: 129) and were more spectacular, with slum areas re-envisaged as ecological theme parks and commercial districts, while Rebero Hill in the south of the city was reimagined as a tourist haven featuring nine-hundred-room hotels.

Kigali was thus redrawn as a sparkling future-city linking Africa's Indian Ocean coast to the tumultuous, war-torn interior of the continent with its thwarted potential and largely untapped markets. This vision was a sort of mirror image of the urban reality that the RPF inherited in 1994, and the extraordinary scope of the RPF's urban vision needs to be considered in that light: after the unimaginable trauma of the genocide that unfolded on the streets of the capital, nothing less than total transformation would be enough to legitimize rule by a minority group of former exiles. These plans were accompanied by a strong emphasis on securitizing urban space through new forms of top-down social organization and surveillance, facilitated by the capillaries of infrastructural power embedded in Rwandan society that the RPF were able to capitalize on (explored in Chapter 8). This emphasis on urban socio-spatial reorganization to some degree parallels the rural social engineering discussed elsewhere (see e.g. Ansoms 2009; Straus & Waldorf 2011).

The sense in which the emerging plans for Kigali were not only visionary but depicted an 'imaginary' city, often interpreted as being in the realm of fantasy, was palpable in the attitude of certain stakeholders, notwithstanding the resolute

[19] Interview with Singaporean planner, 6 December 2009.
[20] Interview with foreign consultant, 11 December 2009.
[21] Interview with presidential adviser, 20 January 2010.
[22] Interview with Singaporean planner, 6 December 2009.

Figure 5.5 Launch of Nyarugenge Master Plan in Kigali, 2009
Photograph © Tom Goodfellow.

commitment and sincerity of others. One planning advisor working in the city volunteered the view that 'the master plan is not a real design for the real city. It is a virtual design for another city, not the actual Kigali that exists.'[23] Similarly, Vanessa Watson singled out Kigali among a range of 'African urban fantasies' as being the most ambitious; it was the only one proposing 'to replace the city with something entirely new' (2014: 3). However, on another level these plans are far more than mere fantasies, given the dramatic impacts they have for urban lives and livelihoods on the ground, as Chapter 7 explores in relation to the reorganization of trade. Moreover, for many of the foreign consultants and policy advisers working in Kigali at the time, the rigidity with which planning was approached constituted a problem. The tendency to conceive of planning as being about 'rules' rather than more flexible 'tools' sometimes generated intense anxiety among public officials, who were fearful of reprimand if they were seen not to be implementing planning documents to the letter.[24] As one international advisor based in a ministry wryly commented in 2009, '[we] are all impaled on the Master Plan.'[25] In this way the principle of pro-formality was ingrained into norms of accountability and professional survival.

---

[23] Interview with UN-Habitat representative in Kigali, 10 February 2010.
[24] Interviews with Kigali-based architects, 2013–2014.
[25] Interview with government official, 19 February 2009.

The comparative politics of urban 'visioning'

For several years prior to the 'urban turn' in Uganda, attention was thus being lavished on its neighbouring capital by the RPF. The comparative dimension did not go unnoticed; by 2010, the newspaper commentaries in the Ugandan capital decrying the state of Kampala on an almost daily basis often explicitly contrasted it with Kigali. Moreover, delegations of Kampala's politicians and bureaucrats made repeated pilgrimages across the border, frequently commenting on their 'amazement' at Kigali's achievements.[26] Elsewhere in the region, including in Nairobi, city planners were also looking to Kigali with deep-seated admiration.[27] Notwithstanding the empowerment of urban technocrats in Kampala from 2011 and urban investments on a massive scale in Addis Ababa, what was taking place in Kigali was quite distinct. It is Kigali that courted—and was rewarded with—international headlines in the late 2000s and 2010s naming it as the African city to watch. The city burnished its reputation as a continental leader as early as 2008, when it was awarded a UN-HABITAT Scroll of Honour Award for 'many innovations in building a model, modern city'.[28] Underpinning this, however, was the eviction of low-income populations on a large scale and often through highly egregious practices (Goodfellow 2014b; Manirakiza 2014; Shearer 2017).

Despite the rise of new urban visions across the region, these embodied distinct political agendas, which involved different emphases on territory and property and produced very different built-environment outcomes. Part of the motivation for the RPF's emphasis on producing a continent-leading capital city of the future, with the production of spatial discipline at its aesthetic core, relates to its broader ongoing pursuit of legitimacy through visibly transformative developmental accomplishments. As an organization perceived as being led by a small minority of foreign-born returnees within the already minority Tutsi ethnic group, the RPF has little 'natural' legitimacy to draw on among the wider Rwandan population (Reyntjens 2004; Longman 2011). As explored further in Chapter 6 and 7, the maintenance of a credible commitment to a tightly disciplined developmental project is central to the mentality of the regime, and both urban visions and tight urban land-use controls provide a highly visible way for the government to demonstrate this. The government believes Kigali plays a special role as somewhere that must 'lead' the rest of the country by example.[29] Moreover, one resource the government does have to draw on is its reputation for clamping down on corruption (Desrosiers & Thomson 2011). While there are certainly forms of corruption and patronage in Rwanda (Booth & Golooba-Mutebi 2012;

---

[26] Conversations with members of Ugandan delegation to Kigali, December 2011.
[27] Conversation with Kenyan urban planner, 9 February 2013.
[28] http://www.unhabitat.org/content.asp?typeid=19&catid=564&cid=5666, accessed 27 April 2011.
[29] Interview with government official, Kigali, 9 February 2009.

Kassa et al. 2017), the eradication of highly *visible* forms of corruption associated with haphazard urban development has been prioritized. This speaks to the deep importance of appearance—as well as reality—of territorial control for the RPF elite; Kigali has in this sense been termed a 'spectacle city' (Rollason 2013).

In Kampala, meanwhile, the NRM entered a high-stakes gamble from 2010 through which it sought new legitimacy with the middle classes, who were increasingly irked by potholes, pervasive street vending, and congestion, at the risk of further undermining its legitimacy both with the urban poor (who were often at the sharp end of KCCA's vision) and the kingdom of Buganda. These tensions ultimately weakened the resolve of the government in implementing its new urban agenda, as evidenced by the widespread perceptions by 2018 that the early gains in urban re-ordering were being reversed,[30] followed by the resignation of an exasperated Jennifer Musisi in October of that year. Much of the divergence in the capacity of the city governments in Kigali and Kampala to physically mould these cities in line with stated government aims comes down to differential distributions of associational power. The weakness of opposition parties but also of broader opposition forces in Rwanda, facilitated both by the character of post-genocide politics (discussed in Chapter 8) and the limited capitalist development (described in Chapter 4), contrasts with the ongoing need to manage opposition forces in Kampala. This has meant that the pressure to maintain various forms of urban rent flows remains very strong in Kampala, operating primarily through modes of political informality that have undermined the major push towards urban formalization and reordering, as explored more in Chapter 7.

In Addis Ababa, meanwhile, the importance of building new sources of legitimacy in the city, given the growing range of urban constituents demanding attention, became crystal clear after 2005. A dual strategy of territorialization and distribution of property was required—and in contrast to Kampala, the imperial and communist legacies bequeathed levels of infrastructural power and reach that enabled the EPRDF to deliver much of this through formal policy channels. To explore further the reshaping of urban landscapes in the three cities over the past two decades, the remainder of this chapter turns to the question of infrastructure. As a growing preoccupation of East African governments and their international development partners, this needs to be situated in the broader turn towards and agenda of infrastructure investment and financing over the past decade.

---

[30] Interview with city and national government officials, May 2018.

5.3 The African 'infrastructure gap' as a twenty-first-century priority

Since the late 2000s, it has become commonplace to read about an 'infrastructure gap' in Africa that is often described in terms such as 'yawning' (ECN 2015) and 'staggering' (World Bank 2010). The realities of limited infrastructure on the continent, particularly its least developed areas, are indisputable.[31] Most striking is how low-income sub-Saharan countries diverge even from other low-income countries, apparently by all key infrastructure measures, and by significant margins. Paved road density in low-income sub-Saharan Africa is less than 25 per cent of that of other low-income countries, and electricity generation capacity only 11 per cent (Addison et al.: 2017: 33). By 2018, it was estimated that 'closing Africa's infrastructure gap' would cost $130–$170bn per year (ADB 2018).

This renewed infrastructure emphasis on the part of international organizations has, not coincidentally, occurred at the same time as a sea change in how global finance interacts with African infrastructure. These changes are rooted in three significant developments over recent decades. The first is the rise of Chinese finance on the continent,[32] with China reportedly accounting for over 30 per cent of the total value of infrastructure projects in Africa by 2013 (Alves 2013; Gharib 2013). China's role is particularly significant in placing infrastructure at the heart of a strategy to combine financial returns and the export of excess construction capacity with geopolitical benefits. The scale of Chinese loans for African transport infrastructure has been especially remarkable, exceeding loans for any other sector and amounting to over $38bn from 2000 to 2015.[33] OECD development finance institutions have not been inattentive to the long-term implications of this, and the stakes were raised further with the unveiling of China's Belt and Road Initiative. Recent moves by the United States to engage much more in infrastructure financing on the continent can be seen as a response, or even as aping China's approach (Tremann 2019; Schindler et al. 2022).

The second key factor is the global financial crisis and its aftermath. As early as 2009, the World Bank argued that 'the global financial crisis has only made infrastructure [in Africa] more relevant'. (World Bank 2010: 15). The shifting orientation of finance towards the global South generally in response to the crisis is part of a wider quest among financial actors to identify, map, and securitize new asset classes given diminishing returns on conventional assets (Hildyard 2016; Fernandez & Aalbers 2017; Whiteside 2019). By 2008 it was already apparent that the private financing of infrastructure 'was re-emerging in the developed world after

---

[31] This section draws extensively on Goodfellow (2020b).

[32] For a relatively recent continent-wide analysis, see Brautigam and Hwang (2016).

[33] China-Africa Research Initiative, October 2018 Data, available at: http://www.sais-cari.org/data-chinese-loans-and-aid-to-africa.

four decades of mainly public sector financing' (Torrance 2008), and this trajectory has widened to encompass countries that until recently were viewed primarily as aid recipients rather than infrastructural investment opportunities.

Meanwhile, infrastructure has been rising up the agenda of foreign aid donors as a development need; after a steady decline from the 1970s, in the late 2000s Overseas Development Aid (ODA) for economic infrastructure in Africa began to rise again as a share of total ODA. Overall aid from OECD DAC countries for economic infrastructure more than trebled from $7.2bn in 2003 to $23.3bn in 2015, with an especially sharp increase after the financial crisis (OECD 2019). This shift dovetailed with the post-crisis quest by global private finance to discover new investment horizons. The third factor is thus the global development agenda that eventually cohered around the sustainable development goals, and following this the Addis Ababa Action Agenda (AAAA) on financing them. The emphasis on bringing in private finance marks a substantial shift from the mainly public financing of the Millenium Development Goals, with a primary purpose of ODA now being to 'de-risk investment' in order to 'transform billions to trillions' (Mawdsley 2018).

Africa shines brighter than any other region as a potential magnet for private infrastructure finance: according to Preqin, a financial intelligence firm specializing in 'alternative assets', infrastructure funds typically target average net returns of 15.8 per cent (12 per cent for developed and 19.3 per cent for developing markets), but returns in Africa are expected to hit 30 per cent (Hildyard 2016: 49–50). Moreover, East Africa shines brightest of all. A 2017 Deloitte report on African construction sector trends notes that 'East Africa continues to stand out; both as a growth region and as one focused on creating a more conducive environment through infrastructure investment' (Deloitte 2017: 3). By the time of the 2019 report, East Africa had the continent's largest share of projects by value. Many of these projects traverse large expanses of rural territory, connecting rapidly growing urban nodes where existing transport links are either non-existent or take the form of ageing and defunct colonial routes (Enns & Bersaglio 2020). The leading position of East Africa in terms of attracting international infrastructure investments thus reflects its frontier status in processes of global urbanization. Increasingly, the region's infrastructure megaprojects involve investments within cities and metropolitan regions as well, which have become priorities of both OECD donors and Chinese agencies in their negotiations with governments in East Africa.[34] Urban infrastructure finance is therefore not hard to come by: on the contrary, it is now potentially on offer from all sides. As the representative of one major donor agency casually remarked when discussing the challenges

---

[34] Interviews with donor representatives and government agencies in China, Ethiopia, and Uganda, 2017–2018.

of enhancing transport systems in the greater Kampala area, 'the finance is the easiest.'[35]

What is less straightforward is the implementation of infrastructure projects and their eventual material, economic, political, and distributional outcomes. As noted in Chapter 2, infrastructure is inherently distributional in nature and a marker and creator of differentiated inclusion (Chu 2014; Harvey 2018); yet it can be repurposed and subverted for uses far removed from the goals of designers (Mrázek 2002; Harvey & Knox 2012). Across the three cities examined here, major infrastructure projects have had distinct political and economic drivers, with easy access to finance in globalized, late-urbanizing contexts being filtered through the distribution of associational power and particular legitimation projects. But the manner of their implementation depends on the nature of state reach, particularly in terms of control over land. Moreover, though their materiality, everyday use, and discursive reframing they can come to play unanticipated roles in urban development and political relations. In order to examine these dynamics further, we examine one particular 'flagship' project in each case that symbolizes dominant trends in urban infrastructure development.

5.4 China and the Ethiopian urban 'renaissance': The light railway in Addis Ababa

As noted above, the urban transformation in Addis has been the most dramatic of all the cities considered here, and possibly in all the major cities of Africa. In the words of one long-term observer, '[no] other capital city on the continent has known such fast-paced and extensive modernization over the last few years' (Lefort 2015: 357). The idea of the 'Ethiopian renaissance', harking back to the distinguished urban past discussed in Chapters 3 and 4, has come increasingly to be connected with the country's urban flourishing and renewal (Kloosterboer 2019; Terrefe 2020; Weldeghebrael 2019; 2020). Meanwhile, Ethiopia has become a key site of Chinese financial flows, many of which have been channelled through infrastructure. As of 2017, China was by far the largest player in East Africa both in terms of infrastructure financing and building: 25 per cent of construction was Chinese-financed, and 54 per cent of all construction was undertaken by Chinese firms (Deloitte 2017).

The annual revenues of Chinese contractors in Ethiopia came second only to those in Angola in sub-Saharan Africa, and Ethiopia is the recipient of the largest amount of Chinese concessional lending on the continent (and second to Angola in terms of overall lending).[36] The largest component of its Chinese loans in recent

---

[35] Interview with donor representative, 26 November 2020.
[36] China-Africa Research Initiative, October 2018 Data, available at: http://www.sais-cari.org/data-chinese-loans-and-aid-to-africa.

Figure 5.6 Addis Ababa LRT after construction
Photograph © Tom Goodfellow.

times have been for transport infrastructure: $4.4bn out of $13.7bn total loans from 2000–2013, or 33 per cent.[37] Most of this was for the new Addis-Djibouti Railway, building directly on the route of the colonial-era railway discussed in Chapter 4. The next most significant Chinese-financed infrastructure project was, however, the Light Rail Transit (LRT) in Addis Ababa (see Figure 5.6): a flagship project conceived in the late years of Prime Minister Meles Zenawi's rule, though largely executed after his death in 2012. The LRT constitutes a fascinating example of an urban infrastructure project that demonstrates both the scale and nature of the government's ambitions and legitimation priorities, and how infrastructure can generate its own unanticipated urban outcomes.[38]

The LRT originated from a proposed Bus Rapid Transit (BRT) system, which was a well-established plan by 2006 (Kassahun and Bishu 2018). The decision to switch from BRT to LRT the following year came directly from federal government, with little explicit justification and reportedly at the behest of Meles who believed it would make more of an impact; the actual decision-making process 'remained a mystery' (Kassahun 2021: 157). Indeed, this project in many ways came to symbolize the urban dimension of the Ethiopian 'renaissance', being

[37] China-Africa Research Initiative, October 2018 Data, available at: http://www.sais-cari.org/data-chinese-loans-and-aid-to-africa.
[38] This section draws extensively on Goodfellow and Huang (2021).

proudly presented as the first light rail system in sub-Saharan Africa and a model for the continent (Nallet 2018). The total cost of the light rail system was $475m, 85 per cent of which was financed by China Exim Bank through a mixed loan (part concessional and part commercial, though the exact terms are confidential).

With the commitment to LRT finalized in the late 2000s, expressions of interest were invited and many international contractors submitted bids. An Italian firm was favoured in preliminary selection, but CREC (a Chinese state-owned enterprise) then came forward with an offer at what they claim was half the cost of the Italian bidders, bolstered by the promise of financing through Exim. What happened next is illustrative of the relative bargaining power on the part of the Ethiopian government relative to CREC. The Chinese firm's design affiliate proposed an alternative LRT route after the contract with them was signed, which involved potentially better integration with the city's zoning plan and expansion process. However, the proposal was rejected by the Ethiopian government on the grounds of cost and length of implementation period. Moreover, a number of requests for additional elements from the Ethiopian side (relating to elevation of parts of the track, a system for emergency braking, and additional electricity cable channels), most of which CREC did not deem necessary, inflated the cost substantially with the result that Exim had to increase the loan by US$60–70m.[39]

Project conception, procurement, and construction was thus fraught with difficulties and conflicts, and the narrative is far from being one of domineering Chinese influence. The Ethiopian government's steering of the project's direction is also evident in the setting of fares, which at the time of writing were 2–6 Ethiopian Birr depending on distance,[40] making the LRT even cheaper than minibus-taxis and thus offering affordable transport to lower-income groups. Significantly, this is much lower than the 40 Birr recommended by CREC,[41] indicating an extremely high level of subsidy. The fares recommended by CREC reflect the fact that the LRT was originally conceived for the middle classes rather than the poor. However, with fears of urban discontent rising and the memory of 2005 still strong, the original plans to make the LRT a middle-class commuter infrastructure were subverted. Increasingly seen as a symbolic project in terms of mass commuting from the peripheries to the city centre, it opened in 2015 after a frenetic push to try and complete it in time for the elections of that year.

Several years after opening, the overall impacts of the LRT are disputed, particularly relative to the BRT option it displaced. It clearly provides a valued service to large numbers of people: daily passenger numbers are estimated at 120,000–150,000.[42] However, the lack of integrated design between the LRT and other

---

[39] These figures were provided by Chinese SOE representatives, though were disputed by ERC. See also Kassahun (2021: 16) on factors that led to increased costs.

[40] USD 0.07–0.2 at 2019 exchange rates.

[41] Interview with SOE representative, 20 March 2018.

[42] Data provided by CREC and ERC, November 2018. See also Kassahun (2021).

transportation modes, as well as with broader urban-planning processes, is a point of ongoing contention. Its rails bisect previously porous streets, with long distances between crossing points, and many people believe it is worsening road traffic by disrupting flow rather than improving it.[43] There is also little if any possibility of it covering its operational costs, let alone generating enough resources to repay the loan. This problem is exacerbated by the limited potential for land value capture linked to the LRT, which was central to the viability of China's own experience of such investments.

Some of the problems associated with the integration into broader transport systems are rooted in institutional gaps between the national and local planning authority, and the fragmented way that the project evolved. The Ethiopian Railway Corporation (ERC), established in 2007 and with the aim of facilitating national and international rail development, took full charge of planning for this city-level infrastructure project in 2010 with very little experience. Opinions vary on how much the Addis Ababa transportation authority was involved in planning and decision-making,[44] but the lack of engagement with local private sector and civil society actors (Kassahun and Bishu 2018) and with the Addis Ababa City Planning Office (Rode et al. 2020) are clear. In fact, the city authority disowned the project just a few years after its opening, with the deputy mayor announcing in November 2018 that the city has learned that LRT 'wasn't the right option', being built on a capacity for power generation the city does not possess. He argued that buses are more suitable and 'more Ethiopian', and the city intends to 'freeze' any extension of the LRT.[45]

This, however, does not necessarily mean that the project is judged a failure by city-dwellers; in fact, the LRT has taken on a life of its own beyond the initial visions of the Ethiopian government or Chinese agencies. Based on survey and interview work in Ayat, a neighbourhood of Addis Ababa at the far eastern end of the LRT, over half of the people in the area use the LRT never or only very rarely, but those who did use it generally did not do so for commuting to work, which was the stated intention of the LRT. Almost four-fifths of users travelled on it for shopping, going to the bank, and social activities, as compared to just 15 per cent who used it to access work. Commuters coming to Ayat from more central areas (who are significant in number, given the area's construction boom) were likely to use it only occasionally or never, opting instead for minibuses and buses.[46] Qualitative responses suggests this was sometimes because some street vendors, construction workers, and small businesspeople were unable to transport goods

---

[43] Various interviews with key stakeholders, 2017–2018; small-scale survey with LRT users, May 2018.

[44] See Boudet et al. (2015) and Nallet (2018) for contrasting perspectives.

[45] Presentation by Solomon Kidane, deputy mayor of Addis Ababa, Urban Age Conference, Addis Ababa, 30 November 2018.

[46] Small-scale exploratory survey with LRT users, May 2018.

and materials on it. People commuting the other way (from Ayat towards the city centre) were even less likely to use it, despite the fact that providing periphery-to-centre commuting was integral to its rationale (Goodfellow & Huang 2021).

It is, however, striking that despite many people not using it, a large majority of all respondents—both residents and workers—were positive about it. Over 80 per cent of all people in the area, whether they used it or not, believed it was positive for the area and good value for money.[47] In all, its usage and value were substantial—and therefore its role in contributing to the project of urban popular legitimation arguably quite significant. But instead of being a commuting option for the middle classes as initially intended, it has been appropriated by lower-income groups as an occasional, useful, and cheap means of accessing urban life. The social legitimation project that it embodied was increasingly turned towards poorer city-dwellers as the governments developmentalist orientation and concerns with urban stability evolved—yet the ways in which they found it useful were unplanned and contingent.

5.5 Kigali's tourist infrastructures of regional ambition

Kigali's infrastructural recovery after the genocide has been remarkable. Alongside the RPF urban vision outlined above and commitment to particular forms of physical development, it is important to situate Kigali's infrastructure against the large amounts of foreign aid flowing through the city since the mid-1990s. Aid played a direct role in the early reconstruction of Kigali, when urban infrastructure accounted for up to 40 per cent of capital expenditure (Uvin 1998: 149). There was an 'aggressive infrastructure rollout' by the state, 'opening new areas of the city for development'.[48] Most of the $1bn of aid flowing through the city by 2010 was not targeted at urban infrastructure, but the overall volume of aid resulted in the heavy presence of the international community in the city, which helped to cement the status of Kigali as a space for both domestic and international elites—and thus the prioritization of urban infrastructure by the RPF government (Goodfellow & Smith 2013).

Also important is Rwanda's sense of its position in the East/Central Africa region and the aspirations for Kigali's role within this, building on the service-sector visions discussed in Chapter 4. Ambitious plans to develop a major $1.3bn international airport at Bugesera, for example, alongside the broader aim to become a logistics hub linking East and Central Africa, and a centre of finance, conference tourism, and higher education, all involve central roles for Kigali.

---

[47] See Goodfellow and Huang 2021 for full details of these findings.
[48] Estate agent, interviewed 9 June 2014.

Rwanda's landlocked location and distance from the coast is seen as both a challenge and an opportunity: it is often said (and doubtless even more often thought)
that its development progress depends in part on the turmoil in neighbouring
countries and neighbouring governments' inability to prevent the flow of human,
natural, and other economic resources towards Kigali. The vision for the city is
thus distinctly regional in scope as well as national.[49] The airport is intended
to serve fourteen million passengers annually when completed in 2032, twice
the seven million currently served by Nairobi's Jomo Kenyatta Airport and also
exceeding the twelve million who pass through Bole Airport in Addis Ababa. Work
on the site is substantially underway, but as with many infrastructure projects of
this scale it has been dogged by challenges relating to funding and viability for
over a decade.

Connected to the Bugesera airport plan is tourism, a further sector central to
the RPF vision, and which drives the centrality of certain kinds of infrastructure
development. A particular focus over the past decade, alongside the promotion
of gorilla tourism and investment in the national airline, Rwandair, has been conference tourism focused on Kigali. The infrastructures that perhaps best exemplify
Kigali's transformation are thus those associated with tourism and, more generally,
international 'visitor' architecture. The attention to conference tourism reflects a
broader aim to 'go beyond gorillas' and establish Rwanda as more than an add-
on destination at the end of an East African safari tour (GoR 2009). By 2010, the
Rwandan Development Board began to see the 'MICE' sector (meetings, incentives, conferences, and events) as a priority area for further support,[50] and the
central government along with Kigali City Council sharpened its focus on the key
sectors needed for its MICE ambitions to succeed. By the end of 2016, Kigali had
3,400 upper- and middle-range hotel rooms available (Behuria and Goodfellow
2019).

Alongside setting up the Rwanda Convention Bureau, the government worked
feverishly to complete the physical centrepiece and symbol of its MICE strategy: the Kigali Convention Centre (see Figure 5.7). The Convention Centre
was initiated in 2007 by three corporate investors—Rwanda Investment Group,
Prime Holdings, and the Rwanda Social Security Board (RSSB). Initially slated
for completion in 2011, it was beleaguered by controversy, escalating costs, and
terminated construction contracts with a series of Chinese contractors, and only
finally opened in June 2016. One source in the construction sector claimed that
the quality of many of the construction materials and interior fittings was so poor
that fittings such as sinks were already rusting in 2015, before construction was
even completed.[51] The desperation to finish it in the face of ongoing delays and

---

[49] It is interesting to note that certain advertisements for the national airline, Rwandair, depict maps
that position Kigali significantly nearer the centre of the continent than is actually the case.
[50] Interview, RDB official, November 2011.
[51] Interview with construction-sector specialist, 19 January 2015.

Figure 5.7 Kigali Convention Centre just before completion
Photograph © Tom Goodfellow.

concerns about quality was reflected in the eventual termination of the last in line of a series of Chinese contracts, and the decision finally to bring in the Rwandan army's engineer regiment to finish the job.[52] By 2015, Kagame was reported to have said in meetings that he was 'fed up' with the Chinese.[53]

Expectations for the Convention Centre were piled high: a government official argued that it was a 'gamechanger for Rwanda's development', while a private consultant characterized it as 'Rwanda's version of the Eiffel Tower. That's how important it is.'[54] The Kigali Convention Centre comprises a five-star Radisson Blu hotel, a 2,600-capacity conference centre, Kigali Information Technology Park and a museum on the bottom floor. With construction costs of over $300m, 40 per cent of which was financed through international debt and the rest through the equity of three domestic investment groups, the Convention Centre is the most expensive building complex in Africa. Its costs were inflated in part by the impetus to ensure environmental sustainability at all stages of the process, which speaks to the RPF's

---

[52] Interview with architect, January 2015; interview with foreign adviser, January 2015.
[53] Interview with foreign adviser, January 2015.
[54] Cited in Behuria and Goodfellow (2019: 592).

desire to situate itself internationally as a champion of sustainable development.[55] The gamble that the Convention Centre represents has in some respects paid off, with the MICE sector thriving and Kigali now second only to Cape Town as the leading city for international meetings[56]—though the broader development benefits of this remain questionable (Behuria & Goodfellow 2019). There have also been many casualties of the government's emphasis on tourism, in the form of mid-range hotels that were built on a large scale from around 2007, with substantial government encouragement, only to be auctioned off by banks a few years later. With many hotel owners severely lacking in clientele and unable to pay the loans, over a hundred hotels were reportedly being auctioned off by 2015.[57] Major international hotels were among the few who can withstand the highly fluctuating demands and long fallow periods.[58]

The above developments reflect the general emphasis on 'going big' that the government has adopted in a range of high-end service sectors (Behuria & Goodfellow 2019), almost as if the spectacle of large-scale urban transformation is an end in its own right. Indeed, if Addis Ababa's light railway along with its housing programme (explored in Chapter 6) evoke mid-twentieth century 'high modernism' in their scale, brutalist appearance, and aspirations for moulding social relations, the tourist infrastructures of Kigali in some respects evoke the postmodern. Rather than being an inward-looking project of social engineering—of which there are certainly ample examples in Rwanda, including its rural villagization programme (Ansoms 2009)—Rwanda's priority mega-infrastructure projects including the Kigali Convention Centre are intended to project an image abroad, symbolizing a specific vision of services-led capitalist development. It epitomizes, to recall a phrase central to Harvey's (1989) definition of postmodernity, the city as an advertisement for itself. Thus as well as evoking Ghertner's (2015) 'rule by aesthetics', Kigali is a city that is internationally projected 'in order to attract the investment which will give body to the simulated spectacle that Kigali presents' (Rollason 2013: 9). At the same time, it also aims to romanticize Rwanda's precolonial past and culture: its central dome was inspired by the King's palace in Nyzanza, with a spiral motif drawn from traditional Rwandan art. Clad onto the hotel part of the Centre, meanwhile, is a pattern of colourful ribbons said to represent 'Rwanda's rich weaving tradition'.[59] Part infrastructure, part real estate, and part symbolism, it is the ultimate pastiche project—including with respect to its architectural stylings.

---

[55] One observer even spoke of a 'simmering hysteria' around the (often ill-defined) concept of sustainable construction in Rwanda (interview with architect, 28 August 2013).

[56] https://tophotel.news/exploring-africas-rising-star-of-conference-hosting-rwanda-infographic/.

[57] 'How Rwanda became the land of a hundred hotel auctions', https://qz.com/africa/544187/how-rwanda-became-the-land-of-a-hundred-hotel-auctions/, accessed 6 April 2020.

[58] Interviews with investors and construction-sector representatives, 2014–2015.

[59] https://www.mindsky.com/magazine/news-and-trends/6-cool-facts-you-didnt-know-about-the-kigali-convention-center-complex.

The broader story of major infrastructure in Kigali is one in which a significant number of donors, investors, and construction firms have been attracted to the country by the government's astute marketing and the very real benefits Kigali offers as a secure place to live and work. But, as with the Convention Centre, the completion of projects has been a big problem. A lack of clear prioritization often creates major delays and funding shortfalls, while multiple donors working through different institutions and with different standards minimize information and skills transfer between projects.[60] The consequence is a sort of 'Tower of Babel' of aid and investment, producing fragmented rather than cohesive development. As management is transferred and splintered among numerous international agencies, little institutional knowledge is captured. In one striking example, an international advisor said that having been tasked with assembling all the relevant studies and documentation on the proposed Bugesera Airport, he found it impossible. Despite repeated visits to the relevant government agencies and even being directed to specific laptops to search out information, many documents appeared to be missing or lost; 'literally no one knows where all the documents are.'[61]

This level of documentary and communicative fragmentation, combined with everyday challenges on the ground from the language of manuals to the specification of standards, further fuel the trend towards 'incoherent emulation' (Behuria 2018). In Kigali, this often takes the specific form of infrastructural pastiche as the government strives to realize the urban agenda on which it has staked its legitimacy, working through a range of sets of institutions and rules associated with the range of funders and supporters on whom its position rests.

5.6 The 'world's most expensive road': The Kampala-Entebbe Expressway

While Kigali has positioned itself as a regional services hub, the more diverse and vibrant economy across the border in Kampala has produced a city that is both more congested and more complex in its infrastructural arrangements. The NRM's success in courting aid and investment over successive decades, combined with Uganda's longstanding significance as a logistics and trade route from central Africa to the Indian Ocean coast, has led to extreme concentration of the economy in Kampala and the corridor linking it to the cites of Jinja and Entebbe (see Chapter 4). As Kampala's economy boomed, its infrastructure was worn down to the point of virtual collapse, as noted in section 5.1. Parts of the city's infrastructure had a substantial refresh in the run-up to hosting the Commonwealth Heads of Government Meeting (CHOGM) in 2007. However, the political dynamics

---

[60] Interviews with foreign investors and local construction firms, Kigali, January 2015.
[61] Interview with foreign adviser, Kigali, 19 January 2015.

discussed earlier fuelled a lack of maintenance and resources for sustained infras-tructural improvement, with the effect that CHOGM's main legacy was a number of large and under-used hotels. Meanwhile, major new transport infrastructure was seen as increasingly urgent by the late 2000s. The EU-funded Kampala North-ern Bypass road was completed in 2009 amid a series of corruption scandals (Wiegratz 2016), but in the 2010s a range of even grander projects were pursued to decongest the Kampala city-region.

Infrastructure investments are notoriously expensive and unprofitable in Uganda; one donor representative remarked that 'you might as well drop the money out of an aeroplane and you would get a better return'.[62] The multiple conflicting interests in land emerging from the land tenure system described in Chapter 3, alongside relatively diffuse distribution of associational power and long legacies of para-formal exchange outside of official state processes, combine to perpetuate and exacerbate the state's lack of infrastructural power to realize such projects. One major project that did make it to completion in the 2010s was the Chinese-funded Expressway from Kampala to the airport at Entebbe, though the path of its implementation is revealing of the underlying distribution of power and limits to government planning capacity in and around the city.

The idea for an expressway connecting Kampala to Entebbe existed since the early 2000s, by which time the pre-existing 10m-wide road was so congested that it could take three hours to travel under 50km. After the Uganda National Roads Authority (UNRA) was inaugurated in 2006, the idea gathered momentum. China First Highway Engineering Company, soon to be merged into the new China Communication Construction Corporation (CCCC), approached the Ugandan government after hearing about the idea in 2009 and then secured a preferen-tial loan offer from Exim Bank. Negotiation around planning and routing mostly took place between UNRA and CCCC; the Ministry of Lands, Kampala Capital City Authority and the government of Wakiso District, through which most of the expressway passes, were barely involved.[63]

Allegations of corruption between UNRA and CCCC were rife, particularly concerning environmental and social safeguards and inflated cost. A Ugandan auditor general's report claimed that the unit cost for the Kampala-Entebbe Expressway was almost double that of other CCCC-constructed roads in Uganda, even after accounting for specific characteristics, and much more expensive than the regional average.[64] Excessive costs were blamed on the lack of competitive bid-ding, duplication of consultancy services, and—inevitably—land acquisition. The cost of this was driven up by rampant speculation by actors able to acquire land along the route prior to government acquisition; some allegedly even developed

---

[62] Interview with donor representative, 3 May 2018.
[63] Various interviews with key stakeholders in Kampala, 2018.
[64] https://observer.ug/news-headlines/46002-entebbe-highway-cost-was-inflated-auditor-general.

properties such as hotels in order to claim compensation not only for buildings but also for lost future earnings.[65] By April 2017, compensation costs had reached over twice the planned figure of UGX100bn.[24] The debate over the cost led to considerable public anger, with claims that it was 'the world's most expensive road' per kilometre hitting the headlines in 2016.[66] Even as early as 2013, sources claimed that one third of the proposed route had been diverted for reasons relating to land acquisition (Gil 2015).

Land acquisition generated not only extensive cost, but major delays. The problem of compensation in Uganda is not just about finding the money, as a one source working for a major donor agency points out; there are also practical challenges involved in actually implementing compensation: 'getting the money actually paid out is an issue—if the property owner is dead and he has many children, who do you write the check out to?' Often title deeds sit with a bank rather than an individual, and it is far from clear who should be compensated given the complexity of tenure systems, contested land rights, and prevalence of absentee landlords.[67] Uganda's 1998 Land Act, celebrated as bringing land to the people and reversing the authoritarian centralism of Amin and Obote, specifies that compulsory acquisition can only happen once fair and adequate compensation has been agreed and paid. Yet given ongoing disputes concerning ownership and payment, this can lead to years and years of delays.

Frustrated with the limitations this posed for major infrastructure investment, in 2017 the government attempted to pass a Constitutional Amendment allowing it to acquire land even while these disputes were ongoing, by depositing an amount they determined to be fair in an escrow account until the dispute was resolved.[68] The desire to strengthen state powers over land reflected a long-term agenda on the part of President Museveni, who said as early as 1995 during a speech launching Uganda's constitution, at which Ethiopia's Prime Minister Meles was present, that he was disappointed he could not nationalize land like Ethiopia.[69] Yet the distribution of associational power and rooting of NRM social legitimacy in *liberating* Uganda from the centralizing tendencies of previous regimes makes anything approaching this impossible. Even the 2017 Constitutional Amendment was withdrawn in the face of resistance. The idea resurfaced in a weakened form in early 2019, through the idea of amending the Land Acquisition Act of 1965 rather than the Constitution. This stipulates that the government would allow seventy-five

[65] Interview with lawyer, Kampala, 21 June 2018.
[66] https://pesacheck.org/is-ugandas-entebbe-expressway-the-costliest-road-per-kilometer-in-the-world-f5e1730758a9.
[67] Interview with donor representative, Kampala, 26 November 2020.
[68] Interview with senior land official, Kampala, 8 May 2018.
[69] Interview with lawyer, Kampala, 21 June 2018.

days to settle a dispute before taking control of compulsorily purchased land.[70] By the end of 2020, however, there were still no signs of this being passed.

The amount loaned by the Chinese—US$350m—combined with strong government buy-in to the project, meant that the Expressway was realized relatively quickly despite these challenges. But even aside from the exorbitant cost per kilometre, the overall benefit of the road is highly uncertain. It effectively 'floats' above other transport infrastructure in the city-region, evidencing little or no embedding in strategic planning processes and no clarity on how it can even pay for itself or generate clear socio-economic returns. The toll—which was central to its rationale and financing—was still not operation at the time of writing. Although many users of the road such as taxi drivers plying the route to the airport held positive opinions of it, their appreciation is partly contingent on the lack of toll payments being in place.[71] As for the impact of the Expressway on surrounding areas, UNRA officials themselves admit that there was no coherent plan for this.[72] The caused frustration among the Chinese agency representatives, who found the lack of planning difficult to comprehend. As well as there being limited planning at the level of central government agencies involved, there was no effective district plan in place at that time for Wakiso, which the Expressway carves in two. Given soaring land values in areas near the Expressway's few entry points, the door was open to further rampant speculation and haphazard development.

Meanwhile, among many people in the wider area, the road has generated intense resentment. The majority of questionnaire respondents claimed they had no opportunity to comment on it in any way; the only reported engagement with implementing authorities was in relation to land valuation for compensation.[73] This lack of consultation meant that most locals did not realize the extent to which they would be shut out of the road—which has only three entry points along its full length—resulting in expectations far removed from the eventual reality. Many people living close to the Expressway but far from its access points are cut off from their own land and livelihoods on the other side, having to take lengthy, traffic-choked detours to get to geographically proximal places. In some areas where the Expressway joins the old Entebbe Road South, properties were destroyed due to inadequate drainage provided in the overall design for the joining of two roads in swampy areas, causing severe flooding. All of these consequences point to the Expressway's extensive 'collateral damage', which cannot be dissociated from the lack of both planning and popular consultation.

[70] 'Govt reintroduces the compulsory land acquisition amendments'. *The New Vision*, 20 March 2019.
https://www.newvision.co.ug/news/1496642/govt-reintroduces-compulsory-land-acquisition-amendments.
[71] This section draws on Goodfellow and Huang (2021); for more details see the full paper.
[72] Interview with UNRA official, 19 October 2018.
[73] This paragraph draws on responses to structured interviews undertaken in January 2019 with thirty-two residents of an area particularly negatively affected by the Expressway.

A number of other features of the road, including aspects of design and material qualities also render using it problematic. Many users had long lists of complaints. Enhanced speed means fuel consumption also increases, and there are no fuel stations or garages along the way, or even places designed for stopping, even though most drivers in Kampala depend on small, regular inputs of fuel. The free-flow also leads to reckless driving, which combined with a lack of street lights and a common complaint of slipperiness in bad weather makes some drivers hesitant to use it.[74] It is widely believed to have substantially worsened congestion around its access point in central Kampala, putting some people off using it at all. Thus the users' appreciation is highly tenuous: the road's smooth exterior, offering a celebrated contrast with the city's potholes, itself generates new and unanticipated problems.

In all, the future potential and utility of the road—which has had highly variable impacts on land value and development prospects depending on proximity to access points, and may not offer a material answer to the city's congestion problems—remain wide open. Many of the problems associated with it echo those affecting major transport infrastructure elsewhere; but the particular difficulties of land acquisition, often extortionate compensation, and extreme disregard for urban planning processes testify to the particularities of Buganda's powerful landed interests and the state's relatively weak levers of infrastructural power. Moreover, the nature of the project itself, and the fact that it was prioritized over other forms of transport infrastructure, also reflect the political context. The concluding section of this chapter examines in a comparative light how politics has shaped infrastructural trajectories in the three cities.

5.7 The comparative politics of urban mega-infrastructure

The above three flagship mega-projects are revealing of the forces shaping these cities in the twenty-first century. At US$300–$500m apiece, all three were phenomenally expensive; the fact that they were realized at all indicates that they were allocated the highest level of priority by their respective governing regimes. A large proportion of the cost was internationally financed in all cases, without which these projects would have been impossible, and concerns about debt repayment have dogged all three. Yet they also symbolize the different developmental and political priorities of each governing regime, the attempts to construct particular forms of legitimacy and the legacies of infrastructural reach.

The Addis LRT is a unique project in Africa. Its scale, destruction of the urban fabric, land acquisition requirements, and cost symbolize both the extent of the government's control over land and the high importance placed by EPRDF in

---

[74] Interviews with taxi drivers and regular users of the expressway, November 2018.

the 2000s on building infrastructures for the burgeoning urban middle classes—the original intended beneficiaries—and subsequently the urban poor. No other project in sub-Saharan Africa (outside of South Africa) has devoted such resources to urban public transport; compare the LRT's $475m for just 34km to the $150m spent on 137km of Bus Raid Transit network in Dar es Salaam (Rizzo 2017: 152). The willingness and ability to borrow this much money to finance a light rail system speaks to the extent of access to Chinese finance in Ethiopia and reflects the EPRDF elite's obsession with overcoming perceptions about Ethiopia's lagging development, and with modernity 'as an end in itself' (Ejigu 2014: 287). Yet it also reflects the growing sense after 2005 that the urban classes are a political force to be reckoned with.

This offers a sharp contrast to Rwanda, where inward-facing projects primarily intended to benefit and build support among ordinary urbanites are notably absent. Instead, resources have been heaped onto outward-facing prestige infrastructure projects, part of the RPF elite's strategic moves to construct a high-end services comparative advantage and secure ongoing legitimacy through developmental transformation. This reflects the very different distribution of associational power in the two countries: the EPRDF government has been focusing on securing itself from maturing threats from within, while the RPF's approach betrays awareness that despite its precarious social legitimacy internally, the associational power of urban opposition is weak. Moreover, it reflects a perception that bolstering the regime's fragile legitimacy requires maintaining its appeal and value to actors outside the country. Equally significant, however, is that such a small economy could mobilize almost half of the resources for the Kigali Convention Centre through domestic equity, by bringing together the country's key investors: an indication of the tightness of economic power within the country and the ability of the ruling elite to marshal this towards a specific, high-risk developmental vision.

The nature of mega-infrastructure development in Kampala differs markedly again. Urban passenger transport infrastructure on anything approaching the scale of the Addis LRT is rendered virtually impossible by the scale and strength of private land rights in the city, as well as resistance to significantly disrupting the informal economy.[75] Moreover, despite some service-sector motivations akin to those in Rwanda, there is nothing in either the distribution of power or the quest for social legitimacy in Uganda that would incentivize an urban services-based investment on the scale of the Kigali Convention Centre. The Expressway, however, was an appealing prospect in a country seen as having a latent regional

---

[75] The need to find ways to incorporate the vast numbers of people working in paratransit (see Goodfellow 2015b; 2017c; Goodfellow and Mukwaya 2021a) is one of the ongoing sticking points in efforts to develop any mass transit, along with the question of land compensation (interviews with various transport-sector representatives, November 2020).

comparative advantage in logistics, held back by inadequate and choked infrastructure. Uganda's urban middle classes and economic elites, whose support for the NRM has always been tenuous at best, were growing increasingly frustrated with Kampala's congestion. The decision to make such a major investment in a single road between the capital and the airport thus reflects the extent to which, since the 2000s, Kampala's infrastructural decay came to impinge on urban elites themselves.[76] Yet the progress of this road—and above all its remarkable economic cost—speaks volumes about the relatively diffuse nature of power in Kampala, with landlords and speculators able to cash in through a bonanza of compensation claims, and the state's infrastructural reach highly constrained in its capacity to plough through an intended route without paying off interests at every turn. That this road cost around twice as much per kilometre as a similar Chinese-financed toll road from Addis Ababa to Adama in Ethiopia, built by exactly the same firm, starkly illustrates this.[77]

Each of these infrastructures exerted is own influence on urban life and urban political economy, mediating the above dynamics of power and legitimacy and setting in train forces on the ground that further shape urban change. This is particularly clear in the case of the Addis LRT, the use of which by (and, increasingly, its association with) poorer urban groups rather than middle-class commuters has fundamentally altered its role in the city. Yet the force of infrastructure and the practices it generates is also exerting influence on urban space around the other two projects, as land values unexpectedly dip in areas next to the Kampala-Entebbe Expressway where dust, flooding, and lack of access have left some of the new real estate—constructed in anticipation of substantial value uplift—empty.[78] In Kigali, meanwhile, the institutional, material, financial, and symbolic pastiche of the Convention Centre has altered the relationship between the RPF government and Chinese firms, while also becoming the most visible symbol of the extent to which the ruling elite is willing to gamble on a very specific vision of its future. An urban landscape littered with prestige projects and half-empty hotels plays its own role in raising the stakes in the RPF's development strategy; the tangible threat of the potentially wasteful 'white elephant' lurks visibly on the horizon, further impelling the ruling elite to hold its resolve in pushing for continued economic and urban transformation.

---

[76] See Muwanga et al. (2020) for a further discussion of the increased elite interest in the city from 2010.

[77] https://www.monitor.co.ug/News/National/Why-Kampala-Jinja-Expressway-delayed/688334-5274626-hun6l4/index.html.

[78] See Goodfellow and Huang (2021) for a fuller discussion.

6

Urban propertyscapes

Introduction

In using gargantuan concrete, steel, and glass formations such as the LRT and
Kigali Convention Centre to bolster their legitimacy internally or externally,
infrastructure projects can serve to territorialize the authority of the regimes that
drive them forward. Yet as well as performing territorializing functions, such
infrastructures have consequences for property. Property and infrastructure exist
in a dynamic, symbiotic relationship: the latter often creates property value, while
property creates a need and demand for infrastructure. However, infrastructure
can also destroy property, and vice versa. Governing regimes often seek to use
infrastructure to create the kinds of property that generate value for the constituents, supporters, and finance that matter most to them—with other forms of
property and infrastructure often sacrificed in the process.

If this amounts to a 'top-down' perspective on the evolution of urban property, we also need to pay due attention to how property evolves from the ground
up, through the practices of urban-dwellers with highly variable amounts of capital, space, and time to invest and build. These practices exist in parallel with
big infrastructure development and government-sponsored urban visions, though
sometimes intersect or collide with them. Whether responding to new infrastructural opportunities or compensating for the lack of them, the creation and
extraction of value in the economy through real estate is proceeding apace across
East Africa's urban areas. This trend is exacerbated by the severe challenges of
attracting investment into manufacturing industry under the conditions of late
urbanization in the region. Yet despite increasing evidence that real estate is pivotal
to economic growth in these contexts, the varying ways that property investment
and development take place East Africa remain under-researched.

This chapter explores the phenomenon of urban property in cities where the
real estate sector has been built over recent decades out of the ashes of protracted
conflict, capital flight, and—in the Ethiopian case—communism. However, in
contrast to economies in which real estate investment is now highly 'financial-
ized', much of this private capital comes not through formal financial channels and
multinational investors but from domestic and diaspora elites, often channelled
in opaque ways. The following section explores the contours of the urban property sector in each city under the political and economic regimes of the EPRDF,

Politics and the Urban Frontier. Tom Goodfellow, Oxford University Press. © Tom Goodfellow (2022).
DOI: 10.1093/oso/9780198853107.003.0006

NRM, and RPF. It then specifically explores some of the incentives and constraints that lead to real estate investment absorbing a substantial amount of domestic and diasporic urban investment. Following this I explore the lineaments of the urban 'propertyscape' in each of the cities, considering what kinds of things tend to get built and how this relates to land regimes and the politics of regulation. I then shift from real estate to a focus on mass housing, examining the evolution and key features of Ethiopia's celebrated condominium housing programme before considering how and why attempts to provide mass housing have either failed to emerge or delivered very little in Kampala and Kigali. The chapter then offers a comparative analysis of the propertyscapes in these cities, and how these are explicable in relation to the distribution of power, pursuit of social legitimacy, and modalities of political informality.

6.1 Real estate out of the ashes

As the NRM, EPRDF, and RPF consolidated their grip on power in Uganda, Ethiopia, and Rwanda, both capital and people poured in. Those with sufficient financial resources sought to establish themselves permanently in urban space as value gradually accreted back to cities devastated by war, genocide, and revolutionary upheaval. While the new regimes in power initially devoted most of their policy energies elsewhere, as described in Chapter 5, the cities began to transform under their feet. However, the evolution of property development differed significantly in the three capital cities.

Earlier chapters have described how Kigali's growth rates exploded in the late 1990s as successive waves of returnees arrived in the city. As a consequence, a new generation of (often foreign-born) Rwandans was increasingly interested in owning their own homes, and new areas of the city were opened up through the infrastructure drive. At this time, however, there was virtually nothing by way of a property development sector; the only agencies engaging in real estate development at scale by 2005 were one state-owned enterprise and the Rwanda Social Security Board.[1] The virtual non-existence of the real estate sector is underlined by the comment of one land administrator at the end of the 2000s, who in discussing the issue of expropriation of property noted that 'the law provides that you hire a valuer, but they aren't there to hire, really.'[2]

For the most part, houses were developed by individuals who contracted small building firms. This included a significant number of 'high-end' residential properties, financed by elites, which were usually built to be rented out. In the context of heightened international donor and NGO presence, there was by the mid-2000s a

---

[1] Various interviews, Kigali, 2014.
[2] Interview with land official, 3 December 2009.

booming rental real estate market largely driven by international personnel. Much of this was in the 'new areas' of the city in the north and north-east urban periphery. While the city authority was still weak in terms of its capacity to fully control and regulate this growth, the relatively early commitment to ordered forms of urban development, considered so central to the RPF's vision of a 'clean slate' in post-genocide Kigali, meant that there was an unusually concerted effort to do so (Goodfellow 2013a).

In contrast, Addis Ababa's experience of imperial (rather than European colonial) rule prior to 1974 bestowed a unique legacy, as noted in Chapter 3. The property market that operated under the emperors, producing Addis Ababa's patchwork landscape of grand houses interspersed with wattle-and-daub huts, was effectively terminated when the Derg took power and nationalized all land and extra houses. When the EPRDF overthrew the Derg in 1991, as the state retained land ownership there was no formal property market to speak of. In the 2000s, however, this began to change as economic growth accelerated and homeownership became a central government objective. As the EPRDF developed its land-leasing policy, private property developers came to play an increasingly important role. In the early 2000s, loans were made available for the purpose of real estate development, as was cheap land.[3]

Meanwhile, as the focal city for the African Union and other international agencies, Addis Ababa's international community grew to sizeable proportions, necessitating both office space in central areas and higher-end housing in the new suburbs. Forms of socio-economic segregation thus began to emerge which were new in Ethiopian history. In terms of the actors engaging in property development, the role of the diaspora has been crucial; Ethiopia's diaspora numbers an estimated 1.5–2 million people (mostly living in the United States), who provide an estimated gross annual income of US$20 billion to the country (Lefort 2015: 368). After the 2008 financial crisis, diaspora Ethiopians were even more likely to invest in property development 'back home' in Addis Ababa.[4]

The development of a real estate sector in Kampala has had somewhat longer to evolve, and Uganda's long civil war did not destroy the foundations of this sector to the same extent as Ethiopia's socialist revolution or Rwanda's economic decapitation through genocide and the flight of domestic elites. Valuers were easier to come by and property development firms were numerous by the 2000s. However, the rapid development of real estate 'hotspots' took place long before the NRM's pivot towards urban policy in the 2010s, at a time when urban planning was especially under-resourced and land-use regulation chronically under-valued by the government. This, combined with the widespread private land ownership bestowed by Buganda's history, provided a larger window of time in which the

---

[3] Property developer, interviewed 30 September 2014.
[4] Construction firm representative, interviewed 29 September 2014.

wealthier members of society could engage in a virtual free-for-all in terms of property development. Whether on *mailo* land, Buganda Kingdom land or public land
sold off or leased out by the city council (often illicitly), the city's planners found
themselves unable to exert any effective development control whatsoever in many
parts of the city.

One area that rapidly became a residential real estate hotspot in the absence
of any effective planning was Muyenga, a wealthy neighbourhood that became
known as the 'rich man's slum'. Desirable in part due to its views over the city and
lake, Muyenga Hill was a spot favoured by the elite after 1986, when rapid and
unplanned real estate development took off as the wealthy capitalized on the newfound security and economic growth. The rush to divide and develop real estate
in Muyenga led to grand houses that could barely be reached by road, some of the
roads having been built over and the remainder being narrow, zig-zagging and
erratic.[5] If there is one feature that characterizes property development in postcolonial Kampala it is the sheer extent of its unplanned nature across the entire
socio-economic spectrum. In 2010, around 50 per cent of the buildings in central
Kampala were in breach of regulations, with the figure likely to be significantly
higher in the suburbs.[6] The situation was so alarming by the mid-2000s that the
Ministry of Local Government set up a Commission of Inquiry into the sale, purchase, and leasing of land by Kampala City Council. The resulting document was
a highly political one, given the context of the central government's growing ani-
mosity towards the opposition run Council; yet claims such as the following were
affirmed rather than denied by actors involved in planning at the city level:[7]

> The emerging picture is shocking. The power to change and alter land use has
> been grossly abused by officials who wantonly approve structures to be built
> over, or close to, sewerage lines, road reserves, wetlands, high voltage power lines,
> recreation grounds, and traffic islands meant for road safety. The scramble for the
> remaining open spaces is similar to the gold rush and Wild West in the United
> States of America, and the unscrupulous methods used are no different.
>
> (MoLG 2006)

When thinking about trajectories of property development in the three cities, it is
clear that the mainstream literature on property development does not travel very
well, being rooted in global North contexts and based on assumptions about the
availability of information on real estate values and transactions (see, for example,
Archer & Ling 1997). In late urbanizing countries with nascent real estate sectors,
most property transactions are unregistered and construction is often informal
(Kombe 2005; Kusiluka, 2012; Mercer 2017). The idea that agents with clear-cut
roles such as landowner, speculator, investor, developer, and valuer work through

---

[5] Interview with land official, Kampala, 20 January 2010.
[6] Interview with building inspector, Kampala, 19 January 2010.
[7] See Goodfellow (2013a) for a fuller discussion of these dynamics in the mid/late 2000s.

established and formalized systems of interaction is misleading in these contexts, where such roles are often much less clear-cut and property relationships characterized by brokerage embedded in social relations and networks (Nkurunziza 2008; Obeng-Odoom 2015). In Kampala for example, an estimated 80 per cent of land transactions involve informal brokers, even where formal estate agents were involved. These actors build up the knowledge and contacts to be able to sabotage property transactions that exclude them, and the blurring of the line between property surveyors and informal brokers creates further obstacles to operating outside this system.[8]

The sphere of urban property development is thus guided by a different range of institutions and 'place entrepreneurs' (Molotch 1993) in contexts where the urban institutional environment is so highly informalized (Simone 2004b; Roy 2011; Kusiluka 2012; Obeng-Odoom 2015). Urban fortunes everywhere are crucially affected by government regulations and institutions (Logan & Molotch 2007) but in low-income, late-urbanizing countries with relatively weak state implementation capabilities, it may not be the formal regulations themselves but the very fact that they are weak and compromised that most shapes the investment environment. A lack of effective systems for land value capture and property taxation is crucial here (Fjeldstad et al. 2017; Goodfellow 2015a). Investors can realize substantial profits 'in places that have weak or non-existent state requirements for developers to contribute to infrastructure costs or to share in the land value increases resulting from real estate development'. (Palmer & Berrisford 2015: 5). To understand why investment is concentrating so intensely on urban real estate in East African cities, but also why this takes different forms in each case, we therefore need to pay close attention to the informal as well as formal incentive structures that affect investment in property.

Incentives and constraints in the emergent real estate industry

A comparative examination of Kigali and Addis Ababa is particularly revealing in terms of how resources are being drawn into the 'secondary circuit' despite very different land regimes, policies, and official incentives. In the former, a whole range of incentives such as tax breaks, one-stop-shop investor services, and subsidized land were put in place to deliberately stimulate investment in the sector,[9] which was seen as part of the broader services-led vision. A range of mortgages with much longer terms than were ever previously offered was also available by the mid-2010s, with one bank even offering 100 per cent (deposit-free) finance for

---

[8] Discussion with Ugandan land experts, Kampala, 10 May 2018.
[9] See Goodfellow (2017a) for a full discussion.

people to build on their land.[10] These measures were also complemented by strong informal incentives, including the virtual absence of property taxation (Goodfellow 2015a; 2017b). Alongside these various measures to stimulate the sector, the government has been directly involved in real estate development through the Rwanda Social Security Board (RSSB), which has a strategic aim of investing 25 per cent of its funds in property. For the most part, this has been extremely high-end. Most striking of all is the 'Vision City' project (reputedly the largest real estate project in East Africa), involving five hundred variable-sized units, none of which can be considered anything but luxurious in the Rwandan context. The most expensive were initially priced at $560,000, with some slightly more modest ones at $370,000. The project, which builds on some smaller RSSB-funded real estate projects ostensibly aimed at 'middle-income' groups but only affordable to the rich, was viewed with almost universal scepticism by all non-RSSB stakeholders consulted.[11] For the RPF-led government, however, Vision City is intended as a landmark 'to provide an inspiration, a model to stimulate more high-quality real estate investment'.[12]

In marked contrast, until the mid-late 2010s there were no formal incentives for real estate developers in Ethiopia, with loans of any kind very hard to come by. Indeed, the government was suspicious of service sectors generally, viewing them as having rent-seeking rather than value-creating tendencies.[13] Yet despite the more hostile formal institutional environment, as in Kigali there are numerous powerful informal incentives to invest in property. High rates of inflation, the lack of a stock market to invest in, an absence of effective taxation of buildings (despite often substantial land lease payments) are all notable factors (Goodfellow 2017b). On top of this-and contrasting with Kigali-despite measures to prevent land speculation, the planning and construction regulations themselves are relatively lax. Building permits are required, but the system of occupation permits (whereby your construction has to be approved for use after being constructed) is barely functional,[14] removing a further barrier to the use of property as a relatively easy source of economic returns.

While there were therefore a range of incentives to invest in property rather than other sectors, there were also powerful constraints to property development in both cases, many of which feature in Uganda as well, and landlocked countries in the region more generally. In Rwanda for example, materials are very expensive, with 60 per cent imported from abroad. Moreover, despite the growing mortgage market, access to finance is highly constrained as interest rates are so high. One

---

[10] Interview with major international bank representative, 20 January 2015.
[11] Interviews with construction-sector, donor, government and civil society representatives, 2014–2015.
[12] Interview with RSSB representative, 3 June 2014.
[13] Interview, 2 October 2016.
[14] Interview, 26 September 2014.

developer described having 'stacks of land all around Kigali' but not being able to use much of it due to the prohibitive 18–20 per cent interest rates.[15] The huge costs faced by developers mean that they expect very high profit margins; at least 20–40 per cent.[16] Ironically, the costs of construction further push people towards the high end of the market, where serious profits are most likely. As one architect observed, 'the only way you can battle the huge cost of finance is to build more expensively.'[17] Meanwhile, the fact that 81 per cent of the population do not earn enough to be able to access any kind of mortgage means there is no effective demand from low and middle-income groups to incentivize developers to build for them. The constraints to property development and the incentives to construct high-end properties are thus two sides of the same coin.

In Ethiopia, meanwhile, a state-controlled banking system prior to 2018 made real estate finance extremely scarce, with state-owned banks prioritizing loans for national development priorities, such as the textile and leather industries, as well as having to use a proportion of their capital to help finance the Grand Ethiopian Renaissance Dam.[18] Further constraining property development is the fact that land is extremely expensive, as the government releases limited amounts of land for leasehold sale, and for commercial projects this is mostly allocated through competitive bidding since 2011. Given these constraints, the majority of property development came either in the form of mega-investments by investors with sufficient upfront cash (including the state itself), or incremental building by individuals and organizations as they acquire money gradually.[19] The diaspora could fall into either category. The incentive for them to invest in property was augmented by the fact that they were prohibited from investing in key sectors exclusively reserved for domestic Ethiopians: insurance, banking, telecommunications, media, and air transport services. Diaspora are known to focus their investments in the service sector, and particularly in the construction of hotels, office blocks, and other forms of real estate.[20] Foreign investors, meanwhile, were for a significant period of time under the EPRDF only allowed to invest in real estate as part of a joint venture with Ethiopians, as in the case of the Chinese-financed apartment complex in Figure 6.1.

This comparison and the following discussion of propertyscapes illustrate that under conditions of late urbanization, incentives for investment to gravitate towards high-end real estate are substantial *regardless* of concerted efforts to channel capital elsewhere (which were marked in Ethiopia but virtually non-existent

---

[15] Interview, 21 January 2015.
[16] Interview, 8 June 2014.
[17] Interview, 5 June 2014.
[18] Interview, 3 October 2014.
[19] See Van Noorloos et al. (2020) for a discussion of incremental housing development and the factors driving and constraining it in the global South generally.
[20] Interview with Ethiopian investment official, 1 October 2014.

Figure 6.1 Poli Lotus International Centre, Addis Ababa
Photograph © Tom Goodfellow.

in Rwanda and Uganda through much of the 2010s). However, variable systems of land tenure and divergent regulatory regimes—linked to fundamentally different distributions of power—mean that the sucking of resources into real estate is generating distinct patterns of urban property development and producing highly differentiated 'propertyscapes' across the three cities. It is to these that we now turn.

6.2 East African propertyscapes: Landlords, bubbles, and skeletons

The fact that these countries are highly dependent on international aid, and that their capital cities play host to numerous international organizations as well second homes for diaspora, shapes patterns of demand for high-end properties. In Kigali, international personnel on inflated salaries combined with a welcoming attitude to property development and the infrastructural 'opening-up' of new areas of the city has had an explosive effect on certain kinds of property development (see Figure 6.2). Rentals dominate the business of the small number of formal estate agents, with few if any houses available to rent below $500 per month in 2015—and this would only obtain a cheap apartment far from the city centre. More commonly, houses in 'new' areas of the city rent for around $2,500, though as much as $4,000 was 'typical' for someone working for the EU or a foreign embassy in 2014.[21] Very top-end properties were on the market for $8,000–$12,000

---

[21] Interview, 6 June 2014.

Figure 6.2 High-end residential property under development, Kigali.
Photograph © Tom Goodfellow.

per month. Clearly, in a country with an annual GDP per capita in current USD of $697,[22] 'not many Rwandese are renting those houses at those prices!'[23]

Given the limitations of both property tax and rental income tax—which from 2002 was decentralized to local authorities that severely lacked the capacity collect it (Goodfellow 2012)—owners of these properties could earn substantial untaxed incomes from such properties, further incentivizing the construction of houses at the top end of the market. Thus 'all firms are fighting for 20 per cent of the market' when 80 per cent of the demand is for low-income housing.[24] By 2013, Rwanda was the most unequal country in East Africa, and among the top 15 per cent most unequal countries in the world by Gini index.[25] It seems beyond doubt that rents from property have played a role in this. The houses financed by RSSB—the pension fund—were primarily bought by people who already owned other houses and were just pursuing rental income, even according to RSSB representatives themselves.[26] By 2014, concerns about an oversupply of office space, too many hotels,

---

[22] World Bank (2015) estimate, available at: http://data.worldbank.org/indicator/NY.GDP.PCAP.CD, accessed 27 July 2016.

[23] Interview, 3 June 2014.

[24] Interview, 21 January 2015.

[25] United Nations Development Programme data, available at: http://hdr.undp.org/en/content/income-gini-coefficient. The Gini Index is admittedly a blunt instrument, as are most indices of inequality, many of which are not available for all countries.

[26] Interview, 3 June 2014.

and 'high-end' housing were growing. Claims were made that 'most office blocks are empty' and that despite the apparent scramble to build more, commercial areas are 'failing'.[27] By 2014, it was apparent that the bubble had already started to burst and rents were falling due to an oversupply of high-end housing, with many houses built for rental ending up on sale.[28]

Despite this, because the effective demand from the low-income urban majority is so constrained, developers continue to build at the high end in the hope of future rental and sale profits—and with little by way of tax disincentives to steer their investment decisions elsewhere. Moreover, while rents may have dipped, there is a floor below which property in these higher-end brackets generally does not fall, leaving prices far beyond the reach of the majority. A bubble economy serving a tiny fraction of the country's property needs, sustained by the circulation of international personnel and the growing wealth of a small economic elite, thus prevails in Kigali. The one major institutional investor, RSSB, has continued to build houses that are clearly unaffordable even to the people who pay into its coffers, such as relatively well-off civil servants. The disconnect is striking: 'Am I buying a house in New York?', joked one such civil servant about the prices.[29] RSSB representatives suggest the houses are aimed at the diaspora, but some Rwandans who have lived among the diaspora are sceptical; 'we don't have a diaspora that rich! They don't know who our diaspora are.'[30]

Meanwhile, the demand for commercial property has remained so tenuous that the government has periodically forced organizations to move into new commercial properties. In 2017, with many offices in flagship commercial buildings in the city centre still empty several years after completion, the government issued a three-month ultimatum to a number of businesses and non-profit organizations around the city a move into these premises.[31] The desire to 'go large' in the property sector despite limited demand echoes the dynamics discussed in relation to MICE and related infrastructure in Chapter 5, and is further epitomized by the size of the plots carved out in 'CBD1'—the area envisaged as the new CBD under the Master Plan, which was referred to several times in the 'Impressions' opening this book. These large, expensive plots proved extremely difficult to sell, as evidenced by the subsequent slashing of prices (see Figure 6.3). The government also compelled people in certain areas of the city to merge their plots in order to meet the minimum plot sizes in the masterplan.[32]

In stark contrast to Kigali, those involved in real estate in Addis believe that there is an enormous amount of unmet demand for residential housing even at

[27] Interview, 19 January 2015; Interview, 3 June 2014.
[28] Interviews, 3 June 2014; 5 June 2014; 6 June 2014.
[29] Interview, 4 June 2014.
[30] Interview, 5 June 2014.
[31] 'Businesses are being forced to move into designated properties', *The Economist*, 2 March 2017.
[32] Interview with senior construction-sector representative, 15 January 2015.

Figure 6.3 RSSB marketing for expropriated city-centre plots in CBD1

Photograph © Tom Goodfellow.

the high end, due to the extreme constraints on real estate discussed above. In 2014, one claimed there was unmet demand for fifty thousand housing units in the $300,000–$400,000 range. All of the real estate companies together were by this time only building an estimated 1,000–1,500 per year, so this demand was nowhere near being met.[33] The diaspora undoubtedly do play a much more central critical role in Addis. One developer affirmed that '75 per cent of our buyers are Ethiopians living in foreign countries, usually the US'.[34] The ongoing demand for high-end residential property is thus much higher than Kigali both because there is a much larger and often wealthier long-term diaspora looking to own homes in the city (as second homes or to rent out), and because the squeeze on developers means that supply is more constrained.

Consequently, relative to other sectors, real estate is extremely profitable for those who have the finance to engage in development in Addis. It is perfectly feasible to make 100 per cent profit on the construction and sale of a house.[35] Finished houses can also command twice or more the price of similar houses sold 'off plan' (i.e. sold prior to construction), due to scepticism about the latter actually finding finance and materializing.[36] Undersupply is such that the first houses built by Ayat Real Estate around the turn of the millennium, which at the time sold for ETB 187,000, were in 2014 being sold on for ETB 4m, with no improvement—in other words there was a *twentyfold* 'unearned increment' in under fifteen years.[37] Other developers said that houses that sold for ETB 3m in 2009 were worth 12m in 2014.[38] Those who purchase houses from developers and sell them on relatively soon are thus able to make enormous profits.

Another striking feature of Addis Ababa's emerging landscape is the extent of commercial real estate development, and in particular the mushrooming of high-rise towers. The fact that construction is second only to government as an employer in Addis Ababa cannot be adequately grasped without considering the scale of commercial property development being undertaken in the city, alongside the housing programme discussed later. Opinions differ on the actual extent of demand for commercial property. The presence of a large number of international organizations in a city that fulfils the role of the diplomatic 'capital of Africa' is clearly significant in accounting for the explosion of commercial development. Yet there is also speculation on the perceived potential for future profits in commercial real estate, and again the lack of any tax disincentive for unused or under-utilized commercial structures is important to consider. Those with the resources to acquire auctioned plots in the city are often keen to 'gamble on the strong demand for office and commercial space', (Duroyaume 2015: 405) regardless of how certain the continued growth of this demand may be.

For diaspora, who until the collapse of the EPRDF in 2019 were prohibited from investing in several key sectors open to other Ethiopians, building office or retail space for rent has been especially appealing. Having foreign nationality and

---

[33] Interview, 29 September 2014.
[34] Interview, 30 September 2014.
[35] Interviews, September–October 2014.
[36] Interview, 29 September 2014.
[37] Interview, 3 October 2014.
[38] Interview, 30 September 2014.

access to international banks, this group has much easier access to finance than other Ethiopians. As Ethiopia turned towards a more market-driven growth model in the 2000s, the promotion of investment by diaspora was central to EPRDF strategy (Chacko & Gebre 2017). Given the diaspora were often hostile to the ruling EPRDF and particularly the TPLF, which many considered authoritarian and a vehicle of ethnic favouritism, property was an important way of ensuring that a group with substantial associational power would not rock the boat. Thus, despite a general antipathy towards real estate investment at the official level, the widespread opportunity to engage in real estate ventures relatively unhindered by taxation helped to keep potentially disruptive diaspora groups content (Goodfellow 2017b). An implicit deal was offered by the government to these 'new entrepreneurs'—'stop politicking and we'll help you get rich' (Lefort 2015: 365).

While there were numerous formal government incentives to invest in industry and none for real estate, evidence clearly shows that most diaspora with resources to invest have channelled these into property. A massive 75 per cent of all investment by diaspora in the period from March 1994 to November 2017 was in real estate and related services. The amount invested in this sector was over *eleven times* more than that invested by diaspora in both manufacturing and agriculture. Two thirds of all diaspora investment was located in Addis Ababa, with much of the remainder being in Oromia.[39] Estimates of how much money has been invested by diaspora into real estate in the last few years range from US$1bn to over $3bn (Lefort 2015: 368). Diaspora are not the only investors of relevance here: the centrality of property development to the city's economy is also starkly illustrated by the fact that 35 per cent of all *domestic* investment projects in Ethiopia in the period between January 1992 and November 2017 were also in real estate and related sectors, a significantly larger number than in any other sector.[40]

To understand the evolution of property development in Addis Ababa over time, and particularly the trend towards high-rise commercial developments, requires considering the successive changes to the land-leasing system discussed in Chapter 3, and the regulatory frameworks around construction. The 2002 revision of the urban land law made it much easier to acquire land at low prices, which stimulated a surge of land speculation, as well as creating the shoots of a construction boom in real estate among people who could battle the financial and regulatory

---

[39] Figures acquired from the Ethiopian Investment Commission, November 2017. This data is updated from that provided in Goodfellow (2017a). Forty-five per cent of all diaspora investment was from diaspora of US or dual US/Ethiopian nationality, with the majority of the remainder coming from Sweden, Canada, and the United kingdom.

[40] Figures acquired from the Ethiopian Investment Commission, November 2017. The actual percentage of domestic resources invested in real estate and related services (as opposed to the percentage of the total number of projects) was significantly lower at 15 per cent, though this is likely to reflect the weight of a smaller number of large strategic investments in agriculture and manufacturing.

obstacles and start developing property.[41] However, the 2011 revision to the law—designed to tighten the system and curtail speculation—led to land prices shooting up by subjecting many leases to auctioning, which incentivized building *upwards* as high as possible to maximize the profitability of a given plot.

A significant degree of informality characterizes such property investments, and the channels through which resources travel to finance the escalating landscape are difficult to establish. As one source noted, 'the question we are all asking is: where is all the money for construction coming from?'[42] One study by a local research organization reportedly showed that just 10–15 per cent of the money ploughed into construction in a five-year period had passed through banks.[43] What is clear is that the current incentive structure, leads to a very large number of *incomplete* structures. This is partly because of the perceived appeal of real estate as a source of profit for anyone able to get involved, even those without the expertise or capacity to finish the job. These are often not 'property developers' in the sense assumed in the conventional real estate literature. One construction engineer noted that many people in other businesses, with no knowledge whatsoever of the sector, effectively become entrepreneurs in unfinished places: they 'see that it's so lucrative so try to invest their profits in real estate. When they run out of funds they re-invest what they have in their [other] business, hoping to make more profit to finish the job, but this rarely happens.'[44]

Further feeding partial construction are the rules regarding how much must be built on a plot of land before title deeds can be transferred, which creates incentives to part-construct buildings so the land is saleable.[45] In reality of course, many plots exchange hands without the requisite percentage of construction having been done, through systems of informal brokerage and exchange. However, the new 'owner' remains insecure until they have undertaken sufficient construction to be able to officially acquire the deed.[46] This regulatory framework combines with the cost of land and lack of savings and investment opportunities to encourage people to channel resources into buildings, even if they cannot be finished when easy finance runs out. The combination of incentives and constraints in place is thus producing 'skeleton cityscapes' of speculative and unfinished construction.[47]

In Uganda, too, research has shown that 'instead of depositing money in bank accounts or investing in instruments such as shares and bonds, most individuals invest in physical structures, such as land and buildings' (Kangave et al. 2016). The

---

[41] Interview with land and property specialist, 1 July 2019.
[42] Interview, 24 September 2014.
[43] Interview, 24 September 2014.
[44] Interview, 29 September 2014.
[45] See Goodfellow (2017a) for a fuller discussion of these regulations.
[46] Interview, 30 September 2014.
[47] These dynamics took a new turn from 2018 after Abiy Ahmed became Prime Minister, with a new focus on an aesthetic of beautification and mega-real estate projects often financed with capital from the Gulf (Terrefe 2020).

situation in Kampala differs from the other two cities however, both due to legacies of private land ownership and weaker government controls over land, as well as the relative absence of specific visions for urban development. If Kigali's property boom has been shaped by an active desire to build a high-end services economy, and Addis' scaffolded towers produced (ironically) in part by efforts to limit land speculation and property development, the evolution of real estate in Kampala has been more haphazard. As noted above, it has been characterized by an urban land value bonanza in which planning officials attempting to exert control are regularly prohibited from entering development sites by the armed guards of the private developers.[48]

Kampala's property development also echoes the more piecemeal, plot-by-plot forms of self-build characteristic of cities across the continent (Sawyer 2014; Karaman et al. 2020). Given limitations on who can access loans in many contexts (depending on, for example, formal employment) and the high rates of interest, self-building is widely preferred among middle classes across Africa—not just in slum areas as often assumed (Gough & Yankson 2011; Mercer 2017; Amoako & Boamah 2017; Gastrow 2020). While the situation in Kigali has involved a substantial amount of building for profit at the very high end of the market, in many cities there is more of a market spread in the self-build sector due to larger pool of people with resources to invest in building for themselves and for different segments of the market, as well as greater tolerance for sprawl. In Kampala this has combined with spectacularly lax regulatory regimes, as exemplified by the example of Muyenga.

The specifics of land tenure in Buganda also play an important role, codified in that fateful 1900 Act and revised multiple times, but with the persistence of the deeply entrenched institution of *mailo* (see Chapter 3) still playing a pivotal role. The multiple overlapping land rights hardwired into this land tenure system differ completely from anything in contemporary Kigali or Addis Ababa. The combination of the freehold rights of *mailo* landowners themselves, and the relative strength of *kibanja* rights held by tenants living on *mailo* land, is unique within the region and underscores both the diffuse distribution of associational power and the lack of the state's infrastructural reach. After the Land (Amendment) Act of 2010, it was even harder than previously for *mailo* landlords to evict tenants, and the Act also created major delays in selling land by allowing *kibanja* holders right of first refusal to amass funds to try and purchase it.[49] Moreover, there are often three key stakeholders on a given plot: the land owner, the *kibanja* holders who own structures on the land, and the tenants in those structures. This further complicates issues of eviction and compensation.[50] The 2010 Amendment Act is

---

[48] Interview with former chief town planner, Kampala, 11 February 2009.
[49] Interview with Baganda landholders, Kampala, 6 May 2018.
[50] Discussion with Ugandan land experts, Kampala, 10 May 2018.

believed to have heightened already intense land disputes, with landlord–tenant deadlock and rising violence a notable feature.[51]

The fact that much *mailo* land is not usable by its owners provokes a range of attempts to extract value from it—including through exploiting opportunities for government compensation, as observed in Chapter 5—as well as fuelling the search for more land by people who wish to acquire plots they can more easily develop. In Kiganda culture (i.e. the culture of the Baganda people), land inheritance usually skips a generation, on the basis that the generation directly below the landowner will be able to live on that land and therefore not need the inheritance.[52] This principle exists in tension with contemporary desires for property, fuelling further attempts to acquire and develop land around the city in an uncontrolled sprawl that has led to Kampala's metropolitan area seeping deep into the surrounding Wakiso District. As ongoing political and administrative struggles frustrate efforts to consolidate a Greater Kampala Metropolitan Area for planning purposes,[53] the city's metropolitan morphology is being enacted on the ground.

The dynamics explored in this section illustrate that while forms of incremental housing financing and development exist in all the cities examined here, with unfinished construction peppering the landscape, their manifestations are very different. The scale and number of high rise skeletons in Addis, the stark disparity between spacious villas and informal settlements (with little in between) in Kigali, and the expansive unregulated development in ever-sprawling Kampala present distinctive urban propertyscapes. In the midst of these is the question of where the majority of people, including the urban poor, actually manage to live given that much of what is produced by private developers in the formal sector remains completely out of their reach.

6.3 The politics of mass housing

The disparity between real estate development and the living conditions of most people, evident across many cities of the global South, is especially stark in the countries considered here. The cost of formally developed housing is far beyond the reach of average incomes: Ethiopia and Rwanda are two of the three countries in Africa where the *very cheapest* formally built house costs over 100 per cent of per capita GDP (the third being Malawi), with Uganda close behind in the 50 per cent–100 per cent category (UNECA 2017: 101). These countries are therefore extreme in terms of the lack of formally provided affordable housing, and consequently many or most of the city population live in various settlements characterized as

---

[51] Interview with lawyer, Kampala, 21 June 2018.
[52] Interview with Baganda landholder, Kampala, 6 May 2018.
[53] Various interviews, Kampala, May and June 2018, and November 2020.

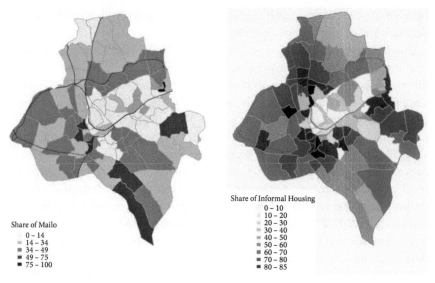

Share of Informal Housing
0 – 10
10 – 20
20 – 30
30 – 40
40 – 50
50 – 60
60 – 70
70 – 80
80 – 85

Share of Mailo
0 – 14
14 – 34
34 – 49
49 – 75
75 – 100

Figure 6.4 Proportion of *mailo* land and proportion of informal housing in different areas of Kampala

Source: Bird and Venables (2020).

'slums'.[54] However, the underlying political economy giving rise to and perpetuating these settlements is again very different in each case. In Kampala, slum areas overlap significantly with *mailo* land, much of which is located in areas outside the former colonial municipality of Kampala (Nuwagaba 2006). Figure 6.4 illustrates the extent of this overlap. Given the legacy of these areas as being beyond the remit of formal planning systems, Baganda landlords (including the kingdom itself, which owns significant chunks of land in the city) had often allowed as many tenants onto their land as possible in order to maximize profits (Bryceson 2008)— a trend which continued at even greater pace in the years of urban growth and relative prosperity under the NRM.

As discussed in Chapter 3, Rwanda lacks the same landlord–tenant relations, having never had tenure relations like those instituted by the 1900 Agreement. Instead, much urban land has been state-owned since 1976, with decades of tolerated development in an informal market layered onto this. Under the RPF however, the government has tried to formalize all plots through its Land Tenure

[54] In all three cases, the percentage of the urban population living in such conditions has declined substantially over the course of the century: between 2000 and 2018 it fell from 78 per cent to 42 per cent in Rwanda, 75 per cent to 48 per cent in Uganda, and 88 per cent to 64 per cent in Ethiopia. This reflects the broader trends in economic growth and development discussed in Chapter 4, but is also difficult to interpret, given varying definitions of 'slum', the fact that these are national rather than city-level statistics and also that large-scale slum clearances have occurred, in Kigali and Addis Ababa particularly. Data retrieved from https://data.unhabitat.org/, accessed 1 December 2020.

Regularization Programme, issuing leasehold titles (usually for just twenty years) to individual families. This process has been fraught with difficulty, not least since it was common for ownership of a plot in Kigali to be claimed by four different people, as well as there often being five or more houses on one plot.[55] City-dwellers' newfound status as leaseholders has offered minimal security in the face of a highly flexible definition of 'public interest' that has regularly been used by the government to clear large swathes of Kigali's land. Since 2007—the year the Conceptual Master Plan was published—the bulldozing of low-income areas in pursuit of a 'slum-free vision' has attracted mounting controversy (Goodfellow 2014b; Manirakiza 2014; Shearer 2017; Nikuze et al. 2019; 2020; Uwayezu & De Vries 2019). Recent efforts to address this through in-kind compensation rather than cash, in the form of resettlement housing on the fringes of the city, have already been criticized on the grounds that resettled communities have limited economic prospects and few resources with which to reconstitute a livelihood (Uwayezu & De Vries 2020b; Nikuze et al. 2020).

In Addis, meanwhile, slum areas involve a very different set of relations, with the majority of low-quality housing not being informal settlements per se but rather *kebele* houses still owned by the state, for which occupants pay a small amount in rent to the local government (see Chapter 3). Largely prohibited by law from making improvements to their own houses under the Derg's hardline communist regime, the conditions in most *kebele* housing became increasingly dilapidated and cramped over time, a situation that continued into the EPRDF period where initially urban housing remained very low on the list of priorities. Aside from a small amount of new rental housing, very little was built under the Derg. *Kebele* housing was progressively supplemented by informal settlements dotted around the city. With the need for mass housing increasingly glaring, in 2004 the EPRDF initiated its Grand Housing Programme, subsequently reimagined as the Integrated Housing Development Programme (IHDP)—one of the most ambitious state-led housing programmes in Africa, unparalleled in scale outside of South Africa. Moreover, as the government has pivoted towards large-scale city-centre renewal since around 2010, *kebele* and informal settlement residents have been evicted for major commercial ventures (as described in detail by Weldeghebrael (2019) and Kloosterboer (2019)), rendering the need for housing for lower-income groups even more pressing.

The Integrated Housing Development Programme in Addis Ababa

Nowhere is the relationship between infrastructure and the creation of property more starkly illustrated than in the case of Ethiopia's massive urban housing

---

[55] Interview with former district mayor, 15 December 2009.

programme—an initiative rooted partly in the pursuit of social legitimacy but which also demonstrates the 'vitality' of infrastructure in exerting its own influence on urban change. Unlike the real estate skeletons discussed above, the huge concrete frames of condominium blocks that have erupted across Addis Ababa are rapidly completed and populated, as the soaring demand for these units has established itself in the form of waiting lists of over a million people. The initial goals of the programme were to construct 400,000 condominium units, create 200,000 jobs, and promote the development of 10,000 micro- and small enterprises (MSEs), enhancing the capacity of the construction sector as well as regenerating inner-city areas and promoting home-ownership for low-income households (UN-HABITAT 2011; Kassahun and Bishu 2018). By late 2019, over 175,000 had been built in Addis Ababa with 132,000 more under construction (Larsen et al. 2019), and a rate of production of around 30,000 units per year.[56] The programme delivers houses via a lottery scheme, and offers three different modalities known as 10/90, 20/80, and 40/60. The first figure in each of these pairings represents the percentage down payment in each case, with the remainder being the amount given to recipients as a loan from the Commercial Bank of Ethiopia that needs to be paid off in instalments over time. The interest for these loans was initially set at 8.5 per cent. Though significantly lower than commercially available rates, this amounts to a substantial burden of debt for households paying off the loan over extended periods.

There is a growing literature on the design, implementation, and relative successes and failures of the IHDP, and there is no space to go into detail on these critiques here.[57] However, this programme has been one of the most unique and transformational aspects of Addis Ababa's development since the mid-2000s, and the politics driving it and generated by it are thus of special comparative significance. Particularly interesting is how the programme itself changed over time, with two salient aspects of this change exerting potentially long-term impacts on the city: the shift from condominiums largely concentrated in the city centre to their rolling out on a massive scale in the city's peripheries (see Figure 6.5), and the shift towards housing the middle classes rather than the poor—both deliberately and unintentionally.

The shift to the peripheries dovetailed with the government's broader focus on urban infrastructure development alongside city-centre renewal, with the broad aim being to renovate the city centre as a major commercial hub and the 'Diplomatic Capital of Africa' (Kloosterboer 2019; Weldeghebrael 2019; 2020) while dispersing people living in cramped central *kebele* housing to new peripheries through an intensifying programme of evictions (Di Nunzio 2022). Thus while

[56] Interview with government adviser, 24 November 2017.
[57] See, for example, UN-HABITAT (2011); Ejigu (2012; 2015); Kassahun and Bishu (2018); Keller & Mukudi-Omwami (2017); Planel & Bridonneau (2017); Tiumelissan & Pankhurst (2013).

Figure 6.5 A peripheral condominium settlement from the air, Addis Ababa
Photograph © Tom Goodfellow.

the first condominium developments under IHDP were in relatively central parts of the city such as Lideta, in the 2010s there was a decisive centrifugal drive outwards to areas framed as 'transition zones'. Locational choices for condominium settlements were to a large extent based on where sufficient land could be acquired at a low enough cost, with relatively sparse populations: essentially the path of least resistance.[58] Even so, dealing with the complexity of land interests in the city's liminal peri-urban zones, combined with the opaque process of making land available for large projects, has produced a haphazard pattern in which the pattern of condominium development often lacks a clear spatial rationale. In some cases, such as the major developments in Tulu Dimtu and, most recently Koye Feche—the largest single condominium site with an astonishing sixty thousand housing units—there is an attempt to link these sites to industrial zones and corridors. However, ironically given the 'integrated' rationale of the housing programme, the attempt to integrate broader spatial and socio-economic considerations into the planning of the condominium settlements came relatively late in the process—in reality, only a few years before the programme started winding down in 2018.[59]

---

[58] Interview with city planning official, 1 December 2017.
[59] This was affirmed by multiple government sources interviewed in 2017 and 2018.

By way of exemplifying the nature and scale of just one peripheral condominium site and its production process, consider these figures from Yeka Abado,
a neighbourhood in the city's north-eastern periphery. In this area 18,169 housing units were developed, housing over 100,000 people in 746 separate housing
blocks across 250 hectares, the majority of which are five storeys high. Two hundred and eight-seven separate contractors were involved in construction, though if
all activities including infrastructure and material supplies are included, a total of
668 micro and small enterprises played a role, employing around twelve thousand
people.[60] This particular site, while one of the larger ones, was less than a third of
the size of Koye Feche. As remarkable as the scale itself is the fact that this area—
while initially selected for its peripheral nature and land availability—no longer
feels peripheral and is a bustling residential and services hub, as well as a highly
desired neighbourhood compared with some others.

When considering how the IHDP went from being a primarily pro-poor intervention to something much more about housing the middle classes, it is important
to note both intended and unintended dimensions of this. As Nallet (2015) Planel
& Bridonneau (2017) point out, the IHDP has to some extent been *consciously*
about the creation of an urban middle class. However, it is also characterized by
two very different ideological registers: an impetus to reduce poverty, rooted in
the EPRDF's developmental mindset and the broader communist legacy, and a
more market-oriented desire to create a property-owning class from whom the
regime could draw enhanced urban social legitimacy. These dual motives are captured in the structuring of the condominium programme, with houses in the 20/80
scheme initially intended for poorer groups and 10/90 ones for the very poorest and displaced, while the 40/60 programme which accelerated after 2013 was
always intended for the middle classes. Yet the fact that the programme as a whole
has increasingly become a middle class one is also related to the real estate dynamics described above; the expense of properties by private developers rapidly priced
out all but the wealthiest in society, falling well short of growing middle class
demand.

In reality the vast majority of the condominiums—which are of the 20/80 type—
have ended up housing groups that could be defined as middle class, or certainly
middle income. This reflects the lack of other middle-class housing production,
the need to have sufficient disposable income to save enough to qualify for the
programme, and the fact that poorer people who won houses under the lottery
scheme (or through relocation schemes) often cannot afford the repayments and
end up renting out the units, or simply prefer to rent out the units to make a profit.
Illegal resales also proceeded apace, despite the fact that resale within the first
five years was prohibited to prevent prices from escalating and ensure that houses

---

[60] Information gathered from the local IHDP office by Dr. Meseret Kassahun, a research collabora-
tor, on 28 January 2018.

allocated to poorer groups remained in their possession.[61] Ultimately, by tying the housing programme to individual forced savings, the programme selected people on two contradictory economic criteria: their relative poverty and their ability to save substantial amounts each month. This helped 'to indirectly circumscribe a middle class of condominium residents' (Planel & Bridonneau 2017: 29). In this sense, if the light rail was a project designed for the middle classes but unexpectedly tilted towards the poor, the condominium programme started as a pro-poor intervention but veered in the other direction.

Even if some kind of class formation has therefore been at work through the large-scale creation of property ownership and facilitation of property rents as an income source, the capacity of condominium dwellers to think and act *as* a class is still very uncertain (Planel & Bridonneau 2017: 32). In Marxist terms, both the condominium owners and tenants may be becoming classes in themselves, but are a long way from constituting a class *for* themselves. This is partly due to the newness of these assets and income streams, but also because of the extensive diversity within the condominium sites—particularly in terms of the relationship between owners and tenants. Tenants now generally constitute at least a third of condominium residents, and sometimes well over half.[62] Even within these two categories there is great diversity, not least due to the varying means by which people come to acquire an apartment; yet there has been rapidly growing sense that tenants and owners are living in different worlds.

The tenants are generally better off economically than the owners, because the most common reason owners rent out their units is that they cannot afford the monthly repayments. However, tenants are also associated with a lack of social cohesion in the settlements and associated problems such as crime. They often live there for fleeting periods and are viewed by owners as having limited interest in forming social ties and supporting community development.[63] Landlord–tenant relations are quite different from those in many cities across the world, in the sense that the unit owners—far from being the exploitative petty capitalists often associated with the private rental sector—are often lottery-winners and less well-off than their tenants, as well as being less socially and geographically mobile.

While the overall profile of occupants differed from initial pro-poor intentions, the programme has had other unanticipated impacts too, illustrating how a dual push to generate infrastructure and property on this scale can produce its own forces in the maelstrom of urban transformation. For example, the poor quality and incompleteness of much of the construction—often arising from the

---

[61] Research conducted for the Living the Urban Periphery project, 2017–2018.

[62] From a randomized sample of 400 condominium residents undertaken as part of our research in the Living the Urban Periphery project, in Tulu Dimtu 62 per cent were owners of their apartments (having won them in the lottery) while 38 per cent were renting. In Yeka Abado only 44 per cent were lottery winners, with 56 per cent being renters.

[63] Findings from qualitative interviews with condominium residents undertaken for the Living the Urban Periphery project, 2018.

sheer number of MSEs involved in any one site—has generated a huge market in repair and internal decor, with residents often paying almost the full price of their unit again on renovation and redecoration.[64] The ability to change how the IHDP works—for example to improve aspects of condominium design—is highly constrained: its integrated nature means that so many actors, processes, financial logics, and commodity chains are built into the system that attempting to adjust it is akin to turning round a juggernaut.[65] A range of practices have therefore evolved around the gaps and inefficiencies of the model. Meanwhile, alongside the formal job-creation scheme embedded in the programme there have also been more spontaneous forms of livelihood creation. Many residents describe how groups of male youth in particular congregate in shared spaces between blocks and spring into action when opportunities inevitably arise to earn a casual wage from issues such as helping people move house, dealing with deliveries, and attending to vehicle breakdowns.[66]

More generally, the nature, extent, and pace of many consequences of the programme—both positive and negative—were unanticipated. In many cases, peri-urban areas transformed into commercial hubs even more rapidly than expected; community-generated initiatives to transform public spaces within the sites took off, with the pooling of resources promoting block-level gardens and security provision;[67] and new forms of (often dysfunctional) social relations based on vertical living and the constant circulation of renters became increasingly normal (Ejigu 2015). As one representative of the Addis Ababa Housing Development Bureau noted, 'The transformation that took place wasn't predicted. Once the infrastructure began, no one anticipated how those areas could grow this fast.'[68]

The political outcomes remain uncertain. While many condominium owners are rendered vulnerable by loan repayments and interest, their professed gratitude to the state for enabling them to become property owners promotes a degree of political quiescence (Planel & Bridoneau 2017). It is notable that while the fear of urban uprising after the 2005 election was pronounced—to the extent that it arguably drove many of the investments discussed in this chapter and the previous one—in the upheavals that have shaken the country from 2014–2021, Addis has mostly been calm. This will be discussed further in Chapter 8, but it bears emphasis that the huge public investment in the city's infrastructure and housing appears to have succeeded in doing much of the political work that was needed *within* the city—even if not in the ways initially intended. As one long-term advisor to the Ethiopian government commented, the programme was never about

[64] Interviews with condominium residents, March 2018.
[65] Interview with housing expert, Addis Ababa, 29 November 2017.
[66] Findings from qualitative interviews with condominium residents undertaken for the Living the Urban Periphery project, 2018.
[67] Interviews with condominium residents, June 2019.
[68] Interview with housing development bureau representative, conducted by Meseret Kassahun for 'Living the Urban Periphery' project, 18 July 2018.

creating a carefully thought-through, sustainable housing model. No amount of criticism of the design failures, mis-targeting, creation of household debt, or negative spatial consequences changes the fact that it was intended to deliver certain political benefits, and in many ways did so.[69]

Housing supply failures in Kigali and Kampala

Given these political benefits, why have other countries in the region with similar economic profiles, and urbanizing at similar rates, *not* pursued programmes of mass urban housing? One reason relates to the fact that demand for such housing among the urban middle classes has been much more muted. In contrast to Addis Ababa where even higher-end real estate supply was very constrained, Kampala and especially Kigali have showed evidence of *oversupply* at the higher end of the market. Consequently, while the latent demand for adequate housing of poorer groups is huge, the effective demand coming from higher- and middle-income groups has been largely satisfied by the private (formal and informal) real estate market. The potential social and political impact of producing mass housing for the middle classes is therefore much smaller. Yet when contemplating why housing at least nominally targeted at lower-income groups does not appear to have been prioritized or feasible in Kampala and Kigali, the four elements of this book's analytical framework are all relevant—though in strikingly different ways in each case.

The contrast between Ethiopia and Rwanda is particularly instructive in relation to the first two factors—the distribution of associational power and pursuit of social legitimacy. The RPF government has observed Ethiopia's housing programme very closely, spending much of the decade between 2010 and 2020 attempting to create appropriate structures and incentives to make affordable housing appealing to investors. Their desire to pursue a private-sector rather than state-led route has, however, proved very limiting when it comes to achieving affordability; advisors to the government conceded that 'we may have to be tolerant [of unaffordability] for an intermittent period.'[70] Moreover, when the government finally passed its regulations and initiated funding streams for 'affordable' housing, an academic study scrutinizing the scheme concluded that the housing units developed would be 'seriously and severely unaffordable for most of the target beneficiaries', in part due to the high profits expected by real estate developers (Uwayezu & de Vries 2020a).[71]

---

[69] Interview with government adviser, Addis Ababa, 24 November 2017.
[70] Interview with international advisor on housing, Kigali, 14 January 2015.
[71] An early exception in terms of providing formal housing to the poor is the settlement at Batsinda, which was based on a model of low-cost housing developed with support from GIZ, and was intended to accommodate people displaced from expropriation in the city centre. This however only resulted

The need for affordable housing is accentuated in Kigali by the limits that strict regulatory enforcement places on informal housing construction. For male youth especially, this also stymies the transition into adulthood, for which constructing a house has traditionally been central (Sommers 2012). However, while the government has had affordable housing on the agenda for well over a decade, it is simply not a political priority in the way it was in Ethiopia. With the threat of popular urban uprising still minimal, and political opposition in the city unable to effectively function, keeping domestic elites onside and providing sufficient profit for international investors is more central to regime survival than actually delivering affordable housing. To the extent that the creation of property within the wider population has been a priority, the government channelled much of this energy into its Land Tenure Regularization Programme. This is significantly weaker than housing as a political instrument, but powerful in terms of consolidating bureaucratic control: a key priority in the regime's overriding concern to promulgate continued legitimacy through narratives of development effectiveness.

Uganda tells a different story. Here the desire to appease urban middle- and lower-income groups is substantial, particularly given the strength of opposition within Kampala and the government's increased concern to politically dominate it (Muwanga et al. 2020). Yet the NRM government has not come even remotely close to developing an affordable housing programme (Haas & Hoza Ngoga 2018). In contrast to Kigali, this is not so much because of the distribution of power or the fact that offering benefits to the non-elite urban population is unimportant for governing legitimacy. Rather, it relates more to the state's lack of infrastructural reach and the salience of particular modalities of political informality that confer benefits on target populations largely through extra-legal processes and sporadic favours instead of programmatic policy. This is starkly illustrated by the fact that the highest-profile issue relating to large-scale housing in the 2000s concerned a flagship housing estate that was *not* built, rather than the actual construction of anything new.

This new project was due to be implemented in Kampala on the site of a was a dilapidated colonial estate known as Nakawa-Naguru (indicated on the right hand side of Figure 3.1 in Chapter 3), built by the colonial government on public land in the 1950s for itinerant labourers (Munger 1951: 17). Nakawa-Naguru was earmarked in the early 2000s for demolition and redevelopment in accordance with the 1994 Structure Plan as a 'satellite town' to draw congestion away from the city centre. After several years of delays, in 2007 a British company (OpecPrime) finally signed a Public-Private Partnership agreement with the government to undertake the area's redevelopment. The $300m proposal involved developing 5,000 housing

in 250 housing units and despite the intention of replicating it across the city, this did not take place (see Goodfellow 2012 and Shearer 2017 for discussions). Construction of 1,040 apartments for another displaced community was also underway in 2019, amid further controversy (Nikuze et al. 2020).

units including 1,747 affordable flats which the displaced tenants would have an option to purchase at subsidized prices.

For the next four years, the project was stalled countless times by petitions from the public and interventions from politicians and the inspector general of government, as the residents of the estate fought against the Ministry of Local Government's efforts to evict them and demolish the existing housing.[72] There was believed to have even been an intervention by the president on behalf of the tenants, even though the redevelopment was always part of the 1994 Kampala Structure Plan and a court ruled that the tenants had no legal grounds to oppose it.[73] In July 2011 the eviction eventually took place, affecting an estimated 1,760 families.[74] In contrast to Kigali and Addis Ababa, evictions on this scale are a rare event in Kampala and it is no coincidence that it occurred just a few months after a presidential election, when concerns over antagonizing constituents were at a relatively low ebb.

In 2013, Museveni laid the foundation stone for construction of the Naguru-Nakawa satellite city estate, amid further fanfare and declarations that he was 'embarrassed' about the many years of delay. However, a further seven years of almost total inaction followed, and in April 2019 the project was cancelled,[75] following claims that the land had been parcelled out to various private interests.[76] In this sense, the city's usual patterns of political informality have prevailed, whereby para-formal 'side payments' in the form of prime land have taken precedence over the use of formal policy measures as a tool of allocating benefits. The fact that virtually nothing had been built on this land by way of housing (even for the evictees), after a process spanning the better part of two decades, could hardly offer a more stark contrast with the housing trajectory in Addis Ababa, where hundreds of thousands of formal housing units have been delivered over the same period.

Particularly striking is the fact that land on which the original Nakawa-Naguru estates sat was not *mailo* but public land. This meant that the long initial delay in evicting the population was not attributable to the formidable obstacles associated with expropriating private land, but more to do with political concerns about evicting urban constituents (and thus feeding broader urban discontent) in the volatile run-up to the 2011 elections. After the eventual eviction, the failure to then ensure the development of the land in line with the proposed 'satellite town' plans reflects the general weakness of infrastructural power in the face of pressures to appease private interests, as the land itself became swallowed into the broader scramble for property. If true that it has been parcelled off to private interests (and previous developments definitely suggest this happens, often covertly,

---

[72] 'Behind the Nakawa-Naguru estates story'. *Sunday Monitor*, 15 February 2009.
[73] 'Naguru-Nakawa land "grabbed" from investor'. *Sunday Monitor*, 15 February 2009.
[74] 'Nakawa-Naguru families stranded as evictions begin', *Daily Monitor*, 5 July 2011.
[75] 'Government retakes Naguru-Nakawa land', *Daily Monitor*, 3 April 2019.
[76] 'Naguru-Nakawa tenants want 50 acres of housing estate land', *New Vision*, 14 October 2018.

with public land),[77] then not only has nothing been done to promote housing for the broader public, but the government has continued to actively weaken its own infrastructural reach by further reducing the pool of public land available in Kampala.

6.4   Reading the politics of urban propertyscapes

The dynamics described in this chapter are intimately linked to the context of late urbanization, in which histories of urban disinvestment are overlain with rapid urban population growth and the disproportionate sucking of capital into the 'secondary circuit' of capital. As we have seen, however, these features of late urbanization have manifested in very different ways in each case. As with the urban visions and infrastructure investments discussed in Chapter 5, these differences are explicable through the nature of politics and political history, and the contemporary priorities and practices this generates at the national and city level. This way of reading urban propertyscapes speaks to the broader literature on landscapes as representing and concretizing social and political relationships and struggles in space (Mitchell 1994; Therborn 2017; Castán Broto 2019). The analysis presented by the following subsections concludes this chapter by bringing such conceptualizations into conversation with a discussion of the distribution of associational power, pursuit of urban legitimacy, and the varying roles of political informality.

Kampala

Uganda has a relatively diffuse distribution of associational power. While the ruling elite has become increasingly narrow, with the bias towards the president's own ethnic group from Ankole becoming more visible over time (Lindemann 2011; Kjær 2015), excluded factions and 'lower-level' elements within the NRM coalition remain relatively strong (Tripp 2010; Golooba-Mutebi & Hickey 2013; Kjær 2015). The Asian businesspeople invited back by Museveni in the 1990s are economically significant but are relatively small in number and not considered politically threatening due to their broad support for the NRM (Rubongoya 2007). Much more significant numerically and politically are various groups excluded from the ruling coalition who have relatively low capitalist capabilities and thus do not benefit significantly from Uganda's (colonial and donor-driven) formal institutional framework of capitalist property rights, yet by virtue of their associational power can command benefits through informal channels. These include Baganda kingdom elites, whose support was crucial to NRM success in the civil war but increasingly feel excluded, and disgruntled military elites with potential capacity to mobilize violence (Kjær 2015; Lindemann 2011). In addition, former

[77] See Goodfellow (2013a) for a discussion.

soldiers and the large numbers of informal workers possess substantial associational power due to their numerical significance as voting blocs, evidenced by their capacity to regularly subvert government regulation in their interests (Goodfellow & Titeca 2012; Goodfellow 2015b).

There are thus a wide range of groups nationally with sufficient associational power to demand benefits and rents. Given the ruling coalition's low (and declining) capacity to effect structural economic transformation (Kjær 2015) there is need for continuous patronage that can deliver more immediate rewards than long-term capitalist investment can offer. This is partly a consequence of a relatively weak legacy of infrastructural reach bequeathed by colonial institutions and exacerbated by the zeal for liberalizing economic reforms noted in Chapter 4—a weakness that also renders mass housing delivery beyond the state's capabilities. In this context, and given the increased need to appease urban groups as well as rural interests, strategies for social legitimation at the city level became more important in the 2000s. Turning a blind eye to regulation and illicit land sales has been one of the cheaper options available (or at least its costs only become apparent in the longer term). The recourse to informal 'side payments' that operate through facilitating urban land access and use, undermining formal institutions and plans, thus became highly significant over successive decades under the NRM. Kampala's physical evolution tells this story in glorious technicolour. As economically powerful interests cluster in the city, the dense constellation of colonial, capitalist, and modernist economic and planning institutions are more of an obstacle to than effective instrument for allocating them benefits, so this instead takes place through a para-formal politics of urban distribution in land and property.

When considering the scale at which this political informality functions, another important dimension concerns the decentralization of governance functions, and how this operates at city level. The NRM's enthusiastic adoption of decentralization from the 1990s enabled opposition figures to be elected to power in Kampala City Council, bringing the struggle between the NRM and opposition forces to the city with increasing intensity, and fuelling the struggle to buy urban support through para-formal land access. These dynamics have changed (but ultimately not diminished) over the past decade, due to both the central government 'takeover' discussed in Chapter 5 and the Land (Amendment) Act, which have raised the stakes and complicated the formal institutional overlaps in terms of managing urban land.

Kigali

In Rwanda, the distribution of associational power differs in fundamental ways. Non-elite social groups and especially the rural and urban poor have substantially less associational power, both due to especially weak foundations of capitalist development, a historical dependence on the state for land rights and access, and the fact that the RPF did not depend on the allegiance of these domestic groups to achieve and consolidate power. Elite factions excluded from the ruling coalition are also relatively weak—not least as they have been ruthlessly exiled, or worse—though in some cases still threaten the regime from abroad (Behuria 2016b). The trauma of genocide, outflow of opposition groups, and strong legal restrictions on political activism also contribute to the relatively low level of holding power of groups outside the ruling coalition (Reyntjens 2013). As such, there is a much smaller range of groups to whom it is necessary to allocate 'side payments'. There are, however, a number of powerful groups *within* the ruling coalition, such as former military figures and wealthy supporters of the regime, with significant individual and associational power. In its attempts to spur capitalist development the RPF regime has largely centralized economic rents, leading to significant elite frictions as many opportunities for individual profits are foreclosed (Behuria 2015a; 2016a). Consequently, the ruling elite faces a situation where, despite the relatively concentrated distribution of power, there is still some demand for side payments because powerful elites within the coalition need to be kept onside and cannot easily enrich themselves through productive capitalist investment.

When it comes to Kigali, then, the ability for elites to enrich themselves through land-based benefits is very important for the ruling elite's ability to maintain legitimacy and stability. Some of the ways in which this is institutionally managed are illuminated vividly by Kigali's spatial evolution, which for the most part has not unfolded through the para-formal processes that prevail in Kampala. Indeed, strictness in regulatory enforcement is remarkable; the idea that 'there is no friend or favour' that can facilitate the breach of urban laws and regulations, while surely exaggerated, repeatedly comes through in the testimonies of international firms.[78] Even wealthy and well-connected Rwanda nationals are sometimes forced to sell their land because they cannot get around regulations preventing them from using it as they wish.[79] Given that there are important factions within the ruling coalition with the associational power to demand benefits, it is perhaps surprising that the kind of para-formal land bonanza evident in Kampala does not appear to have unfolded in Kigali.

To understand why formal institutions for managing land and property have greater force in Kigali therefore requires looking beyond the distribution of power alone, and taking seriously the role of image management, displays of discipline, and 'zero tolerance' to corruption plays in RPF elite ideology and its pursuit of legitimacy (Behuria 2016b; Chemouni 2016). In Kigali specifically, the visible enforcement of rules is part of a broader 'performance' (Rollason 2013) to present

---

[78] Interview with international construction firm A, 15 January 2015. Some international investors even complain that the lack of corruption is quite problematic, making it hard to do business in Rwanda.

[79] Interviews with investors, Kigali, 2009 and 2014.

Rwanda as a developmental success, which is crucial to the RPF regime's survival given its lack of a broad social base. Kigali's propertyscape illustrates that visible adherence to formal institutions is in its own right central to the maintenance of legitimacy. This display of rule-bound development is both inward-facing, due to the potential threats to power that might emerge if perceptions of corruption and disorder among a regime based on an ethnic minority were to spread, and outward-facing. Kigali is, in the government's own account,[80] where Rwanda is most obviously on show to the world, as discussed also in relation to Chapter 5's infrastructures. This dual internal and external threat places limits on the extent to which a para-formal politics of land allocation can be the primary means of appeasing elite interests.

This preoccupation with formal rules does not, however, mean that elites do not garner substantial land-based benefits in Kigali. They clearly do, given the widespread untaxed rents described earlier. There is a further important dimension to the institutional management of Rwanda's distribution of power that helps to explain how the ruling elite can sustain the required allocation of benefits in Kigali without wider recourse to para-formal distribution. Alongside a regulatory regime that constrains the para-formal allocation of benefits, there are many *formal* rules and laws that facilitate land-based benefits—or have the flexibility to do so. Strong legal powers of expropriation, for example, allow for a very expansive definition of 'public interest' through which land can legally be expropriated for profit under certain conditions (Goodfellow 2014b; Manirakiza & Ansoms 2014; Nikuze et al. 2020). Property tax reforms have also been successfully resisted by elites to facilitate maximal profits from real estate, feeding into the rush to develop high-end properties as described above (Goodfellow 2017b). The vesting of authority in a master plan and development agenda that privilege such real estate is also well aligned with the interests of domestic elites seeking profit in the city.

Moreover, some laws and regulations are easily changed without widespread consultation (such as the property tax rate or zoning regulations), and others are also unclear or actively in flux, providing further opportunities for elites to profit *without actively breaking formal rules*.[81] In Kigali after the wave of detailed planning undertaken by Singaporean firm Surbana, the changing of official zoning regulations has constituted an important means through which those with influence can maximize the extraction of value from land. For example, in a certain parts of the city's fringe, land zoned for residential real estate was then suddenly re-zoned as being for forestry only, as noted in the 'impressions' at the start of this book. Some time later, certain plots was again re-zoned for residential development—but only behind closed doors, with no public announcement

---

[80] Interviews with government officials, Kigali, 2010–2011.
[81] Interviews with tax officials, planning officials, and investors, January 2015.

and with allegations that the City Council had attempted to erase previous evidence that the whole area had once been zoned for residential development. This led to widespread suspicion that the re-zoning to forestry enabled certain powerful figures to acquire land very cheaply, before then exerting influence to have it re-zoned back to residential, thus enabling real estate development at a huge profit.[82]

While processes such as this surely involve informal negotiation, this was done in such a way as to *change* the formal institutional framework to facilitate profits, rather than simply to *override* laws and regulation. This capacity to change formal laws relatively easily can itself be seen as a form of side payment, echoing Khan's point that 'informal power can also be used to change formal laws to benefit groups who would otherwise not have benefited' (Khan, 2010: 54). Thus a predominant mode of political informality shaping Kigali's propertyscape is pro-formal: it consists of influence being exerted by actors in order to change formal institutions to reflect their interests, and maintain them as such, rather than to override or discredit the formal institutions. Much about Kigali's urban landscape can be explained with reference to the relatively concentrated distribution of power combined alongside a preference for pro-formal over para-formal politics, given the risks the latter pose to regime legitimacy.

Addis Ababa

Ethiopia's distribution of power is rooted both in legacies of the Imperial and Derg regimes and the complex ethnic calculus of the Ethiopian polity under EPRDF rule. As with Uganda and Rwanda, capitalists have historically been politically weak and lacking in productive capabilities and largely remain so, as discussed in Chapter 4. There are, however, a number of groups that could threaten various forms of mobilization against the EPRDF regime, as became starkly evident in the 2014–2018 crisis that eventually resulted in the dissolution of the EPRDF under Abiy Ahmed. As well as various excluded ethnic groups nationally, Addis Ababa as a multi-ethnic federal city is home to a substantial educated middle class, as well as a more general sense of a distinctly 'Addis' urban identity that to some degree transcends ethnic identifiers (Di Nunzio 2019). Over time the significance of the Addis factor in national politics grew, as the associational power of urban educated classes became evident and prompted distinct legitimation strategies in the city.

Associational power in Ethiopia generally is thus relatively widely distributed, bearing closer resemblance to Uganda than Rwanda. Given this relatively diffuse distribution, Addis Ababa has developed in ways that reflect the need to allow ample opportunities for powerful individuals and groups to profit from urban

---

[82] Personal correspondence with an investor in land, 2013–2015.

land, as evidenced through the unparalleled frenzy of construction in the city. However, the propertyscape in Addis is also marked by very distinct features rooted in its particular political-institutional context and history. A first such feature is the legacy of urban form produced under the emperors and largely frozen under the Derg, in which wealth and poverty intermingled throughout the urban landscape, as well as the subversion of this over the past decade through the dispersal of people to the peripheries and concentration of private capital in the centre.

The fact that Addis Ababa did not have the typical pattern of colonial urbanism, whereby wealthy enclaves and neglected 'native'/slum areas were built into the urban form from the outset, has made the effort to produce a particular kind of 'world-class' central city exceptionally disruptive, transforming the city by tearing apart its socio-spatial fabric (Weldeghebrael 2019; Di Nunzio 2022). The potentially negative political consequences of this have been mitigated in part by the extent to which public goods—in the form of transport and housing targeted very explicitly beyond the urban elite—have been part and parcel of this transformation. As well as being distinctive in terms of its spatial layout, the Addis Ababa inherited by the EPRDF was unusual in having very little of what many cities have in abundance: private property and opportunities to acquire it. The upending of the city's physical landscape was possible partly because it was twinned with the creation and distribution of private property through the housing programme and land-leasing system—something that has been central to building and maintaining legitimacy.

A second distinctive feature is the vertical sprouting of commercial property driven by the particular range of incentives and constraints to property development in Addis Ababa under much of the EPRDF period, including the regulatory framework that incentivized part-construction, the lack of widespread access to finance for real estate, and the highly constrained access to land through the state's monopoly over formal access to it. While these factors were designed in some ways to inhibit certain kinds of property development and speculation, they also drove up the potential profits to be made from land and real estate for those with the capital to invest. The leasing of limited amounts of very high-value land to commercial interests played a particular role in accommodating the profit-making desires of the diaspora, particularly given their inability to invest in other sectors, as well as important domestic elites. This can be seen as part of a political effort to neutralize the potentially destabilizing role of associationally powerful groups hostile to the regime.

Third and most significant of all is the extent to which the state retained key levers of formal institutional control to enable it to distribute the required benefits across urban space. The maintenance of public land ownership, alongside resistance to some of the donor-sponsored liberalization reforms adopted whole-heartedly in Uganda and Rwanda (Markakis 2011; Lavers 2012),[83] meant that the regime inherited and maintained a significant account of infrastructural reach a through range of formal institutional instruments to allocate urban benefits. The fact that many of the benefits distributed to important excluded and marginalized groups could be facilitated by *formal* institutions for land and housing delivery has been crucial to Addis Ababa's spatial trajectory. The condominium housing programme itself is a potent indication of the scale of the formal response to the associational power of the urban masses in Addis Ababa. While it has remained largely latent in recent years, the capacity of major elements of city population to mobilize major dissent and political damage was not forgotten after the massive opposition gains of 2005 and the successful, though fragile, recapturing of the city by the EPRDF in 2010, as discussed further in Chapter 8.

Importantly, while the Ethiopian government has unparalleled capacity to deliver benefits through formal channels and official government programmes, the extent of associational power outside of the ruling coalition makes it more neces-sary than in Kigali to supplement formal mechanisms for allocating benefits with para-formal side payments. The widespread belief that informal negotiation and corruption permeates the process of land leasing,[84] and similar concerns about the manipulation of the auction process to ensure that key constituencies are allocated condominium housing,[85] suggest it is by no means only through official mecha-nisms that the urban cake is divided up. Thus while the government's legitimacy does not rest so thoroughly on informal allocation as in Uganda, it does require para-formal 'supplements' to its official programmes to ensure that benefits to flow to all the requisite groups. Both the formal and informal dimensions of urban land-based clientelism have spatial effects, because they depend on maximizing the use of land to placate the range of interests vying for benefits in the city. The city thus becomes a vast construction site as institutions of all kinds become geared towards fully exploiting the political value of urban land.

---

[83] Much of this changed in 2018 when Abiy Ahmed rose to power, with a very different social base and pivoting towards new external and internal sources of legitimacy (Terrefe 2020), with urban priorities more akin to those in Rwanda.

[84] Various interviews with government officials and investors, September–October 2014.

[85] Various interviews with civil society sources in Addis Ababa, 2017–2018.

7

Working the city

Vendors, 'untouchables', and street fugitives

Introduction

Despite the grand economic aspirations and often radical re-organization of urban space discussed in the preceding chapters, life in all three cities remains characterized by precarious, low-wage, piecemeal livelihoods for the urban majority. In this sense, the cities examined in this book are similar to many across the global South, though they involve some exceptionally high levels of economic informality even by regional standards.[1] This is unsurprising at the frontier of late urbanization, in countries heavily impacted by rapid urban demographic growth alongside legacies of a very limited productive economy. The high proportions of citizens in late urbanizing contexts living and working in under-serviced, highly insecure informal environments is a counterpart to the real-estate-led urban development that exerts such a magnetic pull on scarce capital in late urbanizing contexts, as examined in the previous chapter.

For most people in all these cities, the challenge is therefore one of how to pursue a life—and ideally achieve a better life—in the context of severely limited urban employment opportunities, alongside a host of constraints relating to social hierarchies and political subjugation. To make an urban life and livelihood in such contexts is to seek and maintain diverse networks, tactics, and modes of operating, and to embrace provisionality and improvisation in order to 'get by' (Simone 2004b; 2018; Thieme 2018). It means not simply waiting for opportunity to materialize but making one's own opportunities, through what Di Nunzio (2019) calls 'moving around': exercising conscious agency in the pursuit of transcending present conditions. This often involves combining different income sources simultaneously, making the most of any opportunity that arises and pursuing 'multiple modes of livelihood' (Owusu 2007; Ojong 2011)—or to use a phrase coined by day labourers in Kigali looking for a wage, it is the daily search for *afakijab* (a truncated form of the English 'any fucking job') (Shearer 2017: 118).

---

[1] Rwanda in particular had the highest percentage of informal labour as a proportion of urban labour of any of the countries in Africa recorded in a recent ILO report, with Uganda not far behind (ILO 2018: 91). Statistics from Ethiopia are harder to come by and are generally absent from the databases of the World Bank, ILO, and other international organizations.

Politics and the Urban Frontier. Tom Goodfellow, Oxford University Press. © Tom Goodfellow (2022).
DOI: 10.1093/oso/9780198853107.003.0007

These efforts can involve providing small-scale services (hairdressing, brewing, phone-charging and 'airtime' to name just a few), as well as market vending and street trade, informal transport provision, hustling, sex work, and a range of petty criminal activities. These activities are generally precarious and unstable, and in many cases also stigmatized, putting them out of step with expectations of what urban-dwellers feel they should or could be doing—especially for younger and increasingly educated generations, raised with aspirations of 'modern' employment (Mains 2012; Baral 2018). Indeed, the informal economy is often 'a repository for those with skills but without opportunity' (Simone 2004b: 26). Continued 'moving around' is often the only way to create opportunities and render life meaningful, maintaining an open-ended life in an ongoing attempt to overcome constraints (Di Nunzio 2019).

This chapter explores these livelihood activities and the political practices that generate and sustain them in different contexts, with a particular focus on market vending and street trade. The nature of such activities may look similar on the surface across the three cities examined in this book, in contrast to the evolving differentiation in the built environment. But this belies very different underlying dynamics, particularly regarding how people negotiate the urban economic landscape politically and the opportunities that the political context generates and forecloses. The chapter begins by exploring the broader context of urban 'informality', a concept that matters despite its flaws, because of its discursive endurance and its permeation of policy discourses that condition how urban workers are viewed and treated. Following this, I turn to urban petty trade, which in its various forms is among the most significant options available to urban residents. While urban marketplaces themselves constitute key sites of opportunity—and often of political engagement—for many people, hawking wares or services on the streets constitutes the lifeblood of urban existence. In examining marketplaces and street economies in turn, I consider how the shared economic conditions of late urbanization filter through different government legitimation strategies and varying practices of political informality to generate diverse political streetscapes across the three cities.

7.1 Informality and urban life

In the half century since it was popularized by Keith Hart (1973), the concept of the urban 'informal sector' or 'informal economy' has been subject to relentless critique, but has proved inextinguishable. While critiques of the concept's crude economic dualism soon proliferated (Harriss 1978; Peattie 1987), its popularity was turbo-charged by Hernando De Soto's (1989) 'legalist' approach in *The Other Path*, an ebullient celebration of what people excluded from formal economic work by excess bureaucracy could achieve if laws and regulations were relaxed. This chimed with the deregulatory ideological spirit of the times and the agenda of the Washington-based international financial institutions. In the 1990s the concept remained in constant currency, including through Marxist approaches that rejected the idea that informal work represented 'entrepreneurial triumph', instead framing informality as a strategy of the formal sector to ensure a flexible pool of casual labour (Castells et al. 1989; Meagher 1995; Rizzo 2017), and a consequence of the exclusionary processes associated with the changing global division of labour (Beall 2002). The gendered aspects of informal work have also received increasing attention, with women not only being more likely to work informally but also being disproportionately represented in the riskiest and least well-paid informal jobs (Chen 2001; Chant & Pedwell 2008).

The idea of informality has at best 'modest analytical value' (Lindell 2010: 5), and while definitions abound, the clearest remain those that refer simply to activities that 'lie beyond or circumvent state regulation' in some way (Lindell 2010: 5). Yet debates on informality have been enlivened by waves of fresh thinking from geographers and planners interested primarily in informal settlements, housing, infrastructure and land use rather than employment (e.g. Roy 2005; 2009; McFarlane 2012; Banks et al. 2020). Although the focus of this chapter is on work rather than settlement, much of the recent work conceptualizing more general ideas of 'urban informality' has emerged from discourses concerning the latter. Many (though certainly not all) urban-dwellers who live in informal housing are the same people as those working in informal jobs, with the effect that both home and work life exist in tension with the state's legal and regulatory framework: they are essentially cast as 'informal people' living 'informal lives' (Bayat 1997).

Informality has thus come to refer to a symbolic state of being that is instrumentalized in different ways by governments and other actors. This frequently involves the creation of 'grey spaces' as a technique of power (Yiftachel 2009), whereby the urban majority inhabits a precarious existence that leaves them perpetually 'walking the tightrope' (Lourenço-Lindell 2002) between acceptance and expulsion. In this sense the *designation* of people, their homes, or their work as informal becomes a tool to manipulate the urban poor, however fuzzy the term might be analytically. The very idea of informality has strong political 'currency' in urban political relations (McFarlane & Waibel 2012; Marx & Kelling 2019). In this capacity it has also become increasingly associated with urban aesthetics and the significance of what is considered to appear informal rather than questions of legality or regulatory status itself (Ghertner 2015; Marx & Kelling 2019).

Despite this association of informality with poverty, spatial and economic practices that lied beyond state regulation do not involve the poor in their own separate sphere of activity; rather, they constitute 'a series of transactions that connect different economies and spaces to one another' (Roy 2005: 148; Guha-Khasnobis & Kanbur 2006). Informality is thus seen as an 'organizing logic' that governs the very process of urbanization in many parts of the world (AlSayyad & Roy 2003; McFarlane 2012), deeply rooted in the political economy of urban social and economic relations (Banks et al. 2020). It is, however, the urban poor who generally face the coercion, manipulation, and stigmatization at the hands of state agencies wielding ideas of informality and associated discourses in order to pursue particular developmental, political, and aesthetic projects. There has been growing interest in how urban-dwellers pursue their lives in contexts of informality through day-to-day flexibility, pragmatism, and negotiation with state actors (Simone 2005; Bayat 1997; 2000; Di Nunzio 2019). For some scholars, however, to focus on everyday practices of urban informal life as being somehow generative is to celebrate their agency while underplaying the magnitude and severity of the structural constraints they face (Rizzo 2017; Young 2021b).

This book posits that an appreciation of the deep structural factors constraining urban livelihoods, and an engagement with how people attempt to remake their lives and overcome marginality, can and must be compatible. The condition of late urbanization and global economic system in which this is embedded has to a significant extent generated the pervasive insecurity that characterizes urban existence in much of the global South. These conditions are localized and rendered tangible through national political strategies and capacities (Fox & Goodfellow 2021) but are also refracted through the activities of people striving to survive through provisional, improvised lives (Simone 2004b; 2018). Many city-dwellers are aware that a better urban condition can only come through some higher-level systemic change, and they live in constant hope and expectation of this; yet they also have to no choice but to make their own futures and constantly 'work' the social networks that might give rise to a better future (Di Nunzio 2019).

Building social relations and engaging with what Simone (2018) terms 'ensemble work' in order to eke the best possible life out of the city is thus essential; but it does not necessarily result in certainty about these social relations, or generate concerted forms of collective mobilization. Drawing on a popular jazz metaphor, ensemble work in the urban margins amounts to a profusion of 'melody' rooted in experiences of improvisation (Mains 2019: 17), though the melody this produces is not necessarily subsumed by harmony (Simone 2018: 41). Urban life is, for the poor especially, 'labour-intensive' and involves constantly working on relationships with others, without necessarily producing institutionalized collective politics (Simone 2018: 134–136). Indeed, while maximizing social and political connections is always central to 'working the city' (Bayat 2000; Simone 2004; Meagher 2010; Mains 2012), this does not take the same generic form in any southern, informalized urban context, because the ways that politics and the state penetrate social relations can differ fundamentally. To use Di Nunzio's (2019) term, the urban majority in the three cities examined in this book are characterized by different 'regimes of interconnectedness': in particular, urban informal workers are connected to wider economies and political programmes in different ways in each case. Despite their shared conditions of late urbanization, the collective dimensions of urban street livelihoods play out through varying forms of political informality that connect urban informal workers to structures of power.

The different political dynamics associated with urban informal work in each case need to be situated against Chapter 4's national economic backdrop. In Uganda, after the explosion of the *magendo* economy and its further growth and consolidation under the second Obote government, the informal economy has remained enormous in the NRM period. The extent of informalization by the 1990s was quite striking even by regional standards (Palmer 2004). As we will see in this chapter, under the NRM Kampala's informal economy has been fuelled by the regular suspension of laws and regulations to enable informal activities to thrive, as political actors seek to reconstitute their own power. The formal restructuring of governance under KCCA since 2011 resulted in some significant changes to the engagement between the state and informal operators, but the effects were limited and ultimately short-lived.

In Rwanda, meanwhile, the early post-genocide years in which the city's population mushroomed—against the backdrop of an extremely minimal industrial legacy—inevitably saw a flourishing of the urban informal economy, as people took to the streets to trade and hustle for livelihoods (see Chapter 4). As Shearer notes, in Kigali's popular neighbourhoods 'every inch of ground' was 'involved in the production, circulation and exchange of value' (2017: 55). However, this was to radically change in the 2000s, particularly after the unveiling of the Master Plan from 2007 and subsequent aesthetic and securitizing legitimation project that allowed virtually no space for market vending and informal street trade. Ethiopia's economic legacy also bequeathed low levels of industry and formal employment. Yet when combined with the stronger associational power of urban-dwellers and expectations about the role of the state that date back to the imperial and communist period, this generated particular demands on government that would prove challenging for the EPRDF in the 2000s. After 2005, the state rolled out a remarkable series of responses. To explore these varying experiences of 'working the city', the sections that follow unravel the differential politics of the marketplace and the street economy in each case, and their manifestations in urban space.

7.2 The marketplace: Urban politics etched in economic space

As structural adjustment dissolved formal work opportunities and fuelled the urban informal economy from the 1980s (Meagher 1995; Cross 1998), many urban-dwellers resorted to selling commodities either in marketplaces or on the streets. Facilitated by burgeoning urban populations in need of food and basic goods, and distribution networks that drew in both rural produce and cheap manufactures from abroad, this was a livelihood option that required only a minimal capital outlay. Hence petty trade proliferated in African cities, particularly in the poorest countries where access to finance was scarce and there was little industry. Broadly speaking, petty trade can be divided into two elements with distinct dynamics and characteristics: vending in urban marketplaces and selling or hawking goods on the streets. These activities are also among the most gendered elements of the informal economy, being particularly common for women (Mitullah 2003).

Urban petty trade sits oddly with technical definitions of informality, since urban vendors can rarely be 'beyond' state reach in the manner of, for example, home-based petty commodity producers (Moser 1978); their work is necessarily public so it is difficult to avoid some forms of taxation and state control. When trading legal goods, they often pay some (usually local) taxes but not other (often national) ones, though the degree to which they are actually subject to taxes can be highly arbitrary (Lourenço-Lindell 2002). Meanwhile, the belief that they generate rubbish, obstruct traffic, and comprise a public nuisance underscores their *perceived* informality (Mitullah 2003), though this has little to do with legal or regulatory status. whether or not they are strictly informal, markets are usually governed as though they are (Young 2021a: 199). Vendors, whether in relatively formalized marketplaces or working on the streets, thus occupy a special role in relation both to government discourses about 'cracking down' on informality, and—concomitantly—politicians' populist efforts to court their support.

Relations between vendors and the state therefore tend to be characterized by both conflict and cooperation, either simultaneously or in waves conditioned by shifting political circumstances (Lindell 2008; Resnick 2019). The form this conflict and cooperation takes can vary widely by context. This is not just a question of which regulations are in place: focusing on the regulations themselves, as did de Soto (1989) and other 'legalists', obscures the political economy of how those regulations are used and implemented. The prevailing assumption of such approaches has been that the more ambitious and overbearing the regulations, the more cause for escape and thus the more informality (Lomnitz 1988: 54). However, this does not account for the differing extent to which they are enforced. The conditions of work for petty traders have more to do with politics than with the nature of regulations, which often are very similar across contexts, particularly given that many regulatory and legal frameworks have shared colonial origins. The remainder of this section explores this in relation to marketplace activity in the three cities. These narratives unpick the dynamics of associational and infrastructural power, legitimation, and political informality that explain different market trading environments in each case.

Shifting layers of legitimacy and political informality in Kampala's markets

Uganda's explosion of economic informality from the 1970s onwards led to Kampala being a city in which trade appears to be happening almost everywhere, both inside and outside formal markets. Like most governments, the NRM has long viewed vendors 'as a problem that has to be controlled' (Mitullah 2003: 10), with various national laws and urban ordinances invoked to this end. Prior to the new KCCA urban governance regime from 2011, vendors in legal markets were subject to a combination of monthly rent and daily dues (collectively termed *empooza*), while street trade was regulated through permits. There were also important policy developments from the 1990s concerning how and by whom markets were to be owned and managed, in the context of Museveni's zeal for neoliberalizing reforms. These radically challenged the strong social networks that had been built and maintained within markets since the colonial era (Monteith 2015; 2019). Following the privatization of market services such as revenue and waste collection (Lindell & Appelblad 2009), a drive to privatize marketplaces themselves by selling leases to entrepreneurs emerged around 2005 and caused a huge furore in Kampala's markets, particularly as it coincided with the re-establishment of multi-party political competition in the run-up to the 2006 election. The idea that marketplaces had become a central political issue by the end of the 2000s is well captured by the comment by one observer that '[Markets] are everywhere, they are a mess. It's politics, and nothing else.'[2]

Central to the perceived marketplace 'problem' in Kampala was Owino market,[3] by far the country's largest marketplace. Established in 1971, it spread over seven acres of land with some fifty thousand vendors working within its orbit.[4] A particular controversy surrounding Owino began when Godfrey Kayongo, the marketplace chairman since 1987, was accused by the inspector general of government in a 1997 report of grossly mismanaging funds issued for marketplace development under a World Bank project (IGG 1997). Through deals struck with KCC officials, Kayongo allegedly used his daughter's name to make himself a major shareholder of the construction company awarded the tender to develop the market, which siphoned off funds and violated the approved construction plans (IGG 1997). He was further accused of massively under-reporting the number of market stalls in the market to KCC, in order to retain large proportions of the *empooza* he was responsible for collecting and passing to the city authorities.[5]

In the context of the government's post-2005 drive to sell off the leases to the marketplaces, Kayongo set up another company called the 'Stall and Lockup Owners Association' (SLOA) to collect money from vendors and purchase the lease in their name.[6] As a limited company with a maximum of fifty shareholders, SLOA necessarily excluded most vendors from control over the market and its

[2] Interview with Ugandan academic, 10 February 2009.
[3] At some point in the 2000s this market was formally renamed St. Balikkudembe (a more 'Bugandan' name), but most people still used the original name Owino.
[4] Interview with marketplace leader, 13 October 2009; interview with government minister, 27 January 2010.
[5] Interview with vendors at Owino Market, 13 January 2010.
[6] Interview with marketplace leader, 13 October 2009.

spoils—as some vendors soon realized, subsequently establishing their own rival group[7] with the aim of mobilizing vendors against Kayongo. They considered him an NRM 'stooge', claiming that he 'treats the market as his own property' and abolished marketplace elections in 1993 to make himself 'a dictator—chairman for life!'[8] On taking their grievances to Kayongo, his supporters reportedly beat them with sticks,[9] and Kayongo himself dismissed their activities as being coordinated by 'tycoons' who had co-opted vendors with the aim of preventing them from purchasing the market lease.[10] The conflict between the two groups resulted in continuing efforts by each to seek political patronage and sabotage the other's plans for greater control over the market. Eventually, the rival group that represented a broader base of vendors adopted the position that markets should remain under government control, as vendors could not afford to purchase and redevelop markets themselves. While this group managed to get support from KCCA, eventually Kayongo's SLOA prevailed due to his ongoing patronage from President Museveni (Young 2021a: 208).

Similar dynamics were evident in many of Kampala's lucrative major marketplaces, as the tussle to control their rents unfolded across the city. The fact that this occurred at a time of opening political competition provided significant scope for politicians to enter the marketplace with promises of a better deal for market vendors, often denouncing the privatization policy through populist, anti-formal interventions aimed at bolstering their social legitimacy. This approach was personified above all in Nasser Ssebagala, the city's first directly elected mayor from 1998. Associated for most of his political career with the opposition Democratic Party (DP), Ssebagala built his populist appeal around being the son of a vendor at the city's oldest market, Nakasero (see Figure 7.1), with an agenda to empower vendors. His catchphrase was 'seya', which has been translated as someone who 'wanders' and 'makes visits' (Monteith 2016: 158), but also as a local adaptation of the word 'share' used by the urban poor to denote camaraderie.[11] 'Seya' became his nickname, accompanying his slogan, 'forward with the common man's revolution'.[12] Shortly after being elected, Ssebagala was imprisoned for eleven months in the United States on fraud charges. This only increased his popularity as he was seen as a martyr, as well as a source of wealth that might be shared with his followers; he returned in 2000 to a hero's welcome, ran again for mayor and won decisively in 2006.[13] The markets were crucial sites of support—for example, it is estimated that 90 per cent of Owino market vendors were DP supporters.[14]

---

[7] 'St. Balikkudembe Produce Vendors and Traders Co-Operative Society'.
[8] Kayongo was still in place in 2010, after over two decades.
[9] Interview with vendors at Owino Market, 13 January 2010.
[10] Interview with Godfrey Kayongo, 13 October 2009.
[11] Interview with Ugandan academic, 23 September 2009.
[12] Interview with Ugandan politician, 12 October 2009.
[13] 'MPs declare Seya unfit for Cabinet', *Daily Monitor*, 2 June 2011.
[14] Interview with local trade development officers, Central Division, 5 October 2009.

Figure 7.1 Nakasero market, Kampala
Photograph © Tom Goodfellow.

Despite his promises to empower vendors, once back in power Ssebagala made a dramatic volte-face and embraced the national government's privatization agenda, continuing to negotiate the lease of some of Kampala's markets to politically connected private companies, reportedly for substantial bribes.[15] As anger at his betrayal grew among vendors, President Museveni saw an opportunity to reclaim some urban support and made his own populist counter-move to usurp the mayor's role as the 'saviour' of market vendors. Casting aside the official policy of privatizing markets by announcing support for vendors' taking direct control, this anti-formal pivot led to a surge of NRM support in the marketplaces (Goodfellow & Titeca 2012). Ssebagala too made a further U-turn, reverting to his earlier claims of support for vendors' rights, but this came too late as the sale of Nakasero market to a prominent tycoon had already been processed.[16] Not wanting to lose his own newly acquired political capital in the markets, Museveni met personally with vendors, declared the sale nullified and gave clearance to the vendors to redevelop Nakasero market themselves.[17] In so doing, he managed to significantly

[15] Interviews with Ugandan politician, 12 October 2009; local official, 22 September 2009.
[16] 'Ssebaggala stops the sale of Nakasero Market', *Daily Monitor*, 24 January 2007.
[17] Interviews with local officials, 5 October 2009.

(though temporarily) boost his popularity among a key sector of the population in Kampala, an opposition stronghold.

Each of Kampala's major marketplaces had its own complicated narrative involving corruption, factional in-fighting, and political intervention, often resulting in the casting aside or over-riding of proposed policies of market redevelopment, and with formal City Council structures largely bypassed.[18] Ultimately, multipartyism, decentralization, and privatization combined to both raise the stakes of political struggles over markets and fragment urban governance structures. Ssebaggala himself summed this up candidly:

> This is a capital city, we are fighting with so many interests! So this causes [government] most of the time to break down ... A minister says this, or the president says this ... at the end of the day also we have our interests, because we all are fishing in the same lake.[19]

This 'breaking down' of government can be seen as the consequence of politicians actively pursuing anti-formal strategies and tactics in pursuit of greater legitimacy among vendors to secure their votes. In the midst of all this, the formal institutions of the City Council were increasingly insignificant, despite being legally charged with managing all aspects of petty trade. When asked about why the markets were so disorganized and poorly managed, a city official noted that 'The vendors are strong because they have the vote, [but] we are on the low bargaining side.'[20] This was a term that KCC officials used repeatedly. The fact that the city authority's capacity to bargain was so weak—let alone that bureaucratic officials considered themselves in the business of 'bargaining' at all—speaks volumes not only about their limited infrastructural reach but about how anti-formal politics in Kampala exacerbated the city government's ineffectuality, while generating a range of marketplace rent opportunities for private interests.

Meanwhile, vendors themselves were engaging in a range of 'modalities of struggle' (Lindell & Ampaire 2016) that encompassed not only anti-formal activities such as unauthorized protests and riots (see Chapter 8), but also pro-formal forms of political mobilization. For example, in their appeals to the president, vendors explicitly invoked formal policies and laws such as the Land Act (1998) to claim their rights as 'sitting tenants' in the market. As Monteith explains, they drew upon 'an *impersonal* language of legal "rights"—a tool of their historical exclusion in Kampala—in order to prompt a *personal* intervention from a leader in need of new followers' (Monteith 2016: 63). Thus, while the kinds of interventions sought tended to be informal and often actively anti-formal, such as a presidential statement encouraging vendors to disregard official urban policy or process, these were sometimes leveraged through pro-formal vendor discourse.

---

[18] For a discussion of Kisekka Market, see Chapter 8, and also Baral (2018).
[19] Interview with Nasser Ssebaggala, 15 October 2009.
[20] Interview with local official, 22 September 2009.

Through these recurrent bursts of anti and pro-formal agitation and disruption, vendors managed to achieve an official turnaround, such that vendor-controlled markets became established in government policy by the end of the decade (Lindell & Ampaire 2016: 268). This, however, afforded the leadership of vendors' organizations increased scope to impose strict internal control through further centralizing decision-making and new forms of discipline, leading trust networks to disintegrate within the markets. An environment of heightened confusion and mistrust emerged, particularly in the politically charged context of the 2011 elections. When KCC was replaced by the unelected KCCA, control of the markets reverted to the city government: the hard-won achievement of vendor-controlled markets was reversed. Interestingly, there were not significant protests this time. The capacity to engage concertedly in either pro- or anti-formal politics had severely diminished, and 'politics' itself came to be seen by many vendors as amoral and unstructured—even as a sort of 'madness' (Monteith, 2016; see also Baral 2018). As the new city authority tried to further streamline markets through new forms of pro-formal administration and discipline, bottom-up marketplace politics became increasingly a-formal, mistrustful, and unpredictable in nature, with vendors' capacity to act in concert weakened. Meanwhile, KCCA's control over the markets led to little change on the ground in places like Owino, where Godfrey Kayongo not only consolidated his power but was given the official position of 'presidential advisor on markets' (Young 2021a: 208) amid ongoing complaints from disgruntled vendors about extorted and embezzled fees.[21]

Veterans and missing markets in Kigali's pro-formal push

Efforts to re-organize marketplaces in Kigali tell a very different story. When the RPF turned its attention to managing urbanization in the early twenty-first century, addressing the question of market trade was a clear priority in light of the broader concern with *akajagari* (defined as urban disorderliness, especially among the lower classes). This was something of an obsession for the ruling elite (Shearer 2017). Kigali's main market at the time was Nyarugenge, rehabilitated soon after the genocide by Kigali's first post-1994 mayor, Rose Kabuye. It occupied a central location in the CBD, and as with Owino in Kampala there were concerns about dilapidated infrastructure and over-congestion of the market and surrounding streets. Early in the new millennium, the government decided that the main vending markets should be located outside the city centre where congestion would be less problematic. In 2004, Nyarugenge market was demolished, with

---

[21] https://ugandaradionetwork.net/story/owino-market-gear-up-for-200-million-development-after-museveni-visit; https://ugandaradionetwork.net/story/controversy-as-owino-market-leadership-asks-vendors-to-pay-arrears.

the site then sold in 2006 to Kigali Investment Group, a group of investors close to the RPF regime, to be redeveloped as a multi-storey commercial shopping centre. Meanwhile, the government considered the city's thriving *caguwa* (secondhand clothing) markets to be antithetical to its development vision and set about trying to eradicate them, with the city's largest *caguwa* market at Nyabugogo eventually being razed in 2014 (Shearer 2017).

The government proposed that each of the city's three districts should have one main covered market, open seven days a week and owned by the district, along with being allowed several smaller peripheral open marketplaces. In practice, many of these operated just one day each week. No trading was officially allowed outside these areas.[22] Kimironko Market in Gasabo District was redeveloped to become the city's largest, with one section reserved for people displaced from Nyarugenge. There were inevitably conflicts because so many people wanted to secure a space at Kimironko, and the district claimed to have ensured transparency in allocating spaces through a randomized 'tombola' system. Once the market was considered full (amounting to little over a thousand vendors), no more were admitted. Although still owned by the district authorities, after 2008 the market was managed by the Kigali Veterans Co-operative Society (KVCS), a group of Rwandan Patriotic Army veterans who won the tender to manage all the markets in Gasabo District. Their main responsibility was to collect revenues from the market vendors and ensure security and hygiene, closely supervised by the District authorities.[23]

On one level, how the government approached the 'problem' of marketplaces in Kigali was similar to that in Kampala: selling off plots of prime land in the city centre to private investors linked to the regime, and putting politically linked organizations in charge of revenue collection. However, in terms of both the motivations and urban outcomes of these processes, the two diverged. By contrast with Kampala's markets such as Owino, where funds were embezzled, violent factional conflict rife, and congestion exacerbated as vendor numbers soared, the main district markets were fitted with new infrastructure and their governance was subsumed under district authority. The handing over of the management of all markets in one district to a single army veterans' organization ensured that any efforts to organize market traders were both staunchly pro-formal and pro-RPF. Knowing that markets hold potential as sites of urban mobilization and resistance, state infrastructural power was extended into these spaces through KVCS.

None of this, however, is to say that the management of Kigali's marketplaces was unproblematic. The construction of new marketplaces seriously lagged behind the 'cleaning up' and dispersal of vendors from old ones. As well as devastating many vendors' livelihoods, it also generated the opposite problem from

---

[22] Interview with various city officials, 2009–2010.
[23] Interview with Kimironko Market president, 29 January 2010.

that in Kampala: there simply weren't *enough* markets around to cater for people's needs near to where they lived and worked.[24] Many people living outside the city centre had to travel long distances of three to four kilometres just to obtain basic goods, in an reversal of the situation prior to the 2000s where trade was everywhere.[25] Even Kimironko itself was earmarked for upgrading into a shopping mall in 2016, with vendors given sudden notice of eviction (Finn 2018). In some cases, vendors managed to continue operating even after the destruction of markets— as, for example, when Nyabugogo's *caguwa* vendors rapidly reassembled in a new space at Biryogo several kilometres to the south, following the intervention of a district mayor (Shearer 2017: 142). In much of the city however, regulations around the creation of new spaces for vending were so strictly enforced that the creation of unofficial trading centres was difficult (Sommers 2012; Shearer 2017; Thomson 2018). This was highly problematic given that marketplaces had received the second largest number of votes (ranking above educational facilities and childcare) in a survey preceding the development of the Conceptual Master Plan about the most pressing land-use needs of urban residents (Oz Architecture 2007a: 31).

These dynamics illustrate the extent to which the Rwandan government strives to control numbers of markets and vendors, and its *relative* capacity to organize people through infrastructural reach and pro-formal market governance in the face of blatant evidence that city-dwellers need more markets. While appeasing vendors as a source of social legitimacy was central to marketplace politics in Kampala—at least until the more heavy-handed but short-lived tactics of KCCA after 2011, explored more later—the treatment of vendors in Kigali demonstrates the extent to which transforming urban space has been prioritized over winning the support of poorer groups of urban workers. The constant trumpeting of clean streets, including through its embassy websites around the world (Finn 2018), takes precedence over garnering the support of market vendors and their customers. There was little scope for them to mobilize into associations or unions independently of the state, and vendors consequently had little bargaining power in relation to issues such as the level of market fees, which were a serious burden on vendors, forcing some out of business and limiting their ability to save and accumulate resources even for the few who managed to work in markets.[26] Here the vendors, rather than the city government, were 'on the low bargaining side'. For many, the response was to attempt life as a street trader, spent mostly on the run from police and establishing 'nomadic space' in which to trade (Shearer 2017)—something explored further in the next section.

---

[24] Interview with local trade supervisor, 8 February 2010. Interview with a District Mayor, 15 December 2009.
[25] Interviews with various Rwandan government and civil-society sources, 2009–2010.
[26] Interview with former market traders, 17 December 2009. See also 'Kimisagara vendors irked by high charges' *The New Times*, 12 March 2011.

Not quite 'shaking' Merkato: The endurance
of Africa's biggest marketplace

The geography of market trade in Addis Ababa was permanently reshaped by the creation of Merkato under the Italian occupation, and a consideration of the story of Merkato in recent decades reveals how it has been shaped by the distinctive politics of the city. Reputedly the largest open market in Africa, the area already had around four thousand registered businesses by the 1970s (Ross & Berhe 1974) and its expansion continued under successive regimes, such that by 2016 there were sixty thousand businesses registered in Addis Ketema (the city subdivision in which Merkato is mostly based) ranging from wholesale textiles and clothing to goldsmiths, food produce, household utensils, and services such as restaurants and barbers. The market covers an area of 1.7 square kilometres, organized into *terras* (specialized quarters) for specific kinds of items and services (Truneh 2013; Vrscaj & Lewis 2016). Smaller-scale markets also exist around the city, notably in areas such Megenagna, Arada and more specifically Piazza, which was the central site of market activity prior to the Italian occupation and has remained an area of flourishing commercial activity ever since.

Contemporary Merkato been described as an 'organism' in which the more formal storekeepers exist in symbiotic relationships with market vendors, kiosk owners, 'mobile marketers', and various intermediaries (Vrscaj & Lewis 2016: 122). Over 250,000 people work and live in its orbit, with a further 300,000 commuting there to work or shop daily (Truneh 2013; Vrscaj & Lewis 2016). Although it was originally dominated by Muslims and members of the Guraghe ethnic group, as a magnet for migrants it evolved into a hub of cultural, ethnic, and religious differ-ence, with a substantial degree of mutual tolerance and social harmony (Truneh 2013: 306). Perhaps because of this and the interoperative relations between the elements of the market 'organism', the pitching of traders against street vendors— which has been central to the politics of petty trade in Kampala (as discussed later)—does not have the same currency in Addis Ababa (or at least in Merkato).

Despite this, the area has at times come under substantial pressure both from the city government and major developers. As a consequence of the land-leasing policy adopted in 1993 (see Chapter 3), from the mid-1990s businesses in Merkato were supposed to progressively purchase leases to the land and buildings they had long been using, with lease fees set substantially higher than other parts of the city. This led to significant mobilization against these changes by Merkato-based businesses, spearheaded by the larger ones via the chamber of commerce and the creation of a 'Merkato and Surrounding Special Committee' (Mengistu & an Dijk 2011: 37; Mengistu 2013: 318). These higher-level businesspeople within Merkato possessed both the knowledge and connections to play the formal and pro-formal political game, working through legitimated processes and discourses to make their claims.

Shortly after this, the whole market came under existential threat when a Malaysian investment firm Adorna-Shebele agreed to purchase the lease to the whole area in 1999 and spend US$6bn transforming it into a 'modern' commercial hub and satellite town (Truneh 2013: 308). In an area so lucrative that land values reputedly equal those in New York City (Vrscaj & Lewis 2016: 123), this would have generated substantial government revenue under the lease system as well as injecting massive investment into the wider economy. However, the potential disruption was enormous, necessitating mass relocation on an unprecedented scale. The threat of this deal going through further galvanized social ties and lobbying capacity within the Merkato community, bolstering the political weight of trader and worker associations as they solidified communal bonds and demanded greater voice (Angélil & Siress 2010; Mengistu & van Dijk 2011; Duroyaume 2015).

Eventually, the Malaysian company withdrew on the grounds that the Addis Ababa City Authority refused to commit US$20m towards relocation costs for displaced businesses (Truneh 2013: 308). By the end of 2001, building on a long history of ingenuity rooted in vendors 'dogged struggle for survival' through successive regimes (Zewde 2005: 129), the 'Merkato and Surrounding Special Committee' had become highly effective lobbyists, exerting a significant influence over aspects of both the revised land-lease system and urban-planning framework (Mengistu & van Dijk 2011: 37–38; Yusuf et al. 2009). In their attempts to resist punitively high lease payments, they successfully lobbied for the extension of repayment periods, reduced down-payments, and lower interest rates on leases: changes codified in the Urban Lease Holding Proclamation of 2002. Moreover, they also helped to persuade the city administration to reduce its building height requirements in the revised Master Plan that was underway, successfully insisting that two to three storey buildings be permissible in the area (Angélil & Siress 2010; Mengistu & van Dijk 2011).

The experience of the threat from the Malaysian developer also gave local businesses the confidence to attempt a broader redevelopment of the area themselves through the Merkato Millennium Development Partnership initiated in 2003, supported by German aid. This process was further galvanized by Arkebe Oqubay, the city's mayor from 2003 (later to play a key role in Ethiopia's industrialization strategy), who entered office with a drive to transform Merkato. The market, he said, was 'one big sleeping city. Someone needs to shake Merkato to wake it up from its slumber' (cited in Mengistu 2013: 322). However, the Merkato Millenium Development Partnership achieved little, lacking clear framework for the responsibilities of public versus private actors and producing ongoing disputes and mistrust (Mengistu 2013). After the 2005 election, the project was abandoned and any major redevelopment efforts lost momentum. The government was now acutely attuned to the threat of urban dissent and any major disruptions to Merkato's residents and workers lost their appeal, especially given the evident capacity for the area's business interests to mobilize as a powerful lobby.

While specific plots in the area have periodically been leased for extraordinary amounts of money—one plot was leased for a staggering $15,872 per square metre, higher at the time than the average price for developed real estate in Geneva[27]— Merkato has largely been left to evolve in a more piecemeal way. This contrasts with the ongoing factional clientelist politics of Kampala's marketplaces, and the radical re-organization that swept across Kigali. Rather than being a space in which struggles for both rents and votes in the city were to repeatedly play out (as in Kampala), or a socio-spatial 'problem' over which there was a perceived need to exert concerted top-down pro-formal control (Kigali), the collective constituency and bargaining experience of Merkato's community had bought it a certain degree of autonomy and enhanced associational power. As a consequence, in Merkato there is neither a dominant politics of disrupting extant formal institutions, nor a continuing effort by the regime to 'straighten' the market's practices into line with specific government visions. Faced with the revealed associational power of its vendors, and with higher priority projects around housing and transport to prioritize in pursuit of urban social legitimation, after 2005 the EPRDF had a significant interest in not 'shaking' Merkato in the ways that Arkebe Oqubay initially intended. Rather than stepping forward, the state largely stepped back.

7.3 The street economy: Forbearance, hunting, and hustle

'Street trade' can mean many things. I use it here to encompass three distinct activities, which often have different regulatory frameworks: street vending (where vendors remain stationary, displaying goods on the pavement), hawking (where vendors carry their goods and move around), and kiosks (where traders erect a 'lock-up' structure on the pavement or other open area). People involved in these activities, particularly in the former two categories, are commonly scapegoated by governments for congestion, disease, disorder, and waste generation; indeed, in the worlds of policy they are often among the most reviled city-dwellers (Bromley 2000; Mitullah 2003; Mackie et al. 2014), depicted as being intrinsically 'out of place (Yatmo 2008). Yet they are also the most significant component of urban informal economies in Africa after home-based workers (Brown & Lyons 2010; Ezeadichie 2012). These activities disproportionately involve women, who are therefore particularly vulnerable to the ire of state agencies seeking to assert their authority over urban space.

---

[27] 'Merkato sees another massive bid', Ethiosports, 9 November 2016. https://www.ethiosports.com/2016/11/09/merkato-sees-another-massive-bid/.

While street trade is significant across virtually all cities of the global South, this kind of street-level informal work is an arena for the playing out of politics, and is therefore highly variable and dependent on political context. Streets are not only part of the fabric of hard infrastructure, but spaces in which infrastructural power can be extended and performed, places through which governments pursue particular paths of legitimation, and platforms on which street workers themselves seek to negotiate and improve their position through varying modalities of political informality. The following three subsections comparatively examine the street economy in Kampala, Kigali, and Addis Ababa and the varying ways in which they have been shaped through political interventions and popular responses.

Kampala: 'We remove them, the politicians bring them back'[28]

Though in much of central Kampala it is hard to imagine that the state has ever attempted to regulate street trade, in fact there have long been extensive regulations that Kampala City Council sporadically took drastic action to enforce, even before the shift to KCCA in 2011. Different legal statuses and regulations applied to the different forms of street trade: hawkers, known as *batembeyi*, were legal if they had secured a license, but were obliged by bylaws constantly to keep moving (see Figure 7.2). Street vendors (with a few exceptions such as newspaper sellers) were entirely illegal after an ordinance to this effect was passed in 2006. Kiosk-operators were allowed only in permitted areas.

As most markets in Kampala were informal (or 'ungazetted'), in reality street vending and kiosks exist on a continuum with marketplaces. In considering how the politics of this plays out, consider the following quotation, in which the interviewee adopts the 'voice' of a state representative negotiating with a kiosk owner:

> You put a kiosk there on the roadside and then I come up and say you know what? According to the laws you are not supposed to have any kiosk in the road reserve. You need to have a trading licence, you need to have facilities a, b, c, d, which you do not have—so remove it [...] Maybe you earn 10,000 per day, you tell me, 'Ok I will give you 1,500 a day out of my profit, just to leave me to operate my business.' You get a second, a third [kiosk]. Now, that cumulative resource that I get makes me become a mafia, because I will not be operating alone. We will become a group of people who offer you protection. In the meantime, that grows into a market. After some time it becomes difficult to handle because when anyone tells me that 'you people are responsible for those things, you need to remove them', I've got a group of people who have reached up to maybe 1,000, 2,000, whom I've got

---

[28] Interview with local official, 22 September 2009.

Figure 7.2 A street hawker, Kampala
Photograph © Tom Goodfellow.

to displace, and [...] I've taken money from them. I will not be able to displace them.[29]

Prior to the introduction of KCCA, these challenges were exacerbated by the highly fragmented nature of regulatory enforcement. Responsibility for managing street traders lay with a team of 150 city law officers (CLOs), working from 8am to 5pm and armed only with handcuffs.[30] Any attempt to move street traders on were largely futile, since they returned and set up again after hours. Moreover, there was no guarantee that CLOs' activities would be supported by the police; as the principal CLO in 2010 noted, 'here in Uganda politics takes the upper hand [...] so sometimes the police are ordered not to intervene.'[31] At other times, police actively intervened on the side of the illegal vendors. All of this increased the incentive for CLOs to turn a blind eye for a bribe—but in order to keep up appearances, the periodic charade of attempting to move vendors on would continue.

This was part of a broader pattern through which non-enforcement of trade regulations was fuelled both by regularized patterns of everyday corruption among street-level bureaucrats (Blundo et al. 2006) and by political clientelism in the

---

[29] Interview Ugandan academic, 10 February 2009. Other sources also expressed the view that the actors protecting informal traders 'literally' constituted a mafia (interview with independent planning consultant, 4 February 2009).
[30] Interview with city law officer, 7 January 2010; interview with local official, 22September 2009.
[31] Interview with city law officer, 7 January 2010.

context of Kampala's intensely competitive politics, especially after the opening of multiparty competition in 2005. While street traders were often considered 'thugs' or *bayaye* (see Chapter 4), attempts to establish larger commercial premises in illegal sites were frequently associated with army veterans and other politically favoured groups. According to one source, veterans had 'taken most of the open spaces. They come and sit on them, construct their makeshift buildings … they build markets there, shops, which are not approved by council … without any guided development control whatever.' As former soldiers, these people were described as 'untouchable', with 'blessing from high authorities'.[32] The bond between army veterans and top NRM cadres was very strong even after years of peace and demobilization; yet in contrast to the example from Kigali above, the favours afforded to Kampala's army veterans often took the form of 'untouchability' in relation to their trade activities, rather than an official contract to manage a formal marketplace. Veterans claimed to be 'strange squatters of the ruling party', and whenever there was open space publicly owned by KCC 'these people grab it'. Were it not for the blessing from above, 'it would be easy' to remove them.[33]

Prior to the institution of KCCA, whenever the City Council attempted a more concerted 'cleaning-up' drive, senior politicians would simply shut these efforts down. For example, one morning in September 2008, a team of CLOs arrived in the Wandageya neighbourhood to remove the kiosks built illegally in the road reserve, after issuing several warnings and having their operation approved by the local police commander. At around 10am they began removing the kiosks and loading them onto a truck to ferry them away. However, at 12.30pm, Major General Kale Kayihura—then the Inspector General of Police, the most senior policeman in Uganda—arrived in person. Complaining that the operation was causing a traffic jam, Kayihura demanded that the removal exercise be halted immediately and the kiosks put back. Some of the vendors reportedly wept before Kayihura in gratitude.

These clashes between state agencies can sometimes become alarmingly violent. A few months after the above episode, a fight broke out between CLOs attempting to remove illegal street vendors and some traffic police who intervened in the vendors' defence. Initially the CLOs overcame the traffic police, and sped off to escape in their vehicle. However, their path was subsequently blocked by a group of *boda-boda* (motorcycle taxi) drivers, who had joined the vendors' cause and formed a barrier across the road, as had a growing number of police officers arriving at the scene. The CLOs were soon outnumbered, and one of them was badly beaten by the policemen and *boda-boda* drivers, who were now acting in concert in an attempt to lynch him.[34]

---

[32] Interview with local politician, 6 January 2010.
[33] Interview with local politician, 6 January 2010.
[34] Sources for this account include: interview with Ugandan academic, 23 September 2009; *The New Vision*, 17 September 2008; *Daily Monitor*, 26 September 2008; *The New Vision*, 16 February 2010.

The non-enforcement of regulations that allowed street vending to thrive was therefore not always attributable to street-level bureaucrats taking bribes; it was often a consequence of clientelistic links with political actors, often enacted through the police. Furthermore, some vendors were said to be political agents, given protection in exchange for 'informing' on local activities; they might also be 'poor relatives' and ethnic kin of politicians, who installed them there to secure them some kind of livelihood.[35] One official complained that 'we remove them, the politicians bring them back.'[36] This political guardianship might also be combined with bribes to officials and police, so that basically '*everyone* protects them!'[37] Kampala's streets were thus teeming with people who for one reason or another had become 'untouchable', with *boda boda* drivers themselves forming a particularly stark example, as explored elsewhere (Goodfellow & Titeca 2012; Goodfellow 2015).

These processes of protection evoke Holland's (2016) concept of 'forbearance' (see Chapter 2), rather than weak state enforcement capacity. Since 'forbearance' is by definition a *revocable* leniency towards violations of the law (Holland 2016), it is entirely consistent with sporadic crackdowns. These were particularly targeted at street vendors, considered to be the greatest nuisance (Ahikire & Ampaire 2003). Most notably, in 2002 KCC undertook 'Operation Clean the City' to remove them, partly under pressure from retailers in small shops angered by illegal competition (Ahikire & Ampaire 2003: 45). This elicited some initial compliance but did not last long (Young 2017). Such crackdowns seemed to fulfil the function of reminding 'untouchables' of why they should be grateful that they were usually tacitly permitted to operate.

After the creation of KCCA, however, there was an especially concerted effort at sweeping street vendors away, this time with much more political muscle and resource behind it. The initial effects of this were extreme, with estimates that the number of vendors declined by 80–90 per cent after KCCA began its aggressive programme in 2011; those who attempted to remain on the streets faced a draconian regime of steep fines, arrests, and confiscated goods (Young 2017). During this period, vendors adopted a range of responses from cooperatively relocating to specified (and generally unprofitable) new trading spaces, continuing to bribe officials, taking to streets nocturnally, and attempting to mobilize politically despite increasing legal restrictions (Young 2018). As with the other early moves undertaken by KCCA, the clampdown on street trade involved a gamble on the part of the central government—channelled through its newly centralized city authority under Jennifer Musisi—to court support among the growing urban middle classes, even if this meant sacrificing street vendors: with the 2011 election out of the way,

---

[35] Interview with Ugandan academic, 23 September 2009.
[36] Interview with local official, 1 October 2009.
[37] Interview with trade development officer, 5 October 2009.

the support of the latter was deemed expendable. Moreover, the Kampala City Traders Association, which represents formal shop owners in the city, had long been lobbying against what they perceived as unfair competition from street vendors, and KCCA provided a new opportunity for their voice to be heard (Young 2017).

The aggressive moves against street trade played into the mounting battle between Musisi and the elected (but relatively powerless) Lord Mayor Erias Lukwago. In the period 2011–2016, Kampala became a theatre for even greater political struggles between different wings of the city government than previously, in large part due to the treatment of street vendors. Lukwago's weakened political wing was no longer able to wade in and simply overturn bureaucratic 'cleaning-up' efforts, and he instead ramped up his political mobilization of city-dwellers against Musisi's urban regime (Young 2017; Muwanga et al. 2020). As KCCA's efforts to remove street vendors persisted more vigorously and for longer than at any other point in Kampala's history, vendors responded through intensifying their support to Lukwago. Meanwhile, support for Musisi's urban beautification projects—and with it support for the NRM in Kampala—gradually drained away. It was not only the public that turned against the KCCA project: so too, perversely, did Museveni. According to a senior KCCA official, as the 2016 election loomed, the president 'directly asked us to stop enforcement activities, and within two weeks the sidewalks were full.'[38] This reversal came, however, too late to undo the political damage done. Lukwago increased his vote share to hold the lord mayoralty in 2016, while support to the NRM sunk to historic lows in the city, which Museveni explicitly blamed on Musisi's actions (Young 2017; 2018; Muwanga et al. 2020).

After the 2016 election, Musisi attempted to resurrect her tough stance on street vending but faced heightened and increasingly violent resistance. This period was, according to a KCCA source, '*very* violent. Some KCCA enforcers lost their eyes.'[39] One enforcer was said to have sustained major brain injuries and spent a month in intensive care after a tussle with vendors. Musisi herself blamed vendors' violent resistance on vocal support provided to them by politicians.[40] By 2018, the vendors once again appeared to have the upper hand and the will to regulate and coerce them off the streets had largely dissipated. This culminated in Musisi's resignation in October 2018, citing a consistent lack of support from the central government for her efforts since 2016. These events demonstrate how the project to build the regime's social legitimacy among the urban middle classes failed, in part due to inconsistent support for it from the president, and the long-term stoking of anti-formal politics that fuelled violent contestation of efforts to implement

---

[38] Interview with KCCA official, 3 May 2018.
[39] Interview with KCCA official, 3 May 2018.
[40] 'Musisi: K'la politicians inciting attacks on KCCA law enforcers', *The Observer (Uganda)*, 18 August 2017. https://observer.ug/news/headlines/54461-musisi-k-la-politicians-inciting-attacks-on-kcca-law-enforcers.

a formal street trade regime. With the end of the Musisi project, forbearance again became widespread.

Kigali: 'Donors have been hunting to see where they are gone'

If the harsh circumstances for vendors in Kampala from 2011–2016 were an aberration in Kampala's recent history, these conditions have long been the norm in Kigali. Even before the marketplaces were re-organized, Mayor Theoneste Mutsindashyaka was attempting to clear the city centre of the city's *abazunguzayi* (street traders and hawkers) from the early 2000s, in response to a survey by the Kigali Institute for Science and Technology. This lamented that 94 per cent of the city's enterprises were unregistered, and recommended reconstituting street vendors and hawkers as registered formal workers (KIST 2001). From 2001, aggressive police raids on *abazunguzayi* were regular occurrences (Shearer 2017: 158). Early efforts to realize aspects of Kigali's 2007 Master Plan accelerated the drive to sweep street life away, as the demolition of slums and associated dispersal of residents to the urban fringes transplanted many petty traders' lives out of the centre. Other vendors were relocated into buildings, often to the detriment of trade that depended largely on visibility and positioning. The kiosks that once lined the city centre's streets were likewise removed.[41] The following discussion focuses particularly on the period from 2007 to 2010, which was especially intense in the government's campaign to transform Kigali.

The push to re-organize urban informal workers saw the government embracing the creation of cooperatives and 'sensitizing' the population about the benefits of this organizational form. This re-organization was considered especially pressing given that 67 per cent of the city's population were classified as 'youth'—albeit with an expansive definition that reaches up to thirty-five years of age—many of whom were considered 'idle', 'dispersed', and 'needed something to do' to prevent them 'getting involved in banditry'.[42] This echoes the government's broader fixation on finding something for youth to do, rather than understanding what their priorities are in the context of alarming levels of urban destitution (Sommers 2012). The particularly high prevalence of youth in Kigali—extreme even within a demographically young country and continent—is partly attributable to genocide and refugee return, combined with the migration of young people to the city to seek work that would enable them to build a house and transition to adulthood (Sommers 2012).

The majority of Kigali's population were therefore deemed suitable for organization into 'youth organizations', of which there were forty-seven in 2010, comprising groups from mobile phone 'airtime' vendors, forex traders, carpenters, and

---

[41] Interview with Rwandan civil-society representatives, 2009–2010.
[42] Interview with youth and education inspector, Kigali City, 27 November 2009.

Figure 7.3 A man sweeps streets on the outskirts of Kigali during *umuganda*
Photograph © Tom Goodfellow.

hairdressers to minibus and motorcycle-taxi drivers.[43] From around 2008, through the promotion of cooperatives the government attempted to move people out of petty trade into other activities, from basket-weaving and mushroom-growing to construction. Part of the aim was quite literally to prevent people from 'moving around': Kigali City's Youth and Education Inspector explained that 'we don't want these sellers moving around the city. We want people to be in the same place as it is easy for leadership to find them and help them. [...] So you won't see people working individually.'[44]

This top-down effort to mould livelihoods from individual, unregistered activities to cooperatives served several purposes. As well as in theory increasing earning capacity, pooling risk, and facilitating savings and credit, all these organizations participated in voluntary 'youth activities', such as 'cleaning and greening' urban spaces (see Figure 7.3) as a complement to *umuganda*—Rwanda's monthly compulsory community works day, through which information is filtered up right through the governmental structures from the village level to the province. The youth cooperatives' extra-curricular activities were turned into competitions, whereby they were ranked on their community activities, with those ranked last being 'shamed in public'.[45] Yet cooperatives also helped to render the urban poor

---

[43] List of Kigali City Co-operatives and Associations, acquired from CoK.
[44] Interview with youth and education inspector, Kigali City, 27 November 2009.
[45] Interview with local official, Kigali City, 27 November 2009.

more legible, and organizing them was described by another official as being 'not only an economic issue but a security issue'.[46] While this was justified by officials mostly at a superficial level ('if someone sells bananas on the street he can make an accident'), it also reflects the deeper perceived 'dangers' of *akajagari*: disorderly urbanization. Discourses linking street trade to security are common in campaigns against vendors (Bromley 2000), but have a particular resonance in post-genocide Rwanda. Linking cooperatives to security reflected ongoing efforts to inculcate a 'mindset'—a popular English world in Rwandan government circles—through which security was popularly associated with government-sponsored organization, and indeed with government legitimacy.

However, the rapid shrinkage of informal activity from the city centre's streets cannot simply be accounted for by 're-organization'; there were also various forms of 'disappearing' at play. The government acknowledged that many youths were effectively forced to leave the city due to lack of livelihood options, though they attempted to paint this in a positive light. Consider the following quotation from a former Minister of Infrastructure, which vacillates between conceding that there was little space for the poor in the city and arguing that their situation was actually being improved:

Some young people decided to run away from Kigali because the rent is expensive, jobs are paying less, life is almost impossible for low earners in Kigali. There are no hawkers, there is nowhere you can buy cheap food. So they ran away, they are very upset with the city and the government. They go back to their village but because they have been in town they know what is required here. [...] A few years later they come back in a different shape.

Donors have been hunting to see where they are gone. You don't see them. In Nairobi the people who are left out from development in the urban area go and expand the slum of Kibera. In Rwanda those who are left out, you don't see them [...] They are not even gone ... they have changed mode of production. Those who were selling things in scattered manner are in cooperatives and sell in the marketplace or they sell in a shop. There are many to own one shop, so it's like transforming their little little into one big asset [...] Some run away, some get organized and recycle in city activities [...] but there is no ground in the whole republic where you find people who have been victim of all these processes of change and they are getting worse off. [Donors] think they are *pushed* in the rural area ... but [donors] go to the rural area and they don't see instability from those who are pushed from town [...] they are pushed from selling on the street and they get help to sell in the marketplace where they sell more goods and get help to sell in a more organized way.[47]

---

[46] Interview with economic development officer, Kigali City, 3 December 2009.
[47] Interview with Minister of Infrastructure, 9 December 2009.

Aside from the fact that his claims of 'no hawkers' is a clear exaggeration, the minister's awkward juxtaposition of people being 'left out' from development and yet not worse off, being pushed from the streets and yet not pushed from the city, is very telling. Even some critical voices within civil society acknowledged that the narrative of people working 'in a more organized way' was 'partly true',[48] but this celebrated cooperativization is clearly only part of the story. By one estimation, when 'the so-called re-organization' took place 'around 40 per cent of the people had their livelihoods moved in a planned way ... the rest were just chased away'.[49]

A number of former vendors were relocated in 2007 from Kigali's first major slum clearance at Ubumwe (a city-centre informal settlement next to the upmarket Kiyovu area, known locally as 'Kiyovu Poor') to Batsinda, one of the only low-cost urban housing settlements developed for evictees, with just 250 units (see Chapter 6). Given Batsinda's location far out on the distant urban fringe, most displaced vendors were in reality not making a livelihood via the government-sponsored cooperatives, and could not find other work.[50] Agriculture was not an option, since they owned no land and as lifelong city-dwellers 'would have no idea what to do'.[51] Meanwhile people displaced from Gaculiro (see Figure 7.4), where an even larger eviction was undertaken in 2009 to clear space for the absurdly high-end 'Vision City' project (see Chapter 6), were effectively 'ruralized' and expected to keep cows or cultivate crops on their small plots.[52] In contrast to the minister's statement, displaced communities in both Batsinda and one such rural estate claimed to be earning less than before. Many also had to commute into the city to make a living and paid up to RWF2,000 per day on transport, an enormous financial burden.[53] Some observers believe that people on Kigali's peri-urban fringe were often worse off even than in other *rural* provinces, due to higher living costs and limited scope for agriculture.[54] These problems appear to be persisting with the recent government move to provide evictees with in-kind compensation in the form of houses in peripheral locations (Nikuze et al. 2019; 2020; Uwayezu & De Vries 2020b).

There is also a much darker side to the minimization of visible informality in Kigali. In the shadows of the discourse of 're-organization', those seeking a livelihood on the street were relentlessly hunted, swept away, and detained at Kigali's notorious Gikondo Detention Centre. Based in a warehouse previously belonging to Félicien Kabuga, a high profile genocide fugitive who was finally captured

---

[48] Interview with Rwandan civil-society representative, 11 December 2009.

[49] Interview with Rwandan civil-society representative, 11 December 2009.

[50] Interviews with residents at Batsinda relocation settlement, 17 December 2009.

[51] Interview with local community representative, 17 December 2009.

[52] Interview with community leader in a rural displacement area within the boundaries of Kigali City, 17 December 2009.

[53] Interviews with local leader and with Batsinda residents, 17 December 2009. This was equivalent to around 2 GBP at the time of this particular research in 2009/10.

[54] Interview with local researcher, 8 December 2009.

Figure 7.4 A hawker in Kigali walks through the rubble of a demolished informal settlement

Photograph © Tom Goodfellow.

in France in May 2020, this informal 'transit centre' operating since 2002 became widely known as Kwa Kabuga ('Kabuga's Place').[55] Large numbers of street hawkers were taken there alongside street children, sex workers, and petty criminals. They were often picked up 'just for selling things in the street',[56] taken to Kwa Kabuga without any formal procedure, and kept for up to a month or longer.[57] A former detainee described it as having four separate compounds for street children, petty thieves, women (whose hair was cut off on entry), and 'vagrant' men and street traders, with a meeting place in the centre.[58] Other sources claim that many detainees die due to the poor conditions.[59] Human Rights Watch published a report on the centre in 2006, claiming that it held six hundred people at any time and detailing its lack of legal status, severe overcrowding, lack of medical care, and requirement that detainees pay for basic amenities including water (Human Rights Watch 2006). The report recommended the centre's immediate closure. As of 2015 however, Kwa Kabuga was still in operation and central to ongoing efforts to eliminate street trade (Human Rights Watch 2015; Shearer 2017; Finn 2018). Perhaps

[55] Interview with former detainee at *Kwa Kabuga*, 8 February 2010.
[56] Interview with street hawker (translated from French), 8 February 2010.
[57] Interview with street hawker (translated from French), 8 February 2010.
[58] Interview with former detainee at *Kwa Kabuga*, 8 February 2010.
[59] Interview with independent Rwandese journalist, 3 February 2010. See also Shearer (2017).

the ultimate irony of the clampdown on informality was that informality itself—albeit of a resolutely pro-formal variety that sought to enforce top-down official visions—was perpetuated through the highly informal procedures associated with Kwa Kabuga.

In its sheer determination to eliminate the street economy, Kigali City Council even passed a resolution in 2009 to criminalize the clients of street traders as well as traders themselves.[60] Yet just as the endurance of Kwa Kabuga illustrates the uses of informality in efforts to stamp out informal street trade, it also demonstrates the impossibility of doing so, no matter how many criminalizing laws are put in place. The street economy is ineradicable in Kigali both due to the very small formal economy and the ongoing need for goods and services affordable to a large low-income urban population—especially given the problems with markets noted above. The narrative of zero informal trade is an illusion, and the continued presence of *abazunguzayi* is essential for the survival of the urban poor (Finn 2018; Shearer 2020). This, however, does not negate the distinct impacts that extreme criminalization and relentless chasing has had on the city. In contrast to the normal state of play in Kampala (outside the dramatic interlude of the early KCCA era) the operation of street trade in Kigali has long depended on what Shearer (2017) terms 'nomadic space'. In other words, Kigali's street economy is about being constantly on the run.

Shearer (2017; 2020) describes how police crackdowns on vendors that occurred twice daily in areas around Nyabugogo bus station did not actually prevent such trade occurring, merely displacing it to other streets. The situation escalated when in 2014 and 2016 street traders were actually killed in public by security forces, the second of these being a woman who was beaten to death merely for selling produce. This generated a tipping point after the Ministry of Gender became involved, leading to a process which—ironically given the prior destruction of markets—precipitated a decision to build two new markets nearby (Shearer 2020). Whether this leads to a change in the treatment of street traders more generally remains to be seen. But since they are still seen as presenting a threat to the image of Kigali as the modern services hub presented in Chapter 5, their stigmatization persists, normalizing a nomadic, cat-and-mouse street economy. The use of the Kinyarwanda term *gukatakata* (to zigzag) is particularly evocative here of the need to dodge security forces, potentially at a moment's notice. As Shearer (2020) notes, the language of 'zigzagging' is prevalent in many African cities—perhaps most lucidly evoked by the opening chapter of Quayson's (2014) *Oxford Street, Accra*—but in Kigali takes a distinctive form in the face of the government's constant efforts to fashion the city into straight lines.

This pro-formal drive to structure associational life and keep the street economy on the run, and the consequent fact that that Kigali's street traders cannot

---

[60] 'Nyarugenge to Penalise Vendors' Clients', *The New Times*, 11 September 2009.

engage in autonomous collective mobilization, necessitates zigzagging not only on the streets but in terms of social and political relations; they have to engage in what Simone (2018) terms 'moving sideways' when it comes to social and political interactions, as explored further in Chapter 8. Kigali's street workers need to engage in 'ensemble work' to get by, with resource-pooling characteristic of 'solidarity entrepreneurialism' (Kinyanjui 2014) being essential to survival in this harsh operational environment. Yet direct bargaining with state actors of the kind that generates widespread 'forbearance' in Kampala is impossible in a context where the government has so thoroughly staked its legitimation on ideas of a 'modern' city, implemented through ruthless pro-formal discourse, and in which the urban poor have never managed to substantially grow their associational power.

Addis Ababa: Street hustle and the party-state's employment promise

While government approaches to the street economy in Addis Ababa since the mid-2000s display strong parallels with Kigali, the filtering of these through Ethiopia's particular historical legacies and political dynamics has produced a distinct economic streetscape. A first legacy relates to the salience of government-sponsored education in Ethiopian modern history. The prioritization of education by Haile Selassie (see Chapter 4) was part of a broader expansion of state bureaucracy, which inculcated ideas of meritocracy as well as middle-class urban sensibilities and aspirations (Markakis 1974). This contrasts with what was taking place in most colonized African states at the time. Second and related, the drive to expand education and bureaucracy generated increased dependence on the state. Economic and bureaucratic re-organization under the Derg's communist regime exacerbated this by radically expanding the state's role in employment creation and certain kinds of services (Clapham 1988). Aspirations of socio-economic mobility were connected to access to state education and other forms of state support. This set up expectations that could not be met, trends that continued into the EPRDF period (Mains 2012).

By the 2000s, the dashing of expectations generated by the state's failure to lift urban society out of poverty pervaded Ethiopian cities. Anger about how the hopes generated by the state were constantly 'cut' by the lack of opportunities for urban advancement (Mains 2012) became explosive in the early 2000s, and were radically politicized through the shock of the EPRDF's massive election defeat in Addis Ababa in 2005 (see Chapter 8). After this it was clear that piecemeal approaches to urban labour would not suffice. The regime concluded that it needed to aggressively pursue *both* repression and forms of co-optation through urban employment and other benefits with equal vigour. The legacy of communist social organization, which had largely lapsed since the Derg was overthrown was partially re-activated to facilitate this (Di Nunzio 2019). The EPRDF after 2005 thus pivoted from having little understanding, knowledge, or interest in the urban question (as noted in Chapters 5 and 6) towards a comprehensive attempt at reworking the street economy and stamping out opportunities for the effective mobilization of dissent.

In his rich ethnography of street life and marginality in Addis Ababa, Di Nunzio (2019) explores the tensions, contradictions, and aspirations that shape and constrain the lives of street hustlers. He describes the notion of becoming and being *Arada*. As well as being the name of Addis Ababa's old commercial centre, this term denotes a state of urban existence in a place of diversity, and a certain street smartness and sophistication in navigating city life (Di Nunzio 2019: 30–31). Interestingly, it is term that applies differently to both 'gentlemen' and to 'thugs'. The fact that one word can describe both urban upper/middle classes and an underclass equivalent to Uganda's *bayaye* illustrates the distinctive nature of the socio-economic context in Addis, whereby rich and poor, while separated by a socio-economic gulf, are interlinked through a conception of urban identity and aspiration that is much less clearly established in Uganda or Rwanda. This sense that, while socio-economically segregated, there is still some kind of common identity among the city's population is significant when it comes to understanding the EPRDF's growing fear of the urban classes collectively turning on them.

The Derg's reforms did little to address Ethiopia's fundamental inequalities, and indeed exacerbated inequality of opportunity by attempting to co-opt the cultured urban classes through access to education and state employment (Di Nunzio 2019). The EPRDF regime thus inherited a class of urban poor with few if any formal employment opportunities, which it continued to largely ignore in its early visions for national development. Among these were large numbers of vendors, which in the Ethiopian context often take the form of 'micro-sellers' or *gulit* vendors, a sector of the urban economy largely populated by women selling food produce on a piece of cloth (*gulit*) in the street or open market (Woldu et al. 2013; Mekonen et al. 2016). *Gulit* vendors exhibit extreme vulnerability, often suffering from poor health and education and frequently having to involve their children in income-generating activities in order to survive (Mekonen et al. 2016). While not illegal, their activity is often confined to specific areas; one of the major problems for livelihood generation in the new condominium settlements discussed in Chapter 6 was the strict rules limiting *gulit* activity.[61] Street vendors of other kinds position themselves around the city, often around markets, transport hubs, and churches, selling anything from books and shoes to cigarettes and sweets. A significant number of sites were allocated for vending by the municipal government,

---

[61] Interviews in condominium settlements, March 2018 and June 2019.

though these were often considered to offer limited demand (Ethiopia Etsubdink Sibhat 2014: 41, 45).

Surviving on the streets not only requires smartness but access to the right kinds of relationships and knowledge about when and how to hustle, share, lie, and steal (Di Nunzio 2019). The vast majority of street vendors depend either on loans or other forms of assistance from friends or relatives (Ethiopia Etsubdink Sibhat 2014). This dependence persists in the street economy despite the unveiling of extensive entrepreneurship schemes and the organization of the urban poor into cooperatives. These processes parallel those described in Kigali but with a notably stronger commitment to employment generation and microenterprise development (Di Nunzio 2015; Getahun Fenta Kebede 2015: Gebremariam 2017). The first significant programme was the Urban Youth Development Package, unveiled in 2006 and further built upon by the Micro and Small Enterprise (MSE) Strategy of 2011, and the Revolving Youth Fund initiated in 2016. These programmes were overtly concerned with restoring and consolidating the dominance of the ruling coalition and its developmental project on the streets of the capital (Gebremariam 2017; 2020).

The effects of these entrepreneurship programmes have been very mixed. While in theory street vendors could access them, many are unable to do so because they cannot meet bureaucratic requirements or lack the start-up capital required to enter the specific sectors these schemes are willing to support (Getahun Fenta Kebede 2015: 91–93). Even those who manage to enrol often find themselves unable to transcend their marginality, eventually returning to previous activities (Di Nunzio 2019). It is also striking that social networks exert a much greater influence over the profitability of street vendors' enterprises than levels of education, vocational training, or business experience, with the latter having little impact on profits (Kebede & Odella 2014; Getahun Fenta Kebede 2015).

This is not to say, however, that the EPRDF's employment programmes had no effect on urban socio-economic dynamics. Although these programmes may not have helped the most marginal, the government is considered to have a strong record on reducing urban unemployment (World Bank Group 2016). Yet, as Gebremariam (2020) shows, this relative success is intimately linked to efforts to expand of the infrastructural power of the state, and more specifically the party-state under the EPRDF. The ability to access trading spaces in government-owned commercial buildings or access loan schemes appears to hinge on the willingness of participants in the MSE scheme to sign up as EPRDF members (Gebremariam 2020: 24–25). The effect on city-dwellers' relationships with and expectations of the ruling party was therefore as significant as the economic consequences of these programmes; a new, conditional promise of support seemed to be on offer for those willing to sign up as agents in the extension of EPRDF reach. Recognizing the latent associational power of Addis Ababa's urban poor, these schemes generated what Di Nunzio (2017) terms a 'politics of limited entitlement' which, while of limited significance economically, was in some ways rather effective politically, as explored further in Chapter 8.

The scope of employment generation in Addis Ababa contrasts significantly with Kigali, partly due to these programmes but also because of the employment created by massive infrastructure development and the IHDP housing programme, and broader attitudes to urban commercial activity. It is notable, for example, that the government actively promoted container (or kiosk) shops on the street as a means to a livelihood, which contrasts both with the interplay of restriction and 'forbearance' regarding kiosks in Kampala, and the policy of eliminating them in Kigali. Yet also significant was how after 2005, in contrast to the earlier management of street crime and dissent through prisons and detention camps, which still dominates in Kigali, 'state intervention took place *on the streets*' (Di Nunzio 2019: 115; emphasis in original). Marginality on the streets, and how it was being refashioned into aspiration and putative entrepreneurialism, thus remains visible in all its unevenness and mess. The harassment of street vendors and confiscation of produce by police is widespread (Ethiopia Etsubdink Sibhat 2014; Getahun Fenta Kebede 2015), but the scope for operating on the streets is *relatively* extensive. Many city-dwellers opt for a life of street trade without having to become fully 'nomadic'. Rather than invisibilizing them, the state's drive has been to remake the street economy into 'a terrain of interactions, relations and transactions' compatible with the government's concerns with developmental transformation (Di Nunzio 2019: 116).

7.4 Conclusions

This comparative discussion illustrates how, despite the stated aim of 'modernizing' urban commercial life in all three cases through territorial re-organization, the reality of life as a market trader or street worker in the three cities was quite different. The contrast in approaches to marketplaces in Kampala and Kigali parallels the state–society engagement in the motorcycle-taxi sector, explored elsewhere (Goodfellow 2015). In Kigali, markets were sanctioned only when people other than vendors themselves entered the political fray. Thus the intervention of the Ministry of Gender and Family Promotion, an important ministry in Rwanda's wider legitimation strategy concerning gender equity, was central to an apparent change of direction in attitudes to urban marketplaces. This resonates with the way that motorcycle-taxis were reinstituted only after interventions from middle-class professionals and international voices (Goodfellow 2015). In Kampala, the maintenance of space not only for the operation of street economies but for their continued expansion and flourishing does not require the upper echelons of urban society to get involved. Whether in relation to trade or transport, working the city is a direct negotiation between street-level informal workers and the political classes.

When Kigali's street vendors attempted to resist the regulatory impulses of the state, they were beaten to death by security forces. In Kampala, when a similar hard-line approach to street trade was adopted, it was the security forces themselves who 'lost their eyes'. If the street economy is constantly being disavowed in Kigali (Shearer 2017), in Kampala it has for the most part been avowed by the actions of politicians—even while the rhetoric of 'cleaning up streets' persists. In the face of the clear and overwhelming need for these forms of urban livelihood to persist in all of these cities, the state backs down in Kigali only through pro-formal politics: in other words, when the urban majority are able to leverage the authority of aspirations enshrined in Rwandan government policy, such as gender equality or the need for a baseline of service provision for the city to function. In Kampala, these activities persist primarily through anti-formal politics: the bartering of favours whereby explicit suspension of formal rules and regulations through forebearance is traded for support or cash, constantly, as part of the very fabric of the city's functioning. When an attempt to enforce more pro-formal political culture was attempted in Kampala, the outcome was so disruptive to the government's pursuit of social legitimacy in the city that it was abandoned.

The narrative of the street economy in Addis Ababa differs from both of these cities, albeit in rather more subtle ways. Though the sustained drive to formalize street activity and repress street hustle bears parallels with Kigali, there was an important difference with respect to how marginality itself was reproduced, and the relatively high level of *tolerance* for marginality. In Kigali, as the following chapter documents, the politics of the margins is too potentially threatening to be allowed to breathe. In Addis, marginality was not something that either needed to be or could be visibly eliminated from the city centre; rather, the government has sought ways to accommodate and incorporate it. It was not so central to the legitimation discourse of the EPRDF regime to constantly disappear these people, only allowing them to settle back onto the streets if they 'come back in a different shape'. Rather, the *dependent marginality* of swathes of people on the streets of the city, subjugated and beholden to the state, was part of the demonstration effect of political power. A similar three-pronged approach to the street economy was evident in both Kigali and Addis in terms of brutal policing, political surveillance, and economic organization. In Addis however, the employment-creation component was notably more significant in the face of a large urban population with historically-conditioned aspirations and a demonstrated capacity to revolt.

When comparing with Kampala, the story of Merkato in Addis Ababa is particularly interesting because of the means through which vendors secured long-term gains, including through sustained pro-formal mobilization and engagement with institutional reform. This contrasts with the short-term, unstable outcomes of vendors' agitation in Kampala. The relatively strong bargaining position of Merkato's vendors both reflects the long history of the market and its evolution of a common identity that bolstered collective associational power, and how it managed to leverage this after the political shock of 2005. More generally, the thrusting of politics into the street economy after 2005 in Addis Ababa offers both interesting parallels and important differences with Kampala. While post-2005 Kampala saw opening political competition and efforts by rival political parties to court vendors' support, the insertion of politics into post-2005 Addis was much more about tying the economic fate of urban groups to the political fate of the ruling party, lessening the need for a pure reliance on coercion in the face of potentially explosive resistance. The favours afforded to street actors in Kampala were largely delivered informally—often through anti-formal populist gestures issued direct from State House. Indeed, local NRM leaders discussing the distribution of youth entrepreneurship funds in parts of Kampala complained they were 'tired of being neglected', noting that 'the habit of bypassing party structures must stop'.[62] In Addis, party structures were certainly not bypassed but rather were central to enrolling street workers into formal employment programmes.

In both cases however, this politicization of the street economy began to displace existing trust networks, replacing them with ties to political figures and organizations in ways that undermined the will or collective capacity to mount organized resistance. Despite this, festering dissent surfaced in different ways and with varying intensity in both cities, and even in its own way in the subdued streets and communities of Kigali. It is to these questions of urban politics and their expression through different registers of compliance, engagement, and dissent that we now turn in Chapter 8.

---

[62] Interview with youth-fund beneficiary, January 2019 (conducted by Suzie Nansozi as part of collaborative Cities and Dominance research project).

8

The politics of noise and silence

Negotiation, mobilization, refusal

Introduction

The urban infrastructure megaprojects, real estate booms, housing dynamics, and drives to re-organize street trade discussed in the preceding three chapters have not only had tangible spatial consequences for Addis Ababa, Kampala, and Kigali; they have also been highly consequential for political subjectivity, consciousness, and activism in these cities. Part of the story of the divergent urban trajectories in the three cities relates to how city populations respond to, anticipate, and contest these attempted transformations in very different ways. While contemporary urban political mobilization is often seen as a response to generic processes of neoliberal governance (Mayer 2007; Künkel & Mayer 2011), the nature of political contention in any city is also a function of distinct political projects, and of local practices and norms of political engagement.

The politics of urban transformation are therefore co-constituted by the strategies of elites seeking profit and power, and the popular institutions and practices that evolve in a given city, which can facilitate, contest, constrain, and re-engineer elite visions. This chapter examines the politics of urban popular engagement with, and response to, the changes that elites are attempting to imprint on East African cities. These political practices do not only reflect the needs and calculations of urban groups and individuals; they recondition the terms of urban politics either through demonstrations of associational power or the recursive enactment of particular practices of political informality. These practices can, in turn, shift the distribution of power and realign elites' objectives in pursuit of social legitimacy. Politics is thus not just a central part of any *causal explanation* for patterns of physical urban transformation—the primary focus of preceding chapters—it is also an *outcome* of such transformations.

Urban-dwellers in East Africa today are on average young, relatively educated, pursue multiple and uncertain livelihoods, and have wide access to global communications infrastructures. All of these condition emergent forms of urban politics. This chapter argues that as the governments of the NRM, EPRDF, and RPF achieved relative security across their national territories, the locus of political activism and (actual or potential) rebellion shifted progressively towards urban areas in the 2000s, especially where large-scale employment failed to materialize.

Politics and the Urban Frontier. Tom Goodfellow, Oxford University Press. © Tom Goodfellow (2022).
DOI: 10.1093/oso/9780198853107.003.0008

In this context, urban populations' aspirations and frustrations have been conditioned by exposure to increasing amounts of capital flowing into and through major urban areas, and the stark inequalities generated as the limits of governments' capacity to generate employment and redistribute wealth become ever more apparent.

However, in each of cities examined here, these region-wide trends are refracted through national political systems and legacies, as well as city-level political legitimation strategies, to produce different registers of political engagement. In seeking to understand these contemporary modes of political operation, we must consider the evolution of political cultures in the three countries and how these are localized in cities and perpetuated in everyday life. Practices of urban politics are rooted in histories, but not simply passed down by history; both continuity and change are actively made and remade.

The first part of the chapter explores recent debates on urban politics and how these speak to urban political organization and activism under conditions of rapid urban growth and late urbanization in East Africa. This is followed by a discussion of the evolution of political culture in the three cities and the key historical trends and junctures that have shaped this, building on some of the discussion in Chapters 3 and 4. We then turn to contemporary urban political registers in the three cities, with particular attention to how these have evolved in relation to the efforts to reshape urban informal economies discussed in Chapter 7. Departing from a stylized binary of 'noise' and 'silence', rooted in a comparison of Kampala and Kigali, the chapter then disrupts this device through the case of Addis Ababa, which in displaying a more complex pattern of urban political upheaval and quiescence throws the dynamics in the other two cities into even sharper relief. The chapter then concludes by explaining these different urban political registers with references this book's broader analytical framework.

8.1 The political city in East Africa

Through the scalar, laminated lens adopted in this book, urban politics involves national political relations playing out in urban space but is also a realm of political engagement in which the city itself, and social relations within it, have causal significance. Different academic disciplines have approached urban politics conceptually in very different ways. Three particular strands of literature stand out. In urban political science, which flourished in the mid-twentieth century before falling out of fashion,[1] the focus has primarily been the politics of urban governance processes. This foregrounds the constitution of political parties, civil-society

[1] The 'community power' debates focusing on 'elitism' versus 'pluralism' were deeply rooted in the urban context (Hunter 1953; Dahl 1961), as were later debates on 'urban regimes' (Stone 1989; Stoker & Mossberger 1994). See Stoker (1998) for a succinct overview of changing trends in urban political science.

organizations, and institutions of governance at the city level. Meanwhile in a very different approach to urban politics, geographers and ethnographers have drawn on scholars such as Rancière, Mouffe, and Badiou to foreground political subjectivities and 'forms and choreographies of urban political acting' that challenge dominant discourses and practices (Dikec & Swyngedouw 2017: 2). A third distinct literature involves longstanding debates on urban social movements, often led by sociologists and intersecting with broader work on social movements and 'contentious politics' (Castells 1983; Tarrow 1994; Pickvance 2003; Nicholls 2008; Tilly & Tarrow 2015; Della Porta 2016).

The position and role of the state is a central theme within all these literatures, but sometimes rooted in assumptions that are problematic in East African contexts. For example, the Rancièrean notion that the function of the *political* is to disrupt a post-political 'technocratic consensus' involves assumptions that the formal sphere of governance ('the police') is about the state, while the 'political' is about activities that unfold 'at a distance from the state' (Dikec & Swyngedouw 2017: 4). However, much of the urban political mobilization and subjectivity evident in East African cities is *interlaced with the practices of state agencies and actors*, even this is enacted at the micro level in spaces apparently far from formal arenas of state power (Branch & Mampilly 2015; Phillipps 2016). Rather than political mobilization encountering the state from a distance, it is the *intimacy* between social dynamics and state agencies and their representatives—even if the latter are operating outside their official functions—that shapes many encounters with political contestation and violence (Mbembe 2001). We should not, therefore, assume that processes of formal urban governance are all about the state while informal politics and contentious mobilization are not, taking place instead in some kind of autonomous space. Rather, the 'urban political' (Dikeç & Swyngedouw 2017; Enright & Rossi 2017) in these contexts is often about reproducing certain kinds of state–society reticulations.

Rupture and continuity in the East African 'urban political'

A number of scholars of urban politics have argued that urban social movements had largely been subsumed within the global capitalist order by the early twenty-first century, before being re-politicized over the past decade in response to the shockwaves of the 'Occupy' movement and Arab Spring (Badiou 2012; Hardt & Negri 2012; Žižek, 2012). Yet understanding the 'urban political' in East Africa over the past decade requires looking beyond the influence of, or analogy with, the urban uprisings that flourished after what Enright & Rossi (2017: 2) term 'the long 2011': several years of protest encompassing the Arab Spring, Occupy Movement, and related waves of anti-authoritarian and anti-austerity demonstrations around the world. While some major urban uprisings have occurred (for example in Sudan), these spectacular manifestations of the urban political are not the most significant form of urban contention in the countries considered here in recent times.[2] There is an assumption in much urban politics literature that the 'ordinary' constitutes the working of formally institutionalized arrangements, with episodes of contention forming 'extraordinary' ruptures that seek to overturn the order of things (Kalyvas 2008; Badiou 2012; Dikec & Swyngedouw 2017). However, in many contexts the politics that takes place beyond formally institutionalized arrangements, through varying forms of contention and negotiation, *is itself the politics of the ordinary*. This is a politics which is not institutionalized in a formal sense, but nor is it necessarily 'ruptural' (Dikeç 2015).

Though much of the literature on African urban-based protest has historically been framed in the language of social movements (Mamdani & Wamba-dia-Wamba 1995; Ellis & van Kessel 2009; Larmer 2010; Dwyer & Zeilig 2012), the pattern of urban protest across Africa in recent years mostly represents something quite distinct from the kind of social movements associated with 'the long 2011' and its aftermath (Branch & Mampilly 2015; Mueller 2018). The idea of a large middle class protesting for democratic reforms against authoritarian regimes—the standard trope of the Arab Spring—does not match the reality of many recent sub-Saharan African urban contentious episodes, or indeed some earlier ones (Diouf 2003). While African protests of recent years have frequently been interpreted as calls for democracy by global media, they have often been primarily about basic economic needs and the quest for social and economic opportunity (Mueller 2018: 21–22). Senior protest leaders may have agendas of radical political transformation, but the priorities of 'foot soldiers' who join in are often more diverse and prosaic (Mueller 2018: 22).

This is not to deny that these protests are *political*; just to highlight they do not necessarily fit the mould of the idealized ruptural, emancipatory 'urban political'. The prevalence of unstable alliances, the recurrent switching of sides, and the interplay of political exclusion and inclusion (Philipps 2016; Philipps & Kagoro 2016; Simone 2018) are more prevalent in much sub-Saharan African protest than the coming together of 'the people' in a surge of emancipatory collective subjectivity vis-à-vis a 'distant' state (Dikec & Swyngedouw 2017). The question of who represents the state, and who its real opponents are, is often obscure (Philipps 2016: 601). In this sense, some protest incidents involve what Philipps (2016: 602), drawing on the philosopher Gilbert Simondon, terms 'crystallization': they become collectively political only through the act of protest itself, emerging from a 'metastable pool of potential'. Rather than being movements of pre-existing social groups with established agendas, the social groupings characterizing urban

---

[2] This is not to deny Africa's history of transformative urban protest dating back to anti-colonial struggles in the mid-twentieth century (LeBas 2011; Msellemu 2013; Branch & Mampilly 2015; Gopal 2019), and the wave of pro-democracy protest following in the post-Cold War/structural adjustment period (Bratton & van de Walle 1992; Adekanye 1995; Akinrinade 1999).

contentious politics often take on 'emergent' properties (see Chapter 2) through the very act of engaging in such politics. The politics of protest movements can thus be an *outcome* of prior mobilization, as the call-and-response of contention and governmental reaction evolves.

To understand the practices of the urban political in full means acknowledging the difference between practices that seek to alter the official institutional configuration of urban life, and those that promote institutional and normative *continuity* as people seek to meet basic material needs through the institutions and tactics available to them. Mobilization on the streets, or even quieter forms of negotiation and refusal, are rooted in past experiences and conditioned expectations, which are partly based on collective subjectivities that have 'crystallized' out of previously unstable social dynamics. Through these processes, we see the evolution of different urban political *registers*, which are mutually comprehensible both to city-dwellers making political claims and the political actors responding to them.

Noise and silence as normalized urban political registers

This chapter invokes a heuristic dichotomy between 'noise' and 'silence'[3] to encapsulate particular urban political registers, which I define as *recurrent modes of state-society interaction with particular communicative value in a given urban context*. The idea of urban political registers goes beyond the focus on contentious performances and repertoires in the literature on social movements (Tarrow 1994; Tilly & Tarrow 2015; Della Porta 2016), in the sense that political registers can incorporate forms of politics that are not overtly contentious. The terms 'noise' and 'silence' need to be situated against Albert Hirschman's 'voice', which he characterizes as a means by which customers or citizens may express specific complaints should they be unwilling or unable to 'exit' a political relationship (Hirschman 1970).

As Hirschman notes, in the case of nation-states ruled by dominant parties there may be little opportunity for exit, leaving voice as the only option. However, the use of voice itself depends 'the 'general readiness of a population to complain and on the invention of such institutions and mechanisms as can communicate complaints cheaply and effectively' (Hirschman 1970: 43). The existence of such mechanisms for effective expression of 'voice' cannot be taken as a given, particularly in postcolonial Africa. Across much of the continent, institutions for civil-society campaigning and strategies of peaceful demonstration—despite being championed by key figures such as Nkrumah during the postcolonial struggle—were often

---

[3] See Goodfellow (2013b) for the original discussion. Notwithstanding the figurative rather than literal use of these terms, inverted commas are dropped for the remainder of the chapter to avoid monotony.

demobilized and progressively undermined by postcolonial governments (Branch & Mampilly 2015: 44–45). This raises the question of what happens when *neither* exit nor effective voice are viable. Where state authorities are unresponsive to attempts at exercising voice, the likelihood of such efforts taking the form of a general expression of dissatisfaction or rage, potentially deteriorating into violence rather than the articulation of specific demands, increases. This is what is meant by noise, a term that also reveals itself though widespread vernacular use by residents of Kampala to refer to political disturbance and, in particular, rioting.

However, the absence of both exit and voice as viable political channels might not result in noise if the 'general readiness of a population to complain' is absent or suppressed for some reason—which may be the case even in the presence of political grievances. In this latter situation the population's response can be heuristically characterized as 'silence': an absence of overt exit, voice, *or* noise (though not necessarily an absence of quieter forms of resistance or refusal, as explored later). Hirschman notes that voice is increasingly institutionalized in developed democracies (1970: 42–43). Of societies in which this is not the case, we might ask why and how other forms of political registers can likewise become institutionalized. As will be argued later, through recursive interactions of social groups and state authorities, noise or silence can evolve as normalized political registers that generate powerful self-reinforcing dynamics, repeatedly demonstrating what does or does not deliver results for those with political grievances.

This dichotomy between noise and silence clearly simplifies complex dynamics, beneath which lie more variegated forms of subaltern politics and political subjectivity. As a heuristic device, however, it offers a starting point for exploring urban political registers beyond those we associate with the democratic institutions of exit and voice. Such registers arguably have particular salience in Africa because, as articulated by Fanon (1963), the violence of colonialism on the continent meant that non-violent protest (the ideal type of 'voice') has historically been a hopeless or even dangerous strategy. Yet the line between voice and noise is mutable, and the fact that the order of the 'police' (in Ranciereian terms) *designates* certain forms of politics outside the instituted order explicitly as 'noise' (Swyngedouw 2014: 129), rather than voice or discourse proper, can itself perpetuate noisy political registers.

In this sense, the politics of noise is about people rejecting their allocated place as the 'noisy rabble' while also instrumentalizing this very designation to make claims and meet material needs. On the other hand, silence too is not mere submission or invisibility, and can embody its own forms of quiet refusal. These registers often involve explicit or implicit calls by those who 'do not count' to be counted and recognized (Swyngedouw 2014). The question then is why deliberately quiet or noisy registers are strategically adopted in different urban settings. This is not simply a question of whether the government is authoritarian: both noise and silence are responses to authoritarianism. Understanding the dominance of particular urban political registers is linked to broader modalities of political informality in different settings, the emergent associational power of groups engaged in challenging formal structures, and the infrastructural power of the state to suppress dissent over time. Before exploring contemporary urban political registers, we need to consider the historical evolution of political culture in the different parts of East Africa with which this book is concerned.

8.2   The evolution of urban political cultures

Uganda

Ugandan history has long been characterized by the organization and use of violence, particularly as the kingdoms began to consolidate and compete for regional influence from the seventeenth century (Reid 2002; 2017). As well as approximating some of the dynamics of violent state-formation described by Charles Tilly (1992) in early modern Europe, the valorization of the 'political warrior' in the context of escalating militarization produced long-term patterns of violent challenge to political authority, 'normalising the *coup* in political culture' (Reid 2017: 136). Uganda's precolonial political entities were far from democratic, and this legacy of authoritarianism was distorted, rather than either destroyed or created anew, by colonialism (Mugaju and Oloka-Onyango 2000: 11–12). In the colonial period, the might of the Bugandan state was employed by the British to expand the territory of the protectorate. Meanwhile from the mid-nineteenth century onwards, a second dynamic with more indirect but equally consequential effects for postcolonial politics was economic inequality and its racial and ethnic dimensions.

The colonial government's economic policy laid the foundations for deep political-economic grievances and the manifestation of violent resistance and protest, including in urban areas. The allocation of land on a large scale to Baganda chiefs from 1900 (see Chapter 3), prohibition of Africans engaging in cotton marketing and increasing salience of Asian capitalists (Chapter 4) led to significant anger on the part of exploited Ugandans, most of whom were excluded from the benefits of capitalist development. The first formal quasi-trade unions and associations emerged in the 1930s, but organized agitation was always accompanied by street protest and violence, as in the riots that broke out in Buganda in 1945 and 1949. Interestingly, even at this stage, 'protest could produce results' (Reid 2017: 231) and the colonial regime introduced some measures to bolster the position of African producers in response. The resentment towards the Asians however simmered long after independence, finally exploding in the Idi Amin era.

The 1970s and 1980s are without doubt a critical juncture in Ugandan political culture, layering onto the above dynamics of violence and economic grievance new forms of political claim-making, including through new uses of the print media (Peterson & Taylor 2013). The reality of the political-economic context in 1970s Uganda remains highly contested, partly due to competing historical accounts with a wide range of biases, often overly focused on Amin's personality (Nayenga 1979; Peterson & Taylor 2013). Nevertheless, it was clearly a period of abrupt policy shifts, new forms of political agency, the increasing use of arbitrary violence, and an explosion of the *magendo* (black market) economy (Kasfir 1983; Asiimwe 2013) discussed in Chapter 4.

Amin's populist style played out on the streets, with the redistribution of Asian assets often taking place through pronouncements he and his ministers made literally on street corners, 'surrounded by crowds waving claim forms' (Reid 2017: 237). Amin was a showman who presented himself as both patriot and saviour of the poor, and the use of informal and often arbitrary directives to appeal to particular groups, disseminated through the media, became a staple of political culture under his rule (Peterson and Taylor 2013). This, combined with the levels of violence and militarization which intensified under the Obote II government after Amin's removal (Reid 2017), entrenched forms of state–society interaction that were to endure and in some respects grow under the NRM, despite its rhetoric of revolutionary political change.

Museveni himself proved a master of clandestine political networking, being among the first guerrilla leaders to overthrow an African government (Southall 1988: 64). As a 'donor darling', he was willing to accept economic prescriptions from Washington provided that donors did not meddle in politics (Hansen & Twaddle 1998). This implicit deal was successful; privatization and liberalization proceeded apace while donors allowed Museveni to establish a 'no-party democracy' under the aegis of the NRM (Mujagu and Oloka-Onyango 2000; Carbone 2008). The 'movement' system meant that, until 2005, the only period of multiparty politics in Uganda's history was in the late colonial period of the 1950s, and the early 1960s—which even then was short-lived and lacking in depth (Mujagu and Oloka-Onyango 2000). Transforming Ugandan society proved harder than Museveni anticipated. While the *mafutamingi* mentality was resilient, NRM politicians layered onto it a new form of politics based on their experience of guerrilla struggle and the co-optation of other social groups (Amaza 1998). The combination of decades of socially legitimized black-marketeering and ethnic clientelism with a new cadre of politicians adept in tactical bargaining has indelibly marked Uganda's contemporary political culture.

Meanwhile, the NRM government introduced new dynamics through its enthusiastic pursuit of an agenda of privatization and deregulation, thus ushering in a 'neoliberal moral code' with its emphasis on maximizing individual utility (Wiegratz 2016). This filtered into many aspects of Ugandan society and the economy (Wiegratz et al. 2018). In the 2000s, many officials and politicians were said to arrive in office asking '*nfunila wa?*' (Where do I gain?), and literally demanding of

constituents seeking services '*ovakko ki?*' (What can you give me?).[4] The legitimacy of, and trust in, formal state institutions was very low,[5] and Museveni's
populist efforts to connect personally with social groups led him to attack state
agencies seeking to mediate his power (Carbone 2005: 8). All of this contributed
to a culture of anti-formal politics that conditions the nature of urban political
mobilization. Meanwhile, the continuing use of violent coercion and repression
in the face of political demands meant that Museveni's rule, like that of Amin, was
in some ways yet another manifestation of an older motif of militarism in state–
society relations (Reid 2017). This combination of militarism and anti-formality
contributed to a system that Tapscott (2021) characterizes as 'institutionalised
arbitrariness', embodying the tension between the arbitrary use of state power
and the fact that—as argued later—some aspects of these were actually quite
systematized and predictable.

Rwanda

The evolution of hierarchical structures of social control in Rwanda is generally
thought to date back to the Nyiginya kingdom in the seventeenth century (Vansina
2004), though these deepened under the powerful kings of the late nineteenth and
early twentieth centuries (Des Forges 2011). A central part of the story of contemporary Rwandan culture relates to how the precolonial kingdom's hierarchical
structures were instrumentalized, stratified, and ethnicized through colonial indirect rule (Rumiya 1992; Chrétien 2003; Vansina 2004), leading to a postcolonial
history characterized from the offset by a bifurcated political culture of zero-sum
ethnic (or in some analyses, racial) identification (Newbury 1988; Mamdani 2001;
Straus 2006). Meanwhile, Rwanda is a particularly small and densely populated
polity in which the capacity to surveil the population and manage dissent has been
exploited to the full throughout its history. The bureaucratic reach of state institutions, already remarkable before colonialism, was consolidated under German
and Belgian administrations to the point where by the 1930s there was a sub-chief
in charge of tax collection for a unit as small as 350 individuals (Codere 1973: 20).

In Maquet's (1961) analysis, by the end of the colonial period the very premise
of inequality was seen as a natural condition in Rwandan political culture: people born into what were often seen as the different 'castes' of Tutsi and Hutu
were unequal in endowment and seen to possess different rights and obligations
(Lemarchand 1966). Yet the mid-twentieth century showed that these intrinsic
societal inequalities could be *inverted*. The break with colonialism illustrated the

---

[4] Interview with KCC and Division officials, cited in Makara (2009: 254, 257).
[5] This was particularly true in Kampala, where Afrobarometer data indicates that over half the
population had little or no trust in local government, the ruling party, or the police (Afrobarometer
2010).

capacity for massively ruptural violence to overturn established social relations and shake the foundations of the polity. When the *mwami* (king) died suddenly in 1959 and inter-ethnic violence escalated, Belgium intervened and threw its weight behind the Hutu majority as preparations for independence accelerated (Reyntjens 1985: 268–272). In the summer of that year, national elections were held and PARMEHUTU, the militant Hutu party, won by a landslide. Shortly afterwards the monarchy was abolished and the state declared a Republic. The events of 1959–1961 came to be termed 'the Social Revolution' by the new regime under Gregoire Kayibanda, and were followed by independence from Belgium in 1962. However, in contrast to Ethiopia (discussed later), this was not a revolution proper. Liberation from colonialism and the reversal of ethnic fortunes was not accompanied by a fundamental restructuring of economic relations or governance, with postcolonial Rwanda exhibiting instead substantial institutional continuity (Lemarchand 1966; Reyntjens 1987; Purdeková 2016).

Nevertheless, the capacity to up-end socio-ethnic hierarchies fundamentally shaped the politics of postcolonial Rwanda. Anxiety about the return of Tutsi rule persisted through the pogroms of the early 1960s, and the exclusion of Tutsis from virtually all walks of life, even after Habyarimana came to power in 1973 proclaiming a discourse of national reconciliation that won over much of the international community (Uvin 1998). Beneath the surface of what some international organizations considered an oasis of stability in the late 1970s and early 1980s (Nkuete 1990) was an overbearing, exclusionary, and racist state with more highly developed systems of social control and surveillance than ever before. This was also the time in which state structures became fused with those of a single political party, the National Republican Movement for Democracy, and the government introduced the *numbakumi* system—a local authority responsible for just ten households—as well as new forms of community labour (Purdeková 2016: 66).

The extraordinary degree of state oversight of daily life under Habyarimana's Second Republic is vividly captured by the fact that in 1985, the population of any given local area participated on average in 118 formal state–society encounters annually, including meetings with various local authorities, participation in weekly public works and other structured activities (Kimonyo 2008: 261). This was the level of micro-governance in Rwanda when, under intensifying pressure to democratize, the country tipped into the civil war from 1990 that culminated in the cataclysmic and extraordinarily rapid 1994 genocide. This juncture would again upturn the entire social order, this time resulting in a government largely led by an expatriate Tutsi elite whose lives had been lived in exile.

Post-1994 political culture in Rwanda has generated significant debate. That the population in general exhibits an aversion to confrontational politics is widely agreed, but analysts offer different interpretations of how this relates to the long-term traumatic effects of genocidal violence, the continuity of historical governance norms, and the specificity of contemporary RPF rule (Straus & Waldorf

2011; Reyntjens 2013; Thomson 2013; Purdeková 2015). There is no doubt that longstanding traditions of authority and hierarchy co-exist with a suffocating lack of political space and a raft of post-genocide legislation limiting the capacity for political organization and open contestation (Beswick 2010; Reyntjens 2013). Yet power in contemporary Rwanda also works in intriguing ways, and is not only dependent on the tangible and 'physical' reach of state institutions (Purdeková 2015). In addition to specific policies and regulations are a range of informal processes that build on the institutions of previous regimes to produce what Purdeková terms the state's 'presencing'—the 'density and saturation of local spaces with state presence' (Purdeková 2016: 80).

There is a remarkable paradox between this 'presencing' and the fact that urban youth in Kigali report significant *distance* from government officials, who 'probably have no contact with most youth in their sectors' (Sommers 2012: 151); indeed, many of Kigali's youth 'wanted the government to have a larger presence in their lives' (Sommers 2012: 147). The paradox is explicable in that, for youth in Kigali, *government* itself (in the form of higher-level officials and specific governmental programmes) is remote, even though the *state* makes its presence felt everywhere. Where the state begins and ends is difficult to draw in hard lines, as the local population are drawn into its institutions in myriad ways (Lamarque 2017). The 'thickening' of social monitoring under the RPF is thus something in which the population themselves widely participate, through public displays of attendance and compliance that are explored more later. In this way, state power in Rwanda operates not just as infrastructural reach but as a 'community of affect' (Purdeková 2016: 63).

How all this conditions urban political subjectivity and the possibilities for political action in Kigali specifically have only recently been explored in the academic literature (Goodfellow 2013b; Shearer 2017; Nikuze et al. 2020; Esmail & Corburn 2020). It is significant that mobilization along lines of urban economic interests or identities have been largely absent in Rwanda, having been deliberately submerged in racist ideologies (Hintjens 1999). Moreover, Sommers's research forcefully demonstrates that urban youth in twenty-first-century Rwanda tend to lack the kinds of horizontal networks and collective ties that in many other African cities can be easily mobilized into urban politics (Sommers 2012: 168), with the space for trade-based solidarity organizations having been squeezed out by the top-down government sponsored associations and cooperatives, as described in Chapter 7 (see also Goodfellow 2015 and Rollason 2019 in relation to motorcycle-taxis). These associations push pro-formal modalities of organization from above, while limiting the development of trust networks with the potential to facilitate the autonomous associational power of urban socio-economic groups.

Ethiopia

Any consideration of the evolution of urban political culture in Ethiopia needs to take account of both the sheer historical weight of authoritarianism, with state power in the Abyssinian highlands historically understood in absolute and 'quasi-mystical' terms (Prunier 2015: 244), and how this was both disrupted and ultimately reinforced through the experience of the 1974 Revolution. As the nineteenth-century emperors progressively realized their goals of territorial expansion and modernization of the state, the peasantry both in Abyssinia and conquered surrounding areas were relentlessly repressed (Markakis 2011; Bekele 2015). This subjugation was supported by norms of hierarchy and compliance that had long been central to Amhara culture (Levine 1965b; 1974). This contrasted strongly with societal norms in many of the lowland parts of Ethiopia, where hierarchy was virtually non-existent, rendering the attempt by Abyssinian emperors to assimilate the latter particularly protracted, painful, and violent (Markakis 2011; Clapham 2017).

While the right to make claims on the state was part of political culture under the emperors, the expression of interests in this way had to obey strict social codes, signifying complete deference to authority; indeed, 'the sole legitimate manner of interest articulation in Amhara culture has been the respectful *petition* of a man or spontaneously formed group of men before an authority' (Levine 1965a: 275; emphasis in original). In this regard there was a strong pro-formal culture in Ethiopia, inculcated over centuries. By the twentieth century, norms of hierarchy and deference enabled the last emperor, Haile Selassie, to project an image of total domination so powerful that he was himself largely oblivious to the extent of the simmering dissent that then exploded in the 1960s (Clapham 2015).

The hundreds of thousands of students in Ethiopia's cities and towns by the 1960s (see Chapter 4) increasingly found themselves in a 'social cul-de-sac' as they faced unemployment rates as high as 40–50 per cent (Prunier 2015: 212). The student movement, which became increasingly militant, was both heavily influenced by Marxism-Leninism and fuelled by diasporic Ethiopian student activity in the United States and Europe. Thus while the rural protests of the 1960s remained peripheral, students began to come out onto the streets in 'almost ritual annual demonstrations' from 1965 onwards, 'daring to defy a political order that had managed to secure the cowed submission of a large part of the population' (Zewde 1991: 220). The revolution itself, when it finally came in 1974, was sparked in part by a simultaneous strike by taxi drivers and teachers alongside ongoing student radicalism, and (fatefully in terms of the revolution's ultimate outcome) disaffection in the army's lower ranks (Clapham 2015).

The period of the 'red terror' from 1976–1978 brought urban violence to new levels, with the bloody struggles between the Derg and the student movement and their leading party, the Ethiopian People's Revolutionary Party (EPRP), constituting an 'urban civil war' (Prunier 2015: 220). Although the EPRP was ultimately defeated, the entire episode from the early 1960s through to the late 1970s force-fully demonstrated the growing associational power of the urban classes—as well as the capacity of the state to crush political opposition (Gebremariam & Herrera 2016). The urban political culture bequeathed from this period was one in which longstanding norms of subservience to central authority now co-existed with vivid evidence that ordinary urban-dwellers were a force to be reckoned with: they would no longer be a class that, in Swyngedow's (2014 terms), 'did not count'. This was reflected in the raft of policies that the Derg subsequently rolled out to keep urban-dwellers broadly onside through cheap food and rents (Tiruneh 1993).

Yet the role of violence in political culture had also changed through the revolution and 'Red Terror': rather than being something normal and mundane as it had been previously, beaten into the everyday experience of state–society relations through systems of quasi-feudal oppression, the Derg's 'orgy of violence' meant that violence was no longer an acceptable fact of life that city-dwellers would continually tolerate (Prunier 2015: 229). The 1970s demonstrated that when urban-dwellers rebel in Ethiopia, this cannot be dismissed or bought off with small favours. Rather, it is something dangerous and potentially transformational. Ethiopian political culture had shown itself to be resistant to *gradual* change. These patterns have had substantial implications for the EPRDF era, which are explored later in this chapter, particularly through an examination of how the period after 2005 introduced new forms of political mobilization that complicate any simple distinction between deference and resistance. Building on the historical narratives provided above, the remainder of this chapter explores contemporary urban political registers in each of the three cities as they have manifested in response to the economic and spatial projects discussed in the preceding three chapters.

8.3 Kampala: Normalizing noise

The longstanding culture of militarization and repeated postcolonial political upheavals described above provide an important backdrop for interpreting politics throughout Uganda. However, to fully understand politics in twenty-first-century Kampala specifically, we need to examine how certain urban political registers evolved and reproduced themselves. The popular responses to attempts to radically reorder the city's marketplaces illustrate how a politics of noise not only became a recurrent feature of the engagement between market vendors and the state but also fed into broader patterns of urban political mobilization. These marketplace riots are therefore worth considering in some detail, before we turn to the broader implications of the political register of noise for the politics of protest in Kampala.

The marketplace riots

The most dramatic episodes of marketplace rioting have been associated with Kisekka market, which like Owino and Nakasero (discussed in Chapter 7) was enmeshed in disputes over privatization and redevelopment from the mid-2000s. Kisekka was a large marketplace of almost six thousand registered members devoted to the sale of mechanical goods and vehicle parts. Vendors had organized themselves and secured a twelve-year lease for the market's land in 1999, but in early 2007 the leader of a particular marketplace association clandestinely arranged to sell the lease to a retired army colonel, John Mugyenyi. Mugyenyi, who had allegedly enriched himself through the resource conflicts in the DRC in the 1990s, then came to an arrangement with vendors about which proportion of the land he would develop into a mall and which he would leave for vendors to manage themselves. According to vendors' subsequent accounts this deal was deeply misleading, leaving them with virtually nothing. When they discovered its true terms, many vendors formed a new association and forced the small number of people involved in the fraudulent sale out of the market. They also took the issue to Kampala City Council (KCC—this being before the days of KCCA). However, KCC largely ignored their complaint and many market vendors suspected that Mugyenyi had already bribed officials to do so.[6]

After KCC persistently turned them away, vendors decided that (in their words) they 'had no voice' in relation to formal state structures, and in their own account this is what eventually led them to resort to rioting.[7] The first significant riot was in July 2007, with vendors burning tyres along the roads around the market and causing major disruption. The police entered and violently quelled the riot. Vendors' calls for more control over the market were, however, left unaddressed. Consequently, a second riot broke out later in the year, so violent that Uganda's Inspector General of Police came down personally. The central government was rattled and invoked its new mantra that 'sitting tenants' should be given priority to develop their market, issuing a formal caveat preventing Mugyenyi from taking control despite its earlier tacit support for him. Subsequently, however, KCC staff allegedly bribed by Mugyenyi were said to have forged the signature of the vendors' new leader in a false statement to authorize lifting the caveat, which sparked three more days of riots in February 2008.[8] Following this, there was a formal investigation that came out in the vendors' favour,[9] but then entrenched interests in KCC reportedly found new ways to obstruct the handing of the lease back to the vendors, resulting in a fourth round of riots in 2009. After pressure from the central government,

[6] Interview with Kisekka Market vendors, 18 January 2010.
[7] Interview with Kisekka Market vendors, 18 January 2010.
[8] Interview with Kisekka Market vendors, 18 January 2010.
[9] 'Kisekka Market vendors oppose lifting of caveat' *Daily Monitor*, 25 March 2008; interview with Kisekka Market office managers, 18 January 2010.

Mugyenyi eventually renounced his lease.[10] There was, however, little progress towards vendors' regaining control in 2010, and further rioting broke out in March 2011.[11]

The interesting point about this sequence of events between 2007 and 2011 is how rioting became a relatively normal mode of political interchange through which a large group of urban-dwellers participated in engagement with the state. On the one hand, this affected how markets generally were treated; city officials would commonly explain why they were not even attempting to implement certain KCC policies on the basis that 'there would be riots'.[12] On the other, this reductive association with rioting affected vendors' subjectivity; they came to believe that unless violent events occurred, 'nobody cared about them', leading them to re-appropriate their reputation as rioters as a source of identity (Baral 2018: 169; 173). In a sense, riots 'crystallized' vendors' collective identities (Philipps & Kagoro 2016) cementing 'norm circles' and generating certain forms of political and moral agency, echoing Brisset-Foucault's (2014) findings about earlier waves of rioting in Kampala.

Of course, riots were only periodic occurrences and did not fundamentally change everyday life in the market (Baral 2018); but the ingrained association with rioting made the recourse to violence a powerful register of political engagement. Once it was evident to vendors that rioting was more effective at eliciting a response than voicing complaints to the council, there were clear incentives to riot; yet rioting was not effective *enough* to end the matter, incentivizing more riots to win further attention and concessions. In the context of significant media attention, vendors' expectations that the government would react only to noise, and the government's tendency to respond to bouts of rioting with vague promises, conspired over time to perpetuate it as a form of political dialogue. Rioting was not the sole mode of engagement between vendors and state authorities; nor did all vendors participate or approve (Baral 2018). But efforts to proceed through formal channels were widely perceived by vendors as pointless by 2009, and state agencies were reluctant to engage with or physically enter volatile marketplaces.[13] This gave cycles of rioting a self-reinforcing character as a form of 'parallel participation' in the face of market reforms, which themselves introduced formal lines of participation that were ultimately disempowering (Lindell & Appelblad 2009; Monteith 2016).

While Kisekka was certainly an extreme case, echoes of these dynamics were evident in other markets during the privatization drive, and the infamous 'Buganda riots' (which allegedly started in Kisekka) that broke out across the city in 2009 for entirely different proximate reasons reflected a similar frustration at

---

[10] 'UPDF officer gives up Kisekka market bid', *The Observer*, 17 June 2009.
[11] 'Why Kisekka market vendors keep rioting', *The New Vision*, 12 March 2011.
[12] Interview with local finance official, 28 September 2009.
[13] Interviews with Kisekka Market vendors and various city officials, September 2009–January 2010.

the limits of non-violent voice.[14] A latent capacity for violent mobilization has also characterized the political engagements of other major urban constituencies, including the city's tens of thousands of motorcycle-taxi drivers, whose discursive construction as sources of potential violence is again co-constituted by the state, media, and themselves.[15] Kisekka vendors further flagged their own potential for violence when, in January 2012, they issued the government with 'a seven-day ultimatum' to release suspects from the marketplace who were jailed for involvement in the Buganda riots, erecting banners threatening to 'take to the streets.'[16] Over a five-year period from 2007, a cycle of noise had thus become a central component of the 'public transcript' of Kampala's politics.

From 'Walk to Work' to #freebobiwine

Although riots in Kisekka subsequently declined due to heavy policing,[17] the legacy of this register of noise that evolved in Kampala in the late 2000s is evident both in the events surrounding the 2011 election and subsequent large-scale protests since the rise of opposition figure Robert Kyagulanyi (Bobi Wine) from 2017. Uganda's presidential election in February 2011 was, to the surprise of many, one of the most smoothly executed in the country's history, without the widespread intimidation deployed by government forces in 2001 and 2006 (Kobusingye 2010). However, this peaceful atmosphere did not last long. In mid-April, amid dramatic rises in food and fuel costs arguably linked to Museveni's lavish electioneering,[18] opposition leader Kizza Besigye launched a new pressure group called 'Activists for Change'(A4C), which orchestrated a campaign to take to Kampala's streets. Angered about what he perceived as a third 'stolen' election, he announced a series of 'walk-to-work' protests, in which Ugandans were encouraged to travel to work on foot as a protest against rising fuel prices. Besigye and his allies 'were sure that they would be confronted with the predictable brutal police overreaction', which would draw further attention and crowds to the protests (Branch & Mampilly 2015: 129–30). Sure enough, during one of the first protests in which Besigye walked to work in Kampala with other opposition leaders and a small

---

[14] See Goodfellow and Lindemann (2013) on the politics behind the Buganda riots, which killed at least twenty-seven people.

[15] For extended discussions of the informal politics of this sector, see Goodfellow and Titeca (2012); Goodfellow (2015); Doherty (2020).

[16] 'Vendors give 7 days ultimatum to government to release riot suspects', *Uganda Radio Network*, 11 January 2012.

[17] Despite less overt violence and protest, the market continued to have a fraught and contested history after 2011. For detailed examinations of this, see Baral (2018) and Young (2021b).

[18] Opposition leaders claim that prices trebled in the months after the election (Olara Otunnu, interviewed for NTV Uganda, 20 April 2011, http://www.youtube.com/watch?v=33u_jawhlRk&feature=uploademail).

number of followers, attempts by the police to stop the demonstration resulted in Besigye being shot and injured by a rubber bullet and briefly detained.[19]

A4C vowed to continue protesting every Monday and Thursday, and growing numbers of ordinary urban-dwellers with a range of grievances joined in the increasingly rowdy demonstrations. Besigye was arrested again, this time in an alarmingly violent fashion as he was bundled onto a van and forcibly restrained, all in front of television cameras.[20] The police battled with protestors, resulting in ninety-eight arrests.[21] As a third round of protests loomed, again Museveni began to employ the carrot alongside the stick, making a public display of opening a savings and credit organization for motorcycle-taxi drivers in Kampala, who numbered highly among the protesters.[22] Besigye was unrelenting and the protests continued, with the result that he and other opposition leaders were re-arrested every few days. Eight people had been killed amid escalating violence by 1 May.[23] The biggest demonstration took place on 12 May when Besigye, who had been in Nairobi receiving medical treatment, deliberately returned to Kampala on the day of Museveni's official inauguration. As jubilant crowds followed Besigye's car from Entebbe Airport to Kampala, the police unleashed tear gas, water cannons, and live bullets, injuring scores of supporters and resulting in several further deaths.[24]

The walk-to-work protests reached far beyond the capital, but Kampala was the clear epicentre. The escalation of these events and broad participation of the city's informal workers built on the evolution of perceptions among such groups that government would respond to their marginalization only when they delivered substantial noise. Whatever Besigye's grand designs may have been, both politicians and participants in the protests noted that urban under-employment and the frustration of youth were as central to the protests as support for Besigye;[25] indeed for most, participation had nothing to do with the election result, and the motivations of participants remained nebulous (Branch & Mampilly 2015). One demonstrator observed that the majority of participants were people for whom rioting was a default mode of expression, noting that 'any chance they get, they rise up.'[26] Many battles between police and protesters during the walk-to-work protests took place in Kisekka market, where the army was also deployed on a large scale on some days. Meanwhile the urban middle classes remained largely aloof from the mass action on the streets, and organizers of some small, orderly civil-society demonstrations at the time were at pains to emphasize that their protests were somehow

---

[19] 'Besigye, 48 others injured in demos' *The New Vision*, 14 April 2011.
[20] NTV Uganda report: http://www.youtube.com/watch?v=e86cSOHGnfE&feature=uploademail.
[21] NTV Uganda report: http://www.youtube.com/watch?v=OLTU2iUkSR0&feature=uploademail.
[22] NTV Uganda report: http://www.youtube.com/watch?v=g-bcgnImfeo&feature=uploademail.
[23] http://www.bbc.co.uk/news/world-africa-13255025.
[24] 'Besigye warns govt over "vicious unprovoked" attacks on Ugandans', *The Independent (Uganda)*, 13 May 2011 (http://www.independent.co.ug/?p1781=&option=com_wordpress&Itemid=331).
[25] Various interviews, 2011–2012.
[26] Interview with walk-to-work protestor, 21.03.12.

not political (Branch & Mampilly 2015: 136–140). This further reinforced the association between 'politics' and noise, as if the former implied the latter and 'civil society' wanted to distance itself from this.

The government's behaviour in the face of the walk-to-work protests also echoed its response to earlier rioting by combining sporadic brutality and vague palliative concessions.[27] Rather than unleashing brutality away from the public eye (the primary modus operandi of Idi Amin), Museveni evidently *wanted* people to see the government crackdown, just as he wanted people to hear the concessions he had to offer; he was playing to a gallery that understood this paradoxical register of violence and small favours. Besigye, with years of prior rioting to base his assumptions on, also anticipated violent crackdowns and sought to utilize this to construct himself as a martyr. Meanwhile, for the majority of protestors (over whom he had little control, in the view of some observers)[28] this was an opportunity to express frustration in ways that they had *learned* could provoke some government response.

It was therefore always doubtful that the protests would escalate into anything like an Arab Spring. Rather than becoming transformative and revolutionary events, the walk-to-work protests represented normal politics in Kampala-in which noise is a mutually comprehensible and potentially effective register-writ large. The government deployed the stick significantly more than the carrot in response to these protests; it was short on carrots after an unprecedentedly expensive election, and also the scale of protest scared it into issuing a stark reminder of its capacity to crush opposition. Smaller walk-to-work protests continued in late 2011 and beyond, further entrenching the sense that low-level urban state–society violence was becoming habitual. From this point there was also an upsurge in small-scale protests about other issues, 'fed by a popular perception that protest has new power in the country' as a form of informal negotiation (Branch & Mampilly 2015: 148). Residents of the city even declared to the media that 'it's the demonstration language which this government responds to.'[29]

The propensity for protest to surge into a social uprising that can frighten the regime has further revealed its potential through the figure of Robert Kyagulanyi—aka the popstar Bobi Wine—whose fifteen-year pop career was associated with increasingly angry, politically charged, and anti-Museveni's music. Kyagulanyi's political star rose on the back of historically low levels of votes for the NRM in Kampala and Wakiso District (which largely surrounds the capital) in the 2016 election, resulting from opposition to Jennifer Musisi's disruptive urban modernization drive discussed in Chapter 7. During an April 2017 byelection, Kyagulanyi seized the opportunity to stand for parliament to represent the constituency of

[27] 'Museveni promises to address walk-to-work demands', *The Independent (Uganda)*, 12 May 2011.
[28] Interview with Andrew Mwenda, Capital FM [Uganda], 20 January 2012.
[29] 'Demo looms over roads', *Daily Monitor*, 11 January 2013.

Kyaddondo East in Wakiso and won by a large margin. Explicitly identifying himself with the plight of urban youth, over the next year he successfully supported opposition candidates in several other byelections under the banner of the vague but emotive 'People Power' movement. By mid-2018, the threat that Kyagulanyi posed was clearly alarming the NRM and he was arrested after one particularly violent byelection on charges of possessing firearms and inciting violence, leading to further protests and an international outcry supported by the #freebobiwine campaign on social media.

The government's response to this in the years running up to the January 2021 election involved both heavy repression and repeated attempts to co-opt urban youth, given the extent to which these groups have been attracted to Kyagulanyi and People Power (Muwanga et al. 2020). Attempts at co-optation mostly involved distributing large amounts of cash in informal settlements and suburbs of Kampala, including Kyagulanyi's home turf in Kamwokya, north of the city centre. Youth community groups often formed simply for the purpose of receiving these funds, which were channelled through para-formal processes that operated in parallel to (and unapproved by) the official Youth Livelihoods Fund overseen by the Ministry of Gender, Labour and Social Development. Interviews with recipient groups in 2019 suggest that they were well aware that their capacity to mobilize violent protest could bring cash in their direction.[30] However, receiving these funds was not sufficient to ensure that youth groups would switch to supporting the NRM, and in the end the language of violence was central to the government's effort to see off the threat from Kyagulanyi. In November 2020, shortly before the elections and with Covid-19 restrictions providing an additional pretext for the repression of dissent, horrific levels of violence were unleashed on Kampala residents who were protesting the arbitrary arrest of Kyagulanyi, resulting in at least fifty-four deaths (Human Rights Watch 2021). Neither the co-optation nor repression helped the NRM to win votes in Kampala in 2021; indeed, its levels of support sank lower than ever, despite the large majority Museveni claimed nationally (Goodfellow & Mukwaya 2021b).

The events that have unfolded thus far in the Kyagulanyi era have demonstrated the continued capacity for normalized small-scale protests to feed into a political register that can, at times, be activated into massive waves of popular uprising. They have also demonstrated the continued willingness of the government to unleash shocking levels of public violence on the streets. Unfortunately for Ugandans seeking regime change, the very normalization of noise as a medium of political negotiation makes it more difficult for the larger waves of popular discontent to be truly 'ruptural'—in other words, to fundamentally change the conversation or unseat the regime. The expectations that both government and protesters have about urban protest events are primarily that they will end in some

---

[30] This is based on research for the project Cities and Dominance, funded by the Effective States and Inclusive Development Research Centre (see Muwanga et al. 2020).

kind of settlement between protesters and current political leaders, however unsatisfactory and temporary that might be. Over 70 per cent of Ugandan citizens have never known a president other than Museveni (The Atlantic 2018) and it is very hard for them to imagine his removal as achievable. Urban protest and rioting over the past decade or so has for the most part not been about removing him so much as a means of obtaining small favours, though these will usually be twinned with heavy repression. Through its normalization, the potential for violent urban protest to usher in real change is constantly undermined even as it reasserts itself.

8.4 Kigali: Silence and its limits

Contemporary Kigali is not a place in which noise features as a regular, let alone quasi-institutionalized, political register. The deep historical roots of infrastructural power noted throughout this book clearly play a role in facilitating surveillance and constraining dissent. However, in addition to historical causes of social phenomena we also need to take into account 'constant causes' (Stinchcombe 1968): i.e. the means through which a political culture of silence is perpetuated on a day-to-day basis. For the most part, this has been attributed to limitations directly imposed by the state on public discourse (e.g. Beswick 2010; Gready 2011; Waldorf 2011; Reyntjens 2013; Thomson 2013). This literature emphasizes how the RPF government actively 'prevents the public from expressing its interests' (Longman 2011: 27), instrumentalizing both a history of hierarchical top-down government and the experience of the genocide to do this. Yet Kigali's politics of silence has also been perpetuated in ways other than direct intervention by the state, as Purdeková (2011; 2015; 2016) has argued. Path-dependent patterns of behaviour support widespread compliance with formal rules, even without overt coercion. Simply to ascribe this (as many do) to a 'culture of obedience' in the country[31] is again to fall prey to the fallacy that 'social continuity requires no explanation' (Moore 1966: 485–486). This section explores the self-reinforcing dynamics that perpetuate relative silence in Kigali, particularly with respect to responses to the state-led urban transformation efforts discussed in the past three chapters, before also considering the limits to silence, which is far from absolute and on closer examination reveals itself as nuanced and laced with tones of refusal.

Strategies of silence

The fact that efforts to raze marketplaces and existing settlements in the 2000s and 2010s were not generally met by fierce contestation in Kigali, as they were in Kampala, cannot simply be explained on the grounds that the Rwandan regime is

---

[31] Such a 'culture' is suggested in some of the literature including Prunier (1997) and Straus (2006). It was also noted by various interviewees.

more repressive. Riots and protests in Kampala have all been met with very violent repression, as noted above, and this has not acted as a deterrent to noise there. In Kigali, an aversion to protest is perpetuated as a social norm even in the face of severe urban poverty, exclusion, and displacement. Despite some exceptions to this (discussed later), there is a need to account better for the continuing general absence of protest. The contrast with Kampala in terms of political resistance to radical urban re-organization was starkly evident through diverging attempts to re-order motorcycle-taxi drivers in the late 2000s (Goodfellow 2015),[32] but we can also see this by returning the city's marketplaces.

The marketplace re-organizations in Kigali discussed in Chapter 7 had major implications for vendors' livelihoods, as well as many city-dwellers' access to produce. Yet the closure of Nyarugenge market produced relatively little public outcry, and even some civil-society sources claimed there were very few complaints about the banning of street trade in large parts of the city centre.[33] Vendors adversely affected by the changes persisted in trading carefully where and when they could, aware that they could be thrown into Kwa Kabuga at any point. When asked about the lack of protest, respondents would often reply that it is 'not our way' or 'not our culture' to do so.[34] Behind this, however, lies a rational assessment: in contrast with Kampala, 'it's counter-productive if you try to confront the government directly.'[35] None of this is to say there was no noncompliance; it is rather that disobedience primarily took forms that were covert, and this was as strategic a response to prevailing norms as was the deployment of noise in Kampala. The creation of 'nomadic space' (Shearer 2017) and resort to night hawking[36] are responses more conducive to survival than ramping up noise to try and stimulate favours from politicians.

This relative silence in the face of government oppression is often interpreted, either explicitly or implicitly, through the competing conceptions of power offered by Scott (1990) and Lukes (2005). In other words, Rwandans enact performances of compliance alongside hidden transcripts of resistance in the mould of Scott (Straus & Waldorf 2011; Thomson 2013) or, in contrast, there is actual acquiescence due to internalization of the government's agenda for orderly urbanization, achieved through the 'third dimension' of power (Lukes 2005). Some displaced market traders and residents gave the impression that they *had* been convinced in this way,[37] though for others there is little doubt that Scott's 'internal revolt' was not far below the surface (Shearer 2017). That *both* of these forms of silence

---

[32] See also Rollason (2013; 2019) for rich ethnographic studies of Kigali's *taxi-moto* sector.

[33] Interview with civil-society source, Kigali, 17 February 2009.

[34] Interviews with Kigali residents and workers, November 2009–Feburary 2010.

[35] Interview with NGO representative, Kigali, 25 February 2009.

[36] 'Kigali's night market and its evasive hawkers', *The New Times*, 24 June 2009. 'Kigali's trade-off: Sell and be arrested or starve', *Mail and Guardian*, 6 March 2019.

[37] Interviews with residents of the Batsinda housing project, Kigali, December 2009; interviews with displaced market traders, 17 December 2010.

might co-exist, and that people might respond differently to state power, is entirely compatible with diversity in human character and motivation—but is a point that is missed in analyses focusing solely on generic Rwandan responses to state coercion.

The regime actively pursues both 'containment' (i.e. coercion and control) and 'transformation' (i.e. education, 'mindset' change, and 'sensitization') in its efforts to mould Rwandan subjects (Purdeková 2015). The latter is a constant preoccupation of the state bureaucracy: in the words of one official, 'if you understand something then you will do it better than if someone was to police you.'[38] In response to ongoing attempts at 'mindset change', some people effectively internalize surveillance (Purdeková 2015). Yet given the complex and multi-layered formal and informal structures of policing in Rwanda (Lamarque 2017), the point at which state surveillance and community surveillance evolve into self-surveillance is difficult to discern; indeed, to attempt to do so speaks to longstanding debates on the internalization of social structure and operations of governmentality (Foucault 1975; Bourdieu 1977; Fraser 1981; Archer 1995; 2000). The relatively low levels of formal policing in Kigali (Baker 2007; Lamarque 2017) attest to the fact that high levels of compliance were not so much a consequence of omnipresent state security forces as of socially embedded practices that serve to reinforce norms of community and self-surveillance.

Such practices include *umuganda*, the community works day resurrected from the Habyarimana era that takes place on the last Saturday of every month. As well as facilitating direct state surveillance, it has helped to inculcate a culture of 'checking on your neighbour', and through facilitating 'gossip' has consolidated powerful norms of acceptable and unacceptable behaviour.[39] Meanwhile Rwanda's *Ingando* 'citizenship re-education' camps (Sundberg 2016) as well as the *gacaca* courts established to try genocide perpetrators from 2001–2012 serve to inculcate ideas about the acceptable limits of voice in contemporary Rwandan society (Longman 2009; Beswick 2010). The sense that any grievances should remain in the private rather than public domain was reflected in interesting procedural footnotes accompanying the 2007 World Values Survey. Surveyors found that in Rwanda's urban areas, respondents tended 'to herd the interviewer inside their house, so as to keep confidential the reasons for their visit', in marked contrast to other African cities and despite the Rwandan government having approved the survey.[40]

To the extent that Kigali's politics is silent, this is not therefore because it is constantly and flawlessly policed—which would be beyond even the infrastructural powers of the state under the highly organized RPF—but because (whether

---

[38] Interview with local government source, Kigali, 3 December 2009.
[39] Interview with Rwandan researcher, Kigali, 18 November 2009.
[40] Technical specifications of the Values Surveys: Rwanda. (http://www.wvsevsdb.com/wvs/WVSTechnical.jsp, accessed 16 July 2012).

internally rebelling or not) people understand the *value* of silence. Several authors note how a sense of power and agency is 'reclaimed through silence ... Purposeful silence is both a strategy against being "read" and a direct way to undermine surveillance' (Purdeková 2016: 78; see also Thomson 2013; Rettig 2008). Given Rwanda's history of extremely violent ruptures with uncertain outcomes, a politics of silence also helps to stabilize expectations of daily life and reduce uncertainty amid extremely challenging urban socio-economic conditions for the urban majority.

Pushing the boundaries

Despite all this, there are moments in which attempts at political voice emerge, or compliance itself is conveyed in tones that unsettle dominant registers of silence. Recent work on the eviction of communities from unplanned settlements in Kigali explores situations where some urban claim-making took place, though there are 'carefully delimited silent boundaries' to urban contention that are widely understood (Esmail & Corburn 2020: 34). Esmail & Corburn (2020) frame such boundaries as being spatial and scalar, forming 'discursive limits that urban residents navigate when they contest their relocation in terms of the law, valuation, and procedural irregularity', rather than issuing any open challenge to the political vision for the city embodied in the plans themselves (Esmail & Corburn 2020: 33). Thus, appealing to the law and making claims based on proper legal process—essentially, a pro-formal modality of political contestation—may be possible, but with the district level as the upper-scalar limit of contestation. Protest that could be construed as political and that targets authorities at the city level or above is still off limits. Claims are both localized and rendered procedural, and thus circumscribed within forms of behaviour that aligned with government-sanctioned ideals of 'good citizenship' (Esmail & Corburn 2020: 34).

   In some recent eviction cases there were unusually vocal episodes of contention, such as those that ensued following a recent policy shift that determined all compensation would be in the form of replacement housing (apartments on the urban periphery) rather than cash. In the Kigali neighbourhood of Kangondo, due to be bulldozed for a high-end real-estate project, a clear majority of affected households rejected proposals to assign them a new apartment 10km away. In an unusual development, around four hundred landowners became the 'elites of resistance' and exercised substantial voice by pleading with the minister for local government to give them cash compensation instead, and when this failed took their case to the courts (Nikuze et al. 2020). They were unsuccessful, and the eviction went ahead; but it was nevertheless a clear breaking of the mould of compliance. Two things are, however, notable: first, the grounds on which these complaints were made were pro-formal, again working with established procedure to make claims that might be perceived as reasonable on the Rwanda government's own terms. Second, it was 'better-off' property-owning residents who felt emboldened to make these claims (Nikuze et al. 2020: 15). These recent experiences thus show that while political registers of silence can be transgressed in Kigali, overt transgressions are primarily undertaken through pro-formal processes and only by better-off people with the capacity to engage in such legalistic discourses.

For the majority, responses to coercion, displacement, and other deleterious urban policy moves were registered in more subtle and individual ways, often beneath the surface of silence. This could take the form of decisions to celebrate and venerate values antithetical to those characterizing the government's urban development vision: a form of 'aesthetic dissent' (Gastrow 2017). While adherence to the aesthetics of order and 'modernity' indicate a sort of political complicity in Rwanda, the celebration of *akajagari* (urban disorderliness) is for some Rwandans a way of facing down total political control. As Shearer notes, the constant efforts by the state to hunt vendors and control urban space has fed an 'ideological commitment' to disorder and associated traditional spatial formations among some city-dwellers (Shearer 2017: 35). In the words of one of his sources, '*Akajagari is beautiful*' (Shearer 2017: 33). That spatial disorder can be seen as so rebellious is a reflection of the dominant culture of pro-formality that allows such little room for manoeuvre and generates its own forms of subversion.

Kigali's dominant register of silence does not involve resistance in any meaningful sense, which is known to be largely futile; yet the above dynamics illustrate that it is often saturated with tones of refusal. In feminist theories of visual culture (Campt 2019; Mengesha & Padmanabhan 2019), refusal involves political subjectivities and practices defined not by contention so much as the rejection of the very premises that negate and delegitimize your existence (Simone 2018: 22). What is refused is the project to render the subject 'solely or primarily a "problem to be solved"' (Simone 2018: 22–23). In Kigali, staying silent in the presence of power can enable life to go on while also transmitting a message of refusal 'in the face of an intimate encirclement by the state' (Purdeková 2016: 78).

In this sense, through the purposeful withholding of futile voice and the quiet celebration of *akajagari*, politics and dissent in Rwanda is never truly silenced. But the fact that it does not flourish through and feed on noise is highly significant for how urban-dwellers operate in their individual and collective agency. Refusal is experienced to a significant extent individually and covertly, while networks for mobilization are weak and interpersonal trust has been found by numerous studies to be low (Hintjens 2008; Ingelaere 2009; Sommers 2012; Ingelaere and Verpoorton 2020), suggesting an environment of significant political a-formality.[41]

---

[41] This is not to deny that significant economic risk-sharing institutions exist within the urban informal economy, as Shearer (2017) documents. But this does not seem to translate into substantial broader trust networks in the sphere of political life. The low levels of trust in Rwandan society

With little to be gained and much to be risked through collective mobilization, the urban majority—who remain poor and engaged in daily struggles for survival—eschew making collective noise in favour of 'moving sideways' (Simone 2018), though subtle forms of oppositional practice that are no less political for being quiet.

8.5 Addis Ababa: The politics of total mobilization

Superficially, urban political culture in Ethiopia offers parallels with Rwanda, both in terms of what has been described as the 'public silence' of civil-society organizations (Brechenmacher 2017; Pellerin 2018), and the political restraint among urban youth for several decades after the 1974 revolution. Gebremariam and Herrera (2016) contrast the 'revolutionary generation' of the 1970s with the subsequent 'restrained generation', who in the shadow of the Red Terror grew up with the popular saying 'avoid politics like you would avoid electric shock' (Gebremariam & Herrera 2016: 143). Political engagement became synonymous with violence, and urban Ethiopians in the 1980s and 1990s were 'politically socialized' to avoid contentious politics (Gebremariam & Herrera 2016: 146). Yet in 2005 Addis Ababa was the site of one of the continent's most striking urban uprisings of the early twenty-first century, a juncture so explosive that it may have influenced government responses to subsequent major protests elsewhere on the continent, including Kampala (Branch & Mampilly 2015). Moreover, the wave of protest from 2014 to 2018, much of which was outside of Addis Ababa but clearly triggered by issues relating to the city's expansion, was so tumultuous as to precipitate the eventual downfall of the EPRDF regime. Addis Ababa therefore presents a complex picture in terms of urban political registers, with periods of relative silence and restraint ruptured by violence, as politics itself veers between tight control from above and explosions of dramatic contention.

From restraint to mobilization

Despite a long period of relative restraint after the 1970s, the latent capacity for urban uprising was evident during the early EPRDF years, with student protests in Addis Ababa in 1993 and 2001 and protests in Hawassa in 2002 all being brutally repressed (Branch & Mampilly 2015; Gebremariam 2017). The events of 2005

are perhaps unsurprising in a post-genocide context—though it is remarkable that the proportion of people responding affirmatively to the question, 'It is naïve to trust others' actually increased from 41 per cent in 2002 to 54 per cent in 2006 (Ingelaere 2009: 512). Moreover, although inter-ethnic trust has gradually improved over time since 1994, *intra*-ethnic trust has actually declined for some groups (Ingelaere & Verpoorton 2020).

were however of a different order. The storm was generated by a combination of the EPRDF's neglect of urban-dwellers and obliviousness to their dwindling support, and its decision to open up political space prior to the 2005 election, suddenly giving unprecedented breathing space to a long-stifled civil society (Pellerin 2018). A new opposition movement with a strongly urban and middle-class base, the Coalition for Unity and Democracy (CUD), emerged in 2004 and rapidly gathered strength. Given a long history of vigorous student mobilization and a sizable urban intelligentsia, the temporary opening of political space allowed for opposition movements to draw in middle-class professionals, intellectuals, and civil society in a way that was absent in Kampala's 2011 protests (Branch & Mampilly 2015: 154).

The protests themselves erupted after elections in which the EPRDF lost virtually all their urban seats across the country, including in Addis Ababa, but emerged as the winners nationally. Amid recriminations about the fairness of the electoral process and intimidation of rural voters (Lefort 2007), a ban on demonstrations was issued that was defied first by students before then drawing in taxi drivers, high school children, and street youths in cities across the country in June 2005, eliciting a violent crackdown and at least forty-six deaths (Abbink 2006: 186). Worse was to come in November, after the CUD boycotted entry into the new parliament amid ongoing harassment by the EPRDF regime, culminating in nationwide protests that activated and electrified the 'passive networks' of urban youth (Branch & Mampilly 2015; Di Nunzio 2012). The government responded with a massive and brutal crackdown on protesters, media, and opposition politicians in which as many as forty thousand people were arrested and two hundred killed (Abbink 2006; Aalen & Tronvoll 2009).

To fully understand the subsequent evolution of urban politics in Ethiopia we need to look beyond the protest and immediate response and consider how the EPRDF regime then attempted to strategically counter the threat posed by urban passive networks and their explosive potential. It is well established that the government response combined a ramping-up of repressive strategies to constrain and coerce civil society, the solidification of urban infrastructural power through societal infiltration of the ruling party, and an unfurling of strategies to build support and legitimacy through the deployment of hard infrastructure and other development projects (Duroyaume 2015; Pellerin 2018; Di Nunzio 2019; Weldeghebrael 2020; Gebremariam 2017; 2020). This post-2005 period offers further parallels with Kigali, in the sense that renewed controls over civil society were harsh and offered an impression of regime stability (Pellerin 2018). Yet the registers through which urban politics was enacted differ significantly, and in ways that also help to explain the subsequent upheavals from 2014 onwards.

If Addis Ababa's urban majority largely comprised a 'restrained generation' after the 1970s, there are distinct differences between the nature of this 'restraint' before and after the 2005 juncture. In the period between the Red Terror and the emergence of significant urban protest in the early 2000s, the avoidance of politics was essentially about *disengagement*; this meant literally turning away from politics, especially in the early EPRDF years when the government likewise disengaged from urban populations' concerns (Gebremariam and Herrera 2016; Di Nunzio 2019). After 2005, such disengagement was not possible. This was a new urban world in which policies of mass youth employment, party expansion, and the activation of party-state networks of localized, 'capillary' urban control were rapidly unfurled on the streets, all alongside an aggressively transformational developmental vision (Gebremariam 2017; Di Nunzio 2019; Weldegherael 2020). Under these conditions, the ruling party was not just attempting to alleviate some of the challenges facing the urban poor and to repress them politically, but to actively mobilize them on all fronts. This approach to 'mobilizing the marginalized' in Ethiopian cities was new for the EPRDF, but drew on and reactivated Derg-era forms of mass association (Di Nunzio 2014; 2019). The urban poor themselves increasingly opted to sign up to new government programmes, and often to the ruling party itself, in the hope of both economic opportunity and averting state repression, to the extent that they were not merely participants in ongoing political restraint but mobilized into—and often active *mobilizers* of—a massive political project.

In this regard, urban development itself became a 'politics machine' in Addis Ababa (Di Nunzio 2019: 125) to a much greater extent than has been the case in Kigali. The surveillance and repression that characterize the latter were certainly present, but the over-riding logic has been to draw city-dwellers (and particularly urban youth) deeply into the EPRDF political project by offering them the opportunity to be part of the new urban world it was attempting to deliver—albeit on the EPRDF's terms. From the party-state's perspective, urban youth needed to become central to the developmental narrative and accompanying political organization because the threat they posed had been starkly demonstrated; their ability to ultimately topple regimes, effected in 1974, was refreshed in the popular imagination after 2005. The EPRDF was in stark need of sources of social legitimacy in urban areas, faced with the evident potential of counter-mobilization by *all* sectors of urban society: middle classes, civil society, intelligentsia, and the neglected majority, many of whom had already been targeted for action as dangerous 'vagrant' youth by 2004 (Gebremariam 2017; Di Nunzio 2019). For the middle and 'working' classes,[42] this quest for legitimacy took the form of the housing programme and urban infrastructure drive discussed in Chapters 5 and 6. For poorer and unemployed sectors of urban society, a raft of programmes were unleashed including successive youth employment programmes in 2006, 2011, and 2016 and subsidized food delivery through newly empowered Urban

---

[42] Note that this term does not have the same implications as in the West, referring generally to salaried professionals.

Consumers Co-operatives (Gebremariam 2020). All of this was backed up by the reactivation of the Derg's most local system of administration—the *kebele*—which while clearly performing functions of political domination like the Rwandan equivalent (*umudugudu*) was also essential tool of mobilization rooted in communist organization. From 2011 there was a further attempt to extend the reach of the state even further down than the *kebele* to the level of the household through sub-*kebele* administrations and the 'one-to-five' networks, where in every neighbourhood people were grouped into six and one person was responsible for passing on relevant information from government offices to the other five (Chinigò 2019; Lavers 2020).

The politics of performative loyalty

The above developments meant that urban youth were aggressively mobilized rather than merely *contained*. Between 2005 and 2014, while offering an outward picture of regime stability due to low civil-society activism and urban youth restraint (Pellerin 2018), behind this lay the multifaceted enrolment of the population in party-state networks, often actively pursued by desperate city-dwellers themselves as well as being engineered from the top down (Gebremariam 2020). This is distinct from Rwanda's politics of silence. Without an exit option from the ruling party (a fact made starkly clear by its capturing of 99 per cent of parliamentary seats in 2010 and 100 per cent in 2015 (Arriola & Lyons 2016)) or any meaningful voice (Aalen & Tronvoll 2009), the post-2005 political register was closer to the third concept elaborated by Hirschman, alongside exit and voice: loyalty. Indeed, Di Nunzio (2019) describes how a 'logic of political loyalty' was the dominant register on the streets after 2005, despite being to varying degrees performative and in many respects outright 'fake' (Di Nunzio 2019: 125, 184). While a façade of compliance again offers some parallels with Kigali, the evident associational power of a range of urban groups from informal transport workers to students render an enacted politics of loyalty quite different. In Hirschman's terms, loyalty holds a certain power, and implies a degree of influence because it implies the *possibility* of disloyalty (Hirschman 1970: 82). Though there was clearly no formal exit option in the EPRDF's Ethiopia in the form of a viable opposition party, the possibility of regime overthrow *was* within the bounds of possibility. In this sense, through *mobilizing as loyal* the urban classes could leverage their latent associational power and claim some modest benefits for themselves (Gebremariam 2020).

The difference between Ethiopia and Rwanda's dominant political registers in recent years can thus be conveyed through a distinction between the active mobilization of performative loyalty in Addis Ababa, and pervasive silent compliance—sometimes accompanied by individual acts of refusal—in Kigali. Yet there are also significant contrasts with Uganda, despite parallels between Ethiopia's 2005 protests and events in Kampala. Foremost among these is the extent to which urban uprising in Ethiopia has always represented a potentially existential struggle for control, rather than a form of negotiation. Rather than bargaining, in Ethiopia political struggle was a rigid process with an absolute winner or loser, 'with no room or very little room for compromise and negotiation' (Gebremariam and Herrera 2016: 155). The objective in Addis Ababa in 2005 was to precipitate seismic, total change. In Kampala, the threat of urban protest has been countered partly through off-budget, para-formal moves to buy off urban youth groups with bags of cash, as part of a mutually understood clientelistic bargain. This contrasts markedly with the enrolment of urban youth in Ethiopia after 2005 into official government schemes, supported by pro-formal mechanisms of social control reactivated from previous times.

The change that came to the city after 2005 was indeed dramatic, though it was not regime change but rather a radically new urban orientation of the existing regime. A more fundamental change of personnel at the top would have to wait until the following decade. The wave of protest from 2014 was not, however, initiated by the urban classes and rooted in socio-economic identities as was the case in 2005 (or 1974), but driven primarily by the ethnic identification that the EPRDF had been fomenting since its institution of ethnic federalism. Triggered by the launch of a new plan for the Addis Ababa metropolitan area that would extend the city by 1.1 million hectares into surrounding Oromia, the 'Oromo protests' were initiated by students, initially often in urban areas. They were however fuelled by a long history of Oromo marginalization and agitation that had given rise to demands for greater federal powers or even secession, enacted through the increased salience of social media (Østebø & Tronvoll 2020; Workneh 2020). While there was a lull in the protests in 2015 after the government suspended its plans for the capital's expansion, they resumed in November of that year and rapidly ascended to the level of a social movement throughout 2016, spreading also to parts of the Amhara region and reaching fever pitch in October with the declaration of a State of Emergency on 9 November (Kelacha 2019; Workneh 2020). Further protests erupted in August 2017, leading ultimately to a second state of emergency in February 2018, the resignation of Meles Zenawi's successor Hailemariam Dessalegn and the rise of Abiy Ahmed.[43]

It is striking that Addis Ababa's population was not at the forefront of the protests from 2014 to 2018; indeed the movement barely disturbed the city for much of this period, beyond its contested peripheries with Oromia (where the encroachment of the IHDP housing settlements onto Oromo farmers' land was

---

[43] The events that have further torn Ethiopia apart since Abiy took power, including the devastating war in Tigray and other regions from late 2020, are beyond the scope of this book.

a highly contentious issue).[44] Yet this is not so surprising when one considers the 'modest benefits' available to much of the city's population noted above and in earlier chapters, which had rapidly emerged from the multifaceted EPRDF offensive to win over the city after 2005. All the city's most significant socio-economic groups were being offered something by the regime, and even if these offerings did little to allow them to transcend positions of marginality (Di Nunzio 2019), they helped to orient them away from actively joining the 2014–2018 protests—which being distinctly ethnic in nature were also at odds with the city's multi-ethnic DNA.

The registers of protest in Ethiopia since 2014 represent a 'flipping' of the mobilization of performative loyalty to the EPRDF into the radical counter-claims of loyalty to Oromo nationalism. Though the Oromo protests overwhelmingly played out outside the capital, they ultimately overwhelmed the force of the top-down efforts to buy off urbanites since 2005, precipitating regime collapse. These recent events represent a battle of competing mobilizations: a register in which compliance or protest amount to total domination or total contestation, rather than either noisy negotiations or a conspiracy of political silence. The feast or famine of urban politics in Ethiopia reflects how pro-formal mobilization from both above and below through a comprehensive political project, as seen in the period 2005–2014, can be ruptured as the very networks that enable that mobilization are reversed against the regime. In this register of total mobilization one way or the other, there is no room for noise to serve as mere negotiation, and little value to be found in 'silence'.

8.6 Conclusions

This chapter has analysed the phenomenon of differing registers of urban political protest, which are rooted in the broader political dynamics and socio-economic changes explored in previous chapters. Through an exploration of these registers in Kampala, Kigali, and Addis Ababa, it has shown the analytical limits of 'resistance' as a lens on to urban politics in authoritarian contexts. In any of these cities we might find ample responses to top-down urban transformation that could be termed resistance, but to better understand them we need to analyse registers of urban political struggle in a more granular fashion. In these cities we see struggles that take the form of negotiation through noise, refusal cloaked in silence, and mobilized loyalty to an authoritarian project that contains the seeds of its own overthrow.

These differences show how, despite urban life being both intrinsically composed of 'ensemble work' and inescapably political, this does not necessarily result in concerted political action of the kind associated with sustained social

---

[44] Interviews with condominium residents and government key informants, Addis Ababa, 2018–2019.

movements. Instead it often means 'moving sideways' through different forms of composition and calibration, rather than collective resistance (Simone 2018). These sideways movements might be of the kind examined in Kigali, where community surveillance and subtle political subversion co-exist in constant tension, or the kinds of ensemble enacted through riots in Kampala and their limited material gains. Either way, this is a politics of the ordinary, and a politics in which the state is entangled rather than distant. Moreover, these differences in political registers exist in an iterative, co-constitutive relationship with the real and attempted urban transformations discussed in Chapters 5, 6, and 7. The politics is not simply a response to these transformations, as it has played a role in shaping them; yet nor did it exist fully prior to their unfolding. The differences in political registers are therefore an *inseparable part of a broader story of divergent trajectories of urban development and change.*

These differences are also explicable in relation to the broader explanatory framework of this book. In each case, the distribution of associational power and the dominant political registers evolve in dynamic interaction: the power of social groups can change over time through these registers, yet the evolution of registers also reflect shifts in the distribution of power. In Kampala, urban informal workers have shown time and again their capacity to assert themselves. Yet in doing so through registers of relatively unorganized protest and rioting, which are responded to with violent and divisive state actions, they are constrained in what they can achieve with this power and the extent to which they can augment it through protest. In Addis Ababa, critical junctures of mobilization for ruptural change demonstrated decisively the combined associational power of urban classes, which led to massive state response—though this response itself effectively co-opted some of this associational power. It is therefore unsurprising that the regime change of 2018 was not forced by the city's population, as it could have been if the protests of 2005 had radically escalated, but rather by movements outside the city. In Kigali, meanwhile, the majority of city-dwellers can mobilize very little associational power, partly due to the long-term inhibition of horizontal social relations by an infrastructurally powerful state. Consequently there has been no effort to co-opt the lower urban classes. Their political registers remain merely self-protective, limiting their capacity to assert themselves beyond any gains that might trickle down from the efforts of the more well-favoured middle-class professionals.

Amid these registers and the relations of power they reflect and recalibrate, the formal sphere of politics takes on different roles and meanings. In Addis Ababa, the skill with which formal government programmes and urban associational life has been mobilized since 2005, supported by a range of pro-formal institutions, is remarkable. Only in the moments of uprising and regime overthrow does this seem to collapse into its opposite. Yet anti-formal politics—that which challenges formal institutions of governance—persists daily in ordinary but very different ways in Kampala and Kigali. In Kampala, anti-formality is the central public trope of politics, as urban-dwellers mobilize often violently against policies they perceive as unfair, and opportunistic political actors then themselves sometimes mobilize against those same policies. Here anti-formal politics is open, expected, and central to politicians' strategies for social legitimation: it has to be *visible* to even mean anything. In Kigali, by contrast, an anti-formal sensibility exists at the level of subjectivity, but the urban poor for the most part lack the associational power to take it to the streets and realize it in practice. Simultaneously harbouring anti-formal impulses and publicly enacting the relentless pro-formal social institutions on which the regime subsists creates a sense of dissonance and suspicion, to the effect that *collective* politics in Kigali is largely a-formal in nature, characterized by limited trust and acts of refusal in place of collective dissent.

PART IV
CONCLUSIONS

9

Politics and the urban frontier

This book has examined specific domains of urban development—urban visions and large-scale infrastructure, property and housing, vendors' livelihoods, and urban political registers—by threading its three-way comparison throughout every chapter. This comparative exposition is central to the book's core aims, which involve concurrently folding together threads of similarity and unravelling patterns of difference, in pursuit of a broader understanding of urban change in the most rapidly and dynamically urbanizing region of the world. In this concluding chapter I return to the key elements of the book's comparative analytical framework, examining the distinct real causal forces shaping the three cities, but also attending to their scaled intersections. As the previous four chapters have shown, divergences among the cities in each of these domains can be explained by drawing to varying degrees across the analytical factors discussed in Chapter 2, and situating these against histories of territorialization, property in land, and operations of capital. In the sections that follow, I summarize the key arguments of this book with reference to its framing concepts, and offer some concluding thoughts.

9.1 Capital in the time and place of late urbanization

Capital and its operations in the context of late urbanization account for some of the most salient similarities across the three cities today. The re-ordering of cities through the globalization of capital flows has been a central trope of urban theorizing for decades (Friedmann & Wolf 1982; Taylor 1982; Sassen 1994; Keil 1998; Brenner & Theodore 2002). More recently, a body of work has considered some of the more specific ways that global capital reconfigures cities of the global South, or majority world (Simone 2004b; Robinson 2006; Roy 2009; Parnell & Robinson 2012; Ghertner 2015; Schindler 2017; Simone & Pieterse 2017; Fernandez & Aalbers 2020). However, despite the important contributions of the literature examining 'Southern' dynamics of capitalist urbanization, there is still a tendency to flatten dynamics across global South countries. Much of what happens within them is attributed to the generic operations of global capital in postcolonial settings, with less attention to the highly varied ways in which this unfolds in specific regions and national territories. Significant work has touched on the specificities of neoliberal urban development in China (Wu 2008; He & Wu; 2009;

Politics and the Urban Frontier. Tom Goodfellow, Oxford University Press. © Tom Goodfellow (2022).
DOI: 10.1093/oso/9780198853107.003.0009

Lim 2014), where capitalism is operating through very obviously distinct institutional histories. There is also an emerging literature on comparative capitalist urbanization within Africa (Otiso & Owusu 2008; Pitcher 2017). This book seeks to contribute to these endeavours, but emphasizes that there are particular dynamics of globalized capitalism that operate at the level of regions *within* Africa, and which help us to understand patterns of urban development.

As a region characterized more than any other by late urbanization, East Africa offers distinct opportunities for capital such as rapidly growing urban consumer markets, large pools of cheap labour, new frontiers for real-estate development, and major limitations in infrastructure that require external financing. Combined with its geographic and geopolitical characteristics, this positions it as both at the leading edge of the continent's construction activity and FDI growth (Deloitte 2017; UN-HABITAT 2018; Enns & Bersaglio 2020) and affords it a particularly privileged position in China's Belt and Road Initiative (Johnston 2019; Otele 2020; Lesutis 2021). Meanwhile, partly due to longstanding dependence on agriculture and histories of conflicted state formation that intertwine its relatively late urban transition, most of its countries are still highly dependent on international aid. East African cities thus have a *regionally specific relationship to contemporary global capitalism.*

However, this book has also argued that there are limits to how much dynamics of capital alone can explain varying trajectories of urban development. All of the region's major cities are penetrated by capital, and all of their governing regimes aspire to attract capitalist investment. Yet this produces very different physical and sociopolitical outcomes in each case. It is therefore insufficient to say, for example, that the Kigali's transformations can be explained with reference to exogenous transformations in global policy and finance and have little 'Rwandan' specificity (Shearer 2017: 71). In fact, minimal global finance accrues to Rwanda compared to other countries in the region. The specific ways that the Rwandan government attempts to position Kigali in this globalized environment, and how this intersects with domestic and political context, have consequences for how capital is deployed in the city and for what it can or cannot achieve. The filters of politics at national and urban scales are crucial for explaining what happens in these cities—which, as this book has demonstrated, exhibit many stark differences in terms of the kinds of housing, infrastructure, and structural economic transformation occurring. Thus, notwithstanding the significance of the generic capital perversions that characterize conditions of late urbanization, we cannot reduce these outcomes to the vicissitudes of global capital. These need to be 'grounded' (Rizzo 2017), and political analysis offers us vital tools for this grounding.

9.2 Associational and infrastructural power

Against this backdrop of global capitalism and the regional context of late urbanization, the distribution of associational power in each country diverges substantially for historical reasons, explored in Part II of this book. In all three cases the process of urbanization has ultimately political ruptures. This generated a more concerted focus on urban investment, as the significance of urban-dwellers and urban property interests grew as an element of the national political economy. Beyond this, however, the power distribution within the three countries diverged, with varying distributional consequences. These consequences were partly produced by the different ways in which the distribution of associational power intersects with the infrastructural power of the state. I now review these two dimensions of power and their urban ramifications in each case.

Rwanda had the lowest level of urbanization in the world in 1990, at just 5.4 per cent of the total population. This proportion leapt up to 15 per cent a decade later, following the extraordinary events of the genocide, and has since increased much more slowly, reaching 17 per cent by 2019.[1] This remarkable trebling of the urban share of the population after the civil war and genocide underlines the significance of this rupture for relations of power within the country at large. While on the one hand the RPF period has intensified an existing situation in which cities were sites of power associated with bureaucratic elites, it also marks a major transformative shift. The pre-existing elite was replaced almost wholesale by a new one, largely of refugee and diasporic origin, with a staunchly international outlook and limited internal social legitimacy. As more returnees poured in and aid-backed growth supported a small elite and urban middle class, it was elite factions within the RPF-led coalition, as well as both domestic and international investors, that grew their associational power. The urban majority, traumatized by genocidal conflict, cowed by restrictive legislation, and with little history of unionization and activism to build on, have been largely unable to augment theirs.

Meanwhile, the ruling coalition has capitalized on a strong legacy of infrastructural power rooted in the centralized authority of state institutions in Rwanda's precolonial kingdom, bolstered by colonialism. This intensified systems of centralized land management and population control, while also contributing to the progressive undermining of social networks outside the state. This created a virtuous cycle for the state in which infrastructural power was bolstered and the associational power of ordinary Rwandans simultaneously thwarted. These

---

[1] World bank data, available at https://databank.worldbank.org, accessed 3 December 2020. The same source is used for the figures for Ethiopia and Uganda which follow. Like all urbanization figures, these need to be treated with scepticism given their dependence on different local measures and processes, but they nevertheless indicate general trends.

dynamics, combined with the specific urban legitimation strategies reviewed below, have generated an effort to realize a specific model of urban development. While only partially successful in relation to its stated aims, the *attempt* to implement this vision has been highly consequential in producing Kigali's distinct urban landscape.

In Ethiopia, the increase in urban population from 12.6 per cent of the total in 1990 to 21 per cent in 2019 has led to a gradual rise in the associational power of the urban classes, which has been most notable in Addis Ababa since in the early 2000s. With urban middle classes having been cultivated under the later years of Haile Selassie's regime, and students playing a key role in the 1974 revolution, this sense of actual and latent urban collective power has been heightened by the growing numbers of poor and often jobless city-dwellers with the capacity to destabilize. The EPRDF's decisions about urban investment, and the devotion of huge energy and resources to mobilizing urban youth though successive entrepreneurship schemes, were rooted in its recognition of the maturing and potentially existential threat that Addis Ababa's population posed to its existence. Meanwhile, diaspora based outside the country also held substantial associational power, to a greater extent than in either Rwanda or Uganda given the estimated two million diasporic Ethiopians (many of them in the global North) harbouring both hostility to the regime and capital to invest 'back home'. In the end, the EPRDF lavished so much attention on Addis Ababa between 2005 and 2015 that it co-opted many previously excluded or ignored urban groups and largely neutralized the urban threat. It did so at the expense of other poles of associational power, where grievances were left to fester, as the dramatic unravelling of the country's stability since 2016 has harshly exposed.

In managing this distribution of power, the EPRDF pursued a strategy that produced particularly dramatic urban transformations in Addis Ababa in the early twenty-first century. But accounting for its ability to do this also requires acknowledging the relatively strong infrastructural power of the state, at least in the 'highland core' and across much of the 'highland periphery' of the country, including Addis Ababa. Yet unlike in Rwanda, efforts to consolidate territory through Ethiopia's imperial regimes did not involve unbroken consolidation of infrastructural power within one tightly organized hierarchical kingdom. The impetus to centralize 'despotic' power was more important, and advanced further, than the capillaries of infrastructural power in the imperial period. If anything, the most significant attempt to build heightened infrastructural power was under the Derg from the 1970s, where there was a colossal effort to further enhance central control through the institution of the *kebele* system and wresting of authority over land away from the nobles and petty capitalists. Despite this, the EPRDF did not inherit the levels of infrastructural power that the RPF did. As it attempted to turn itself into a vanguard agent of economic transformation

(Weis 2016), it was only after 2005 that it sought to consolidate infrastructural power within Addis Ababa, reactivating Derg-era systems of social control. Infrastructural power has thus been important for the EPRDF's project in the city-but has its limits, as reflected in the repurposing and unpredictable outcomes of its infrastructure investments, and the backing off from large scale market redevelopments.

The proportion of Ugandans living in cities has seen even more significant increases over the last two decades, rising from 11 per cent in 1990 to 24.3 per cent in 2020, with most of this happening since 2000. An already complex distribution of power in a fragmentary multi-nation postcolonial polity was rendered even more so by the increased political significance of urban groups over time. A context where Baganda landowners, foreign investors, military figures, returnee Asian capitalists, newly enriched urban elites, aid-financed public-service bosses, and educated middle classes are all vying for attention and influence, alongside a large urban informal workforce, does not incentivize or facilitate a coherent urban strategy of the kinds that have been seen in Kigali in Addis Ababa. In fact, it has produced dramatic swings between projects designed to appeal to one set of interests and others aimed in the opposite direction, generating substantial contradictions and tensions. Kampala is thus scattered with discrete and unintegrated projects. In this landscape, ordinary people living and working informally have enough associational power to command favours and exemptions, but not so much as to impel the government to prioritize their needs over other sectional interests through the kinds of mass transit and housing projects witnessed in Addis Ababa.

Moreover, the state is relatively lacking in infrastructural power to implement such projects. Colonial Uganda was assembled from numerous kingdoms and zones, some only weakly integrated into the protectorate, though the country's territorial integrity was protected through internationally sanctioned borders. While Buganda had strong legacies of central authority and hierarchy, these were not as thoroughly bolstered by the British as were those in Rwanda under German and Belgian rule. In Kampala specifically, they were complicated by the bifurcation of authority between the kingdom's institutions and the colonial state, the undermining of traditional land management through *mailo*, and the introduction of a foreign class of mostly Asian capitalists. Moreover, in the postcolonial period infrastructural power was further weakened by the collapse of state institutions under Idi Amin, two decades of civil conflict, and then the deliberate strategies of deregulation, privatization, and state retrenchment under the NRM. This left Uganda with not only an increasingly diffuse and unruly distribution of associational power, but also weak levers of state infrastructural reach. Attempts to bolster this under KCCA since 2011 achieved only limited change. While these power dynamics are clearly reflected in the differences between Kampala's landscape and those that evolved in Kigali and Addis Ababa, to understand better how and why specific developments in these cityscapes were prioritized we need to also consider the specific pursuit of urban social legitimacy in each case.

9.3 The politics of urban legitimation

Like many states on the continent, the rulers of newly independent states in East Africa—as well as the modernizing late-imperial regime in Ethiopia—were widely seen as representing a tiny urban middle class, and thus 'alienated the majority rural population, which lost its trust in the state' (Bereketeab 2020: 65). However, this situation was effectively reversed in Uganda and Ethiopia when, in 1986 and 1992 respectively, the rebel-led regimes of the NRM and EPRDF capitalized on that sense of rural resentment to march to power in Kampala and Addis Ababa. By the last decade of the twentieth century, these states were therefore governed by regimes with a very limited social base in the cities, and heightened but internally variable degrees of rural legitimacy. As these regimes took control, crises of urban legitimacy manifested in the early twenty-first century that would require sustained efforts to co-opt key sections of the urban population.

These efforts to build social legitimacy in the urban realm played out very differently in the two cities. Relatively strong legacies of infrastructural power enabled the EPRDF to roll out a range of government programmes, building the social and infrastructural foundations of urban legitimacy in order to render the opposition-infused city of Addis Ababa governable. In Kampala, urban opposition was substantial but fragmentary, and had never been demonstrated with the force and cohesiveness of the Ethiopian experiences in 1974 and 2005. However, relatively open democratic competition at city level meant that opposition parties dominated the city government, and throughout the first decade of the twenty-first century the NRM sought legitimacy among the urban population through sustained efforts to discredit the city government. The pursuit of social legitimacy among urban informal workers often took the form of anti-formal, populist interventions, fostering a broader culture of anti-formal politics in the city. In contrast to the EPRDF's mammoth programmes of housing and infrastructure development, youth entrepreneurship, and formal subsidies, Museveni and the NRM pursued legitimacy through informal favours, 'forebearance' in the face of regulation, and personalized interventions. This political culture was ultimately to prevail over the effort to initiate a more transformative programme for urban reform under KCCA from 2011.

In Rwanda the pursuit of legitimacy has differed substantially again, explicable in part through the origins of the RPF regime. The RPF did not march to power with heightened rural legitimacy; its war was fought largely from across the border in Uganda, in the interests of a victimized ethnic group comprising around 15 per cent of the population. Although it gained substantial credit for ending the 1990–1994 civil war and genocide, the sense of a floating elite that lacked roots among the rural masses was augmented as the regime consolidated into a core group largely associated with returnee Tutsis in the early 2000s. Moreover, the flooding in of 'old caseload' returnees into Kigali after 1994, many previously living in exile for their entire lives and indebted to the RPF for their return, created a significant urban RPF constituency among the new middle classes and expatriate elites.

The RPF consequently espoused an urban 'modernization' agenda from an earlier stage than the EPRDF or NRM. Yet the class of urbanites on which its legitimacy depended was not the urban popular classes or informal workers, who remained associationally and politically weak. Legitimacy has not been much sought with the urban poor, whose role in the RPF project is either to become middle class or leave the city until they are 'ready' to do so, in contrast to Addis Ababa where the existence of the poor needs to be institutionally afforded even while it is circumscribed. The RPF's pursuit of urban legitimacy has instead been focused externally on the international investment and donor community, and internally on its new upwardly mobile urban constituents, as well as a military and economic elite with the latent associational power to destabilize it from within. This relatively small urban constituency of elite and middle-class residents is well catered for by private-sector housing and service delivery; hence there has never been the political impetus to invest in mass state-produced housing, which is a significant political instrument in Addis Ababa and some other countries on the continent such as Angola (Croese 2017).

Table 9.1 summarizes the dynamics discussed in this and the preceding section. However, focusing on the state, arrangements of power at the national level, and the urban legitimation strategies of ruling elites can offer only a partial explanation

Table 9.1 Associational power, infrastructural power, and urban legitimation

	Uganda	Ethiopia	Rwanda
Distribution of associational power	Diffuse	Diffuse	Narrow
Reach of state infrastructural power	Weak	Strong	Very strong
Urban legitimation strategy	Populist overtures to urban poor and informal workers; sporadic appeals to urban middle class through 'modernization'; elite free-for-all in access to informal land rents	State-led provision of mass public goods and infrastructure, targeted at urban middle classes and urban poor; elite and diasporic access to urban land rents through formal and informal means	Development 'outputs' including service delivery and tight spatial regulation, targeted at middle-class investors and donors; facilitation of formal elite leverage over land rents

for how these cities are transforming. These factors have certainly shaped urban visions, top-down strategies, and investments; but how they play out depends on the situated practices associated with urban infrastructural change, and on registers of urban politics.

9.4 Practicing infrastructure

Large-scale infrastructures generated by the state or through public–private partnerships, and supported by infrastructural power, do not constitute the primary infrastructures of everyday urban life. In these three cities (as in most cities of the global South) urban energy, water, sanitation, waste management, drainage, and transport is produced not only through state or large-scale private infrastructure but through 'heterogeneous infrastructure configurations' (Lawhon et al. 2018): a range of decentralized, incremental, informal, and fragmentary socio-technical arrangements (Silver 2014; McFarlane & Silver 2017b; Castán Broto 2019; Cirolia 2020). Fascinating accounts of these arrangements are provided by Bjerkli (2005) and Cirolia et al. (2021) in relation to waste management and sanitation in Addis Ababa, Shearer (2017) in relation to water in Kigali, and Sseviiri et al. (2020) in relation to solid-waste management in Kampala—to name just a few. In this book, however, I have considered specific large-scale infrastructure investments not only because of what they reveal about elite strategies and the politics of major spatial reorienting, but also because they enable a consideration of how infrastructure writ large inscribes its own patterns on the city.

In Kigali, even when the outward-facing prestige infrastructure epitomized by the Convention Centre and Bugesera Airport project yields some success in terms of international imaging, it also has other profound consequences for urban development. These range from the vast resources such projects suck away from the rest of the economy, to how they recalibrate relations with international financiers and firms, and the reproduction of operational silos and blockages of capacity and skill transfer in the construction sector. Yet in being so visible and symbolic, they also generate particular expectations of progress locally. These are often frustrated, especially since the very same projects illuminate the gulf between lavish government investment priorities and the everyday enrolment of the population into public works such as local road building, street cleaning and greening, enforced through social infrastructures of hierarchy and control. This gap between the peopled economy of urban social control, and the operations of infrastructure capital floating above, is a defining feature of Kigali; it remains to be seen whether it can be bridged to produce a more solid and integrated urban economy, and whether it provides ground for further political ruptures.

In Kampala, the infrastructures bequeathed by the precolonial period and colonial rule were much more fragmented both nationally and within the city itself, as noted above. Colonial dualism generated hard constraints on infrastructural reach in Kampala, leaving a legacy that makes the implementation of infrastructure projects particularly challenging. There has been a less concerted and sustained infrastructural overhaul than in the other two cities, both in consequence of this legacy and because displacing large numbers of ordinary city-dwellers is seen as too threatening to the regime's social legitimacy. All this makes Kampala a fruitful terrain in which to explore heterogeneous configurations (Lawhon et al. 2018; McFarlane & Silver 2017a; Sseveri et al. 2020). But this infrastructural context, combined with the diffuse distribution of associational power, also means that on the occasions when new large-scale infrastructures are generated there is a maelstrom of contending forces that seek, often successfully, to capitalize on them for private gain.

Consequently we see here that infrastructure as a mediant of elite strategy is often very *unfaithful* to the play of power and legitimation that drives it. The Kampala-Entebbe Expressway has parcelled out benefits and costs in ways that no more align with any grand plans for the road than the route itself aligns with its original proposed course. In addition to the scramble for land prior to government acquisition, flooding, the saturation of certain neighbourhoods with dust, changes to value, and ruptures to commuting patterns unforeseen and unconsidered have altered the terms of the road. It is therefore playing a role in the making of Kampala's metropolitan area that was not clearly written by any of its designers.

The wresting of control over land in Ethiopia by the Derg in 1975, and the forging of networks of social control and infrastructural power through the bloody years of Red Terror and beyond, left an important legacy for the rolling-out of infrastructure within Addis Ababa. It meant that once the EPRDF pivoted towards an urban agenda in the 2000s, land could be acquired for major infrastructure more easily than in either of the other cases, and implemented at remarkable speed. Yet the state cannot enforce the use of these public infrastructures in specific ways, and they have provided opportunities for urban groups to turn physical infrastructures to their own ends.

The Addis Ababa light railway mediated the ruling elite's *political* strategy quite faithfully but skewed the socio-economic and spatial agenda as it became something of a 'wild card' in the city's economy of mobility. Just as Collier (2011) argued in *Post-Soviet Social* that it was difficult to impose neoliberal logics onto the lively physical and social infrastructures of the former USSR, the intense socio-spatial mix of Addis Ababa that evolved under the emperors was not easily re-routed into a core–periphery commuter dynamic envisaged for the light railway. Instead, the urban poor reframed this infrastructure for patterns of family, social, and commercial use rather than the inward commute from new suburbs to city centre that was envisaged, with middle-class commuters staying in their cars. Rather than heralding the rise of Addis Ababa's middle classes, it contributed to the situation in which being poor is legitimized and subsidized, while still being difficult to transcend.

The condominium housing programme again delivered urban political dividends, although it simultaneously exacerbated tensions in Oromia, which proved fatal to the EPRDF. But even given its relative fidelity as a political instrument within the city, the middle-class pivot of the housing programme and the pervasiveness of a short-term rental economy meant that rather than generating new suburbs of settled homeowners, a new and fluctuating socio-economic mix was produced. For many poorer people winning apartments through the lottery, vertical living, and a lack of shared external areas for cooking and slaughter (Ejigu 2012; 2015), combined with peripheral location and prohibitive loan repayments, led them to return to informal settlements and rent out or illegally sell their apartments. For those who remain, the material and infrastructural shortcomings of the housing, alongside rising middle-class aesthetic tastes, have generated a substantial economy in repair and decoration. But as the government continued to build ever more condominiums, residential churn intensified as tenants frequently 'hop' from one new condominium to another more convenient one. Relocation itself has consequently become central to the economy in these settlements. Many of these dynamics were unanticipated, illustrating how investments in the built environment can foster transformation beyond the designs and powers of ruling elites or state planners, as new forms of community are made, broken, and remade across the city.

9.5   Political informality and registers of dissent

The same 'gigantic process of communication and learning' that serves to construct or undermine legitimacy for political actors (Merelman 1966) also serves to inculcate particular social and political norms over time. At the scale of the city, where everyday interpersonal and state–society interactions are frequent and often intense, these norms and how they interact with formal institutions of governance play their own roles in urban development and change. Informal politics conditions urban governance and processes of urban development everywhere, of course, and is as central to the politics of Kigali as Kampala. Yet dominant *modalities* of informal politics and their functions differ substantially, with important urban ramifications.

Some of the most significant differences in the street-level economies of Addis Ababa and Kampala can be explained with reference to political informality and its intersection with infrastructural power. The previously discussed factors cannot alone explain these differences. The need to build legitimacy among urban groups including the youth, in the face of weak support for the ruling party in the capital, has been strong in both cities; and relatedly, the distribution of associational power is broad and challenging to manage in both national contexts. Yet in Ethiopia, efforts to deliver youth employment played out through aggressive pro-formal politics in the guise of official entrepreneurship schemes enforced through party structures. In Uganda, almost the opposite occurred: while there were numerous official entrepreneurship schemes, these were relatively insignificant. Instead, benefits to equivalent groups were largely allocated through para-formal systems in which politicians directly dispensed cash to youth groups, and the latter mobilized to leverage these interventions. As observed in Chapter 7, far from the benefits to urban youth being delivered through pro-formal party hierarchies, local NRM operatives in Kampala said they were fed up of the president's 'habit of bypassing party structures' in the context of the distribution of youth funds.

Beyond these para-formal systems, a predominant means through which political actors interfaced with urban groups in Kampala was through anti-formal interventions and 'forbearance' in the face of law and regulation. Urban constituencies including market vendors, motorcycle-taxi drivers, ex-soldiers, and even informal settlement-dwellers were all sometimes referred to as 'untouchable'. Through mobilizing themselves into groups or associations—even if fleetingly, as with the ever-changing kaleidoscope of organizations in the motorcycle-taxi sector[2]—these groups often play on their large numbers and capacity for 'noise' to demand favours. In the fast and loose world of Kampala's politics, the easiest way for political actors to respond is through individual and sporadic favours that work by virtue of denigrating formal public institutions. Many such interventions come from the president himself, who is notoriously hardworking in his dedication to responding to demands, mostly in ways that perpetuate this anti-formal culture. The president, in the words of one observer is 'not a person but a system'; and in this system 'lawlessness is a reward for political loyalty'.[3] This system has left the city authorities very often on the 'low bargaining side', with a politics that, in the words of a seasoned *boda boda* driver, 'all comes down to individual benefits, not collective goods'.[4]

While urban-dwellers often claim benefits in Kampala through anti-formal channels, in Kigali such an approach is counterproductive. In fact, as discussed in Chapters 7 and 8, substantial gains initiated from below in Kigali seem only to come when people engage in pro-formal politics, by leveraging aspirations and policies enshrined in government policy and law. A tendency for actors to operate through pro-formal politics in Kigali also exists at the highest levels of society, as evident when we consider the urban land sector. Para-formal systems of informal land allocation and exchange exist in all three cities, as in much of the world. These are never easily displaced by official land institutions and reforms, particularly when limited capitalist production renders land so preeminent in the urban economy, and therefore an arena of particularly powerful vested interests. Yet in Kigali, the appearance of ordered formality has been particularly central to government

---

[2] This is as much the case in 2020 as it was in 2009; despite one particular organization consolidating some degree of control of in the interim, this collapsed and the sector remains as organizationally fragmented as ever. See Goodfellow and Mukwaya (2021a).

[3] Interview, Kampala, 10 June 2014.

[4] Interview with branch co-ordinator, 21 June 2018.

legitimation strategies; hence elites need to take official rules and systems more seriously. Maintaining a high degree of visible concordance to formal rules means that rather than attempting to merely *override* laws and regulations in the interests of personal gain, elites are more inclined towards a pro-formal politics that involves negotiation to get these formal rules *changed*. This has been evident for example with respect to the reduction of property tax rates and revising of zoning regulations.

By virtue of being institutionalized, political norms—whether para-formal, anti-formal, or pro-formal—are necessarily resistant to change. Attempting to engineer change in the them from above requires both determination and substantial infrastructural power. This is why anti-corruption measures, which are essentially an effort to replace para-formal norms with pro-formal ones, are so difficult to implement—but also why such reforms have been relatively successful in Rwanda. However, the attempt to eradicate para-formal systems can also be damaging to trust networks. Modern Rwandan history can be interpreted as a history of successive attempts to eradicate trust networks that are beyond the purview of the state. This contributes to the persistence of an everyday urban environment characterized by low levels of trust, not so much in state institutions (as in Uganda), but in fellow citizens. Challenging the political order under these conditions is extremely difficult. That is what inculcating pro-formality is about. In Rwandan history, major political ruptures have only occurred through bloodshed, sometimes on a biblical scale; and even then the fundamentals of the system remain largely unchanged. In ordinary times, registers of dissent are generally individualized as acts of refusal, performed in the context of a trust deficit through a logic of relative silence.

If Kigali's street actors were widely reproducing a climate of silence and self-surveillance, those in Addis were instead treading the line between hope for improvement and the constant reiteration of the constraints to realizing that hope (Mains 2012; Di Nunzio 2019). The city's history of dramatic urban uprising produced a struggle of competing mobilizations, in which the EPRDF coalition managed to gain an upper hand within the city boundaries from 2005 until its eventual demise from 2018. But the threat of protest in Addis has, at least since 1974, always been very real; and from above this represents the danger of total mobilization and potential overthrow. While it was not in Addis that this eventually materialized in the mid-late 2010s, the scale of dissent mobilized in Ethiopia from 2014-2018 did indeed eventually bring down the regime.

9.6 Territory, property, and social contracts on the global urban frontier

Simone has argued of African cities that despite their diverse heritage and experience, 'in the face of global economic restructuring, the particular economic arrangements, cultural inclination, and forms of external engagement that largely made African cities different from each other are being unraveled' (Simone 2004b: 17). This is the condition of late urbanization, which has generated a set of pressures, constraints, and powerful ideas that drive to *homogenize*. And yet difference persists, even within a region such as East Africa that shares so many historical and socio-economic characteristics, and which more than any other has been navigating a shared tidal wave of urban growth since the late twentieth century. In fact, as this book has shown, difference in some domains of urban life not only persisted but became more accentuated in the first two decades of the twenty-first century.

East Africa is therefore a particularly salient region for those who care about urban socio-economic progress and justice, and about the capacity of societies to navigate their own urbanization path in the face of the relentless drive of global capitalism and the weight of their own histories, which never lessens but only grows. The differences that have emerged among the cities examined here are inevitably shaped by varying histories, but they are not victims of them. Active policy decisions have generated consequential transformations to the urban landscape and the urban operations of capital, from the decision to revolutionize structures of home ownership through mass housing in Addis Ababa, to the determination to become a continental leader in conference tourism in Kigali, or the wholesale embrace of economic deregulation in Kampala. Such decisions matter, but they are only part of the story. Both state structures and physical structures filter and divert the priorities of governments, and the ways in which city populations respond to efforts to mould them in line with urban visions plays its own, often unscripted, role.

These three cities on the global urban frontier have experimented with new forms of territory and property, producing different kinds of limited and contested social contracts between state and society. Some of the territorial projects have been pursued with a fervour and effectiveness that is striking, but also disturbing in terms of its consequences for city populations' inclusion in the making of their conditions of existence. Reshaping urban territory has been a notable feature of cities across the global South in the twenty-first century, as Schindler (2015) notes. Yet since these territorial projects are intrinsically political, they can't easily be separated from efforts to control populations and redraw the terms of the social contract.

Stamping 'renaissance' and high modernist gigantism on the city in Addis Ababa was part of a project to mark the city as EPRDF territory from 2005. It has illustrated the extent to which urban transformations outside of the archetypal trappings of late neoliberalism and late urbanization are possible, but also that they can be politically 'owned', despite the unruly socio-economic realties that spiral out of them. The EPRDF's urban project amounted to an offer of an authoritarian social contract in Addis Ababa. In Kigali, working with the grain of a historical legacy of societal hierarchy and infrastructural reach has enabled a powerful new urban story of regulatory control, environmental protection, and the centralization of rents for a future-oriented services economy. Because of the largely external and elite orientation of this vision, it has continued to deliver political dividends without the need for any kind of broader urban social contract.

Meanwhile, Kampala illustrates that in a contested city where the prospects for urban territorialization are weak, given a history of dualized control and state corrosion, the urge of ruling elites to control populations depends on manipulations of property alongside a language of overt violence. Attempts to manage the city via relations of property are evident in the recursive redrawing of rights between landlord and tenant, offering something to both but not enough to satisfy either. These multiple interests in urban property can at times produce negotiated solutions to questions of expropriation and resettlement (Marx et al. 2020); there is little option but to negotiate when an intransigent approach along the lines of those adopted by governing regimes in Ethiopia and Rwanda are all but impossible. This reflects the broader fact that in Kampala, where associational power is so diffuse and unruly, ongoing bargaining over the social contract is unavoidable, and a feature of daily life. Yet the fragmentary and sometimes arbitrary nature of these efforts, combined with recourse to violence, means any social contract is also constantly undermined.

It may be necessary to admit that, despite their celebrated economic achievements in the wake of devastating conflicts, the main lessons that we can draw from this comparative study of East African cities are cautionary ones. The position of Ethiopia in 2022 demonstrates that no matter how much you re-orient the engine of the state towards co-opting urban constituents through infrastructure, property and conditional employment programmes, this cannot substitute for an open, flexible, and inclusionary politics at the national level. A regime unravelled in Addis Ababa after 2018 not because of failures in its approach to managing the urban question (problematic though aspects of its approach were), but because its determination to deliver a new economy and new city could not compensate for its inability to meet the broader challenges of national integration and political opening. In Uganda and Rwanda, the regimes remain in place. The former is threatened more immediately by the vigorous urban dissent it has actively provoked; the latter by the spectre that its economic achievements might prove to be a brittle shell, still hard today but, once cracked, hyper-vulnerable to political implosion.

For states to take a prominent role in governing the process of urban growth in Africa is surely desirable, given the consequences of decades of laissez-faire urbanization, and the need to make clear policy choices in a world of mounting environmental crisis. But even while states have been and continue to be central to the trajectories described here, urban populations have not stood idly by. Nor are they likely to do so as some ruling elites in the region dramatically alter their course. The fact that Abiy Ahmed's government in Ethiopia has turned firmly towards an agenda of greater liberalization, with built environment aspirations now mirroring global aesthetics and a hunger for spectacular real estate (Terrefe

2020), reveals the force of globalized capital under late urbanization and the difficulty of sustaining the EPRDF's more heterodox path. Yet it is far from clear that Ethiopians will embrace this shift.

East African states have shown, sometimes with deservedly celebrated results but also with evident injustices and hubris, that driving distinct paths through late urbanization is possible. At a time when the world needs to re-think how cities work in fundamental ways, we need now to learn from East Africa, and from its varied experiences of trying to manage the pressures of extraordinarily intense urbanization. Its experience shows that transforming territory and property—both of which are hard-won achievements that can bring substantial gains to certain urban groups—is not enough to guarantee the political inclusion that our common urban future clearly demands. East African countries can also learn from each other, and from elsewhere, about the kinds of urban social contracts that might be possible under late urbanization. None of the cities have yet found a path to sustainable socio-political relations under the conditions they find themselves in; but then again, few if any other countries have had to build social contracts and foster political inclusion under such extreme conditions. This is the next challenge the region faces It is a challenge as old as the hills, though rendered anew in this increasingly urbanized context, with its economic and environmental challenges more pressing than ever. In this sense, East Africa remains the world's most vital urban laboratory.

Bibliography

Aalbers, M. B. (2007) Geographies of Housing Finance: The Mortgage Market in Milan, Italy. *Growth and Change* 38(2): 174–199.

Aalders, J. T. (2021). Building on the Ruins of Empire: The Uganda Railway and the LAPSSET Corridor in Kenya. *Third World Quarterly* 42(5): 996–1013.

Aalen, L. & Tronvoll, K. (2009). The End of Democracy? Curtailing Political and Civil Rights in Ethiopia. *Review of African Political Economy* 36(120): 193–207.

Abbink, J. (2006). Discomfiture of Democracy? The 2005 Election Crisis in Ethiopia and its Aftermath. *African Affairs* 105(419): 173–199.

Abebe, Z. B. (2018). Developmental State and Ethnic Federalism in Ethiopia: Is Leadership the Missing Link? *Leadership and Developing Societies* 3(1): 95–127.

Abulof, U. (2016). Public Political Thought: Bridging the Sociological–philosophical Divide in the Study of Legitimacy. *The British Journal of Sociology* 67(2): 371–391.

Acharya, A. (2014). Global International Relations (IR) and Regional Worlds: A New Agenda for International Studies. *International Studies Quarterly* 58(4): 647–659.

Acuto, M. (2013). City Leadership in Global Governance. *Global Governance* 19(3): 481–498.

Acuto, M. (2022). *How to Build a Global City: Recognising the Symbolic Power of a Global Urban Imagination*. Ithaca: Cornell University Press.

Adam, A. G. (2014). Land Tenure in the Changing Peri-urban Areas of Ethiopia: The Case of Bahir Dar City. *International Journal of Urban and Regional Research* 38(6): 1970–1984.

Adam, A. G. (2020). Understanding Competing and Conflicting Interests for Peri-urban Land in Ethiopia's Era of Urbanization. *Environment and Urbanization* 32(1): 55–68.

Adams, A. V., Johansson de Silva, S., & Razmara, S. (2013). Improving Skills Development in the Informal Sector: Strategies for Sub-Saharan Africa. Washington, DC: The World Bank.

ADB (African Development Bank); OECD; UNDP; UNECA (United Nations Economic Commission for Africa) (2012). African Economic Outlook, 2012: Promoting Youth Employment. African Development Bank: Abidjan.

ADB (2018). African Economic Outlook 2018. African Development Bank: Abidjan.

Addison, T., Pikkarainen, V., Rönkkö, R., & Tarp, F. (2017). Development and Poverty in Sub-Saharan Africa. WIDER Working Paper No. 2017/169. Helsinki: UNU-WIDER.

Adekanye, J. B. (1995). Structural Adjustment, Democratization and Rising Ethnic Tensions in Africa. *Development and Change* 26(2): 355–374.

Agnew, J. (1995). The Hidden Geographies of Social Science and the Myth of the 'Geographical Turn'. *Environment and Planning D: Society and Space* 13: 379–380.

Agnew, J. A. (2013). Arguing with Regions. *Regional Studies* 47(1): 6–17.

Ahikire, J., & Ampaire, C. (2003). Vending in the City: A Gendered Perspective (CBR Working Paper Series). CBR Working Paper Series. Kampala: Centre for Basic Research.

Ahmed, Hussein S. (1996) Exchange, Trade and the Development of Urbanism in Somalia. PhD thesis, University of Georgia.

Ake, C. (1996). Democracy and Development in Africa. Washington, DC: Brookings Institution Press.

Akinrinade, S. (1999). Democracy and Security in Africa: Towards a Framework of Understanding. *Journal of Contemporary African Studies* 17(2): 217–244.

Alagappa, M. (1995). *Political Legitimacy in Southeast Asia: The Quest for Moral Authority*. Stanford University Press.

Alan G. & Gugler, J. (1992). *Cities, Poverty and Development: Urbanization in the Third World*. Oxford: Oxford University Press.

Allen, J. (2003). *Lost Geographies of Power*. Oxford: Blackwell.

Almond, G. A. (1956). Comparative Political Systems. *The Journal of Politics* 18(3): 391–409.

AlSayyad, N. & Roy, A. (eds) (2003). *Urban Informality: Transnational Perspectives from the Middle East, Latin America, and South Asia*. Lanham, MD: Lexington Books.

Alves, A. C. (2013). China's 'win-win' cooperation: Unpacking the impact of infrastructure-for-resources deals in Africa. *South African Journal of International Affairs* 20(2): 207–226.

Amaza, Oondoga O. (1998). *Museveni's Long March: From Guerrilla to Statesman*. Kampala: Fountain Publishers.

Amin, A. (2004). Regions Unbound: Towards a New Politics of Place. *Geografiska Annaler: Series B, Human Geography* 86(1): 33–44.

Amin, A. (2014). Lively Infrastructure. *Theory, Culture & Society* 31(7–8): 137–161.

Amin, A. & Thrift, N. (2002). *Cities: Reimagining the Urban*. Cambridge: Polity Press.

Amin, A. & Thrift, N. (2017). *Seeing Like a City*. Chichester: John Wiley & Sons.

Amin, S. (1980). *Class and Nation: Historically and in the Present Crisis*. London: Heinemann.

Amis, P. (2006). Urban Poverty in East Africa: Nairobi and Kampala's Comparative Trajectories. In Byrceson, D & D. Potts, *African Urban Economies: Viability, Vitality or Vitiation?* Basingstoke: Palgrave Macmillan, pp. 169–183.

Amoako, C. & Boamah, E. F. (2017). Build as You Earn and Learn: Informal Urbanism and Incremental Housing Financing in Kumasi, Ghana. *Journal of Housing and the Built Environment* 32: 429–448.

Amsden, A. H. (1989). *Asia's Next Giant: South Korea and Late Industrialization*. Oxford: Oxford University Press.

Anand, N., Gupta, A., & Appel, H. (eds) (2018). *The Promise of Infrastructure*. Durham, NC: Duke University Press.

Anderson, D. & Rathbone, R. (eds) (2000). *Africa's Urban Past*. Woodbridge: James Currey Publishers.

André, C. & Platteau, J-P. (1998). Land Relations under Unbearable Stress: Rwanda Caught in the Malthusian Trap. *Journal of Economic Behavior and Organization* 34: 1–47.

Angélil, M. & Siress, C. (2010). Addis through the Looking-glass. *disP-The Planning Review* 46(182): 8–13.

Angelo, H. & Wachsmuth, D. (2015). Urbanizing Urban Political Ecology: A Critique of Methodological Cityism. *International Journal of Urban and Regional Research* 39(1): 16–27.

Angelo, H. & Wachsmuth, D. (2020). Why Does Everyone Think Cities Can Save the Planet? *Urban Studies* 57(11): 2201–2221.

Ansoms, A. (2008). Striving for growth, bypassing the poor? A critical review of Rwanda's rural sector policies. *The Journal of Modern African Studies*, 46(1), 1–32.

Ansoms, A. (2009). Re-engineering Rural Society: The Visions and Ambitions of the Rwandan Elite. *African Affairs* 108(431): 289–309.

Appadurai, A. (2015). Mediants, Materiality, Normativity. *Public Culture* 27(2 76): 221–237.

Appel, H., Anand, N., & Gupta, A. (2018). Introduction: Temporality, Politics and the Promise of Infrastructure. In Anand, N., Gupta, A., & Appel, H. (eds) *The Promise of Infrastructure*. Durham, NC: Duke University Press, pp. 1–39.

Apter, D. E. 1967. *The Political Kingdom in Uganda: A Study in Bureaucratic Nationalism*. Princeton, NJ: Princeton University Press

Archer, M. S. (1995). *Realist Social Theory: The Morphogenetic Approach*. Cambridge: Cambridge University Press.

Archer, M. S. (2000). *Being Human: The Problem of Agency*. Cambridge: Cambridge University Press.

Archer, W. A. & Ling, D. C. (1997). The Three Dimensions of Real Estate Markets: Linking Space, Capital, and Property Markets. *Real Estate Finance* 14(3): 7–14.

Arendt, H. (1970). *On Violence*. New York: Harcourt, Brace, Jovanovich.

Arrighi, G. (2002). The African Crisis. *New Left Review* 15: 5.

Arriola, L. R. & Lyons, T. (2016). Ethiopia: The 100% Election. *Journal of Democracy* 27(1): 76–88.

Asiimwe, G. B. (2013). From monopoly marketing to coffee magendo: responses to policy recklessness and extraction in Uganda, 1971–79. *Journal of Eastern African Studies* 7(1), 104–124.

Asiimwe, G. B. (2018). The Impact of Neoliberal Reforms on Uganda's Socio-economic Landscape. In Wiegratz, J., Martiniello, G., & Greco, E. (eds) *Uganda: The Dynamics of Neoliberal Transformation*. London: Zed Books. 145–177.

Auerbach, A. M., LeBas, A., Post, A. E., & Weitz-Shapiro, R. (2018). State, society, and informality in cities of the Global South. *Studies in Comparative International Development* 53(3): 261–280.

Austin, G., Frankema, E., & Jerven, M. (2016). Patterns of Manufacturing Growth in Sub-Saharan Africa: From Colonization to the Present. CEPR Discussion Paper No. DP11609. London: Centre for Economic Policy Research.

Ayenew, M., 1999. The City of Addis Ababa: Policy Options for the Governance and Management of a City with Multiple Identity. Discussion paper. Addis Ababa: Forum for Social Studies.

Ayoob, M. (1995). *The Third World Security Predicament: State Making, Regional Conflict, and the International System*. Boulder, CO: Lynne Rienner Publishers.

Azari, J. R., & Smith, J. K. (2012). Unwritten Rules: Informal Institutions in Established Democracies. *Perspectives on Politics* 10(1): 37–55.

Badiou, A. (2012) *The Rebirth of History: Times of Riots and Uprisings*. London: Verso.

Bähre, E. & Lecocq, B. (2007). The Drama of Development: The Skirmishes behind High Modernist Schemes in Africa. *African Studies* 66(1): 1–8.

Baker, B. (2007). Post-war policing by communities in Sierra Leone, Liberia, and Rwanda. *Democracy and Security* 3(2): 215–236.

Banks, N., Lombard, M., & Mitlin, D. (2020). Urban Informality as a Site of Critical Analysis. *The Journal of Development Studies* 56(2): 223–238.

Baptista, I. (2013). The Travels of Critiques of Neoliberalism: Urban Experiences from the 'Borderlands'. *Urban Geography* 34(5): 590–611.

Baral, A. (2018). Bad Guys, Good Life: An Ethnography of Morality and Change in Kisekka Market (Kampala, Uganda). PhD dissertation, Acta Universitatis Upsaliensis.

Baral, A. (2019). 'Like the Chicken and the Egg': Market Vendors and the Dilemmas of Neoliberal Urban Planning in Re-Centralised Kampala (Uganda). *kritisk etnografi: Swedish Journal of Anthropology* 2(1–2): 51–66.

Barker, R. (1990). *Political Legitimacy and the State*. Oxford: Oxford University Press.

Bates, R. H. (2014). *Markets and States in Tropical Africa: The Political Basis of Agricultural Policies*. Berkeley, CA: University of California Press.

Batungi, N. 2008. *Land Reform in Uganda: Towards a Harmonised Tenure System*. Kampala: Fountain Publishers.

Bayat, A. (1997). Un-civil Society: The Politics of the 'Informal People'. *Third World Quarterly* 18(1): 53–72.

Bayat, A. (2000). From Dangerous Classes 'to Quiet Rebels': Politics of the Urban Subaltern in the Global South. *International Sociology* 15(3): 533–557.

Bazaara, N. P. (1997). Agrarian Politics, Crisis and Reformism in Uganda, 1962–1996. PhD thesis, Queens University, Ontario.

Beall, J. (2002). Globalization and social exclusion in cities: Framing the Debate with Lessons from Africa and Asia. *Environment and Urbanization* 14(1): 41–51.

Beetham, D. (1991). *The Legitimation of Power*. Basingstoke: Palgrave Macmillan.

Behuria, P. (2015a). Between Party Capitalism and Market Reforms: Understanding Sector Differences in Rwanda. *The Journal of Modern African Studies*: 53(3): 415.

Behuria, P. (2015b). Committing to Self-reliance and Negotiating Vulnerability: Understanding the Developmental Change in Rwanda. PhD dissertation, SOAS University of London.

Behuria, P. (2016a). Centralising Rents and Dispersing Power While Pursuing Development? Exploring the Strategic Uses of Military Firms in Rwanda. *Review of African Political Economy* 43(150): 630–647.

Behuria, P. (2016b). Countering Threats, Stabilising Politics and Selling Hope: Examining the Agaciro Concept as a Response to a Critical Juncture in Rwanda. *Journal of Eastern African Studies* 10(3): 434–451.

Behuria, P. (2018). Learning from Role Models in Rwanda: Incoherent Emulation in the Construction of a Neoliberal Developmental State. *New Political Economy* 23(4): 422–440.

Behuria, P. (2019a). *African Development and the Marginalisation of Domestic Capitalists*. Manchester: Effective States and Inclusive Development Research Centre

Behuria, P. (2019b). Twenty-first Century Industrial Policy in a Small Developing Country: The Challenges of Reviving Manufacturing in Rwanda. *Development and Change* 50(4): 1033–1062.

Behuria, P., Buur, L., & Gray, H. (2017). Studying Political Settlements in Africa. *African Affairs* 116(464): 508–525.

Behuria, P., & Goodfellow, T. (2017). The disorder of 'miracle growth'in Rwanda: Understanding the limitations of transitions to open ordered development. In Pritchett, L., Sen, K., & Werker, E. (Eds.). (2017). *Deals and Development: The Political Dynamics of Growth Episodes*. Oxford: Oxford University Press. 217–249.

Behuria, P. & Goodfellow, T. (2019). Leapfrogging Manufacturing? Rwanda's Attempt to Build a Services-led 'Developmental State'. *The European Journal of Development Research* 31(3): 581–603.

Bekele, S. (2015). Monarchical restoration and territorial expansion: the Ethiopian state in the second half of the nineteenth century. In Prunier G. & Ficquet E. (eds) *Understanding Contemporary Ethiopia*. London: Hurst. 159–182.

Bennett, J. (2004). The Force of Things: Steps toward an Ecology of Matter. *Political Theory* 32(3): 347–372.

Bennett, J. (2010). *Vibrant Matter: A Political Ecology of Things*. Durham, NC: Duke University Press.

Berdegué, J. A., Escobal, J., & Bebbington, A. (2015). Explaining Spatial Diversity in Latin American Rural Development: Structures, Institutions, and Coalitions. *World Development* 73: 129–137.

Bereketeab, R. (2020). State Legitimacy and Government Performance in the Horn of Africa. *African Studies* 79(1): 51–69.

Berhe, M. G. (2020). *Laying the Past to Rest: The EPRDF and the Challenges of Ethiopian State-Building.* London: Hurst.

Berman, B. J. & Leys, C. (eds) (1994). *African Capitalists in African Development.* Boulder, CO: L. Rienner Publishers.

Bernstein, H. (2004). 'Changing before our Very Eyes': Agrarian Questions and the Politics of Land in Capitalism Today. *Journal of Agrarian Change* 4(1–2): 190–225.

Beswick, D. (2010). Managing dissent in a post-genocide environment: the challenge of political space in Rwanda. *Development and Change* 41(2): 225–251.

Bhambra, G. K., Gebrial, D., & Nişancıoğlu, K. (2018). *Decolonising the University.* London: Pluto Press.

Bhan, G. (2019). Notes on a Southern Urban Practice. *Environment and Urbanization* 31(2): 0956247818815792.

Bhaskar, R. (2007/1975). *A Realist Theory of Science.* London: Verso.

Bird, J. & Venables, A. J. (2020). Land Tenure and Land-use in a Developing city: A Quantitative Spatial Model Applied to Kampala, Uganda. *Journal of Urban Economics* 119: 103268.

Bizimana, N. 1989. *White Paradise, Hell for Africa?* Berlin: Edition Humana.

Bjerkli, C. L. (2005). The Cycle of Plastic Waste: An Analysis on the Informal Plastic Recovery System in Addis Ababa, Ethiopia. Masters thesis, Geografisk institute.

Blomley, N. (2016). The Territory of Property. *Progress in Human Geography* 40(5): 593–609.

Blundo, G., de-sardan, J. P. O., Arifari, N. B., & Alou, M. T. (2006). *Everyday Corruption and the State: Citizens and Public Officials in Africa.* London: Zed Books.

Blyth, M. (2002). *Great Transformations: Economic Ideas and Institutional Change in the Twentieth Century.* Cambridge: Cambridge University Press.

Bonnet, F., Vanek, J., & Chen, M. (2019). Women and Men in the Informal Economy: A Statistical Brief. Geneva: International Labour Office. http://www.wiego.org/sites/default/files/publications/files/Women%20and%20Men%20in%20the%20Informal20.

Boone, C. (1990). The Making of a Rentier Class: Wealth Accumulation and Political Control in Senegal. *The Journal of Development Studies* 26(3): 425–449.

Boone, C. (2003). *Political Topographies of the African State: Territorial Authority and Institutional Choice.* Cambridge: Cambridge University Press.

Boone, C. (2014). *Property and Political Order in Africa: Land Rights and the Structure of Politics.* Cambridge: Cambridge University Press.

Boone, C. & Wahman, M. (2015). Rural Bias in African Electoral Systems: Legacies of Unequal Representation in African Democracies. *Electoral Studies* 40: 335–346.

Booth, D. & Golooba-Mutebi, F. (2012). Developmental Patrimonialism? The Case of Rwanda. *African Affairs* 111(444): 379–403.

Boudet, L., Gendreau, L., & Marchand, Q. (2015) Les transports à Addis Abeba. Report, Université de Rennes 1, France.

Bourdieu, P. (1977). *Outline of a Theory of Practice.* Cambridge: Cambridge University Press.

Bourdieu, P. (1990). *The Logic of Practice.* Stanford, CA: Stanford University Press.

Boyce, J. K. & Ndikumana, L. (2001). Is Africa a Net Creditor? New Estimates of Capital Flight from Severely Indebted Sub-Saharan African Countries, 1970–96. *Journal of Development Studies* 38(2): 27–56.

Boyer, D. (2018). 'Infrastructure, Potential Energy, Revolution'. In Anand, N., Gupta, A., & Appel, H. (eds) *The Promise of Infrastructure*. Durham, NC: Duke University Press, pp. 223–244.

Branch, A. & Mampilly, Z. (2015). *Africa Uprising: Popular Protest and Political Change*. London: Zed Books.

Branch, D. (2011). *Kenya: Between Hope and Despair, 1963–2010*. New Haven, CT: Yale University Press.

Bratton, M. (2007). Formal versus Informal Institutions in Africa. *Journal of Democracy* 18(3): 96–110.

Bratton, M. & Van de Walle, N. (1992). Popular Protest and Political Reform in Africa. *Comparative Politics* 24(4): 419–442.

Brautigam, D. & Hwang, J. (2016). Eastern Promises: New Data on Chinese Loans in Africa, 2000 to 2014. China Africa Research Initiative Working Paper No. 4. Baltimore, MD: Johns Hopkins University.

Brechenmacher, S. (2017). *Civil Society under Assault: Repression and Responses in Russia, Egypt, and Ethiopia*. Washington, DC: Carnegie Endowment for International Peace.

Brenner, N. (2000). The Urban Question: Reflections on Henri Lefebvre, Urban Theory and the Politics of Scale. *International Journal of Urban and Regional Research* 24(2): 361–378.

Brenner, N. (2004). *New State Spaces: Urban Governance and the Rescaling of Statehood*. Oxford: Oxford University Press.

Brenner, N. (2019). *New Urban Spaces: Urban Theory and the Scale Question*. Oxford: Oxford University Press.

Brenner, N., Madden, D. J., & Wachsmuth, D. (2011). Assemblage Urbanism and the Challenges of Critical Urban Theory. *City* 15(2): 225–240.

Brenner, N., Peck, J., & Theodore, N. (2010). Variegated Neoliberalization: Geographies, Modalities, Pathways. *Global Networks* 10(2): 182–222.

Brenner, N. & Schmid, C. (2014). The 'Urban Age' in Question. *International Journal of Urban and Regional Research* 38(3): 731–755.

Brenner, N. & Schmid, C. (2015). Towards a New Epistemology of the Urban? *City* 19(2–3): 151–182.

Brenner, N. & Theodore, N. (2002). Cities and the Geographies of 'Actually Existing Neoliberalism'. *Antipode* 34(3): 349–379.

Brett, E. A. (1973). *Colonialism and Underdevelopment in East Africa: The Politics of Economic Change, 1919–1939*. London: Heinemann.

Brisset-Foucault, F. (2014). What Do People Do When They Riot? Patterns of Past and Present Street Politics in Uganda. *Patterns of Past and Present Street Politics in Uganda*. African Studies Association 2014 Conference Paper.

Bromley, R. (2000). Street Vending and Public Policy: A Global Review. *International Journal of Sociology and Social Policy* 20(1/2): 1–28.

Brown, A. and Lyons, M. (2010). Seen But Not Heard: Urban Voice and Citizenship for Street Traders . In Lindell, I. (ed.) *Africa's Informal Workers: Collective Agency, Alliances and Transnational Organizing*. London: Zed Books. 3345.

Brown, S. (2005). Foreign Aid and Democracy Promotion: Lessons from Africa. *The European Journal of Development Research* 17(2): 179–198.

Bryant, L. R. (2014). *Onto-cartography*. Edinburgh: Edinburgh University Press.

Bryceson, D. & Potts, D. (eds) (2006). *African Urban Economies: Viability, Vitality or Vitiation?* Basingstoke: Palgrave Macmillan

Bryceson, D. H. (2006). Introduction. In Bryceson D. H. and Potts, D. (eds) *African Urban Economies: Viability, Vitaliy or Vitiation?* Basingstoke: Palgrave Macmillan. 3–28.

Bryceson, D. F. (2008). *Creole and Tribal Designs: Dar es Salaam and Kampala as Ethnic Cities in Coalescing Nation States*. Crisis States Research Centre Working Paper No. 35. London: London School of Economics and Political Science.

Buettner, T. (2015). Urban Estimates and Projections at the United Nations: The Strengths, Weaknesses, and Underpinnings of the World Urbanization Prospects. *Spatial Demography* 3(2): 91–108.

Bunnell, T., Goh, D. P., Lai, C. K., & Pow, C. P. (2012). Introduction: Global urban frontiers? Asian cities in theory, practice and imagination. *Urban Studies*, 49(13), 2785–2793.

Burton, A. (2001). Urbanisation in Eastern Africa: An Historical Overview, *c*.1750–2000. *AZANIA: Journal of the British Institute in Eastern Africa* 36(1): 1–28.

Burton, A. (2005). *African Underclass: Urbanisation, Crime and Colonial Order in Dar es Salaam*. Oxford: L James Currey.

Burton, A. (2017). Urbanization in East Africa, circa 900–2010 CE. In *Oxford Research Encyclopedia of African History*. Oxford: Oxford University Press. Available at: https://oxfordre.com/africanhistory/view/10.1093/acrefore/9780190277734.001.0001/acrefore-9780190277 734-e-31.

Büscher, K. (2018). African Cities and Violent Conflict: The Urban Dimension of Conflict and Post-conflict Dynamics in Central and Eastern Africa. *Journal of Eastern African Studies* 12(2): 193–210.

Byerley, A. (2005). Becoming Jinja: The Production of Space and Making of Place in an African Industrial Town. PhD thesis, Stockholm University.

Byerley, A. (2011). Ambivalent Inheritance: Jinja Town in Search of a Postcolonial Refrain. *Journal of Eastern African Studies* 5(3): 482–504.

Campt, T. M. (2019). Black visuality and the practice of refusal. *Women & Performance: a journal of feminist theory* 29(1): 79–87.

Carbone, G. M. (2005). 'Populism'visits Africa: the case of Yoweri Museveni and no-party democracy in Uganda. Crisis States Research Centre Working Paper No. 73. London: London School of Economics and Political Science.

Carbone, G. M. (2008). *No-party democracy?: Ugandan politics in comparative perspective*. Boulder: Lynne Rienner Publishers.

Castán Broto, V. C. (2019). *Urban Energy Landscapes*. Cambridge: Cambridge University Press.

Castells, M. (1983). *The City and the Grassroots: A Cross-cultural Theory of Urban Social Movements*. Berkeley, CA: University of California Press.

Castells, M. (1972). *The Urban Question. A Marxist Approach*. London: Edward Arnold.

Castells, M., Portes, A., and Benton, L. A. (eds) (1989). *The Informal Economy: Studies in Advanced and Less Developed Countries*. Baltimore, MD: Johns Hopkins University Press.

Cawthra, G. & Luckham, R. (eds) (2003). *Governing Insecurity: Democratic Control of Military and Security Establishments in Transitional Democracies*. London: Zed Books.

Chacko, E. & Gebre, P. H. (2017). Engaging the Ethiopian Diaspora: Policies, Practices and Performance. In Mangala, J (ed). *Africa and its Global Diaspora*. Basingstoke: Palgrave Macmillan. 219–249.

Chami, F. A. (1994). The First Millennium AD on the East Coast: A New Look at the Cultural Sequence and Interactions. *Azania: Archaeological Research in Africa* 29(1): 227–237.

Chami, F. A. (1998). A Review of Swahili Archaeology. *African Archaeological Review* 15(3): 199–218.

Chant, S. & Pedwell, C. (2008). Women, Gender and the Informal Economy: An Assessment of ILO Research, and Suggested Ways Forward. Geneva: International Labour Organisation.

Charney, I. (2001) Three Dimensions of Capital Switching within the Real Estate Sector: A Canadian Case Study. *International Journal of Urban and Regional Research* 25(4): 740–758.

Cheeseman, N. (2015). *Democracy in Africa: Successes, Failures, and the Struggle for Political Reform*. Cambridge: Cambridge University Press.

Cheeseman, N. & Klaas, B. P. (2018). *How to Rig an Election*. New Haven, CT: Yale University Press.

Cheeseman, N. & Larmer, M. (2015). Ethnopopulism in Africa: Opposition Mobilization in Diverse and Unequal Societies. *Democratization* 22(1): 22–50.

Chemouni, B. (2016). The Politics of State Effectiveness in Burundi and Rwanda: Ruling Elite Legitimacy and the Imperative of State Performance. PhD dissertation, London School of Economics and Political Science.

Chen, M. 2001. Women and Informality: A Global Picture, the Global Movement . *SAIS Review* 21(1): 71–82.

Childe, V. G. (1950). The Urban Revolution. *The Town Planning Review* 21(1): 3–17.

Chinigò, D. (2019). 'The Peri-urban Space at Work': Micro and Small Enterprises, Collective Participation, and the Developmental State in Ethiopia. *Africa: The Journal of the International African Institute* 89(1): 79–99.

Chitonge, H. (2015). *Economic Growth and Development in Africa: Understanding Trends and Prospects*. London: Routledge.

Chitonge, H. (2018). Capitalism in Africa: Mutating Capitalist Relations and Social Formations. *Review of African Political Economy* 45(155): 158–167.

Chitonge, H. & Mfune, O. (2015). The Urban Land Question in Africa: The Case of Urban Land Conflicts in the City of Lusaka, 100 Years after its Founding. *Habitat International* 48: 209–218.

Chittick, H. N. & Rotberg, R. I. (1975). *East Africa and the Orient: Cultural Syntheses in Precolonial Times*. New York: Africana.

Chittick, N. (1965). The 'Shirazi' Colonization of East Africa. *The Journal of African History* 6(3): 275–294.

Chittick, N. (1974). *Kilwa: An Islamic Trading City on the East African Coast*. Nairobi: British Institute in East Africa.

Chome, N. (2020). Land, Livelihoods and Belonging: Negotiating Change and Anticipating LAPSSET in Kenya's Lamu County. *Journal of Eastern African Studies* 14(2): 310–331.

Chrétien, J. P. (2003). *The Great Lakes of Africa: Two Thousand Years of History*. New York: Zone Books.

Chu, J. Y. (2014). When Infrastructures Attack: The Workings of Disrepair in China. *American Ethnologist* 41(2): 351–367.

Cirolia, L. R. (2020). Fractured Fiscal Authority and Fragmented Infrastructures: Financing Sustainable Urban Development in Sub-Saharan Africa. *Habitat International* 104: 102233.

Cirolia, L. R., Hailu, T., King, J., da Cruz, N. F., & Beall, J. (2021). Infrastructure Governance in the Post-networked City: State-led, High-tech Sanitation in Addis Ababa's Condominium Housing. *Environment and Planning C: Politics and Space*, 23996544211037063.

Clapham, C. (1996). *Africa and the International System: The Politics of State Survival*. Cambridge: Cambridge University Press.

Clapham, C. (1988). *Transformation and Continuity in Revolutionary Ethiopia*. Cambridge: Cambrige University Press.

Clapham, C. (2006). Ethiopian Development: The Politics of Emulation. *Commonwealth and Comparative Politics* 44(1): 137–150.

Clapham, C. (2015). The Era of Haile Selassie. In Prunier G. & Ficquet E. (eds) *Understanding Contemporary Ethiopia*. London: Hurst. 183–208.

Clapham, C. S. (2017). *The Horn of Africa: State Formation and Decay*. Oxford: Oxford University Press.

Clapham, C. (2018). The Ethiopian Developmental State. *Third World Quarterly* 39(6): 1151–1165.

Clare, N., Habermehl, V., & Mason-Deese, L. (2018). Territories in Contestation: Relational Power in Latin America. *Territory, Politics, Governance* 6(3): 302–321.

Codere, H. (1973). *The biography of an African society: Rwanda 1900-1960: based on forty-eight Rwandan autobiographies*. Brussels: Musée Royal de l'Afrique Centrale.

Cohen, A. (1969). *Custom and Politics in Urban Africa: A Study of Hausa Migrants in Yoruba Towns*. London: Routledge.

Collier, S. J. (2011). *Post-Soviet Social: Neoliberalism, Social Modernity, Biopolitics*. Princeton, NJ: Princeton University Press.

Collier, P. (2015). 'Africa: New Opportunities, Old Impediments'. *Economic Affairs*, 35(2): 169–77.

Colson, E. (1971). The Impact of the Colonial Period on the Definition of Land Rights. *Colonialism in Africa* 3: 193–215.

Comaroff, J.L. 1998. Reflections on the Colonial State in South Africa and Elsewhere: Factions, Fragments, Facts, Fictions. *Social Identities* 4(3): 321–361.

Connah, G. (1987). *African Civilizations: Precolonial Cities and States in Tropical Africa*. Cambridge: Cambridge University Press.

Connah, G. (2015). *African Civilizations: An Archaeological Perspective*. Cambridge: Cambridge University Press.

Connell, R. (2007). *Southern Theory: The Global Dynamics of Knowledge in Social Science*. Cambridge: Polity Press.

Connelly, S. (2011). Constructing Legitimacy in the New Community Governance. *Urban Studies* 48(5): 929–946.

Coole, D. (2005). Rethinking Agency: A Phenomenological Approach to Embodiment and Agentic Capacities. *Political Studies* 53(1): 124–142.

Coole, D. & Frost, S. (2010). *New Materialisms: Ontology, Agency, and Politics*. Durham, NC: Duke University Press.

Cooper, F. (1977). *Plantation Slavery on the East Coast of Africa*. New Haven, CT: Yale University Press.

Cooper, F. (1994) Conflict and Connection: Rethinking Colonial African History. *American Historical Review* 99 (5): 1516–1545.

Cooper, F. (1996). *Decolonisation and African Society: The Labor Question in French and British Africa*. Cambridge: Cambridge University Press.

Cooper, F. (2002). *Africa since 1940: The Past of the Present*. Cambridge: Cambridge University Press.

Cooper, F. (2017). From Enslavement to Precarity? The Labour Question in African History. In Adebanwi, W. (ed.) *The Political Economy of Everyday Life in Africa: Beyond the Margins*. Oxford: James Currey. 45–76.

Cooper, F. & Frederick, C. (1996). *Decolonization and African Society: The Labor Question in French and British Africa*. Cambridge: Cambridge University Press.

Coquery-Vidrovitch, C. (1975). Research on an African Mode of Production. *Critique of Anthropology* 2(4–5): 38–71.

Coquery-Vidrovitch, Catherine. (1993) *Histoire des villes d'Afrique noire des origines à la colonisation*. Paris: Albin Michel.

COWI (2020). *Physical Development Plan for the Jinja-Kampala-Mpigi Regional Corridor: Situation Analysis Report.* Kongens Lyngby, Denmark: COWI.

Crewett, W., Bogale, A., & Korf, B. (2008). Land Tenure in Ethiopia: Continuity and Change, Shifting Rules, and the Quest for State Contorl. CAPRi Working Paper No. 91. Washington, DC: IFPRI.

Croese, S. (2017). State-led housing delivery as an instrument of developmental patrimonialism: The case of post-war Angola. *African Affairs,* 116(462), 80–100.

Cross, J. C. (1998). *Informal Politics: Street Vendors and the State in Mexico City.* Stanford, CA: Stanford University Press.

Crummey, D. (1971). The Violence of Tewodros. *Journal of Ethiopian Studies* 9(2): 107–125.

Dahl, R. A. (1961). *Who Governs? Democracy and Power in an American City.* New Haven, CT: Yale University Press.

Davis, D. E. (2009). Non-state Armed Actors, New Imagined Communities, and Shifting Patterns of Sovereignty and Insecurity in the Modern World. *Contemporary Security Policy* 30(2): 221–245.

Davis, H. D. (1962). The Economic Development of Uganda. Working paper No. 10112.Washington, DC: The World Bank.

De Boeck F. (2011). Inhabiting Ocular Ground: Kinshasa's Future in the Light of Congo's Spectral Urban Politics. *Cultural Anthropology* 26(2): 263–286.

De Boeck, F. (2015). Divining the City: Rhythm, Amalgamation and Knotting as Forms of Urbanity. *Social Dynamics* 41(1): 47–58.

De Soto, H. (1989). *The Other Path: The Invisible Revolution in the Third World.* New York: Harper and Row.

De Waal, A. (2013) The Theory and Practice of Meles Zenawi. *African Affairs* 112(446): 148–155.

Deleuze, G. & Guattari, F. (1988). *A Thousand Plateaus: Capitalism and Schizophrenia.* London: Bloomsbury Publishing.

Della Porta, D. (2016). *Where Did the Revolution Go? Contentious Politics and the Quality of Democracy.* Cambridge: Cambridge University Press.

Della Porta, D. & Diani, M. (2006). *Social Movements: An Introduction.* Oxford: Wiley.

Deloitte (2017). A Shift to More But Less. Africa Construction Trends Report. Available at: https://www2.deloitte.com/content/dam/Deloitte/ao/Documents/energy-resources/Africa_Construction_Trends_Reports.pdf. Accessed 27 November 2020.

Deloitte (2019). 2019 Commercial Real Estate Industry Outlook. Available at: https://www2.deloitte.com/content/dam/Deloitte/us/Documents/financial-services/us-fsi-dcfs-2019-cre-outlook.pdf. Accessed 21 February 2019.

Demissie, F. (2008). Situated Neoliberalism and Urban Crisis in Addis Ababa, Ethiopia. *African Identities* 6(4): 505–527.

Desrosiers, M. E. & Thomson, S. (2011). Rhetorical Legacies of Leadership: Projections of 'Benevolent Leadership' in Pre-and Post-genocide Rwanda. *The Journal of Modern African Studies.* 49(3) 429–453.

Dessalegn R. (2009). *The Peasant and the State: Studies in Agrarian Change in Ethiopia 1950s–2000s.* Addis Ababa: Addis Ababa University Press.

Des Forges, A. (1999). *Leave None to Tell the Story.* New York: Human Rights Watch.

Des Forges, A. (2011). *Defeat is the only bad news: Rwanda under Musinga, 1896–1931.* Madison: University of Wisconsin Press.

DFID (2007). Phase 1 of the National Land Tenure Reform Programme (Nltrp) in Rwanda: Technical Annex. Kigali: Ministry of Natural Resources.

Dikeç, M. (2005). Space, Politics, and the Political. *Environment and Planning D: Society and Space,* 23(2): 171–188.

Di John, J. & Putzel, J. (2009). Political Settlements: Issues paper. Governance and Social Development Resource Centre Discussion Paper: University of Birmingham.

Di Nunzio, M. (2012). "We are good at surviving": street hustling in Addis Ababa's inner city. *Urban Forum* 23(4): 433–447.

Di Nunzio, M. (2014). 'Do Not Cross the Red Line': The 2010 General Elections, Dissent, and Political Mobilization in Urban Ethiopia. *African Affairs* 113(452): 409–430.

Di Nunzio, M. (2015). What Is the Alternative? Youth, Entrepreneurship and the Developmental State in Urban Ethiopia. *Development and Change* 46(5): 1179–1200.

Di Nunzio, M. (2017). Marginality as a Politics of Limited Entitlements: Street Life and the Dilemma of Inclusion in Urban Ethiopia. *American Ethnologist* 44(1): 91–103.

Di Nunzio, M. (2019). *The Act of Living: Street Life, Marginality, and Development in Urban Ethiopia*. New York: Cornell University Press.

Di Nunzio, M. (2022). Evictions for development: Creative destruction, redistribution and the politics of unequal entitlements in inner-city Addis Ababa (Ethiopia), 2010–2018. *Political Geography* 98, 102671.

Dikeç, M. (2005). Space, Politics, and the Political. *Environment and Planning D: Society and Space* 23(2): 171–188.

Dikeç, M. (2015) *Space, Politics, and Aesthetics*. Edinburgh: Edinburgh University Press.

Dikeç, M. & Swyngedouw, E. (2017). Theorizing the Politicizing City. *International Journal of Urban and Regional Research* 41(1): 1–18.

Diouf, M. (1996). Urban Youth and Senegalese Politics: Dakar 1988–1994. *Public Culture* 19: 225–249.

Diouf, M. (2003). Engaging Postcolonial Cultures: African Youth and Public Space. *African Studies Review* 46(2): 1–12.

Doherty, J. (2020). Motorcycle Taxis, Personhood, and the Moral Landscape of Mobility. *Geoforum*. Available at: https://www.sciencedirect.com/science/article/abs/pii/S0016718520300920.

Doornbos, M. (2001). 'Good governance': The Rise and Decline of a Policy Metaphor? *Journal of Development studies* 37(6): 93–108.

Doner, R. F., Ritchie, B. K., & Slater, D. (2005). Systemic Vulnerability and the Origins of Developmental States: Northeast and Southeast Asia in Comparative Perspective. *International Organization* 59(2): 327–361.

Donham, D. & James, W. (1986). *The Southern Marches of Imperial Ethiopia*. Cambridge: Cambridge University Press.

Dorsey, Learthen. (1994). *Historical Dictionary of Rwanda*. Metuchen, New Jersey and London: The Scarecrow Press.

Dovey, K., Shafique, T., van Oostrum, M., & Chatterjee, I. (2021). Informal settlement is not a euphemism for 'slum': what's at stake beyond the language?. *International Development Planning Review* 43(2): 139–150.

Doyle, S. (2006). 'From Kitara to the Lost Counties: Genealogy, Land and Legitimacy in the Kingdom of Bunyoro, Western Uganda. *Social Identities* 12(4): 457–460.

Duroyaume, P. (2015). 'Addis Ababa and the Urban Renewal in Ethiopia'. In Prunier G. & Ficquet E. (eds) *Understanding Contemporary Ethiopia*. London: Hurst. 395–413.

Dwyer, P. & Zeilig, L. (2012). *African Struggles Today: Social Movements since Independence*. Chicago: Haymarket Books.

Dyson, T. (2010). *Population and Development: the Demographic Transition*. London: Bloomsbury Publishing.

Easterling, K. (2014). *Extrastatecraft: The Power of Infrastructure Space*. London: Verso Books.

ECN (2015). Spanning Africa's Infrastructure Gaps: How Development Capital Is Transforming Africa's Project Build-out. The Economist Corporate Network. Available at: http://ftp01.economist.com.hk/ECN_papers/Infrastructure-Africa.

Ejigu, A. (2015). Places on Becoming: An Ethnographic Case Study of a Changing City and its Emerging Residential Environments. PhD dissertation, KTH Royal Institute of Technology.

Ejigu, A. G. (2012). Socio-spatial Tensions and Interactions: An Ethnography of the Condominium Housing of Addis Ababa, Ethiopia. In Robertson, M. (ed) *Sustainable cities: Local solutions in the global South.* Rugby: Practical Action Publishing: 97–112.

Ejigu, A. G. (2014). History, Modernity, and the Making of an African Spatiality: Addis Ababa in Perspective. *Urban Forum* 25(3): 267–293.

Ekeh, P. P. (1975). Colonialism and the Two Publics in Africa: A Theoretical Statement. *Comparative Studies in Society and History,* 17(1), 91–112

Elden, S. (2010). Land, Terrain, Territory. *Progress in Human Geography* 34(6): 799–817.

Elden, S. (2013). *The Birth of Territory.* London: University of Chicago Press.

Elder-Vass, D. (2010). *The Causal Power of Social Structures: Emergence, Structure and Agency.* Cambridge: Cambridge University Press.

Elkan, W. & Van Zwanenberg, R. (1975). How People Came to Live in Towns. *Colonialism in Africa* 4: 655–672.

Ellis, S. & I. van Kessel (eds.) (2009). *Movers and Shakers: Social Movements in Africa.* Leiden: Brill.

Englebert, Pierre. 2002. Born-again Buganda or the Limits of Traditional Resurgence in Africa. *The Journal of Modern African Studies* 40(3): 345–368.

Enns, C. & Bersaglio, B. (2020). On the Coloniality of 'New' Mega-infrastructure Projects in East Africa. *Antipode* 52(1): 101–123.

Enright, T. & Rossi, U. (eds) (2017). *The Urban Political: Ambivalent Spaces of Late Neoliberalism.* New York: Springer.

Erdmann, G., & Engel, U. (2007). Neopatrimonialism reconsidered: Critical review and elaboration of an elusive concept. *Commonwealth & Comparative Politics* 45(1): 95–119.

Erlebach, R. (2006). The Importance of Wage Labour in the Struggle to Escape Poverty: Evidence from Rwanda. PhD thesis, University of London.

Esmail, S. & Corburn, J. (2020). Struggles to Remain in Kigali's 'Unplanned' Settlements: The Case of Bannyahe. *Environment and Urbanization* 32(1): 19–36.

Evans, P. B. (1995). *Embedded Autonomy: States and Industrial Transformation.* Princeton, NJ: Princeton University Press.

Evans, P. B., Rueschemeyer, D., & Skocpol, T. (eds) (1985). *Bringing the State Back In.* Cambridge: Cambridge University Press.

Ezeadichie, N. (2012). Home-Based Enterprises in Urban Spaces: An Obligation for Strategic Planning? *Berkeley Planning Journal* 25(1): 44–63.

Ezemenari, K., Kebede, E., & Lahiri, S. (2008). The Fiscal Impact of Foreign Aid in Rwanda: A Theoretical and Empirical Analysis. Washington, DC: The World Bank.

Fanon, F. 1963. *The Wretched of the Earth.* New York: Grove Press.

Farías, I. (2011). The Politics of Urban Assemblages. *City* 15(3–4): 365–374.

Farías, I. & Bender, T. (eds) (2012). *Urban Assemblages: How Actor-network Theory Changes Urban Studies.* London: Routledge.

Fei, D, Liao, C (2020) Chinese Eastern industrial zone in Ethiopia: Unpacking the enclave. *Third World Quarterly* 41(4): 623–644.

Ferguson, J. (2006) *Global Shadows: Africa in the Neoliberal World Order.* Durham, NC: Duke University Press.

Fernandez, R. & Aalbers, M. B. (2017). Housing and Capital in the Twenty-first Century: Realigning Housing Studies and Political Economy. *Housing, Theory and Society* 34(2): 151–158.

Fernandez, R. & Aalbers, M. B. (2020). Housing Financialization in the Global South: In Search of a Comparative Framework. *Housing Policy Debate* 30(4): 680–701.

Finn, B. (2018). Quietly Chasing Kigali: Young Men and the Intolerance of Informality in Rwanda's Capital City. *Urban Forum* 29(2): 205–218.

Fischer, A. M. (2015). The End of Peripheries? On the Enduring Relevance of Structuralism for Understanding Contemporary Global Development. *Development and Change* 46(4): 700–732.

Fischer, A. M. (2019). Bringing Development Back into Development Studies. *Development and Change* 50(2): 426–444.

Fjeldstad, O. H., Ali, M., & Goodfellow, T. (2017). Taxing the Urban Boom: Property Taxation in Africa. CMI Insight.

Fleetwood, S. (2001). Causal Laws, Functional Relations and Tendencies. *Review of Political Economy* 13(2): 201–220.

Fletcher, R. (1986). Settlement Archaeology: Worldwide Comparisons. *World Archaeology* 18(1): 59–83.

Foucoult, M. (1975). *Discipline and Punish*. Paris: Gallimard.

Fourchard, L. (2011). Between World History and State Formation: New Perspectives on Africa's Cities. *The Journal of African History* 52(2): 223–248.

Fox, S. (2012). Urbanization as a Global Historical Process: Theory and Evidence from Sub-Saharan Africa. *Population and Development Review* 38(2): 285–310.

Fox, S. (2014). The Political Economy of Slums: Theory and Evidence from Sub-Saharan Africa. *World Development* 54: 191–203.

Fox, S. (2017). Mortality, Migration, and Rural Transformation in sub-Saharan Africa's Urban Transition. *Journal of Demographic Economics* 83(1): 13–30.

Fox, S. & Goodfellow, T. (2016). *Cities and Development*. London: Routledge.

Fraser, N. (1981). Foucault on Modern Power: Empirical Insights and Normative Confusions. *Praxis International* 1(3): 272–287.

Fox, S., & Goodfellow, T. (2021). On the Conditions of 'Late Urbanisation'. *Urban Studies*, 00420980211032654.

Freund, B. (2007). *The African City: A History*. Cambridge: Cambridge University Press.

Mengistu, F. and van Dijk, M. P. (2011). The Challenges of Public–Private Partnerships: The Case of Merkato Millennium Development Partnership (MMDP). In Bongwa, A., Kassahun, S., & van Dijk, M. P. (eds) *Decentralization and Service Delivery in Ethiopia*. Rotterdam: Shaker Publishing BV. 28–56.

Mengistu, F. (2013). Institutional Interfaces and Actors' Behavior in Transitional Real Estate Markets of Addis Ababa. PhD thesis, International Institute of Social Studies of Erasmus University (ISS).

Friedmann, J. & Wolff, G. (1982). World City Formation: An Agenda for Research and Action. *International Journal of Urban and Regional Research* 6(3): 309–344.

Furtado, C. (1983). *Accumulation and Development: The Logic of Industrial Civilization*. London: St. Martin's Press.

Gagliardone, I. (2014). New Media and the Developmental State in Ethiopia. *African Affairs* 113(451): 279–299.

Gandy, M. (2005). Cyborg Urbanization: Complexity and Monstrosity in the Contemporary City. *International Journal of Urban and Regional Research* 29(1): 26–49.

Gandy, M. (2006). Planning, Anti-planning, and the Infrastructure Crisis Facing Metropolitan Lagos. In *Cities in Contemporary Africa*. New York: Palgrave Macmillan. 247–264.

Gann, L. H. (1975). Economic Development in Germany's African Empire'. In Duigan, P. and Gann, L. H. (eds) *Colonialism in Africa*. Cambridge: Cambridge University Press. 216–239.

Garvin, D. (2020). Constructing Race through Commercial Space: Merkato Ketema under Fascist Urban Planning. *Journal of Modern Italian Studies* 25(2): 118–148.

Gastrow, C. (2017). Aesthetic Dissent: Urban Redevelopment and Political Belonging in Luanda, Angola. *Antipode* 49(2): 377–396.

Gastrow, C. (2020) 'Housing middle classness: formality and the making of distinction in Luanda. *Africa*, 90(3): 509–528.

Gebre-Egziabher, T. & Yemeru E. A. (2019) Urbanization and Industrial Development in Ethiopia. In Cheru, F., Cramer, C., and Oqubay, A. (eds) *The Oxford Handbook of the Ethiopian Economy*. Oxford: Oxford University Press. 785–805.

Gebregziabher, T. N. (2019a). Ideology and Power in TPLF's Ethiopia: A Historic Reversal in the Making? *African Affairs* 118(472): 463–484.

Gebregziabher, T. N. (2019b). Soldiers in Business: The Pitfalls of METEC's Projects in the Context of Ethiopia's Civil–Military Relations. *Review of African Political Economy* 46(160): 261–278.

Gebregziabher, T. N. & Hout, W. (2018). The Rise of Oligarchy in Ethiopia: The Case of Wealth Creation since 1991. *Review of African Political Economy* 45(157): 501–510.

Gebremariam, E. B. (2017). The Politics of Youth Employment and Policy Processes in Ethiopia. IDS Bulletin 48(3): 33–50.

Gebremariam, E. B. (2020). The Politics of Dominating Addis Ababa (2005–2018). ESID Working Paper No. 148. Manchester: University of Manchester.

Gebremariam, E. B., & Herrera, L. (2016). On silencing the next generation: Legacies of the 1974 Ethiopian revolution on youth political engagement. *Northeast African Studies* 16(1): 141–166.

Gebresenbet, F., & Kamski, B. (2019). The paradox of the Ethiopian Developmental State: bureaucrats and politicians in the sugar industry. *Journal of contemporary African studies* 37(4): 335–350.

Geddes, B. (1994). *Politician's Dilemma: Building State Capacity in Latin America*. Berkeley, CA: University of California Press.

Geiger, D. (2009). Turner in the Tropics: The Frontier Concept Revisited. PhD dissertation, Universität Luzern.

Gerlach, M. L. (1992). *Alliance Capitalism*. Berkeley: University of California Press.

Gerschewski, J. (2013). The Three Pillars of Stability: Legitimation, Repression, and Co-optation in Autocratic Regimes. *Democratization* 20(1): 13–38.

Geshekter, C. L. (1993). Somali Maritime History and Regional Sub-cultures: A Neglected Theme of the Somali Crisis. AAMH.

Gharib, M. 2013. '6 Surprising facts about Chinese aid to Africa', available at: https://www.one. org/us/blog/6-surprising-facts-about-chinese-aid-to-africa/. Accessed 21 February 2019.

Ghertner, D. A. (2015). *Rule by Aesthetics: World-class city making in Delhi*. Oxford: Oxford University Press.

Giannecchini, P., & Taylor, I. (2018). The eastern industrial zone in Ethiopia: Catalyst for development?. *Geoforum* 88: 28–35.

Gibbon, P., & Ponte, S. (2005). *Trading down: Africa, Value Chains, and the Global Economy*. Philadelphia: Temple University Press.

Giddens, A. (1984). *The Constitution of Society: Outline of the Theory of Structuration*. Cambridge: Polity Press.

Gil, N. (2015). UNRA Kampala-Entebbe Expressway: Uganda's First Toll Road. Unpublished report. Available at: https://personalpages.manchester.ac.uk/staff/nuno. gil/Teaching%20case%20studies/Uganda%20National%20Roads%20Authority%20Part %20A.pdf

Gilbert, A. (2007). The return of the slum: does language matter?. *International Journal of urban and regional Research* 31(4): 697–713.

Gilbert, A., & Gugler, J. (1992). *Cities, Poverty, and Development: Urbanization in the Third World* (Second Edition). Oxford: Oxford University Press.

Gillespie, T. (2016). Accumulation by Urban Dispossession: Struggles over Urban Space in Accra, Ghana. *Transactions of the Institute of British Geographers* 41(1): 66–77.

Gillespie, T. (2020). The Real Estate Frontier. *International Journal of Urban and Regional Research* 44(4): 599–616.

Gluckman, M. (1960). Tribalism in Modern British Central Africa. *Cahiers d'études africaines* 1(1): 55–70.

Goldfrank, B. & Schrank, A. (2009). Municipal Neoliberalism and Municipal Socialism: Urban Political Economy in Latin America. *International Journal of Urban and Regional Research*, 33(2), 443–462.

Goldman, M. (2011). Speculative Urbanism and the Making of the Next World City. *International Journal of Urban and Regional Research* 35(3): 555–581.

Goldman, M. & Narayan, D. (2021). Through the Optics of Finance: Speculative Urbanism and the Transformation of Markets. *International Journal of Urban and Regional Research* 45(2): 209–231.

Gollin, D., Jedwab, R., & Vollrath, D. (2016). Urbanization with and without Industrialization. *Journal of Economic Growth* 21(1) :35–70.

Golooba-Mutebi, F. & Hickey, S. (2013). Investigating the Links between Political Settlements and Inclusive Development in Uganda: Towards a Research Agenda. ESID Working Paper No. 20. Manchester: University of Manchester.

Golubchikov, O. (2010). World-city-entrepreneurialism: globalist imaginaries, neoliberal geographies, and the production of new St Petersburg. *Environment and Planning A* 42(3): 626–643.

Gombay, C. (1994). Eating Cities: Urban Management and Markets in Kampala. *Cities* 11(2): 86–94.

Goodfellow, T. (2010). The Bastard Child of Nobody: Anti-planning and the Institutional Crisis in Contemporary Kampala. Crisis States Research Centre Working Papers Series No. 2 (67). London: London School of Economics and Political Science.

Goodfellow, T. (2012). *State effectiveness and the politics of urban development in East Africa: A puzzle of two cities, 2000-2010*. PhD dissertation, London School of Economics and Political Science.

Goodfellow, T. (2013a). Planning and development regulation amid rapid urban growth: Explaining divergent trajectories in Africa. *Geoforum* 48: 83–93.

Goodfellow, T. (2013b). The institutionalisation of "noise" and "silence" in urban politics: Riots and compliance in Uganda and Rwanda. *Oxford Development Studies* 41(4): 436–454.

Goodfellow, T. (2014a). Legal manoeuvres and violence: Law making, protest and semi-authoritarianism in Uganda. *Development and Change* 45(4): 753–776.

Goodfellow, T. (2014b). Rwanda's political settlement and the urban transition: expropriation, construction and taxation in Kigali. *Journal of Eastern African Studies* 8(2): 311–329.

Goodfellow, T. (2015a). Taxing the Urban Boom: Property Taxation and Land Leasing in Kigali and Addis Ababa. ICTD Working Paper No. 38. Brighton: Institute for Development Studies.

Goodfellow, T. (2015b). Taming the 'Rogue' Sector: Studying State Effectiveness in Africa through Informal Transport Politics. *Comparative Politics* 47(2): 127–147.

Goodfellow, T. (2017a). Urban Fortunes and Skeleton Cityscapes: Real Estate and Late Urbanization in Kigali and Addis Ababa. *International Journal of Urban and Regional Research* 41(5): 786–803.

Goodfellow, T. (2017b). Taxing Property in a Neo-developmental State: The Politics of Urban Land Value Capture in Rwanda and Ethiopia. *African Affairs* 116(465): 549–572.

Goodfellow, T. (2017c). Double Capture'and De-Democratisation: Interest Group Politics and Uganda's 'Transport Mafia. *The Journal of Development Studies*, 53(10), 1568–1583.

Goodfellow, T. (2018). Seeing Political Settlements through the City: A Framework for Comparative Analysis of Urban Transformation. *Development and Change*, 49(1), 199–222.

Goodfellow, T. (2020a). Political Informality: Deals, Trust Networks, and the Negotiation of Value in the Urban Realm. *The Journal of Development Studies* 56(2): 278–294.

Goodfellow, T. (2020b). Finance, infrastructure and urban capital: The political economy of African 'gap-filling'. *Review of African Political Economy*, 47(164), 256–274.

Goodfellow, T. & Huang, Z. (2021). Contingent Infrastructure and the Dilution of 'Chineseness': Reframing Roads and Rail in Kampala and Addis Ababa. *Environment and Planning A: Economy and Space* 53(4): 655–674.

Goodfellow, T., & Jackman, D. (2020). *Control the Capital: Cities and Political Dominance.* ESID Working Paper No. 135. Effective States and Inclusive Development Research Centre: University of Manchester.

Goodfellow, T., & Lindemann, S. (2013). The Clash of Institutions: Traditional Authority, Conflict and the Failure of 'Hybridity' in Buganda. *Commonwealth & Comparative Politics* 51(1): 3–26.

Goodfellow, T. & Mukwaya, P. I. (2021a). *The Political Economy of Public Transport in Greater Kampala: Movers, Spoilers and Prospects for Reform.* Kampala: Frederich Ebert Stiftung.

Goodfellow, T. and Mukwaya, P. I. (2021b). Museveni Has Failed to Win Over Young, Urban Ugandans: Why He's Running Out of Options. *The Conversation.* 28 January. Available at: https://theconversation.com/museveni-has-failed-to-win-over-young-urban-ugandans-why-hes-running-out-of-options-154081. Accessed 7 December 2021.

Goodfellow, T. & Smith, A. (2013). From Urban Catastrophe to 'Model' City? Politics, Security and Development in Post-conflict Kigali. *Urban Studies* 50(15): 3185–3202.

Goodfellow, T., & Titeca, K. (2012). Presidential intervention and the changing 'politics of survival'in Kampala's informal economy. *Cities* 29(4): 264–270.

Goody, J. (1971). *Technology, Tradition and the State in Africa.* London: Routledge.

Gopal, P. (2019). *Insurgent Empire: Anticolonial Resistance and British Dissent.* London: Verso Books.

Gore, C. D., & Muwanga, N. K. (2014). Decentralization is Dead, Long Live Decentralization! Capital City Reform and Political Rights in K ampala, U ganda. *International Journal of Urban and Regional Research* 38(6): 2201–2216.

Gotham, K. F. (2006) The Secondary Circuit of Capital Reconsidered: Globalization and the US Real Estate Sector. *American Journal of Sociology* 112(1): 231–275.

Gough, K. V. & Yankson, P. (2011). A Neglected Aspect of the Housing Market: The Caretakers of Peri-urban Accra, Ghana. *Urban Studies* 48(4): 793–810.

Gouvernement Belge (1960): Rapport sur l'Administration du Ruanda-Urundi. Brussels.

Governement of Rwanda. 2013. Economic Development and Poverty Reduction Strategy: 2013–2018. Kigali: Ministry of Finance and Economic Planning.

Government of Rwanda (GoR). 2009. Sustainable Tourism Development Master Plan for Rwanda. Kigali: Government of Rwanda

Graham, S. & McFarlane, C. (eds) (2014). *Infrastructural Lives: Urban Infrastructure in Context*. London: Routledge.

Gramsci, A. (1971). *Selections from the Prison Notebooks*. London: Lawrence and Wishart.

Gray, H. (2013). Industrial Policy and the Political Settlement in Tanzania: Aspects of Continuity and Change since Independence. *Review of African Political Economy* 40(136): 185–201.

Gray, H. (2018). *Turbulence and Order in Economic Development: Institutions and Economic Transformation in Tanzania and Vietnam*. Oxford: Oxford University Press.

Gray, H. & Whitfield, L. (2014). Reframing African Political Economy: Clientelism, Rents and Accumulation as Drivers of Capitalist Transformation'. Working Paper Series (159). London: International Development, LSE.

Gready, P. (2011). Beyond "You're with us or against us": civil society and policymaking in post-genocide Rwanda. In Straus, S & Waldorf (eds). *Remaking Rwanda: State Building and Human Rights after Mass Violence*. London: University of Wisconsin Press.

Green, E. D. (2006). Ethnicity and the Politics of Land Tenure Reform in Central Uganda. *Commonwealth and Comparative Politics* 44(3): 370–388.

Green, E. (2010). Patronage, District Creation, and Reform in Uganda. *Studies in Comparative International Development* 45(1): 83–103.

Green, Reginald. 1981. Magendo in the Political Economy of Uganda: Pathology, Parallel System, or Dominant Sub-mode of Production? Discussion Paper No. 164. Falmer: Institute of Development Studies, University of Sussex.

Guha-Khasnobis, B. & Kanbur, R. (eds) (2006). *Linking the Formal and Informal Economy: Concepts and Policies*. Oxford: Oxford University Press.

Guidi I. & Valle C., 1937: Programma urbanistico per Addis Abeba. *Architettura* 12: 755–768.

Guma, P. K. (2021). Recasting Provisional Urban Worlds in the Global South: Shacks, Shanties and Micro-Stalls. *Planning Theory & Practice* 22(2): 211–226.

Guma, P. K. & Monstadt, J. (2021). Smart City-making? The Spread of ICT-driven Plans and Infrastructures in Nairobi. *Urban Geography* 42(3): 360–381.

Gutkind, P. C. W. (1963). *The Royal Capital of Buganda: A Study of Internal Conflict and External Ambiguity*. Berlin: De Gruyter Mouton.

Haas, A. & Hoza Ngoga, T. (2018) Where Are Kampala's Missing Houses? Africa at LSE (25 April 2018). Available at: https://blogs.lse.ac.uk/africaatlse/2018/04/25/where-are-kampalas-missing-houses/. Accessed 26 May 2022.

Halvorsen, S. (2019). Decolonising Territory: Dialogues with Latin American Knowledges and Grassroots Strategies. *Progress in Human Geography* 43(5): 790–814.

Hansen, H. B., & Twaddle, M. (Eds.). (1991). *Changing Uganda: The Dilemmas of Structural Adjustment & Revolutionary Change*. Oxford: James Currey.

Hansen, H. B. & Twaddle, M. (1998). *Developing Uganda*. Oxford: James Currey.

Hardt, M. & Negri, A. (2012) *Declaration*. Allen, TX: Argo Navis.

Harrison, G. (2010). *Neoliberal Africa: The Impact of Global Social Engineering*. London: Bloomsbury Publishing.

Harrison, G. (2020). *Developmentalism: The Normative and Transformative within Capitalism*. Oxford: Oxford University Press.

Harriss, B. (1978). Quasi-Formal Employment Structures and Behaviour in the Unorganized Urban Economy, and the Reverse: Some Evidence from South India. *World Development* 6 (9–10): 1077–1086.

Harriss-White, B. (2010) Work and Wellbeing in Informal Economies: The Regulative Roles of Institutions of Identity and the State. *World Development* 38(2): 170–183.

Hart, K. (1973). Informal Income Opportunities and Urban Employment in Ghana. *The Journal of Modern African Studies* 11: 61–89.

Hartman, J. B. (2020). Review of Brenner, N. *New Urban Spaces: Urban Theory and the Scale Question. The AAG Review of Books* 9(1): 15–17, DOI: 10.1080/2325548X.2021.1843907.

Harding, A., & Blokland, T. (2014). *Urban Theory: a Critical Introduction to Power, Cities and Urbanism in the 21st Century.* Thousand Oaks: Sage Publications.

Harvey, D. (1978) The Urban Process under Capitalism: A Framework for Analysis. *International Journal of Urban and Regional Research* 2(1/4): 101–131.

Harvey, D. (1985). *The Urbanization of Capital: Studies in the History and Theory of Capitalist Urbanization.* Baltimore: Johns Hopkins University Press.

Harvey, D. (1989). *The Condition of Postmodernity.* Oxford: Blackwell.

Harvey, P. & Knox, H. (2012). The Enchantments of Infrastructure. *Mobilities* 7(4): 521–536.

Harvey, P. (2018). Infrastructures in and out of Time: The Promise of Roads in Contemporary Peru. In Anand, N., Gupta, A., & Appel, H. (eds) *The Promise of Infrastructure.* Durham, NC: Duke University Press. 80–101.

Hauge, J. & Chang, H.-J. (2019). The Concept of a 'Developmental State' in Ethiopia. In Cheru, F. et al. (eds) *The Oxford Handbook of the Ethiopian Economy.* Oxford: Oxford University Press. 824–841.

Hay, C. (2011). Ideas and the Construction of Interests. In Béland, D. & Cox, R. H. (eds) *Ideas and Politics in Social Science Research.* Oxford: Oxford University Press. 65–82.

He, S. & Wu, F. (2009). China's Emerging Neoliberal Urbanism: Perspectives from Urban Redevelopment. *Antipode* 41(2): 282–304.

Helmke, G. & Levitsky, S. (2004). Informal Institutions and Comparative Politics: A Research Agenda. *Perspectives on Politics* 2(4): 725–740.

Henderson, E. A. (2015). *African Realism? International Relations Theory and Africa's Wars in the Postcolonial Era.* Lanham, MA: Rowman & Littlefield.

Herbst, J. (2000). *States and Power in Africa: Comparative Lessons in Authority and Control.* Princeton, NJ: Princeton University Press.

Hettne, B. (2005). Beyond the 'New' Regionalism. *New Political Economy* 10(4): 543–571.

Heynen, N., Kaika, M., & Swyngedouw, E. (eds) (2006) *In the Nature of Cities: Urban Political Ecology and the Politics of Urban Metabolism.* New York: Routledge

Hickey, S. (2013a). Thinking about the Politics of Inclusive Development: Towards a Relational Approach. ESID Working Paper No. 1. Available at SSRN: https://ssrn.com/abstract=2425235 or http://dx.doi.org/10.2139/ssrn.2425235.

Hickey, S. (2013b). Beyond the Poverty Agenda? Insights from the New Politics of Development in Uganda. *World Development* 43: 194–206.

Hickey, S., Bukenya, B., & Sen, K. (2015). *The Politics of Inclusive Development: Interrogating the Evidence.* Oxford: Oxford University Press.

Hildyard, N. (2016). *Licensed Larceny: Infrastructure, Financial Extraction and the Global South.* Manchester: Manchester University Press.

Hintjens, H. M. (1999). Explaining the 1994 genocide in Rwanda. *The Journal of Modern African Studies*, 37(2): 241–286.

Hintjens, H. (2008). Post-genocide Identity Politics in Rwanda. *Ethnicities* 8(1): 5–41.

Hirschman, A. O. (1970). *Exit, voice, and loyalty: Responses to decline in firms, organizations, and states.* Cambridge, MA: Harvard University Press.

Holland, A. C. (2016). Forbearance. *American Political Science Review* 110(2): 232–246.

Home, R. (1990). Town Planning and Garden Cities in the British Colonial Empire 1910–1940. *Planning Perspectives* 5: 23–37.

Home, R. (1997). *Of Planting and Planning: The Making of British Colonial Cities.* London: E & FN Spon, an imprint of Chapman & Hall.

Honwana, A. M. (2012). *The Time of Youth: Work, Social Change, and Politics in Africa.* Sterling: Kumarian Press.

Hook, W. (2021). *China's Overseas Lending for Transport Projects: Successes, Challenges, and Recommendations.* New York: People-Oriented Cities.

Hoornweg, D. & Pope, K. (2017). Population Predictions for the World's Largest Cities in the 21st Century. *Environment and Urbanization* 29(1): 195–216.

Horner, R. & Hulme, D. (2019). From International to Global Development: New Geographies of 21st-century Development. *Development and Change* 50(2): 347–378.

Horton, M. & Middleton, J. (2000). *The Swahili: The Social Landscape of a Mercantile Society.* Oxford: Blackwell

Horvath, R. J. (1969). The Wandering Capitals of Ethiopia. *The Journal of African History* 10(2): 205–219.

Hudson, R. (2007). Regions and Regional: Uneven Development Forever? Some Reflective Comments upon Theory and Practice. *Regional Studies* 41(9): 1149–1160.

Hudson, D. & Leftwich, A. (2014). From Political Economy to Political Analysis. DLP Research Paper No. 25. Birmingham: Developmental Leadership Program.

Human Rights Watch. (2006). *Swept Away: Street Children Illegally Detained in Kigali, Rwanda.* New York: Human Rights Watch.

Human Rights Watch (2015). *Why Not Call This Place a Prison? Unlawful Detention and Ill-treatment in Rwanda's Gikondo Detention Center.* New York: Human Rights Watch.

Human Rights Watch (2021). One Year Later, No Justice for Victims of Uganda's Lethal Clampdown. Available at: https://www.hrw.org/news/2021/11/18/one-year-later-no-justice-victims-ugandas-lethal-clampdown. Accessed 7 December 2021.

Humphrey, C. 2005. Ideology in Infrastructure: Architecture and Soviet Imagination. *Journal of the Royal Anthropological Institute* 11(1): 39–58.

Hunter, F. (1953). *Community Power Structure: A Study of Decision Makers.* Chapel Hill, NC: UNC Press Books.

Hyden, G. (1983). *No shortcuts to Progress: African Development Management in Perspective.* Berkeley: University of California Press.

ICAS (2010). Business Access to Land in Rwanda: Issues and Recommendations. Washington, DC: Investment Climate Advisory Services, World Bank Group.

IGG. (1997). *Report on Allleged Corruption in Owino Market.* Kampala: Inspector General of Government, Republic of Uganda.

ILO. (1972). *Employment, Incomes and Equality: A Strategy for Increasing Productive Employment in Kenya.* Geneva: International Labour Office.

ILO (2018). Women and Men in the Informal Economy: A Statistical Picture. Third edition. Geneva: International Labour Organization.

Ingelaere, B. (2009). 'Does the Truth Pass across the Fire without Burning?' Locating the Short Circuit in Rwanda's Gacaca Courts. *The Journal of Modern African Studies* 47(4): 507–528.

Ingelaere, B. & Verpoorten, M. (2020). Trust in the Aftermath of Genocide: Insights from Rwandan Life Histories. *Journal of Peace Research* 57(4): 521–535.

Jaganyi, D., Njunwa, K., Nzayirambaho, M., Rutayisire, P. C., Manirakiza, V., Nsabimana, A., et al. (2018). *Rwanda: National Urban Policies and City: Profiles for Kigali and Huye*. Butare: University of Rwanda.

Jamal, Vali. 1991. The Agrarian Context of the Uganda Crisis. In Hansen, H. B. & Twaddle, M. (eds) *Changing Uganda: The Dilemmas of Structural Adjustment and Revolutionary Change*. Oxford: James Currey. 81–96.

Jedwab, R., Kerby, E., & Moradi, A. (2017). How Colonial Railroads Defined Africa's Economic Geography. In Michalopoulos, S. & Papaioannou, E. (eds) *The Long Economic and Political Shadow of History, Volume III: Africa and Asia*. London: Centre for Economic Policy Research. 87–97.

Jefremovas, V. (2002). *Brickyards to Graveyards: From Production to Genocide in Rwanda*. Albany: State University of New York Press.

Jembere, A. (2000). *An Introduction to the Legal History of Ethiopia; 1434–1974*. Munster: LIT-Verlag.

Johnson, C. (1982). *MITI and the Japanese Miracle: The Growth of Industrial Policy, 1925–1975*. Stanford, CA: Stanford University Press.

Johnston, L. A. (2019). The Belt and Road Initiative: What Is in It for China? *Asia & the Pacific Policy Studies* 6(1): 40–58.

Joireman, S. (2000). *Property Rights and Political Development in Ethiopia and Eritrea*. Oxford: James Currey.

Joireman, S. F. (2008). The Mystery of Capital Formation in Sub-Saharan Africa: Women, Property Rights and Customary Law. *World Development* 36(7): 1233–1246.

Jones, B. (2008). *Beyond the State in Rural Uganda*. Edinburgh: Edinburgh University Press.

Jones, G. A. & Corbridge, S. (2010). The Continuing Debate about Urban Bias: The Thesis, its Critics, its Influence and its Implications for Poverty-reduction Strategies. *Progress in Development Studies* 10(1): 1–18.

Jørgensen, J. J. (1981). *Uganda: A Modern History*. London: Croom Helm.

Joseph, R. A. (1987). *Democracy and Prebendal Politics in Nigeria*. Cambridge: Cambridge University Press.

Kalyvas, A. (2008). *Democracy and the Politics of the Extraordinary*. Cambridge: Cambridge University Press.

Kanai, J. M. & Schindler, S. (2019). Peri-urban Promises of Connectivity: Linking Project-led Polycentrism to the Infrastructure Scramble. *Environment and Planning A: Economy and Space* 51(2): 302–322.

Kangave, J., Nakato, S., Waiswa, R., & Zzimbe, P. (2016). Boosting Revenue collection through taxing high net worth individuals: The case of Uganda. ICTD Working Paper No. 45. Brighton: Institute for Development Studies.

Kanyeihamba, G. W. (1974). Urban Planning Law in East Africa: With Special Reference to Uganda. *Progress in Planning* 2: 1–83.

Karaman, O. (2013). Urban Neoliberalism with Islamic Characteristics. *Urban Studies* 50(16): 3412–3427.

Karaman, O., Sawyer, L., Schmid, C., & Wong, K. P. (2020). Plot by plot: Plotting urbanism as an ordinary process of urbanisation. *Antipode* 52(4): 1122–1151.

Karugire, S. (1980). *A Political History of Uganda*. London: Heinemann Educational.

Kasfir, N. (1976). *The Shrinking Political Arena: Participation and Ethnicity in African Politics, with a Case Study of Uganda*. Berkeley, CA: University of California Press.

Kasfir, N. (1983). State, Magendo, and Class Formation in Uganda . *Commonwealth and Comparative Politics* 21(3): 84–103.

Kasfir, N. (2005). Guerrillas and Civilian participation: The National Resistance Army in Uganda, 1981–86. *The Journal of Modern African Studies* 43(2): 271–296.

Kasozi, A. B. K. (1994). *The Social Origins of Violence in Uganda, 1964–1985.* Montreal: McGill-Queen's University Press.

Kassa, F. (2014). Informal Transport and its Effects in the Developing World: A Case Study of Addis Ababa, Ethiopia. *Journal of Transport Literature* 8(2): 113–133.

Kassa, S., Stahl, C., & Baez-Camargo, C. (2017). Social Norms, Mental Models and other Behavioural Drivers of Petty Corruption-the Case of Rwanda. Policy Brief No. 3. Basel: Basel Institute on Governance.

Kassahun, M. (2021). The governance of Addis Ababa Light Rail Transit. In Bekker, Croese and Pieterse (Eds). *Refractions of the National, the Popular and the Global in African Cities.* Cape Town: African Minds. 149–172.

Kassahun, M., & Bishu, S. G. (2018). *The governance of Addis Ababa City turn around projects: Addis Ababa light rail transit and housing.* Nairobi: Partnership for African Social & Governance Research.

Kebede, G. F. (2015). Social Capital and the Urban Informal Economy: The Case of Street Vendors in Addis Ababa, Ethiopia. PhD dissertation, University of Trento.

Kebede, G. F. & Odella, F. (2014). The Economic Returns of Network Resources to the Urban Informal Economy: Evidence from Street Vendors in Addis Ababa, Ethiopia. *European Journal of Sustainable Development* 3(3): 357–357.

Kefale, A. (2011). The (Un)Making of Opposition Coalitions and the Challenge of Democratization in Ethiopia, 1991–2011. *Journal of Eastern African Studies* 5(4): 681–701.

Keil, R. (1998). Globalization Makes States: Perspectives of Local Governance in the Age of the World City. *Review of International Political Economy* 5(4): 616–646.

Keller, E. J. & Mukudi-Omwami, E. (2017). Rapid Urban Expansion and the Challenge of Pro-poor Housing in Addis Ababa, Ethiopia. *Africa Review* 9(2): 173–185.

Kelsall, T. (2013). *Business, Politics, and the State in Africa: Challenging the Orthodoxies on Growth and Transformation.* London: Zed Books.

Kelsall, T. (2018). Towards a Universal Political Settlement Concept: A Response to Mushtaq Khan. *African Affairs* 117(469): 656–669.

Kelsall, T., Schulz, N., Ferguson, W. D., vom Hau, M., Hickey, S., & Levy, B. (2022). *Political Settlements and Development: Theory, Evidence, Implications.* Oxford University Press.

Kendall, H. (1955). *Town Planning in Uganda: A Brief Description of the Efforts Made by Government to Control Development of Urban Areas from 1915 to 1955.* Crown Agents for Oversea Governments and Administrations.

Kenyatta, J. (1938/2015). *Facing Mount Kenya: The Traditional Life of the Gikuyu.* Nairobi: East African Educational Publishers.

Keogh, G., and D'Arcy, É. (1994). Market Maturity and Property Market Behaviour: A European Comparison of Mature and Emergent Markets. *Journal of Property Research* 11(3): 215–235.

Khan, M. (1995). State Failure in Weak States: A Critique of New Institutionalist Explanations. In *The New Institutional Economics and Third World Development.* London: Routledge. 85–100.

Khan, M. (2010). Political settlements and the governance of growth-enhancing institutions. Unpublished manuscript. London: School of Oriental and African Studies.

Khan, M. H. (2018). Political Settlements and the Analysis of Institutions. *African Affairs* 117(469): 636–655.

Khisa, M. (2013). The making of the 'informal state'in Uganda. *Africa Development* 38(1&2): 191–226.

Kilby, P. (1975) Manufacturing in Colonial Africa. In Duigan, P. and Gann, L. H. (eds) *Colonialism in Africa* (Vol 4). Cambridge: Cambridge University Press. 470–501.

Kimari, W. (2021). The story of a Pump: Life, Death and Afterlives within an Urban Planning of "Divide and Rule" in Nairobi, Kenya. *Urban Geography* 42(2): 141–160.

Kimonyo, J. P. (2008). *Rwanda, un génocide populaire*. Paris: Éditions Karthala.

King, A. D. (1976). *Colonial Urban Development: Culture, Social Power and Environment*. London: Routledge.

Kinyanjui, M. N. (2014). *Women and the Informal Economy in Urban Africa: From the Margins to the Centre*. London: Zed Books.

KIST (2001). Kigali Economic Development Survey. Kigali: Kigali Institute of Science and Technology.

Kitabire, D. (1994). The Supply Side Response to Structural Adjustment Policies in Uganda. Report Commissioned for EC Country Study.

Kiwanuka, M. S. (1972). *History of Buganda: From the Foundation of the Kingdom to 1900*. New York: Holmes & Meier.

Kjær, A. M. (2015). Political Settlements and Productive Sector Policies: Understanding Sector Differences in Uganda. *World Development* 68: 230–241.

Kloosterboer, M. H. (2019). The 'New'Addis Ababa: Shantytown or Global City? An Assessment of Large-scale Inner-city Renewal, Redevelopment and Displacement for the Construction of a 'New'Addis Ababa. PhD dissertation, University of Glasgow.

Kobusingye, O. (2010). *The Correct Line?: Uganda Under Museveni*. Milton Keynes: AuthorHouse.

Kohli, A. (2004). *State-directed Development: Political Power and Industrialization in the Global Periphery*. Cambridge: Cambridge University Press.

Kombe, W. J. (2005). Land-use Dynamics in Peri-urban Areas and their Implications on the Urban Growth and Form: The Case of Dar es Salaam, *Tanzania Habitat International* 29: 113–135.

Künkel, J. & Mayer, M. (eds) (2011) *Neoliberal Urbanism and its Contestations—Crossing Theoretical Boundaries*. Basingstoke: Palgrave Macmillan.

Kurimoto, E. (1995). Trade Relations between Western Ethiopia and the Nile Valley during the Nineteenth Century. *Journal of Ethiopian Studies* 28(1): 53–68.

Kusiluka, M. M. (2012) Agency Conflicts in Real Estate Investment in Sub-Saharan Africa: Exploration of Selected Investors in Tanzania and the Effectiveness of Institutional Remedies. Schriften zur Immobilienökonomie, 63. Cologne: Immobilienmanager-Verlag.

Kusimba, C. M. (1999). *The Rise and Fall of Swahili States*. Lanham, MD: AltaMira Press.

Kusimba, C., Kusimba, S. B., & Agbaje-Williams, B. (2006). Precolonial African Cities. Urbanism in the preindustrial world: Cross-cultural approaches. Tuscaloosa: University of Alabama Press.

Kusimba, C. M., Kusimba, S. B., & Dussubieux, L. (2013). Beyond the Coastalscapes: Preindustrial Social and Political Networks in East Africa. *African Archaeological Review* 30(4): 399–426.

Kuteesa, F., Mutebile, E. M., Whitworth, A., and Williamson, T. (2010). *Uganda's Economic Reforms: Insider Accounts*. Oxford: Oxford University Press.

Lagarde, C. (2015). 'Rwanda: Taking on the Future, Staying Ahead of the Curve'. Speech made in the Parliament of Rwanda. Kigali, Rwanda.

Lamarque, H. (2017). Insulating the Borderlands: Policing and State Reach in Rwanda. PhD dissertation, SOAS, University of London.

Lancione, M. (2019). Weird Exoskeletons: Propositional Politics and the Making of Home in Underground Bucharest. *International Journal of Urban and Regional Research* 43(3): 535–550.

Lane, R. (1992). Political Culture: Residual Category or General Theory? *Comparative Political Studies* 25(3): 362–387.

Larbi, W. O., Antwi, A., & Olomolaiye, P. (2004). Compulsory Land Acquisition in Ghana—Policy and Praxis. *Land Use Policy* 21(2): 115–127.

Larkin, B. (2013). The Politics and Poetics of Infrastructure. *Annual Review of Anthropology* 42: 327–343.

Larmer, M. (2010). Social Movement Struggles in Africa. *Review of African Political Economy* 37(125): 251–262.

Larsen, L., Yeshitela, K., Mulatu, T., Seifu, S., & Desta, H. (2019). The Impact of Rapid Urbanization and Public Housing Development on Urban Form and Density in Addis Ababa, Ethiopia. *Land* 8(4): 66.

Lateef, K. S. (1991). Structural Adjustment in Uganda: The Initial Experience. In Hansen, H. B. & Twaddle, M. (1991). *Changing Uganda: The Dilemmas of Structural Adjustment and Revolutionary Change.* Oxford: James Currey. 91–106.

Latour, B. (2005). *Reassembling the Social: An Introduction to Actor-network Theory.* Oxford: Oxford University Press.

Lauria, M. (Ed.). (1997). *Reconstructing Urban Regime Theory.* Thousand Oaks: Sage Publications.

Lavers, T. (2012). 'Land grab'as development strategy? The political economy of agricultural investment in Ethiopia. *Journal of Peasant Studies* 39(1): 105–132.

Lavers, T. (2018). Responding to Land-based Conflict in Ethiopia: The Land Rights of Ethnic Minorities under Federalism. *African Affairs* 117(468): 462–484.

Lavers, T. (2020). State Infrastructural Power and Social Transfers: The Local Politics of Distribution and Delivering 'Progress' in Ethiopia. ESID Working Paper No. 147. Manchester: Effective States and Inclusive Development Research Centre.

Lavers, T. & Hickey, S. (2015). Investigating the Political Economy of Social Protection Expansion in Africa: At the Intersection of Transnational Ideas and Domestic Politics. Working Paper No. 47. Manchester: Effective States and Inclusive Development Research Centre.

Law, J. (1992). Notes on the Theory of the Actor-network: Ordering, Strategy, and Heterogeneity. *Systems Practice* 5(4): 379–393.

Lawhon, M., Nilsson, D., Silver, J., Ernstson, H., & Lwasa, S. (2018). Thinking through Heterogeneous Infrastructure Configurations. *Urban Studies* 55(4): 720–732.

Lawhon, M. & Truelove, Y. (2020). Disambiguating the Southern Urban Critique: Propositions, Pathways and Possibilities for a More Global Urban Studies. *Urban Studies* 57(1): 3–20.

LeBas, A. (2011). *From Protest to Parties: Party-building and Democratization in Africa.* Oxford: Oxford University Press.

Lefebvre, H. (1970) *La révolution urbaine [The Urban Revolution].* Paris: Gallimard.

Lefebvre, H. (2003). *The Urban Revolution.* Minneapolis: University of Minnesota Press.

Lefort, R. (2007). Powers–*Mengist*–and Peasants in Rural Ethiopia: The May 2005 Elections. *The Journal of Modern African Studies* 45(2): 253–273.

Lefort, R. (2015) The Ethiopian Economy: The Developmental State vs the Free Market. In Prunier, G. & Fiquet, É. (eds) *Understanding Contemporary Ethiopia.* London: Hurst. 357–394.

Lemanski, C. (ed.) (2019). *Citizenship and Infrastructure: Practices and Identities of Citizens and the State.* London: Routledge.

Lemarchand, R. (1966). Power and Stratification in Rwanda: A Reconsideration. *Cahiers d'Etudes Africaines*. 6(Cahier 24), 592–610.

Lemarchand, R. (1982). The World Bank in Rwanda: The Case of the Office de Valorisation Agricole et Pastorale du Mutara (OVAPAM). African Studies Program, Indiana University.

Leonardi, C. & Santschi, M. (2016). *Dividing Communities in South Sudan and Northern Uganda: Boundary Disputes and Land Governance.* Nairobi: Rift Valley Institute.

Lesutis, G. (2021). Infrastructural Territorialisations: Mega-infrastructures and the (Re) Making of Kenya. *Political Geography* 90: 102459.

Levine, D. (1965a). Ethiopia: Identity, Authority, and Realism. In Pye, L. W. & Verba, S. (eds) *Political Culture and Political Development.* Princeton, NJ: Princeton University Press. 245–281.

Levine, D. N. (1965b). *Wax and Gold: Tradition and Innovation in Ethiopian Culture.* Chicago: University of Chicago Press.

Levine, D. N. (1974). *Greater Ethiopia: The Evolution of a Multiethnic Society.* Chicago: University of Chicago Press.

Leys, C. (1996). *The Rise and Fall of Development Theory.* Bloomington, IN: Indiana University Press.

Lim, K. F. (2014). 'Socialism with Chinese characteristics' Uneven development, variegated neoliberalization and the dialectical differentiation of state spatiality. *Progress in Human Geography* 38(2): 221–247.

Linden, I. (1977). *Church and Revolution in Rwanda.* Manchester: Manchester University Press.

Lindell, I. (2008). The multiple sites of urban governance: insights from an African city. *Urban Studies* 45(9), 1879–1901.

Lindell, I. 2010. Introduction: The Changing Politics of Informality—Collective Organizing, Alliances and Scales of Engagement. In Lindell, I. (ed.) *Africa's Informal Workers: Collective Agency, Alliances and Transnational Organizing.* London: Zed Books. 1–31.

Lindell, I., & Appelblad, J. (2009). Disabling governance: Privatisation of city markets and implications for vendors' associations in Kampala, Uganda. *Habitat International* 33(4): 397–404.

Lindell, I., & Ampaire, C. (2016). The untamed politics of urban informality: "gray space" and struggles for recognition in an African city. *Theoretical Inquiries in Law* 17(1): 257–282.

Lindell, I., Ampaire, C., & Byerley, A. (2019). Governing Urban Informality: Re-working Spaces and Subjects in Kampala, Uganda. *International Development Planning Review* 41(1): 63–84.

Lindemann, S. (2011). Just another change of guard? Broad-based politics and civil war in Museveni's Uganda. *African Affairs*, 110(440): 387–416.

Lipset, S. (1959). Some Social Requisites of Democracy. *American Political Science Review* 53(1): 69–105.

Lipton, M. (1977). *Why Poor People Stay Poor: A Study of Urban Bias in World Development.* Temple Smith: Australian National University Press.

Little, K. (1973). *African Women in Towns: An Aspect of Africa's Social Revolution.* Cambridge: Cambridge University Press.

Livingstone, I. (1998). Developing Industry in Uganda in the 1990s. In Hansen, H. B. & Twaddle, M. (eds) *Developing Uganda.* Oxford: James Currey. 38–58.

Logan, J. R. & Molotch, H. L. (2007). *Urban Fortunes: The Political Economy of Place.* 20th anniversary edition. Berkeley, CA: University of California Press.

Lomnitz, L. A. (1988). Informal exchange networks in formal systems: a theoretical model. *American Anthropologist* 90(1): 42–55.

Longman, T. (2009). An Assessment of Rwanda's Gacaca Courts. *Peace Review* 21(3): 304–312.

Longman, T. (2011). Limitations to Political Reform: The Undemocratic Nature of Transition in Rwanda. In Straus, S. & Waldorf, L. (eds) *Remaking Rwanda: State Building and Human Rights after Mass Violence*. Madison: University of Wisconsin Press. 25–47.

López, J. and Scott, J. (2000). *Social Structure*. Buckingham: Open University Press.

Louis, W. R. (1963.) *Ruanda-Urundi, 1884–1919*. Oxford: Clarendon Press.

Lourenço-Lindell, I. 2002. *Walking the Tight Rope: Informal Livelihoods and Social Networks in a West African City*. Stockholm: Acta Universitatis Stockholmiensis.

Lucas, J. (1998). The Tension between Despotic and Infrastructural Power: The Military and the Political Class in Nigeria, 1985–1993. *Studies in Comparative International Development* 33(3): 90–113.

Lufumpa, C. L., Letsara, N., & Saidi, S. (2017). Infrastructure Development Index. In Ncube, M. & Leyeka Lufumpa, C. (eds) *Infrastructure in Africa: Lessons for Future Development*. Bristol: Policy Press. 25–88.

Lukes, S. (2005) *Power: A Radical View*. Second Edition. Basingstoke: Palgrave Macmillan.

Lund, C. (2006). Twilight Institutions: Public Authority and Local Politics in Africa. *Development and Change* 37(4): 685–705.

Lund, C. (2008). *Local Politics and the Dynamics of Property in Africa*. Cambridge: Cambridge University Press.

Lund, C. (2013). The Past and Space: On Arguments in African Land Control. *Africa* 83(1): 14–35.

Lund, C. & Boone, C. (2013). Introduction: Land Politics in Africa—Constituting Authority over Territory, Property and Persons. *Africa* 83(1): 1–13.

Lwasa, S. (2010). Adapting Urban Areas in Africa to Climate Change: The Case of Kampala. *Current Opinion in Environmental Sustainability* 2(3): 166–171.

Mabogunje, A. L. (1969). *Urbanization in Nigeria*. New Yok: Holmes & Meier.

Mabogunje, A. L. (1990). Urban Planning and the Post-colonial State in Africa: A Research Overview 1. *African Studies Review* 33(2): 121–203.

Mackie, P. K., Bromley, R. D., & Brown, A. M. (2014). Informal Traders and the Battlegrounds of Revanchism in Cusco, Peru. *International Journal of Urban and Regional Research* 38(5): 1884–1903.

MacLeod, G. (2002). From Urban Entrepreneurialism to a "Revanchist City"? On the Spatial Injustices of Glasgow's Renaissance. *Antipode* 34(3): 602–624.

Mafeje, A. (1998). *Kingdoms of the Great Lakes Region: Ethnography of African Social Formations*. Kampala: Fountain Publishers.

Mafeje, A. (2003). *The Agrarian Question, Access to Land, and Peasant Responses in Sub-Saharan Africa*. Geneva: United Nations Research Institute for Social Development.

Mahoney, J. & Thelen, K. (eds) (2010). *Explaining Institutional Change: Ambiguity, Agency, and Power*. Cambridge: Cambridge University Press.

Mains, D. (2012). *Hope Is Cut: Youth, Unemployment, and the Future in Urban Ethiopia*. Philadelphia, PA: Temple University Press.

Mains, D. (2019). *Under Construction: Technologies of Development in Urban Ethiopia*. Durham, NC: Duke University Press.

Makara, S. (2009). Decentralisation and Urban Governance in Uganda. PhD thesis, University of Witwatersrand.

Makokha, K. A. (2001). Uganda Country Report: A Synthesis of the Four SAPRI Studies. Kampala: Structural Adjustment Participatory Review Initiative.

Mamdani, M. (1985). A Great Leap Backwards: A Review of Goran Hyden's No Shortcut to Progress. *Ufahamu: A Journal of African Studies* 14(2).

Mamdani, M. (1990). Uganda: Contradictions of the IMF Programme and Perspective. *Development and Change* 21(3): 427–467.

Mamdani, M., & Wamba-dia-wamba, E. (eds) (1995.) *African Studies in Social Movements and Democracy.* Dakar: Codesria.

Mamdani, M. (1983). *Imperialism and Fascism in Uganda.* London: Heinemann Educational Books.

Mamdani, M. (1996). *Citizen and Subject.* Princeton, NJ: Princeton University Press.

Mamdani, M. (2001). When Victims Become Killers: Colonialism, Nativism, and the Genocide in Rwanda. Princeton, NJ: Princeton University Press.

Manirakiza, V. (2014.) Promoting Inclusive Approaches to Address Urbanization Challenges in Kigali. *African Review of Economics and Finance* (6)1: 161–180.

Manirakiza, V., & Ansoms, A. (2014). 'Modernizing Kigali': the struggle for space in the Rwandan urban context. In A. Ansoms & T. Hilhorst (eds), *Losing your land: Dispossession in the Great Lakes.* Woodbridge and Suffolk, UK: James Currey.

Mann, M. (1984). The Autonomous Power of the State: Its Origins, Mechanisms and Results. *European Journal of Sociology* 25(2): 185–213.

Mann, M. (1986). *The Sources of Social Power, Vol. 1: A History of Power from the Beginning to AD 1760.* Cambridge: Cambridge University Press.

Mann, M. (2008). Infrastructural Power Revisited. *Studies in Comparative International Development* 43(3–4): 355.

Maquet, J. J. (1961). *The Premise of Inequality in Ruanda: a study of political relations in a Central African kingdom.* London: International African Institute.

Maquet, J. J. (2018). *The Premise of Inequality in Ruanda: a study of political relations in a Central African kingdom.* London: Routledge.

Markakis, J. (1974). *Ethiopia: Anatomy of a Traditional Polity.* Oxford: Oxford University Press.

Markakis, J. (2011). *Ethiopia: The Last Two Frontiers.* Woodbridge: Boydell & Brewer.

Markakis, J. & Ayele, N. (1986). *Class and Revolution in Ethiopia.* Trenton, N.J.: Red Sea Press.

Marston, S. A., Jones, J. P., & Woodward, K. (2005). Human Geography without Scale. *Transactions of the Institute of British Geographers* 30(4): 416–432.

Marvin, S., Luque-Ayala, A., & McFarlane, C. (Eds.). (2015). *Smart Urbanism: Utopian Vision or False Dawn?.* Routledge.

Marx, C., Johnson, C., & Lwasa, S. (2020). Multiple Interests in Urban Land: Disaster-induced Land Resettlement Politics in Kampala. *International Planning Studies*, 25(3): 289–301.

Marx, C. & Kelling, E. (2019). Knowing Urban Informalities. *Urban Studies* 56(3): 494–509.

Matfess, H. (2015). Rwanda and Ethiopia: Developmental Authoritarianism and the New Politics of African Strong Men. *African Studies Review* 58(2): 181–204.

Mawdsley, E. (2018). 'From Billions to Trillions' Financing the SDGs in a World 'beyond Aid'. *Dialogues in Human Geography* 8(2): 191–195.

Maxon, R. (1994). *East Africa: An Introductory History.* Morgantown, W.V.: West Virginia University Press.

Mayer, M. (2007). Contesting the neoliberalization of urban governance. In Leitner, H., Peck, J., & Sheppard, E. S. (eds). *Contesting neoliberalism: Urban frontiers.* New York: Guilford Press. 90–115.

Mayer, P. (1962). Migrancy and the Study of Africans in Towns 1. *American Anthropologist* 64(3): 576–592.

Mbembe, A. (1992). Provisional Notes on the Postcolony. *Africa* 62(1): 3–37.

Mbembe, A. (2001). *On the Postcolony.* Berkeley, CA: University of California Press.

Mbembe, A. J. (2016). Decolonizing the University: New Directions. *Arts and Humanities in Higher Education*, 15(1): 29–45.

Mbembe, J. A. & Nuttall, S. (2004). Writing the World from an African Metropolis. *Public Culture* 16(3): 347–372.

McCann, E. (2011). Urban Policy Mobilities and Global Circuits of Knowledge: Toward a Research Agenda. *Annals of the Association of American Geographers* 101(1): 107–130.

McCann, J. C. (1995). *People of the Plow: An Agricultural History of Ethiopia, 1800–1990*. Madison: University of Wisconsin Press.

McCarthy, J. (2005). Scale, Sovereignty, and Strategy in Environmental Governance. *Antipode* 37(4): 731–753.

McAuslan, P. (ed) (2003). *Bringing the Law Back in: Essays in Land, Law and Development*, Aldershot: Ashgate.

McFarlane, C. (2011a). Assemblage and Critical Urbanism. *City* 15(2): 204–224.

McFarlane, C. (2011b). On Context: Assemblage, Political Economy and Structure. *City* 15(3–4): 375–388.

McFarlane, C. (2012). Rethinking Informality: Politics, Crisis, and the City. *Planning Theory & Practice* 13(1): 89–108.

McFarlane, C., & Rutherford, J. (2008). Political Infrastructures: Governing and Experiencing the Fabric of the City. *International Journal of Urban and Regional Research* 32(2): 363–374.

McFarlane, C. & Silver, J. (2017a). Navigating the City: Dialectics of Everyday Urbanism. *Transactions of the Institute of British Geographers* 42(3): 458–471.

McFarlane, C. & Silver, J. (2017b). The Political City: 'Seeing Sanitation' and making the Urban Political in Cape Town. *Antipode* 49(1): 125–148.

McFarlane, C. & Waibel, M. (eds) (2012). *Urban Informalities: Reflections on the Formal and Informal*. London: Routledge.

McGregor, J., & Chatiza, K. (2019). Frontiers of Urban Control: Lawlessness on the City Edge and Forms of Clientalist Statecraft in Zimbabwe. *Antipode* 51(5): 1554–1580.

Mcloughlin, C. (2015). When Does Service Delivery Improve the Legitimacy of a Fragile or Conflict-affected State? *Governance* 28(3): 341–356.

Meagher, K. (1995). Crisis, Informalization and the Urban Informal Sector in Sub-Saharan Africa . *Development and Change* 26(2): 259–284.

Meagher, K. (2010). *Identity Economics: Social Networks and the Informal Economy in Nigeria*. Woodbridge: Boydell & Brewer.

Meagher, K. (2016). The Scramble for Africans: Demography, Globalisation and Africa's Informal Labour Markets. *The Journal of Development Studies* 52(4): 483–497.

Médard, H. & Doyle, S. (eds) (2007). *Slavery in the Great Lakes Region of East Africa*. Athens, OH: Ohio University Press.

Meehan, P. & Goodhand, J. (2018). Spatialising Political Settlements. *Accord* (4): 14–19.

Mekonen, K. D., Genetu, Y. P., & Legese, F. M. (2016). Women's Livelihood in the Informal Sector: Analysis of Micro Sellers or 'Gullit' in Addis Ababa City, Ethiopia. *Journal of Developing Country Studies* 6(8): 64–79.

Mekonnen, G. (2019). The Dynamics of Anti-Government Protest in Ethiopia from 2015 to 2018: From Hidden to Public resistance. International Affairs and Global Strategy, 72: 12–18.

Mengesha, L. G., & Padmanabhan, L. (2019). Introduction to Performing Refusal/Refusing to Perform. *Women & Performance: a journal of feminist theory* 29(1): 1-8.

Mercer, C. (2017). Landscapes of Extended Ruralisation: Postcolonial Suburbs in Dar es Salaam, Tanzania. *Transactions of the Institute of British Geographers* 42(1): 72–83.

Merelman, R. (1966). Learning and Legitimacy. *American Political Science Review* 60: 553–561.

Mezzadra, S., and B. Neilson. (2015). "Operations of Capital." *South Atlantic Quarterly* 114 (1): 1–9.

Michael, M. (2016). *Actor-network Theory: Trials, Trails and Translations.* London: Sage Publications.

Middleton, J. (1992). *The World of the Swahili: An African Mercantile Civilization.* New Haven: Yale University Press.

Middleton, J. (2004). *African Merchants of the Indian Ocean: Swahili of the East African Coast.* Long Grove: Waveland Press.

Miller, D. (2012). Territorial Rights: Concept and Justification. *Political Studies* 60(2): 252–268.

Mills, C. W. (1956). *The Power Elite.* Oxford: Oxford University Press.

MININFRA (2008). National Urban Housing Policy for Rwanda. Ministry of Infrastructure, Republic of Rwanda, Kigali.

Mitchell, W. J. T. (ed) (1994). *Landscape and Power.* Chicago: University of Chicago Press.

Mitullah, W. V. (2003). Street vending in African cities: A synthesis of empirical finding from Kenya, Cote d'Ivoire, Ghana, Zimbabwe, Uganda and South Africa. Background Paper for the 2005 World Development Report.

Mkandawire, P. T. & Soludo, C. C. (1999). Our Continent, our Future: African Perspectives on Structural Adjustment. Dakar: CODESRIA Publications.

Mkandawire, T. (2002). The Terrible Toll of Post-colonial 'Rebel Movements' in Africa: Towards an Explanation of the Violence against the Peasantry. *The Journal of Modern African Studies* 40(2): 181–215.

Mkandawire, T. (2005). Maladjusted African Economies and Globalisation. *Africa Development* 30(1): 1–33.

MoFED (Ministry of Finance and Economic Development) (2006). A Plan for Accelerated and Sustained Development to End Poverty (PASDEP). Addis Ababa: Federal Democratic Republic of Ethiopia.

Moghalu, K. 2013. Africa as the 'Last Frontier'. AllAfrica.com, 15 August 2013. Accessed 4 March 2020.

MoLG. 2006. The Report of the Commission of Inquiry into the Sale, Lease and Purchase of Land by Kampala City Council. Kampala: Ministry of Local Government, Republic of Uganda.

Molotch, H. (1993) The Political Economy of Growth Machines. *Journal of Urban Affairs* 15(1): 29–53.

Monteith, W. (2015). A 'Market for the People'? Changing Structures of Governance and Participation in a Ugandan Marketplace. *Development* 58(1): 58–64.

Monteith, W. (2016). Heart and Struggle: Life in Nakasero Market 1912–2015. PhD dissertation, University of East Anglia.

Monteith, W. (2019). Markets and Monarchs: Indigenous Urbanism in Postcolonial Kampala. *Settler Colonial Studies* 9(2): 247–265.

Moore, B. (1966). *Social Origins of Dictatorship and Democracy: Lord and Peasant and the Making of the Modern World.* Boston, MA: Beacon Press.

Moser, C. O. (1978). Informal sector or petty commodity production: dualism or dependence in urban development?. *World Development* 6(9-10): 1041–1064.

Mouffe, C. (2005). *The Return of the Political.* London:Verso.

Moyo, S. (2018). Debating the African Land Question with Archie Mafeje. *Agrarian South: Journal of Political Economy*, 7(2): 211–233.

Mrázek, R. (2002). Engineers of Happy Land: Technology and Nationalism in a Colony. Princeton: Princeton University Press.

Msellemu, S. A. (2013). Common Motives of Africa's Anti-colonial Resistance in 1890–1960. *Social Evolution & History* 12(2): 143–155.

Mueller, L. (2018). *Political Protest in Contemporary Africa*. Cambridge: Cambridge University Press.

Mujagu J & J Oloka-Onyango (eds) (2000). *No-Party Democracy in Uganda: Myths and Realities*. Kampala: Fountain Publishers.

Mukholi, D. (1995). A Complete Guide to Uganda's Fourth Constitution: History, Politics, and the Law. Kampala: Fountain Publishers.

Mukwaya, P., Bamutaze, Y., Mugarura, S., & Benson, T. (2012). Rural–Urban Transformation in Uganda. *Journal of African Development* 14(2): 169–194.

Mukwaya, P. I., Sengendo, H., & Lwasa, S. (2010). Urban Development Transitions and their Implications for Poverty Reduction and Policy Planning in Uganda. *Urban Forum* 21(3): 267–281.

Mumford, L. (1964). Authoritarian and Democratic Technics. *Technology and Culture* 5(1): 1–8.

Munger, E. S. (1951*). Relational Patterns of Kampala, Uganda*. Research Paper No. 27: University of Chicago.

Munyaneza, D. (1994). Insertion des artisans du secteur non-structure de Kigali dans l'economie et l'espace urbains. Rwanda National Archive.

Musahara, H. & Huggins, C. (2005). Land Reform, Land Scarcity and Post-conflict Reconstruction: A Case Study of Rwanda. In Clover, J. (ed.) *From the Ground up: Land Rights, Conflict and Peace in Sub-Saharan Africa*. The Hague: Institute for Security Studies. 269–346.

Museveni, Y. K. (1997). *Sowing the Mustard Seed: The Struggle for Freedom and Democracy in Uganda*. Oxford: Macmillan.

Mushemeza, E. D. (2007). *The Politics and Empowerment of Banyarwanda Refugees in Uganda 1959–2001*. Kampala: Fountain Publishers.

Mutibwa, P. M. (2008). *The Buganda Factor in Uganda Politics*. Kampala: Fountain Publishers.

Muwanga, N. K., Mukwaya, P. I., & Goodfellow, T. (2020). Carrot, stick and statute: Elite strategies and contested dominance in Kampala. ESID Working Paper No. 146. Manchester, UK: The University of Manchester.

Mworoha, E. (1981). Redevances et prestations dans les domaines royaux du Burundi precolonial. *Publications de la Société française d'histoire des outre-mers* 5(2): 751–768.

Mworoha, É. & Mukuri, M. (2004). Problématique de la périodisation historique pour la région des Grands Lacs. *Afrique histoire* 2(1): 67–83.

Myers, G. A. (2003). *Verandahs of Power: Colonialism and Space in Urban Africa* . Syracuse: Syracuse University Press.

Nagendra, H., Bai, X., Brondizio, E. S., & Lwasa, S. (2018). The Urban South and the Predicament of Global Sustainability. *Nature Sustainability* 1(7): 341–349.

Nallet, C. (2015). Classes moyennes éthiopiennes: étude empirique d'une assignation catégorielle incertaine. PhD dissertation, University of Bordeaux.

Nallet, C. (2018). The Challenge of Urban Mobility: A Case Study of Addis Ababa Light Rail, Ethiopia. Report. Paris: Institut Français des Relations Internationales.

Nayenga, P. F. (1979). Myths and Realities of Idi Amin Dada's Uganda. *African Studies Review* 22(2):as 127–138.

Negash, T. (2003). The Zagwe Period Re-interpreted: Post-Aksumite Ethiopian Urban Culture. Uppsala: Uppsala Universitet, The Development of Urbanism from a Global Perspective.

Nelson, J. M. (1979). *Access to power: Politics and the urban poor in developing nations*. Princeton: Princeton University Press.

Newbury, C. (1988). *The Cohesion of Oppression: Clientship and Ethnicity in Rwanda, 1860–1960*. New York: Columbia University Press.

Newbury, C. (2011). High modernism at the ground level. In Straus, S. & Waldorf, L. (eds) *Remaking Rwanda: State Building and Human Rights after Mass Violence.* Madison: University of Wisconsin Press. 223–239.

Newbury, D. & Newbury, C. (2000). Bringing the Peasants Back In: Agrarian Themes in the Construction and Corrosion of Statist Historiography in Rwanda. *American Historical Review* 105(3): 845.

Newbury, M. C. (1978). Ethnicity in Rwanda: The Case of Kinyaga. *Africa* 48(1): 17–29.

Nezehose, J. B. 1990. Agriculture rwandaise: Problématique et perspectives. Kigali: INADES—Formation, Rwanda.

Ngoga, T. H. (2019). A Quick, Cost-effective Approach to Land Tenure Regularisation: The Case of Rwanda. London: International Growth Centre.

Nicholls, W. J. (2008). The Urban Question Revisited: The Importance of Cities for Social Movements. *International Journal of Urban and Regional Research* 32(4): 841–859.

Nikuze, A., Sliuzas, R., & Flacke, J. (2020). From Closed to Claimed Spaces for Participation: Contestation in Urban Redevelopment Induced-Displacements and Resettlement in Kigali, Rwanda. *Land* 9(7): 212.

Nikuze, A., Sliuzas, R., Flacke, J., & van Maarseveen, M. (2019). Livelihood Impacts of Displacement and Resettlement on Informal Households: A Case Study from Kigali, Rwanda. *Habitat International* 86: 38–47.

Njoh, A. J. (2008). Colonial Philosophies, Urban Space, and Racial Segregation in British and French Colonial Africa. *Journal of Black Studies* 38(4): 579–599.

Njoh, A. J. (2009). Urban Planning as a Tool of Power and Social Control in Colonial Africa. *Planning Perspectives* 24(3): 301–317.

Nkuete, J. 1990. Une Experience Économique En Afrique Centrale: Le Rwanda. Yaounde: Editions SOPECAM.

Nkurunziza, E. (2006). Two States, One City? Conflict and Accommodation in Land Delivery in Kampala, Uganda . *International Development Planning Review* 28(2): 159–180.

Nkurunziza, E. (2008). Understanding Informal Urban Land Access Processes from a Legal Pluralist Perspective: The Case of Kampala, Uganda. *Habitat International* 32(1): 109–120.

Nugent, P. (2012). *Africa Since Independence.* Basingstoke: Macmillan International Higher Education.

Nuwagaba, A. (2006). Dualism in Kampala: Squalid Slums in a Royal Realm. In Bryceson, D. F. & Potts, D. (eds) *African Urban Economies: Viability, Vitality or Vitiation?* Houndmills: Palgrave Macmillan. 151–168.

Nwulia, M. D. (1975). The Role of Missionaries in the Emancipation of Slaves in Zanzibar. *The Journal of Negro History* 60(2): 268–287.

Obbo, C. (1991). The language of AIDS in rural and urban Uganda. *African Urban Quarterly* 6(1–2): 83–92.

Obeng-Odoom, F. (2015). Informal Real Estate Brokerage as a Socially Embedded Market for Economic Development in Africa. In Abdulai, R. T., Obeng-Odoom, F., Ochieng, E., & Maliene, V. (eds) *Real Estate, Construction and Economic Development in Emerging Market Economies.* London: Routledge. 224–238.

Obeng-Odoom, F. (2020). Property, Institutions, and Social Stratification in Africa. Cambridge: Cambridge University Press.

Ochieng, W. R. & Maxon, R. M. (eds) (1992). *An Economic History of Kenya.* Nairobi: East African Publishers.

Ochonu, M. E. (Ed.). (2018). *Entrepreneurship in Africa: A Historical Approach*. Bloomington: Indiana University Press.

O'Connor, A. (1983). *The African City*. London: Hutchinson.

O'Connor, A. M. (1965). New Railway Construction and the Pattern of Economic Development in East Africa. *Transactions of the Institute of British Geographers*, 21–30.

OECD 2019. OECD data by sector. Available at: https://data.oecd.org/oda/oda-by-sector.htm

Ojong, N. (2011). Livelihood Strategies in African Cities: The Case of Residents in Bamenda, Cameroon. *African Review of Economics and Finance* 3(1): 8–25.

Okuku, J. A. (2006). The Land Act (1998) and Land Tenure Reform in Uganda. *Africa Development* 31(1): 1–26.

Oloka-Onyango, J. (1997). The question of Buganda in contemporary Ugandan politics. *Journal of Contemporary African Studies* 15(2): 173–189.

Olsen, G. R. (1998). Europe and the Promotion of Democracy in Post Cold War Africa: How Serious Is Europe and for What Reason? *African Affairs* 97(388): 343–367.

Omolo-Okalebo, F. (2011). The Evolution of Town Planning Ideas, Plans and their Implementation in Kampala City 1903–2004. PhD dissertation, KTH Royal Institute of Technology.

Ong, A. (2006). *Neoliberalism as Exception: Mutations in Citizenship and Sovereignty*. Durham, NC: Duke University Press.

Onoma, A. K. (2009). *The Politics of Property Rights Institutions in Africa*. Cambridge: Cambridge University Press.

Oqubay, A. (2015). *Made in Africa: Industrial Policy in Ethiopia*. Oxford: Oxford University Press.

Oqubay, A. (2018). Industrial Policy and Late Industrialization in Ethiopia. Abidjan, Côte d'Ivoire: African Development Bank.

Oqubay, A. (2019). Industrial Policy and Late Industrialization in Ethiopia. In Cheru, F., Cramer, C., & Oqubay, A. (eds) *The Oxford Handbook of the Ethiopian Economy*. Oxford: Oxford University Press. 605–629.

O'Reilly, P. (2019). Agency, Ideas and Institutions: The East African Community in the Emerging Economic Order. PhD dissertation, University of York.

Østebø, T. & Tronvoll, K. (2020). Interpreting Contemporary Oromo Politics in Ethiopia: An Ethnographic Approach. *Journal of Eastern African Studies* 14(4): 1–20.

Otele, O. (2020). China, Region-centric Infrastructure Drives and Regionalism in Africa. *South African Journal of International Affairs*. Online first, doi: 10.1080/10220461.2020.1856179.

Oteng-Ababio, M. (2016). Beyond Poverty and Criminalization: Splintering Youth Groups and 'Conflict of Governmentalities' in Urban Ghana. *Ghana Journal of Geography* 8(1): 51–78.

Otiso, K. M. & Owusu, G. (2008). Comparative Urbanization in Ghana and Kenya in Time and Space. *GeoJournal* 71(2–3): 143–157.

Ouma, S. (2016). From financialization to operations of capital: Historicizing and disentangling the finance–farmland-nexus. *Geoforum* 72: 82–93.

Owusu, F. (2007). Conceptualizing Livelihood Strategies in African Cities: Planning and Development Implications of Multiple Livelihood Strategies. *Journal of Planning Education and Research* 26(4): 450–465.

Oya, C. (2019). Building an Industrial Workforce in Ethiopia. In Cheru, F., Cramer, C., & Oqubay, A. (eds) *The Oxford Handbook of the Ethiopian Economy*. Oxford: Oxford University Press. 668–686.

Oz Architecture (2007). Kigali Conceptual Master Plan. Kigali: Ministry of Infrastructure.

Paller, J. W. (2014). Informal Institutions and Personal Rule in Urban Ghana. *African Studies Review* 57(3): 123–142.

Paller, J. W. (2019). *Democracy in Ghana: Everyday Politics in Urban Africa*. Cambridge: Cambridge University Press.

Palmer, R. (2004). The informal economy in sub-Saharan Africa: Unresolved issues of concept, character and measurement. *Occasional Paper No. 98*. Ediburgh: Centre of African Studies, Edinburgh University.

Palmer I. & Berrisford, S. (2015). Urban Infrastructure in Sub-Saharan Africa—Harnessing Land Values, Housing and Transport. Final report. Cape Town: African Centre for Cities.

Pankhurst, R. (1961). Menelik and the Foundation of Addis Ababa. *The Journal of African History* 2(1): 103–117.

Pankhurst, R. (1969). Notes for the History of Gondar. *Ethiopia Observer* 12(3): 177–227.

Pankhurst, R. (1996). Post-World War II Ethiopia: British Military Policy and Action for the Dismantling and Acquisition of Italian Factories and Other Assets, 1941–2. *Journal of Ethiopian Studies* 29(1): 35–77.

Parnell, S. (2016). Defining a Global Urban Development Agenda. *World Development* 78: 529–540.

Parnell, S. & Robinson, J. (2012). (Re)theorizing Cities from the Global South: Looking beyond Neoliberalism. *Urban Geography* 33(4): 593–617.

Parr, J. (2005). Perspectives on the City-region. *Regional Studies* 39(5): 555–566.

Pastor, M., Lester, T. W., & Scoggins, J. (2009). Why Regions? Why Now? Who Cares? *Journal of Urban Affairs* 31(3): 269–296.

Pausewang, S. (1983). *Peasants, Land and Society: A Social History of Land Reform in Ethiopia*. Munich: Weltforum Verlag.

Pausewang, S., Tronvoll, K., & Aalen, L. (2002). *Ethiopia since the Derg: A Decade of Democratic Pretension and Performance*. London: Zed Books.

Peattie, L. (1987). An Idea in Good Currency and How It Grew: The Informal Sector. *World Development* 15(7): 851–860.

Peck, J. (2005). Struggling with the Creative Class. *International Journal of Urban and Regional Research* 29(4): 740–770.

Peck, J. (2015). Cities beyond Compare? *Regional Studies* 49(1): 160–182.

Peck, J., Theodore, N., & Brenner, N. (2009). Neoliberal Urbanism. *The SAIS Review of International Affairs* 29(1): 49–66.

Peck, J., Theodore, N., & Brenner, N. (2010). Postneoliberalism and its Malcontents. *Antipode* 41: 94–116.

Peck, J., Theodore, N., & Brenner, N. (2013). Neoliberal Urbanism Redux? *International Journal of Urban and Regional Research* 37(3): 1091–1099.

Pellerin, C. L. (2018). *The politics of public silence: civil society–state relations under the EPRDF regime*. PhD dissertation, London School of Economics and Political Science.

Peterson, D. R., & Taylor, E. C. (2013). Rethinking the state in Idi Amin's Uganda: the politics of exhortation. *Journal of Eastern African Studies* 7(1): 58–82.

Philipps, J. (2016). Crystallising Contention: Social Movements, Protests and Riots in African Studies. *Review of African Political Economy* 43(150): 592–607.

Philipps, J. & Kagoro, J. (2016). The Metastable City and the Politics of Crystallisation: Protesting and Policing in Kampala. *Africa Spectrum* 51(3): 3–32.

Pickvance, C. (2003). From Urban Social Movements to Urban Movements: A Review and Introduction to a Symposium on Urban Movements. *International Journal of Urban and Regional Research* 27(1): 102–109.

Pitcher, M. A. (2017). Varieties of Residential Capitalism in Africa: Urban Housing Provision in Luanda and Nairobi. *African Affairs* 116(464): 365–390.

Planel, S. & Bridonneau, M. (2017). (Re)making Politics in a New Urban Ethiopia: An Empirical Reading of the Right to the City in Addis Ababa's Condominiums. *Journal of Eastern African Studies* 11(1): 24–45.

Porter, L. (2010) *Unlearning Colonial Cultures of Planning.* Farnham: Ashgate.

Porto-Gonçalves, C. W. (2012). *A reinvenção dos territories na América Latina/Abya Yala.* Mexico: Universidad Autónoma de México.

Pottier, J. (1993). Taking Stock: Food Marketing Reform in Rwanda, 1982–89. *African Affairs* 92(366): 5–30.

Pottier, J. (2002.) *Re-imagining Rwanda: Conflict, Survival and Disinformation in the Late Twentieth Century.* Cambridge: Cambridge University Press

Potts, D. (2006). 'Restoring Order'? Operation Murambatsvina and the Urban Crisis in Zimbabwe. *Journal of Southern African Studies* 32(2): 273–291.

Potts, D. (2007). The State and the Informal in Sub-Saharan African Urban Economies: Revisiting Debates on Dualism. Crisis States Working Paper Series, 2. London: London School of Economics and Political Science.

Potts, D. (2018). Urban Data and Definitions in Sub-Saharan Africa: Mismatches between the Pace of Urbanisation and Employment and Livelihood Change. *Urban Studies* 55(5): 965–986.

Poulantzas, N. A. (1980). *State, Power, Socialism.* London: Verso.

Pouwels, R. L. (2002). *Horn and Crescent: Cultural Change and Traditional Islam on the East African Coast, 800–1900.* Cambridge: Cambridge University Press.

Pratt, A. C. (2011). The Cultural Contradictions of the Creative City. *City, Culture and Society* 2(3): 123–130.

Pritchett, L., Sen, K., & Werker, E. (Eds.). (2017). *Deals and Development: The Political Dynamics of Growth Episodes.* Oxford: Oxford University Press.

Prunier, G. 1983. Le Magendo: Essai sur quelques aspects marginaux des échanges commerciaux en Afrique orientale. *Politique Africaine* 9: 53–62.

Prunier, G. (1997). *The Rwanda Crisis: History of a Genocide.* New York: Columbia University Press.

Prunier, G. (1998). The Rwandan Patriotic Front. In Clapham, C. (ed.) *African Guerrillas.* Oxford: James Currey. 119–133.

Prunier, G. (2008). *Africa's world war: Congo, the Rwandan genocide, and the making of a continental catastrophe.* Oxford: Oxford University Press.

Prunier, G. (2015). 'The Ethiopian Revolution and the Derg Regime'. In Prunier G. & Ficquet E. (eds) *Understanding Contemporary Ethiopia.* London: Hurst. 2019–232.

Purdeková, A. (2011). 'Even If I Am Not Here, There Are So Many Eyes': Surveillance and State Reach in Rwanda. *The Journal of Modern African Studies* 49(3): 475–497.

Purdeková, A. (2015). *Making Ubumwe: Power, State and Camps in Rwanda's Unity-Building Project.* New York: Berghahn Books.

Purdeková, A. (2016). 'Mundane Sights' of Power: The History of Social Monitoring and its Subversion in Rwanda. *African Studies Review* 59(2): 59–86.

Pye, L. W. & Verba, S. (1965). *Political Culture and Political Development.* Princeton, NJ: Princeton University Press.

Quayson, A. (2014). *Oxford Street, Accra: City Life and the Itineraries of Transnationalism.* Durham, NC: Duke University Press.

Radnitz, S. (2011). Informal Politics and the State. *Comparative Politics* 43(3): 351–371.

Rahmato, D. (1984.) *Agrarian Reform in Ethiopia.* Uppsala: Scandinavian Institute of African Studies.

Rakodi, C. (ed.) (1997). *The Urban Challenge in Africa: Growth and Management of its Large Cities*. Tokyo: United Nations University Press.

Rancière, J. (1995). Politics, Identification, and Subjectivization. In Rajchman, J. (ed.) *The Identity in Question*. New York: Routledge. 63–70.

Rancière, J. (1998). *Disagreement*. Minneapolis: University of Minnesota Press.

Rancière, J. (2004). Introducing Disagreement. *Angelaki: Journal of the Theoretical Humanities* 9(3): 3–9.

Randall, V., & Svåsand, L. (2002). Party Institutionalization in New Democracies. *Party Politics*, 8(1): 5–29.

Rankin, K. N. (2011). Assemblage and the Politics of Thick Description. *City* 15(5): 563–569.

Rao, V. (2006). Review Essay: Slum as Theory: The South/Asian City and Globalization. *International Journal of Urban and Regional Research* 30(1): 225–232.

Rasmussen, M. B., & Lund, C. (2018). Reconfiguring Frontier Spaces: The Territorialization of Resource Control. *World Development* 101:mc 388–399.

Regan, A. J. (1998). 'Decentralisation policy: reshaping state and society'. In Hansen, H. B. & Twaddle, M. (eds) *Developing Uganda*. Oxford: James Currey. 159–75.

Reid, R. (2001). Warfare and Urbanisation: The Relationship between Town and Conflict in Pre-colonial Eastern Africa. *AZANIA: Journal of the British Institute in Eastern Africa* 36(1): 46–62.

Reid, R. (2002). *Political power in pre-colonial Buganda: economy, society and warfare in the nineteenth century*. Oxford: James Currey.

Reid, R. J. (2011). *Frontiers of Violence in North-East Africa: Genealogies of Conflict since c.1800*. Oxford: Oxford University Press.

Reid, R. J. (2017). *A History of Modern Uganda*. Cambridge: Cambridge University Press.

Reid, R. & Medard, H. (2000). Merchants, Missions and the Remaking of the Urban Environment in Buganda c.1840–90. In Anderson, D. & Rathbone, R. (eds) *Africa's Urban Past*. London: James Currey. 98–108.

Resnick, D. (2012). Opposition parties and the Urban Poor in African Democracies. *Comparative Political Studies*, 45(11), 1351–1378.

Resnick, D. (2014a). *Urban Poverty and Party Populism in African Democracies*. Cambridge: Cambridge University Press.

Resnick, D. (2014b). Urban Governance and Service Delivery in African Cities: The Role of Politics and Policies. *Development Policy Review* 32(s1): s3–s17.

Resnick, D. (2019). The Politics of Crackdowns on Africa's Informal Vendors. *Comparative Politics* 52(1): 21–51.

Resnick, D. (2020). The politics of urban governance in sub-Saharan Africa. *Regional & Federal Studies* 31(1): 1–23.

Rettig, M. (2008). Gacaca: truth, justice, and reconciliation in postconflict Rwanda?. *African Studies Review* 51(3): 25–50.

Reyntjens, F. (1985). *Pouvoir et droit au Rwanda. Droit public et évolution politique, 1916-1973* (Vol. 117). Brussels: Musée Royal de l'Afrique Centrale.

Reyntjens, F. (2004). Rwanda, Ten Years on: From Genocide to Dictatorship. *African Affairs* 103(411): 177–210.

Reyntjens, F. (2013). *Political governance in post-genocide Rwanda*. Cambridge: Cambridge University Press.

Reyntjens, F. (1987). Chiefs and burgomasters in Rwanda: The unfinished quest for a bureaucracy. *The Journal of Legal Pluralism and Unofficial Law* 19(25-26): 71–97.

Richards, A. (1963). Some Effects of the Introduction of Individual Freehold into Buganda. In Biebuyuk, D. (ed.) *African Agrarian Systems*. Oxford: Oxford University Press. 267–280.

Ripstein, A. (2017). Property and Sovereignty: How to Tell the Difference. *Theoretical Inquiries in Law* 18(2): 243–268.

Rizzo, M. (2017). *Taken for a Ride: Grounding Neoliberalism, Precarious Labour, and Public Transport in an African Metropolis*. Oxford: Oxford University Press.

Robertson, C. C. (1997). *Trouble Showed the Way: Women, Men, and Trade in the Nairobi Area, 1890–1990*. Bloomington, IN: Indiana University Press.

Robi, S (forthcoming). *Integrating the urban–industrial nexus in the disintegrating Ethiopian Party-State*. PhD thesis, University of Sheffield, UK.

Robinson, J. (2006). *Ordinary Cities: Between Modernity and Development*. London: Routledge.

Robinson, J. (2011). Cities in a World of Cities: The Comparative Gesture. *International Journal of Urban and Regional Research* 35(1): 1–23.

Robinson, J. (2016). Thinking Cities through Elsewhere: Comparative Tactics for a More Global Urban Studies. *Progress in human geography*, 40(1), 3–29.

Robinson, J. & Roy, A. (2016). Debate on Global Urbanisms and the Nature of Urban Theory. *International Journal of Urban and Regional Research* 40(1): 181–186.

Rode, P., Terrefe, B., & da Cruz, N. F. (2020) Cities and the Governance of Transport Interfaces: Ethiopia's New Rail Systems. *Transport Policy* 91: 76–94.

Rodgers, D. (2006). The State as a Gang: Conceptualizing the Governmentality of vVolence in Contemporary Nicaragua. *Critique of Anthropology* 26(3): 315–330.

Rodgers, D. & O'Neill, B. (2012). Infrastructural Violence: Introduction to the Special Issue. *Ethnography* 13(4): 401–412.

Rodney, W. (1972). *How Europe Underdeveloped Africa*. London: Bogle-L'Ouverture Publications.

Rodrik, D. (2016). Premature Deindustrialization. *Journal of Economic Growth* 21(1): 1–33.

Rollason, W. (2013). Performance, Poverty and Urban Development: Kigali's Motari and the Spectacle City. *Afrika Focus* 26(2).

Rollason, W. (2019). *Motorbike People: Power and Politics on Rwandan Streets*. Lanham, MD: Lexington Books, Rowman and Littlefield.

RoR. (1990). *Mongraphie De La Prefecture De La Ville De Kigali*. Kigali: Republique Rwandaise.

RoR. (2000). *Rwanda Vision 2020*. Kigali, Rwanda: Government of Rwanda

RoR. (2004). *National Land Policy*. Kigali: Ministry of Lands, Environment, Forests, Water and Mines, Republic of Rwanda.

RoR (2009). Strategic Road Map for Land Tenure Reform in Rwanda. Kigali: Ministry of Natural Resources, Republic of Rwanda.

Ross, J. & Berhe, Z. (1974). Legal Aspects of Doing Business in Addis Ababa: A Profile of Mercato Businessmen and their Reception of New Laws. *The Journal of Legal Pluralism and Unofficial Law* 6(10): 1–46.

RoU (2006). The Report of the Commission of Inquiry into the Sale, Lease and Purchase of Land by Kampala City Council. Kampala: Ministry of Local Government, Republic of Uganda.

Roy, A. (2005). Urban Informality: Toward an Epistemology of Planning. *Journal of the American Planning Association* 71(2): 147–158.

Roy, A. (2009). The 21st-century Metropolis: New Geographies of Theory. *Regional Studies* 43(6): 819–830.

Roy, A. (2011). Slumdog Cities: Rethinking Subaltern Urbanism. *International Journal of Urban and Regional Research* 35(2): 223–238.

Roy, A. (2016). Who's Afraid of Postcolonial Theory? *International Journal of Urban and Regional Research* 40(1): 200–209.

Roy, A. & Ong, A. (eds) (2011). *Worlding Cities: Asian Experiments and the Art of Being Global*. Chichester: John Wiley & Sons.

Rubin, M. (2018). At the Borderlands of Informal Practices of the State: Negotiability, Porosity and Exceptionality. *The Journal of Development Studies* 54(12): 2227–2242.

Rubongoya, J. (2007). *Regime Hegemony in Museveni's Uganda: Pax Musevenica*. New York: Palgrave Macmillan.

Rueschemeyer, D. & Evans, P. B. (1985). The State and Economic Transformation: Towards an Analysis of the Conditions Underlying Effective Intervention. In Evans, P. B., Rueschemeyer, D., & Skocpol, T. (eds) *Bringing the State Back In*. Cambridge: Cambridge University Press. 44–77.

Rumiya, J. (1992). *Le Rwanda Sous le Régime du Mandat Belge* (1916-1931). Paris: L'Harmattan.

Sagashya, D. & English, C. (2009). *Designing and Establishing a Land Administration System for Rwanda: Technical and Economic Analysis*. Kigali: National Land Centre Ministry of Natural Resources (MINIRENA).

Sager, T. (2011). Neo-liberal Urban Planning Policies: A Literature Survey 1990–2010. *Progress in Planning* 76(4): 147–199.

Samuel, I. (2021). Land and Property in Pre-colonial Africa: Land Ownership, Land Sales and the Shortfalls of the 'Land-abundant Africa' Theories'; *African History Extra* blog. Available at: https://isaacsamuel.substack.com/p/land-and-property-in-pre-colonial#footnote-35. Accessed 24 November 2021.

Sandbrook, R. & Cohen, R. (1975). *The Development of an African Working Class*. Oxford: Oxford University Press

Sassen, S. (1994). Cities in a World Economy. London: Sage Publications.

Saul, J. S. & Leys, C. (1999). Sub-Saharan Africa in Global Capitalism. *Monthly Review* 51(3): 13.

Sawyer, L. (2014). Piecemeal Urbanisation at the Peripheries of Lagos. *African Studies* 73(2): 271–289.

Scharpf, F. W. (1999). *Governing in Europe: Effective and Democratic?*. Oxford: Oxford University Press.

Schatz, E. (2004). What Capital Cities Say about State and Nation Building. *Nationalism and Ethnic Politics* 9(4): 111–140.

Schensul, D. (2008). From Resources to Power: The State and Spatial Change in Post-apartheid Durban, South Africa. *Studies in Comparative International Development* 43(3–4): 290.

Schindler, S. (2015). Governing the twenty-first century metropolis and transforming territory. *Territory, Politics, Governance* 3(1): 7–26.

Schindler, S. (2017). Towards a Paradigm of Southern Urbanism. *City* 21(1): 47–64.

Schindler, S., DiCarlo, J., & Paudel, D. (2022). The new Cold War and the rise of the 21st-century infrastructure state. *Transactions of the Institute of British Geographers* 47(2): 331–346.

Schmelzle, C. (2012). Evaluating Governance: Effectiveness and Legitimacy in Areas of Limited Statehood. SFB-Governance Working Paper No. 26. Berlin: DFG Research Centre (SFB).

Schmid, C., Karaman, O., Hanakata, N. C., Kallenberger, P., Kockelkorn, A., Sawyer, L., et al. (2018). Towards a New Vocabulary of Urbanisation Processes: A Comparative Approach. *Urban Studies* 55(1): 19–52.

Schmidt, V. A. (2008). Discursive Institutionalism: The Explanatory Power of Ideas and Discourse. *Annual Review of Political Science* 11(1): 303–326.

Schmidt, V. A. (2013). Democracy and Legitimacy in the European Union Revisited: Input, Output and 'Throughput'. *Political Studies* 61(1): 2–22.

Scott, J. C. (1990). *Domination and the Arts of Resistance: Hidden Transcripts*. New Haven, CT: Yale University Press.

Scott, J. C. (1998). *Seeing Like a State*. New Haven, CT: Yale university Press.

Scott, A. & Storper, M. (2003). Regions, Globalization, Development. *Regional Studies* 37(6–7): 579–593.

Scott, A. J. & Storper, M. (2015). The Nature of Cities: The Scope and Limits of Urban Theory. *International Journal of Urban and Regional Research* 39(1): 1–15.

Scott, J. C. (2008). *Seeing Like a State*. New Haven: Yale University Press.

Selassie, A. G. (2003). Ethnic Federalism: Its Promise and Pitfalls for Africa. *Yale Journal of International Law* 28: 51.

Sellers, J. M. (2005). Re-placing the Nation: An Agenda for Comparative Urban Politics. *Urban Affairs Review* 40(4): 419–445.

Seyoum, S. (2000). Land Alienation and the Urban Growth of Bahir Dar'. In Anderson, D. & Rathbone, R. (eds) *Africa's Urban Past*. London: James Currey. 235–245.

Sharp, D. (2019). Difference as Practice: Diffracting Geography and the Area Studies Turn. *Progress in Human Geography* 43(5): 835–852.

Shearer, S. (2017). *The Kigali Model: Making a 21st Century Metropolis*. PhD thesis, Duke University.

Shearer, S. (2020). The city is burning! Street economies and the juxtacity of Kigali, Rwanda. *Urban Forum* 31(3): 351–371

Sibhat, E. E. (2014). Cause and Effect of Informal Sector: The Case of Street Vendors in Addis Ababa, Ethiopia. Masters thesis: Universitetet i Nordland, Bodø.

Silver, J. (2014). Incremental Infrastructures: Material Improvisation and Social Collaboration across Post-colonial Accra. *Urban Geography* 35(6): 788–804.

Simmons, A. J. (1999). Justification and Legitimacy. *Ethics* 109(4): 739–771.

Simone, A. (2004a). People as Infrastructure: Intersecting Fragments in Johannesburg. *Public Culture* 16(3): 407–429.

Simone, A. (2004b) *For the City Yet to Come: Changing African Life in Four Cities*. Durham, NC: Duke University Press.

Simone, A. (2005). Urban Circulation and the Everyday Politics of African Urban Youth: The Case of Douala, Cameroon. *International Journal of Urban and Regional Research* 29(3): 516–532.

Simone, A. (2010). https://scholar.google.com/citations?view_op=view_citation&hl=en&user=v5xoj0IAAAAJ&cstart=100&pagesize=100&sortby=pubdate&citation_for_view=v5xoj0IAAAAJ:u9iWguZQMMsC. London: Routledge.

Simone, A. (2018). *Improvised Lives: Rhythms of Endurance in an Urban South*. Chichester: John Wiley & Sons.

Simone, A. & Pieterse, E. (2017). New Urban Worlds: Inhabiting Dissonant Times. Chichester: John Wiley & Sons.

Sinclair, P. J. J. (1995). The Origins of Urbanism in Eastern and Southern Africa: A Diachronic Perspective. In Sahlstrom, B. & Ådal, K. (eds) *Islamic Art and Culture in Africa*. Uppsala: Acta Universitatis Upsaliensis. 99–110.

Sirven, P. (1984). La sous urbanisation et les villes du Rwanda et du Burundi. Thèse de doctorat en géographie, University of Bordeaux III.

Smith, N. (1992). Geography, Difference and the Politics of Scale. In Doherty, J., Graham, E., & Malek, M. (eds). *Postmodernism and the Social Sciences*. London: Palgrave Macmillan. 57–79.

Smith, N. (2002). New Globalism, New Urbanism: Gentrification as Global Urban Strategy. *Antipode* 34(3): 427wa–450.

Soifer, H. (2008). State Infrastructural Power: Approaches to Conceptualization and Measurement. *Studies in Comparative International Development* 43(3–4): 231.

Soifer, H. & Vom Hau, M. (2008). Unpacking the Strength of the State: The Utility of State Infrastructural Power. *Studies in Comparative International Development* 43(3–4): 219.

Sommers, M. (2012). *Stuck: Rwandan Youth and the Struggle for Adulthood.* Athens, GA: University of Georgia Press.

Southall, A. W. (1967) Kampala-Mengo. In Miner, H. (ed.) *The City in Modern Africa.* New York: Frederick A. Praeger. 297–332.

Southall, A. (1971). The impact of imperialism upon urban development in Africa. In Turner, V. (ed) In Duigan, P. and Gann, L. H. (eds) *Colonialism in Africa.* Cambridge: Cambridge University Press. 216–255.

Southall, A. (1988). The recent political economy of Uganda. In Hansen. HB & Twaddle. M (eds) *Uganda Now.* Oxford: James Currey. 54–69.

Southall, A. W. & Gutkind, P. C. (1957). *Townsmen in the Making. Kampala and its Suburbs. Townsmen in the Making. Kampala and its Suburbs.* Kampala: East African Institute of Social Resesarch.

Spear, T. (2000a). Early Swahili History Reconsidered. *The International Journal of African Historical Studies* 33(2): 257–290.

Spear, T. (2000b). Swahili History and Society to 1900: A Classified Bibliography. *History in Africa* 27: 339–373.

Spencer, M. E. (1970). Weber on Legitimate Norms and Authority. *The British Journal of Sociology* 21(2): 123–134.

Sseviiri, H., Lwasa, S., Lawhon, M., Ernstson, H., & Twinomuhangi, R. (2020). Claiming Value in a Heterogeneous Solid Waste Configuration in Kampala. *Urban Geography* 43(1) : 59–80.

Ssonko, D. K. (2008). The Impact of Structural Adjustment Programmes on Uganda (with Particular Reference to Uganda Management Institute) PhD dissertation, University of Glasgow.

Star, S. L. (1999). The Ethnography of Infrastructure. *American Behavioral Scientist* 43(3): 377–391.

Stein, H. (1992). Deindustrialization, Adjustment, the World Bank and the IMF in Africa. *World Development* 20(1): 83–95.

Stepputat, F. & Hagmann, T. (2019). Politics of Circulation: The Makings of the Berbera Corridor in Somali East Africa. *Environment and Planning D: Society and Space* 37(5): 794–813.

Stinchcombe, A. (1968). *Constructing Social Theories.* New York: Harcourt.

Stoker, G. (1998). Theory and Urban Politics. *International Political Science Review* 19(2): 119–129.

Stoker, G. & Mossberger, K. (1994). Urban Regime Theory in Comparative Perspective. *Environment and Planning C: Government and Policy* 12(2): 195–212.

Stone, C. N. (1989). *Regime Politics: Governing Atlanta, 1946–1988.* Lawrence, KA: University Press of Kansas.

Stone, C. N. (1993). Urban Regimes and the Capacity to Govern: A Political Economy Approach. *Journal of Urban Affairs* 15(1): 1–28.

Storey, A. (1999). Economics and Ethnic Conflict: Structural Adjustment in Rwanda. *Development Policy Review* 17(1): 43–63.

Storey, G. (2006). *Urbanism in the Preindustrial World: Cross-cultural Approaches.* Tuscaloosa: University of Alabama Press.

Straus, S. (2006). *The Order of Genocide: Race, Power, and War in Rwanda.* Ithaca, NY: Cornell University Press.

Straus, S. & Waldorf, L. (eds) (2011). Remaking Rwanda: State Building and Human Rights after Mass Violence. Madison: University of Wisconsin Press.

Stren, R. (1993). 'Urban Management' in Development Assistance: An Elusive Concept. *Cities* 10(2): 125–138.

Sundberg, M. (2016). *Training for Model Citizenship: An Ethnography of Civic Education and State-Making in Rwanda.* New York: Springer.

Swyngedouw, E. (2000). Authoritarian Governance, Power, and the Politics of Rescaling. *Environment and Planning D: Society and Space* 18(1): 63–76.

Swyngedouw, E. (2004). *Social Power and the Urbanization of Water: Flows of Power.* Oxford: Oxford University Press.

Swyngedouw, E. (2014). Where Is the Political? Insurgent Mobilisations and the Incipient 'Return of the Political'. *Space and Polity* 18(2): 122–136.

Swyngedouw, E. & Heynen, N. C. (2003). Urban Political Ecology, Justice and the Politics of Scale. *Antipode* 35(5): 898–918.

Tapscott, R. (2021). *Arbitrary States: Social Control and Modern Authoritarianism in Museveni's Uganda.* Oxford: Oxford University Press.

Tareke, G. (2009). *The Ethiopian Revolution: War in the Horn of Africa.* New Haven: Yale University Press.

Tarrow, S. G. (1994). Power in movement: Social movements and contentious politics. Cambridge: Cambridge University Press.

Tarrow, S. (2012). *Strangers at the Gates: Movements and States in Contentious Politics.* Cambridge: Cambridge University Press.

Taylor, P. J. (1982). A Materialist Framework for Political Geography. *Transactions of the Institute of British Geographers* 7(1): 15–34.

Temple, P. (1968) *The Growth of Kampala: An Historical Geographical Review.* Kampala: East African Institute of Social Research.

Terrefe, B. (2020). Urban Layers of Political Rupture: The 'New' Politics of Addis Ababa's Megaprojects. *Journal of Eastern African Studies* 14(3): 375–395.

The Atlantic (2018). The Pop Star Risking Death to Bring Change. 21 September. Available at: https://www.theatlantic.com/international/archive/2018/09/bobi-wine-uganda/570907/. Accessed 7 December 2021.

Therborn, G. (2017). *Cities of Power: The Urban, the National, the Popular, the Global.* London: Verso Books.

Thieme, T. A. (2018). The Hustle Economy: Informality, Uncertainty and the Geographies of Getting By. *Progress in Human Geography* 42(4): 529–548.

Thompson, J. B. (1984). *Studies in the Theory of Ideology.* Berkeley, CA: University of California Press.

Thomson, S. (2013). *Whispering truth to power: Everyday resistance to reconciliation in postgenocide Rwanda.* Madison: University of Wisconsin Pres.

Thomson, S. (2018). *Rwanda: from genocide to precarious peace.* New Haven, CT: Yale University Press.

Tilly, C. (1992). *Coercion, Capital and European States, AD 990–1992.* Oxford: Blackwell.

Tilly, C. (2005). *Trust and Rule.* Cambridge: Cambridge University Press.

Tilly, C. & Tarrow, S. G. (2015). *Contentious Politics.* Oxford: Oxford University Press.

Tiruneh, A. (1993). *The Ethiopian Revolution 1974–1987: A Transformation from an Aristocratic to a Totalitarian Autocracy.* Cambridge: Cambridge University Press.

Tiumelissan, A. & Pankhurst, A. (2013). Moving to Condominium Housing? Views about the Prospect among Children and their Families in Addis Ababa and Hawassa. Young Lives Working Paper No. 106. Oxford: Young Lives.

Todd, Z. (2016). An Indigenous Feminist's Take on the Ontological Turn: 'Ontology' Is Just Another Word for Colonialism. *Journal of Historical Sociology* 29(1): 4–22.

Torrance, M. I. (2008). Forging glocal governance? Urban infrastructures as networked financial products. *International Journal of Urban and Regional Research* 32(1): 1–21.

Tremann, C. 2019. The New U.S. Africa Strategy Fixates on China While Mimicking Beijing's Approach. *World Politics Review*. Accessed 6 February 2020. https://www.worldpoliticsreview.com/articles/27426/the-new-u-s-africa-strategy-fixates-on-china-whilemimicking-beijing-s-approach.

Tripp, A. M. (1997). *Changing the Rules: The Politics of Liberalization and the Urban Informal Economy in Tanzania*. Berkeley, CA: Univesity of California Press.

Tripp, A. M. (2010). *Museveni's Uganda: Paradoxes of Power in a Hybrid Regime*. Boulder: Lynne Rienner.

Tronvoll, K. (2011). The Ethiopian 2010 Federal and Regional Elections: Re-establishing the One-party State. *African Affairs* 110(438): 121–136.

Troutt, E. (1994). Land Markets in Central Province, Uganda. PhD thesis, University of Wisconsin.

Tsai, L. L. (2007). Solidary Groups, Informal Accountability, and Local Public Goods Provision in Rural China. *American Political Science Review* 101(2): 355–372

Tsing, A. L. (2003). Natural Resources and Capitalist Frontiers. *Economic and Political Weekly* 38(48): 5100–5106.

Tukahebwa, G. B. (1998). Privatization as a Development Policy. In Hansen, H. B. & Twaddle, M. (eds) *Developing Uganda*. Oxford: James Currey. 59–97.

Tumwebaze, P. (2014). 'World Bank Hails Rwanda's Growth'. New Times, Rwanda. 10 April.

Twaddle, M. (1993). *Kakungulu and the Creation of Uganda, 1868–1928*. London: James Currey.

UNDESA (2018). World Urbanization Prospects: The 2018 Revision. United Nations, Department of Economic and Social Affairs, Population Division. Custom data acquired via website. Available at: https://population.un.org/wup/DataQuery/. Accessed 23 October 2021.

UNECA (2017). Economic Report on Africa 2017: Urbanization and Industrialization for Africa's Transformation. Addis Ababa: UN Economic Commission for Africa.

UN-HABITAT. (2011). Condominium Housing in Ethiopia: The Integrated Housing Development Programme. Nairobi, Kenya.

UN-HABITAT (2017). The State of Addis Ababa 2017: The Addis Ababa We Want. Nairobi: UN-HABITAT.

UN-HABITAT (2018). The State of African Cities 2018. Nairobi: UN-HABITAT.

Uvin, P. (1998). Aiding Violence: The Development Enterprise in Rwanda. Boulder, CO: Kumarian Press.

Uwayezu, E. & de Vries, W. T. (2019). Expropriation of Real Property in Kigali City: Scoping the Patterns of Spatial Justice. *Land* 8(2): 23.

Uwayezu, E. & de Vries, W. T. (2020b). Can In-Kind Compensation for Expropriated Real Property Promote Spatial Justice? A Case Study Analysis of Resettlement in Kigali City, Rwanda. *Sustainability* 12(9): 3753.

Uwayezu, E. & Vries, W. T. D. (2020a). Access to Affordable Houses for the Low-income Urban Dwellers in Kigali: Analysis Based on Sale Prices. *Land* 9(3): 85.

Van Hoyweghen, S. (1999). The Urgency of Land and Agrarian Reform in Rwanda. *African Affairs* 98(392): 353–372.

Van Leeuwen, M. (2001). Rwanda's Imidugudu programme and earlier experiences with villagisation and resettlement in East Africa. *The Journal of Modern African Studies* 39(4): 623–644.

Van Noorloos, F., Cirolia, L. R., Friendly, A., Jukur, S., Schramm, S., Steel, G., & Valenzuela, L. (2020). Incremental Housing as a Node for Intersecting Flows of City-making: Rethinking the Housing Shortage in the Global South. *Environment and Urbanization* 32(1): 37–54.

Vanolo, A. (2014). Smartmentality: The Smart City as Disciplinary Strategy. *Urban Studies* 51(5): 883–898.

Vansina, J. (2004). Antecendents to Modern Rwanda: The Nyiginya Kingdom. Madison: University of Wisconsin Press.

Vaughan, S. & Gebremichael, M. (2011). Rethinking Business and Politics in Ethiopia. London: Africa Power and Politics Programme.

Vaughan, S. (2003). Ethnicity and Power in Ethiopia. PhD thesis, University of Edinburgh.

Vaughan, S. & Tronvoll, K. (2003). *The Culture of Power in Contemporary Ethiopian Political Life*. Stockholm: Sida.

Venugopal, R. (2015). Neoliberalism as Concept. *Economy and Society* 44(2): 165–187.

Verba, S. (1965). Comparative Political Culture. In Pye, L. W. & Verba, S. (eds) *Political Culture and Political Development*. Princeton, NJ: Princeton University Press. 512–560.

Verpoorten, M. (2012). Leave None to Claim the Land: A Malthusian Catastrophe in Rwanda?. *Journal of Peace Research* 49(4): 547–563.

Verwimp, P. (2000). Development Ideology, the Peasantry and Genocide: Rwanda Represented in Habyarimana's Speeches. *Journal of Genocide Research* 2(3): 325–361.

Vidal, C. (1974). Économie de la société féodale rwandaise. *Cahiers d'études africaines*, 14(53): 52–74.

Vidal, C. (1984). Enquêtes sur l'histoire et sur l'au-dela Rwanda, 1800–1970. *L'Homme* XXIV(3–4): 61–82.

Von Schnitzler, A. (2013). Traveling Technologies: Infrastructure, Ethical Regimes, and the Materiality of Politics in South Africa. *Cultural Anthropology* 28(4): 670–693.

Von Schnitzler, A. (2016). *Democracy's Infrastructure: Techno-politics and Protest after Apartheid*. Princeton, NJ: Princeton University Press.

Vrscaj S. K. and Lewis, L. L. (2016). Mercato. In Angélil, M. & Hebel, D. (eds) Cities of Change— Addis Ababa: Transformation Strategies for Urban Territories in the 21st Century. Second edition. Basel: Birkhäuser. 121–126.

Wade, R. (1990). *Governing the Market: Economic Theory and the Role of Government in East Asian Industrialization*. Princeton, NJ: Princeton University Press.

Walby, S. (2007). Complexity Theory, Systems Theory, and Multiple Intersecting Social Inequalities. *Philosophy of the Social Sciences* 37(4): 449–470.

Waldorf, L. (2011) Instrumentalising genocide: the RPF's campaign against "Genocide Ideology". In Straus, S. & Waldorf, L. (eds) *Remaking Rwanda: State Building and Human Rights after Mass Violence*. London: University of Wisconsin Press.

Waller, D. (1993). Rwanda: Which Way Now? Oxfam GB.

Wallman, S., & Bantebya-Kyomuhendo, G. (1996). *Kampala Women Getting By: wellbeing in the time of AIDS*. Oxford: James Currey Limited.

Watson, V. (2009a). 'The Planned City Sweeps the Poor away … ': Urban Planning and 21st-century Urbanisation. *Progress in Planning* 72(3): 151–193.

Watson, V. (2009b). Seeing from the South: Refocusing Urban Planning on the Globe's Central Urban Issues. *Urban Studies* 46(11): 2259–2275.

Watson, V. (2013). Planning and the 'Stubborn Realities' of Global South-east Cities: Some Emerging Ideas. *Planning Theory* 12(1): 81–100.

Watson, V. (2014). African Urban Fantasies: Dreams or Nightmares? *Environment and Urbanization* 26(1): 215–231.

Watson, V. (2020). Digital Visualisation as a New Driver of Urban Change in Africa. *Urban Planning* 5(2): 35–43.

Waugh, C. (2004.) *Paul Kagame and Rwanda: Power, Genocide and the Rwandan Patriotic Front.* Jefferson: McFarland and Company.

Weber, Max. 1922/1968. *Economy and Society.* Edited by Guenther R. & Wittich, C. Berkeley, CA: University of California Press.

Weiler, J. H. (2012). In the Face of Crisis: Input Legitimacy, Output Legitimacy and the Political Messianism of European Integration. *Journal of European Integration* 34(7): 825–841.

Weis, T. (2014). Dominant Parties and the Private Sector in Sub-Saharan Africa: A Typology of Approaches. *Zeitschrift für Vergleichende Politikwissenschaft* 8(3–4): 263–281.

Weis, T. (2016). Vanguard Capitalism: Party, State, and Market in the EPRDF's Ethiopia. PhD dissertation, University of Oxford.

Wekwete, K. (1997). Urban Management: The Recent Experience, the Urban Challenge in Africa: Growth and Management of its Large Cities. In Rakodi, C. *The Urban Challenge in Africa.* New York: UNU Press. 587–603.

Weldeghebrael, E. H. (2020). The Framing of Inner-city Slum Redevelopment by an Aspiring Developmental State: The case of Addis Ababa, Ethiopia. *Cities* 125: 102807. Available at: https://www.sciencedirect.com/science/article/abs/pii/S0264275118301884.

Weldeghebrael E. H. (2019). Inner-city Redevelopment in an Aspiring Developmental State: The Case of Addis Ababa Ethiopia. PhD thesis, University of Manchester.

West, H. (1972). *Land Policy in Buganda.* Cambridge: Cambridge University Press.

Weyland, K. (2001). Clarifying a Contested Concept: Populism in the Study of Latin American Politics. *Comparative Politics*, 34(1): 1–22.

Whiteside, H. (2019). Advanced Perspectives on Financialised Urban Infrastructures. *Urban Studies* 56(7): 1477–1484.

Whitfield, L. (2018). *Economies after Colonialism: Ghana and the Struggle for Power.* Cambridge: Cambridge University Press.

Whitfield, L., & Staritz, C. (2021). The learning trap in late industrialisation: Local firms and capability building in Ethiopia's apparel export industry. *The Journal of Development Studies* 57(6): 980–1000.

Whitfield, L., Therkildsen, O., Buur, L., & Kjær, A. M. (2015). *The Politics of African Industrial Policy: A Comparative Perspective.* Cambridge: Cambridge University Press.

Wiegratz, J. (2010). Fake capitalism? The dynamics of neoliberal moral restructuring and pseudo-development: the case of Uganda. *Review of African Political Economy* 37(124): 123–137.

Wiegratz, J. (2016). *Neoliberal Moral Economy: Capitalism, Socio-cultural Change and Fraud in Uganda.* Lanham, MA: Rowman & Littlefield.

Wiegratz, J., Martiniello, G., & Greco, E. (eds) (2018). *Uganda: The Dynamics of Neoliberal Transformation.* London: Zed Books.

Wimmer, A. & Glick Schiller, N. (2002). Methodological Nationalism and beyond: Nation–state Building, Migration and the Social Sciences. *Global Networks* 2(4): 301–334.

Winner, L. (1980). Do Artifacts Have Politics? *Daedalus* 109(1): 121–136.

Woldu, T., Abebe, G., Lamoot, I., & Minten, B. (2013). Urban Food Retail in Africa: The Case of Addis Ababa, Ethiopia. Ethiopia Strategy Support Program II Working Paper, 50. Washington, D.C.: International Food Policy Research Institute (IFPRI).

Woodward, D. (1996). The IMF, the World Bank and Economic Policy in Rwanda: Economic, Social and Political Implications. Report for Oxfam UK, Oxford.

Workneh, T. W. (2020). Social Media, Protest, and Outrage Communication in Ethiopia: Toward Fractured Publics or Pluralistic Polity? *Information, Communication & Society* 24(3): 309–328.

World Bank (2010). Africa's Infrastructure: A Time for Transformation. Washington, DC: World Bank.

World Bank Group. 2015. Ethiopia Urbanization Review: Urban Institutions for a Middle-Income Ethiopia. Washington, DC: World Bank.

World Bank Group (2016). Ethiopia: Priorities for Ending Extreme Poverty and Promoting Shared Prosperity. Washington, DC: World Bank.

World Bank. (2017). *Rwanda Economic Update, August 2017: Sustaining Growth by Building on Emerging Export Opportunities*. Washington, D. C.: World Bank.

Wrigley, C. C. (1957). Buganda: An Outline Economic History. *The Economic History Review* 10(1): 69–80.

Wu, F. (2008). China's Great Transformation: Neoliberalization as Establishing a Market Society. *Geoforum* 39(3): 1093–1096.

Wunsch, J. S. (2001). Decentralization, Local Governance and 'Recentralization'in Africa. *Public Administration and Development: The International Journal of Management Research and Practice* 21(4): 277–288.

Yatmo, Y. A. (2008). Street Vendors as 'Out of Place' Urban Elements. *Journal of Urban Design* 13(3): 387–402.

Yiftachel, O. (2009). Theoretical Notes On Gray Cities: The Coming of Urban Apartheid? *Planning Theory* 8(1): 88–100.

Young, G. (2017). From Protection to Repression: The Politics of Street Vending in Kampala. *Journal of Eastern African Studies* 11(4): 714–733.

Young, G. (2018). De-democratisation and the Rights of Street Vendors in Kampala, Uganda. *The International Journal of Human Rights* 22(8): 1007–1029.

Young, G. (2021a). Development, Division and Discontent in Informal Markets: Insights from Kampala. *Review of African Political Economy* 48(168): 196–216.

Young, G. (2021b). Neoliberalism and the State in the African City: Informality, Accumulation and the Rebirth of a Ugandan Market. *Critical African Studies* 13(3): 305–320.

Yusuf, B., Tefera, S., & Zerihun, A. (2009). Land Lease Policy in Addis Ababa. Addis Ababa: Chamber of Commerce and Sectoral Association.

Zenawi, M. (2012). States and Markets: Neoliberal Limitations and the Case for a Developmental State. In Noman, A., Botchwey, K., Stein, H., & Stiglitz, J. E. *Good Growth and Governance for Africa: Rethinking Development Strategies*. Oxford: Oxford University Press. 140–174.

Zewde, B. (1984). Economic Origins of the Absolutist State in Ethiopia (1916–1935). *Journal of Ethiopian Studies* 17: 1–29.

Zewde, B. (1991). *A History of Modern Ethiopia 1855–1991*. Suffolk: https://en.wikipedia.org/wiki/James_Currey" ø"James Currey

Zewde, B. (2002). *Pioneers of Change in Ethiopia: The Reformist Intellectuals of the Early Twentieth Century*. Oxford: James Currey.

Zewde, B. (2005). The City Centre: A Shifting Concept in the History of Addis Ababa. In Simone, A. and Abdelghani, A. (eds) *Urban Africa: Changing Contours of Survival in the City*. London: Zed Books. 122–123.

Žižek, S. (2012). *The Year of Dreaming Dangerously*. London: Verso.

Zwanenberg, R. M., & King, A. (1975). *An Economic History of Kenya and Uganda 1800–1970*. London: Macmillan.

Index

References to footnotes are indicated by the footnote number following the page number e.g 16n9.